Citizenship in Britain

There are increasing concerns about changes in society and the economy which are undermining the effectiveness of democracy and weakening traditional conceptions of citizenship. What does it mean to be a British citizen in the early part of the twenty-first century? This book presents the first major empirical study of citizenship in Britain, comprising surveys of political participation and voluntary activities, and of the beliefs and values which underpin them. As well as presenting new data, the authors provide a sophisticated discussion of the concept of citizenship, and the consequences of a lack of civic engagement in a modern democracy. They examine why some people are 'good' citizens when others are 'bad' and they explore the consequences of citizenship for policy-makers and democracy. Comprehensive and accessible, this book makes a major contribution to our understanding of civic attitudes in Britain today and will appeal to students, researchers and policy-makers.

CHARLES PATTIE is Professor of Geography at the University of Sheffield. His publications include *From Votes to Seats: The Operation of the UK Electoral System since 1945* (with R. J. Johnston, D. F. L. Dorling and D. J. Rossiter, 2001) and *Scotland Decides: The Devolution Issue and the Scottish Referendum* (with James Mitchell, David Denver and Hugh Bochel, 2000).

PATRICK SEYD is Emeritus Professor of Politics at the University of Sheffield. His recent publications include *New Labour at the Grassroots: The Transformation of the Labour Party Membership* (with Paul Whiteley, 2002) and *High Intensity Participation: The Dynamics of Party Activism in Britain* (with Paul Whiteley, 2002).

PAUL WHITELEY is Professor of Government at the University of Essex. His recent publications include *New Labour at the Grassroots: The Transformation of the Labour Party Membership* (with Patrick Seyd, 2002) and *High Intensity Participation: The Dynamics of Party Activism in Britain* (with Patrick Seyd, 2002) and *Political Choice in Britain* (with Harold Clarke, Marianne Stewart and David Sanders).

Citizenship in Britain

Values, Participation and Democracy

Charles Pattie, Patrick Seyd and Paul Whiteley

CAMBRIDGE
UNIVERSITY PRESS

PUBLISHED BY THE PRESS SYNDICATE OF THE UNIVERSITY OF CAMBRIDGE
The Pitt Building, Trumpington Street, Cambridge, United Kingdom

CAMBRIDGE UNIVERSITY PRESS
The Edinburgh Building, Cambridge CB2 2RU, UK
40 West 20th Street, New York, NY 10011–4211, USA
477 Williamstown Road, Port Melbourne, VIC 3207, Australia
Ruiz de Alarcón 13, 28014 Madrid, Spain
Dock House, The Waterfront, Cape Town 8001, South Africa

http://www.cambridge.org

First published 2004

Printed in the United Kingdom at the University Press, Cambridge

Typeface Plantin 10/12 pt.   *System* LATEX 2ε   [TB]

A catalogue record for this book is available from the British Library

Library of Congress Cataloging in Publication data
Pattie, C. J., 1962–
Citizenship in Britain: values, participation and democracy / Charles Pattie,
Patrick Seyd and Paul Whitely.
    p.   cm.
Includes bibliographical references and index.
ISBN 0 521 82732 9 – ISBN 0 521 53464 X (pb.)
1. Citizenship – Great Britain.   2. Political participation – Great Britain.
3. Citizenship – Great Britain – Public opinion.   4. Political participation –
Great Britain – Public opinion.   5. Public opinion – Great Britain.
I. Seyd, Patrick.   II. Whiteley, Paul.   III. Title.
JN906.P38   2004
323.6′0941 – dc22   2004045177

ISBN 0 521 82732 9 hardback
ISBN 0 521 53464 X paperback

'You gave us the finger and guess what, we want you to keep on doing it. We don't want your money, just your finger. 40,000 of you pulled your finger out, clicked on our website and emailed Nestlé asking them to reduce their whopping $6million claim against the Ethiopian people, which they have! All it takes is one of your fingers to help us create the biggest petition in the world. Join the Big Noise. Make Fair Trade Fair.Com. Text 'MTF7' + your name to 81003 or call Oxfam on 08700101047.'

(Advert in Guardian, 31 May, 2003)

'If you want to change the world put your money in fair trade chocolate and start volunteering.'

(Yann Martel, author of Life of Pi, Booker Prize winner, Guardian,
23 October 2002)

'A public is neither a nation, nor a generation, nor a community . . . a public is a kind of gigantic something, an abstract and deserted void which is everything and nothing.'

(W. H. Auden quoting Kierkegaard)

Contents

Figures

Tables

Acknowledgements

This book is one of the products of the Economic and Social Research Council's 'Democracy and Participation' programme. The programme was established in 1999 to examine the current state of British democracy and participation: twenty-one projects were funded, including the Citizen Audit (grant award number L215252025). We are very grateful to ESRC for its financial support. Additional funding came from Barclays Bank, which provided a sum of money to be used as prizes to those in our sample who completed the mail questionnaire. We thank the Bank, and Sir Peter Middleton in particular, for this support. ESRC officers Gary Williams and Jennifer Edwards deserve a special note of thanks for their help during the period in which the programme was funded.

The survey work, on which our findings are based, was conducted by three organisations. The face-to-face interviewing was carried out by Field Control. We thank Frances Loveless, her headquarters staff, in particular Pol Burton, and her team of interviewers for their professional services. Coding of the face-to-face interview data was carried out by Business Geographics. The dispatch and coding of the mail questionnaires was in the hands of Data Research Services. Tim Conway, who was the project Research Officer for two years, coordinated the survey research work. We are particularly obliged to Amanda Rivis and Andrew Leverton, very well-trained graduate students in the Department of Psychology at the University of Sheffield, who, at a late stage in the research project, resolved some technical difficulties which had arisen with the data. Andrew devoted considerable time and commitment to the project, even when he had broken his leg quite badly, and we hope that the experience he gained on this project will provide the launch for a deservedly successful career in social science research.

Numerous drafts of the questionnaires were devised and revised in the foyer of the Palace Hotel in Tachikawa during the time that Patrick Seyd and Paul Whiteley were visiting Chuo University in Tokyo, at the invitation of Steven Reed. The hotel staff were rather bewildered by the fact that for day after day two of their guests sat for hours on end in the lobby surrounded by questionnaires and piles of paper and made repeated requests for coffee and tea. Their tolerance and service were much appreciated.

We are grateful to our fellow grant-holders in the ESRC's 'Democracy and Participation' programme for their comments on our findings at the regular meetings held to discuss ongoing work on the twenty-one projects. In addition, papers were presented to the annual meetings of the Political Studies Association (PSA), the Elections, Parties and Public Opinion (EPOP) section of the PSA, and the American Political Science Association (APSA) and we are grateful to our academic colleagues for their observations and advice. Finally, we are grateful to Robert Putnam and his Cambridge colleagues for the invitation to present some of our findings to the 'social capital' seminar at the University. The critical but positive comments from Robert Putnam and his colleagues were of considerable value immediately prior to the completion of the manuscript.

During the two-year project we have received support and advice from numerous academic colleagues, especially Anthony King and Ron Johnston, and to them all we are grateful. Last, but by no means least, we are very grateful to our wives – Eilidh, Ros and Sue – for their understanding support during the time that we have been involved in this project. Needless to say, we are solely responsible for the contents.

Sheffield and Colchester
August 2003

Preface

'We should not, must not, *dare not*, be complacent about the health
and future of British democracy. Unless we become a nation of engaged
citizens, our democracy is not secure.'

(Lord Chancellor, in an address to the Citizenship Foundation, 27 January
1998. His emphasis. Quoted in *Education for Citizenship and the Teaching of
Democracy in Schools*. Final Report of the Advisory Group on Citizenship,
September 1998, London: Qualifications and Curriculum Authority, p. 8)

Comments such as those of the Lord Chancellor, quoted above, in
which he warns about British democracy and appeals for engaged citizens have not been a common feature of British political discourse until
relatively recently. For much of the twentieth century British democracy
was assumed to be healthy. Furthermore, the term 'citizen' appeared to
be inappropriate in the British context. The British were more likely to
be dutiful and respectful subjects rather than engaged citizens.

There are numerous reasons, both political and social, why British
democracy and citizenship have become important features of contemporary political debate. These include membership of the European Union,
the introduction of human rights legislation, the devolution of powers
within the state, the increasingly heterogeneous nature of the population,
the greater movement of populations across state boundaries, concerns
about the prevalence of anti-social behaviour, and the threats to both personal safety and personal liberties arising from international terrorism.

For much of the twentieth century both elite and mass opinion was
confident that the political system worked well and individual rights
were effectively protected by its institutions and procedures. Respect for
these traditional political institutions and procedures was reflected in
the absence of any fundamental reforms immediately after the Second
World War. Whereas the culmination of the war heralded an abrupt shift
in domestic policies as post-war governments accepted greater responsibility for managing the economy and providing universal levels of social
welfare, by contrast major reforms to political institutions and procedures
did not occur. Apart from a modification to the delaying powers of the

House of Lords, state institutions remained unchanged. The highly centralised political system was maintained and the powers and procedures of
Parliament, the Civil Service, and local government remained essentially
the same as before. The lack of change reflected an overwhelming belief
that the political system was efficient and required no major upheaval. A
confidence, verging on complacency, was the prevailing sentiment.

Such confidence in the political system seemed justified. The publication of a comparative, five-nation study of civic attitudes (Almond and
Verba, 1963) revealed that the British were trusting of each other and of
their political system, were satisfied with their political system and took
pride in their political institutions. The authors concluded that Britain
could be described as 'a deferential civic culture' in which

The participant role is highly developed. Exposure to politics, interest, involvement, and a sense of competence are relatively high. There are norms supporting
political activity, as well as emotional involvement in elections and system affect.
And the attachment to the system is a balanced one: there is general system pride
as well as satisfaction with specific governmental performance. (1963: 455)

Such positive conclusions regarding the British political system could
not be reached today. Levels of political involvement and public interest
have declined, as have levels of public trust in politicians. The lack of
public confidence in the current political system is shared by many within
the political elite. Here we quote just two recent examples of elite concern.
The first is taken from the retirement speech of the Speaker of the House
of Commons, Betty Boothroyd (2000), in which she stated

I know from my postbag how much disillusionment about the political process
there is among the general public. The level of cynicism about Parliament, and
the accompanying alienation of many of the young from the democratic process,
is troubling. It is an issue on which every member of the House should wish to
reflect. It is our responsibility, each and every one of us, to do what we can to
develop and build public trust and confidence.

The other example comes from the authoritative House of Commons
Select Committee on Public Administration (2001) which stated

Not since the extension of the suffrage in 1918 has there been such a low level
of participation in the electoral process. The reasons for it may be debated, but
not its seriousness for our democracy. We find it extraordinary that this collapse
in electoral participation, put alongside other evidence on civic disengagement,
has not been treated as a civic crisis demanding an appropriate response.

By the 1990s reform of political institutions had become a feature of
inter-party argument. In the years preceding the 1997 general election
the Labour Party sought to capitalise on public concern by portraying

the Conservatives as an *ancien régime* attached to old institutions, and proposed that a new modernised regime would introduce major institutional changes. After the Labour Party's electoral success in 1997, these reforms were duly introduced. For example, the devolution of powers to Scotland and Wales, and the election of these devolved institutions by a more proportional electoral system; the incorporation of the European Convention on Human Rights into a Human Rights Act; and the introduction of a Freedom of Information Act.

Very fundamental changes to the working of the British state have recently been introduced. Critics claim, however, that these reforms are too limited and will not resolve some of Britain's fundamental, structural problems (Beetham et al., 2002). After examining contemporary public attitudes, Bromley, Curtice and Seyd (2001: 200) argue that 'Britain faces a crisis of confidence and participation that is far deeper than any programme of constitutional reform is capable of reversing.'

Declining public confidence in, and respect for, conventional political institutions and procedures has provided a stimulus to alternative forms of politics. Recent well-publicised exercises in protest, particularly against road and airport runway developments, fuel taxes, a ban on fox hunting, and the US-led war in Iraq suggest a greater public willingness to engage in direct action or street demonstrations. Riots in 2001 in Bradford and Oldham provided additional evidence of public disenchantment, particularly among young ethnic minorities, with traditional methods of political participation.

There is solid evidence of voter apathy and distrust of politicians, but we have little knowledge or understanding of people's contemporary attitudes towards citizenship. Which is one reason why the Economic and Social Research Council established its Democracy and Participation programme and why, as part of that programme, it commissioned a Citizen Audit. The findings of the Citizen Audit are the subject of this book.

1   What is Citizenship?

Introduction

This book is about citizenship in contemporary Britain. It addresses the
question: 'what does it mean to be a British citizen in the early part of
the twenty-first century?' Answering this question leads to a number of
subsidiary questions like 'what does it mean to say that someone is a good
citizen?'; 'what determines the values and behaviours which constitute
citizenship?'; and 'what does citizenship mean for the wider society and
the effectiveness of the political system?'

Important changes are taking place in Britain in the relationship
between the citizen and the state. The meaning of citizenship, the relationship between citizens and government and problems of representation and accountability in the modern state have all become the focus of
research in recent years (Andrews, 1995; Brubaker, 1992; Etzioni, 1995;
Spinner, 1994; van Gunsteren, 1998). In Britain there are general questions to be asked about the effectiveness of democracy and the role of
the citizen in government in the twenty-first century (Parry, Moyser and
Day, 1992; Beetham, 1994). Similarly, there are changing conceptions
about the role of citizenship in promoting effective policy-making and
the effects of a strong civic tradition on the performance of the political system as a whole (Putnam, 1993; Van Deth et al., 1999; Weir and
Beetham, 1999).

Against this background there are increasing concerns about changes
in society which are undermining the effectiveness of democracy and
weakening traditional conceptions of citizenship. These changes include a
decline in feelings of community and solidarity in the public (Bellah et al.,
1985); growing public cynicism about politics and a widespread disaffec-
tion with political institutions (Knight and Stokes, 1996; Nye, Zelikow
and King, 1997); a decline in the institutions which underpin civil society
and democracy such as political parties (Whiteley and Seyd, 2002); and
a long-term decline in electoral turnout in the great majority of democratic states (Dalton and Wattenberg, 2000). In the light of these concerns

1

citizenship as a topic for research has undergone something of a renaissance in recent years. Writing a generation ago Van Gunsteren argued that 'the concept of citizenship has gone out of fashion among political thinkers' (1978: 9). This is certainly no longer true since there has been an upsurge in research into citizenship which is now examined from a variety of alternative disciplinary perspectives (Heater, 1990; Clarke 1996; Van Gunsteren, 1998).

In addition to academic debates, citizenship has become a central concern to politicians and policy-makers, faced with difficult social and economic problems arising from changes in society and in politics. Government ministers have been preoccupied with a civic renewal agenda as a means of raising participation, reducing crime and promoting voluntary activity (Blunkett, 2001, 2003). Citizenship studies have been introduced into the schools curriculum for the first time as a compulsory subject. The curriculum focuses on topics such as developing political knowledge, promoting the skills of enquiry and communication and stimulating participation (Department for Education and Employment, 1999; Crick, 2002).

There are a number of reasons why the topic of citizenship has come back into vogue. The first is that for the normative theorists citizenship raises basic questions about the relationship between the individual and the state, issues debated since classical times which are central to the concerns of political philosophers such as Locke and Hobbes. As the relationship between the individual and the state changes and is influenced by issues like new nationalisms, globalisation, mass immigration, multiculturalism and environmental stress, the nature of citizenship is explored by normative theorists who are trying to understand the ethical problems raised by these changes.

Such issues are of great concern to empirical political theorists as well and provides a second reason why citizenship is a topic of such contemporary interest. Since the earliest comparative work on the civic culture by Almond and Verba (1963), political scientists have been trying to understand the nature of the values, attitudes and forms of participation which underpin civil society. The concept of civil society takes centre stage in the analysis of citizenship and refers to the formal and informal relationships between people which can be broadly defined as political but which operate outside the institutions of the state. When party members campaign in local elections, when individuals join an interest group, when concerned citizens go on a protest march, or when volunteers help out in their local hospital, all of these constitute support for civil society. Without this, democracy could not function effectively.

There is a paradox at work here; on the one hand, democracy is triumphant throughout the world with new waves of democratisation occurring in Eastern Europe, Latin America and Asia (Huntington, 1991; Vanhanen, 1997). But on the other hand, fewer citizens are willing to turn out and vote in many of these democracies, when electoral participation is essential for the operation of democratic politics (Dalton and Wattenberg, 2000; Norris 2002). We see this decline in voting rather clearly in Britain where the turnout in the 2001 general election of 59 per cent was the lowest in modern British history. Clearly, there is something happening to contemporary citizenship which is bringing this about.

A third source of interest in the concept of citizenship comes from students of policy-making, particularly social welfare policy-making. With welfare systems under stress in all advanced industrial societies, arising from demographic changes such as an ageing population together with growing demands for state support for various groups, there is a potential 'fiscal crisis of the state'(O'Connor 1973). On the one hand, there are growing demands for spending on health, transport, education and pensions. On the other hand, there is a declining ability to deliver these benefits in the face of tax resistance by electorates. At the heart of welfare policy is a social contract binding citizens to each other both contemporaneously and across the generations. This contract involves a willingness of some individuals and groups to make sacrifices in order to support others. If citizenship is weak then this social contract will be weak, and governments will not be able to deliver on their promises.

A fourth source of interest in citizenship comes from the growth in immigration and in the growth of multiculturalism which that produces. As society becomes more heterogeneous then citizenship potentially becomes more problematic. When nearly all the citizens of a given country share the same ethnic, historical and cultural backgrounds, that makes the task of building the social contract relatively straightforward, though this does not of course eliminate political conflicts. In contrast, when citizens of a country have very heterogeneous identities deriving from different ethnic, cultural and religious backgrounds, particularly if these identities involve fundamental disagreements about values, then the task of building a social contract is much harder.

A fifth factor in the debates about citizenship is the weakening of state power brought about by globalisation, and for Britain the growing consolidation of policy-making in the European Union. If the state is circumscribed in its policy actions by supra-national authorities, even when those relationships bring concrete benefits to its citizens, this creates a democratic deficit and problems of accountability. Citizens unable to hold their governments to account in the long run may withdraw their allegiance from those governments. The problem can be eased if the new supra-national authorities can be made accountable, but as is well known this is highly problematic. Moreover, it is made even more problematic by the role of multinational corporations in the contemporary world. In recent years these corporations have often succeeded in obtaining benefits from government in the form of tax concessions and subsidies while at the same time avoiding tax contributions (Steinmo, 1993). The real problem here is the weakening of state authority which means that the social contract cannot be enforced effectively.

Another aspect of the same issue is the growth of sub-national political movements seeking autonomy and in some cases independence from national governments. In Britain the Labour government has already embarked on devolution for Scotland and Wales and is currently grappling with the problems of managing devolution to the regions. But this is just one aspect of an issue of growing importance across Europe, whether it is Flemish autonomy in Belgium, Catalan autonomy in Spain, Basque autonomy in France and Spain, or northern regional autonomy in Italy. The growth in demands for such regional autonomy may enhance democratic accountability in some respects, but it makes the task of building a national social contract harder. It can also produce a politics dominated by issues of identity, where there is fundamental disagreement about the locus of state authority, as is true in the case of Canada for example. In this situation it becomes ever more difficult to enforce the social contract.

Taken together these factors amount to a formidable array of reasons why citizenship should be taken seriously as a topic for contemporary research. In this book we aim to examine these questions empirically, with the aid of a series of surveys of the population of Great Britain carried out in 2000 and in 2001. We approach the issue of citizenship from an empirical perspective, since we believe that many of the contemporary philosophical debates about the nature of citizenship have lost touch with the political reality of societies and governments trying to grapple with these problems.

To illustrate this point, we cite Rawls' highly acclaimed book, *A Theory of Justice* (1971). As is well known Rawls argues that if people chose a set of principles for determining the kind of society they wish to live in from behind a 'veil of ignorance', that is ignorance about their own position in the social hierarchy, they would choose two founding principles. Firstly, they would favour liberty for all, and secondly redistribution which would advantage the least well-off at the expense of the most affluent. These ideas have received an enormous amount of attention in the literature and they are very interesting, but their relevance for addressing actual issues of inter-generational redistribution, multiculturalism, tax resistance and declining participation is debatable. The 'veil of ignorance' neither exists nor could it exist, thus the utility of these ideas for policy-makers faced with the task of grappling with these problems is highly questionable. We believe that it is much better to address these questions with the help of a firm understanding of what people think and how they behave, rather than with an abstract normative thought experiment.

In the rest of this chapter we review the history of the concept of citizenship with the aim of arriving at a definition of citizenship which can be used to illuminate the analysis in subsequent chapters. This leads into a section which discusses contemporary debates about the problems of citizenship, and this is followed by a section setting out the model of citizenship which will inform the rest of the book. Finally, we finish off by summarising the argument in the various chapters of the book. We begin with a review of the concept of citizenship as it has developed since ancient times.

A history of the concept of citizenship

The word citizen has its origins in the Latin word *civitas*, but the modern conception of citizenship has its origins in ancient Greek civilisation which pre-dates the Roman empire. The idea first emerged in the Greek city states between about 700–600 BC and was a logical consequence of the development of the *polis*, or the political system of the Greek city state (Clarke, 1994: 4–6). The Greeks relied on slaves to free them from the drudgery of day-to-day toil and this allowed them the time to address issues of general concern to the whole society and thereby to become active citizens. Solon, the ruler of Athens in 594 BC, was the first to give legal expression to the emerging ideas of citizenship. His laws do not survive in detail, but it is known that he classified citizens into four categories, depending on their wealth and status, and their influence on government depended on their position in this classification scheme. The lowest class, called *Thetes*, for example, were allowed to serve as jurors although not to hold public office. This was a crucially important historical development since it meant that even the most humble of citizens participated in the administration of justice. It was said that Solon made laws that were deliberately vague, so that cases had to be settled on their merit by the jurors. This served to give all citizens substantial influence over the government of the city state (Clarke, 1994: 40).

Aristotle codified the idea of citizenship in his *Politics*, a text written some time after Solon's rule. Aristotle defines the citizen as a person who both rules and is ruled. He writes: 'There is nothing more that characterises a complete citizen than having a share in the judicial and executive part of the government' (quoted in Clarke, 1994: 44). What makes the citizen distinctive is that he joins with others to make decisions and then subsequently respects the authority of these mutually agreed decisions.

Participation legitimates decision-making which is a key requirement of active citizenship. This system required that participants should be peers or roughly equal in status, something achieved by narrowly prescribing who was and who was not a citizen. For Aristotle, the citizen had to be a male of known genealogy, a patriarch, a warrior and a property owner, where this was defined in terms of owning slaves and controlling a household (Pocock, 1998). His formulation depended on a rigid distinction between the public realm, the *polis*, and the private realm, the *oikos*. Women and slaves were part of the latter and controlled exclusively by the individual householder. The *polis* was the domain of public affairs determined by active citizens and participation was regarded as a good in itself. Thus citizens participated not merely to solve the common problems of the city state, but because such participation was an essential component of the good life.

At the heart of Aristotle's conception of citizenship is the idea that those who own and control property should collectively make and adjudicate the laws which ultimately determine how that property is disposed. The idea that voters required a property qualification before they could be allowed to participate survived well into the twentieth century in Britain, and was justified in much the same terms as Aristotle used. The argument was that only property owners can be stakeholders, and as a consequence they should be the only people allowed to make important political decisions. Aristotle characterised this idea in the following terms:

it is necessary that the freemen who compose the bulk of the people should have absolute power in some things; but as they are neither men of property nor act uniformly upon principles of virtue, it is not safe to trust them with the first offices of the state, both on account of their iniquity and their ignorance. (quoted in Clarke, 1994: 46)

The sociologist Max Weber had an interesting explanation of the origins of this notion of citizens as self-governing stakeholders. He argued that it arose out of the military organisation of the ancient and medieval cities. He pointed out that cities were first and foremost defensive groupings, requiring the participation of individuals who owned their own weapons and were competent to bear arms to defend themselves. As a consequence it was difficult for a small oligarchy to monopolise and retain power if it required the services of large numbers of armed freemen to defend the city. He wrote:

Military discipline meant the triumph of democracy because the community wished and was compelled to secure the cooperation of the non-aristocratic masses and hence put arms and along with arms political power, into their hands. (quoted in Shafir, 1998: 46)

While it was the Greeks who first developed the principles underlying active citizenship, the Greek conception was necessarily limited to the community of the city state. The Romans faced the task of codifying a concept of citizenship which could apply to their entire empire, which formed the bulk of the then known world. The Roman conception of citizenship is best illustrated by the case of Saint Paul who when arrested in Tarsus for preaching the gospel claimed the rights of a Roman citizen. In doing this he was claiming certain legal protections and rights that were not available to non-citizens and the claim actually prevented him from being flogged.

Originally, *civis Romanus* meant someone who participated in the various self-governing assemblies associated with the Roman republic in much the same way as in Greece. But it came to mean legal status rather than just a political status based on participation, giving the recipient legal rights and immunities which could not be abrogated by the arbitrary actions of others. In this way the Roman empire was able to develop a conception of citizenship which could generalise beyond the largely face-to-face groups of the city state. It undoubtedly enhanced Rome's ability to retain the allegiance of a very disparate group of tribes throughout the empire, since citizenship was commonly bestowed on cooperative elites from these tribes. In this way citizenship became a powerful instrument for integration within the empire.

The decline of the Roman empire fragmented citizenship, but the core features of the Greek conception, namely that individuals from similar backgrounds should participate as stakeholders for the purpose of influencing judicial and legislative decision-making, survived in the medieval cities. Feudalism with its hierarchical structure and ascriptive criteria for defining status did not encourage citizenship in this sense, but the values and activities associated with the concept survived in the medieval guilds, and among the citizen soldiers who were periodically required to defend their cities. Weber writes: 'The typical citizen of the medieval guild city is a merchant or craftsman: he is a full citizen if he is also a householder' (quoted in Shafir, 1998: 47). Weber argued that the medieval guilds pursued a 'town economy' whose objectives were both to promote and transmit occupational skills and also to expand their markets by dominating the surrounding countryside. Often this was achieved by making the use of the town market compulsory for the population in the hinterland.

When democracy gradually developed in Britain over a long period of time, it was characterised by a conflict between aristocratic land-owning interests rooted in feudalism on the one hand, and trading, craft and later on nascent manufacturing interests on the other. This conflict was decisively settled in favour of the latter by the English Civil War of the early seventeenth century, just as it was later settled in France by the French Revolution.

Once parliamentary sovereignty had triumphed in Britain, the story of the evolution of citizenship and democracy is one of extending the franchise and representation to wider and wider groups, eventually abandoning the property qualification which had been the hallmark of citizenship since ancient times. In a very influential article the sociologist T. H. Marshall set out a theory of the evolution of citizenship in Britain (see Marshall and Bottomore, 1992). Marshall was writing shortly after the Second World War and in the context of the creation of the welfare state by the 1945–51 Labour government.

In Marshall's view the development of citizenship in Britain was a process involving three distinct phases. It first involved the establishment of civil rights such as the right to own property, equal access to justice, habeas corpus, free speech, freedom of assembly and religion and the freedom to organise trade unions codified by the repeal of the Combination Acts. Roughly speaking these rights were in place by the end of the eighteenth century. In Marshall's view, civil rights included the right to work, which had in Elizabethan times been curtailed by the Statute of Artificers, confining certain occupations to certain social classes, and by the apprenticeship system which he saw as an instrument of exclusion as much as one of education and training. The growth of ideas of free trade opposed such local monopolies, and the common law together with legislation removed such barriers to the right to work. With this in mind Marshall wrote: 'By the beginning of the nineteenth century this principle of economic freedom was accepted as axiomatic' (Marshall and Bottomore, 1992: 11).

The story of civil rights was one of the gradual addition of new rights to those which already existed, albeit only for adult males. The remnants of feudalism lingered on in the countryside long after they had disappeared from the towns. Thus the expansion of civil rights can be seen as a process in which citizenship, which had been sustained in the medieval cities, expanded out to encompass the entire nation and to incorporate a broader range of rights.

The second phase of the growth of citizenship in Marshall's account was the growth of political rights, principally the right to vote, the right to run for office and to participate fully in the politics of the community. The formative period for this was the early nineteenth century, starting with the Parliamentary Reform Act of 1832. In Marshall's view the growth of political rights differed from the growth of civil rights since it consisted not in creating new rights, but rather in the granting of old rights to new sections of the population. The 1832 Reform Act was limited in that it extended the franchise to less than a fifth of the adult male population, but it was an important precedent in recognising that the franchise should be extended beyond the elite groups represented in the eighteenth-century House of Commons. He argued:

It is clear that if we maintain that in the nineteenth century citizenship in the form of civil rights was universal, the political franchise was not one of the rights of citizenship. It was the privilege of a limited economic class, whose limits were extended by each successive Reform Act. (Marshall and Bottomore, 1992: 13)

This process culminated in the Act of 1918 which adopted universal manhood suffrage and thus dropped the property qualification which had been the hallmark of citizenship since the time of the ancient Greeks. A few years later the franchise was extended to all adult women, which completed the process of defining political rights in terms of membership of the community, rather than in terms of the ownership of property.

If the eighteenth century was the source of civil rights and the nineteenth century political rights, for Marshall the twentieth century was the source of social rights. By social rights he meant principally economic welfare and social security, although he defined these in very broad terms:

By the social element I mean the whole range from the right to a modicum of economic welfare and security to the right to share to the full in the social heritage and to live the life of a civilised being according to the standards prevailing in society. The institutions most closely connected with it are the educational system and the social services. (Marshall and Bottomore, 1992: 8)

The original source of these social rights was membership of local communities and functional associations, a source supplemented by the Poor Law and a system of wage regulation which was locally administered. Marshall noted that system, which had its origins in Elizabethan times, was severely undermined by free trade ideology which accompanied the growth of civil rights. The 1834 Poor Law Act, for example, restricted the scope of the Elizabethan Speenhamland system of poor relief, and established the principle of 'less eligibility', i.e. the proposition that payments should always be lower than the minimum market wage available in a locality. Thus the growth of civil rights served to undermine traditional social rights. He wrote:

The Poor Law treated the claims of the poor, not as an integral part of the rights of the citizen, but as an alternative to them – as claims which could be met only if the claimants ceased to be citizens in any true sense of the word. (Marshall and Bottomore, 1992: 15)

Marshall makes a similar point about the right to education, which was not seen as an integral part of citizenship during the formation of civil and political rights. He concluded that as far as social rights were concerned it was 'not until the twentieth century that they attained equal partnership with the other two elements of citizenship' (Marshall and Bottomore, 1992: 17).

Marshall's argument has subsequently been very influential in debates about citizenship, but it has not gone unchallenged. There is now a range of studies which suggest that Marshall's analysis is far from being a universal model, so that the idea of citizenship being a cumulative linear process from civil to social rights is highly contestable. The first significant welfare reforms in Britain introduced by Lloyd George when he was the Chancellor of the Exchequer in the Liberal government prior to the First World War, openly copied the example of Bismarck's Germany (Heclo, 1974; Steinmo, 1993: 59). Bismarck had introduced welfare payments in the German empire explicitly in order to undermine support for the socialists and to reinforce the allegiance of the working class to his authoritarian state. At the time most citizens of Germany lacked basic political and civil rights. Similarly, Michael Mann (1987) has argued that in some societies social rights have been seen as direct substitutes for civil rights rather than as complements to them. Thus fascist and communist regimes provided little or no civil rights, but quite extensive social rights, particularly in the case of the Soviet-style communist regimes.

Fraser and Gordon (1998) suggest that the strong civil rights tradition of the United States, with its emphasis on individual rights and the sanctity of contracts, has served to inhibit the development of social rights. In this case even low wage earners have an anti-welfare ideology, as they explain:

The widespread fear that 'welfare' recipients are 'getting something for nothing' is an understandably embittered response from those who work hard and get little; their own paltry remuneration becomes their norm and they see themselves cheated by welfare clients rather than by their employers. (1998: 125)

Thus Marshall's 'linear, cumulative model' of the development of citizenship is problematic, but it is nonetheless a starting point for debates about contemporary citizenship in Britain.

Beiner (1995) divides contemporary theorising about citizenship into three classes: liberal, communitarian and republican theories of citizenship. Liberal theories emphasise the importance of the individual and see the political community as a mechanism for maximising individual welfare. Individuals must cooperate together to solve various collective action problems and they do this through the medium of the state which provides a forum for solving such problems. In this perspective citizenship is about reconciling the interests of the individual and the state within a legal framework. The emphasis is on equal rights, to ensure that civil, political and social rights are enjoyed equally by all members of society. As Janoski and Gran (2002) explain:

> At a foundation level, all citizenship rights are legal and political because citizenship rights are legislated by governmental decision-making bodies, promulgated by executive orders, or enacted and later enforced by legal decisions. (2002: 13)

Communitarian theories, on the other hand, emphasise the importance of both groups and communities in binding individuals together in order to produce coherent state policies (Etzioni, 1995). Cultural solidarity among those who share a common history or tradition confers identity on otherwise atomised individuals and it is this identity which is the basis of citizenship. Tonnies' famous treatise on Gemeinschaft and Gesellschaft published in 1887 is often seen as the starting point of this tradition (Tonnies, 1957). For Tonnies, 'community' referred to a relatively small cohesive traditional world of direct ties, while 'society' referred to a large-scale, fragmented and individualistic world of indirect ties. For communitarians citizenship arises from culturally defined communities which exist prior to the formation of the state. The latter is thought to derive its authority from these communities. Relationships in such communities transcend the utilitarian calculations of individuals which are the basis of liberal conceptions of citizenship.

Finally, republican theories emphasise the importance of the community as a whole in the form of the state as the key agency for creating identity and sustaining allegiance (Van Gunsteren, 1998). In this view individualistic or communitarian theories are a threat to effective citizenship, the former because atomised individuals may not be able to overcome their conflicts of interest sufficiently to organise effective collective action, and the latter because special interests will dominate the agenda if they are not subsumed under some wider collective identity. In either case these defects will paralyse the state and prevent it from achieving its objectives.

In reality these are conceptual frameworks for talking about citizenship rather than theories of the origins, characteristics and determinants of contemporary citizenship. They help in the task of trying to conceptualise citizenship, but they are of little use in explaining why individuals have certain attitudes or behave in certain ways towards their fellow citizens.

To some extent this framework has been eclipsed by new challenges to traditional theories of citizenship and we examine some of these next.

Contemporary debates about citizenship

There are three important contemporary debates about the nature of citizenship which have preoccupied writers in recent years. These are about transnational citizenship and a possible decline in the nation-state arising from globalisation; issues concerning multiculturalism and the growth of heterogeneous populations in many countries; and also feminist perspectives on citizenship which challenge traditional theories for being male-dominated or patriarchal. All three represent challenges to existing notions of citizenship.

In relation to transnational citizenship, Yasemin Soysal (1998) has assembled an array of evidence which shows how citizenship rights are no longer tied to national and territorial boundaries. Foreigners who are long-term residents of European states or resident aliens in the United States possess substantial rights and privileges even though they are not citizens in the conventional sense. Tomas Hammer (1986) suggested that members of these groups should be described as *denizens* rather than citizens. In his view citizenship should be regarded as a set of concentric circles with the inner circle based on nationality and the outer circle on denizenship. The idea here is that there is a growing separation of citizenship rights from the territorial dimension of state membership. Denizens acquire rights by virtue of living and working in countries other than by birth or naturalisation. Classical notions assume that all citizens are entitled to the same rights, providing that they are members of a nation-state. Transnational citizenship means that different individuals will have different rights, depending on their status. Thus legal permanent residents will have greater rights than political refugees but not necessarily the same rights as those with dual nationality. In this way different categories of citizenship have come into existence. In one sense this is a return to Solon's original model, in which citizenship implies a series of statuses which can be held either temporarily or permanently by different people at different times.

The process of globalisation and the increase in the number of transnational institutions and agreements have reduced the autonomy of the nation-state in controlling these migrant denizens (Held, 1989). There was a tremendous upsurge of refugees seeking access to the European Union from the former Yugoslavia when that country fragmented into civil war in the 1990s. A similar pattern was repeated after the war against the Taliban in Afghanistan. The European Union has sought to increase barriers to the entry of economic migrants, but the member states appear to have had limited success in stemming the tide of refugees.

The powers of the nation-state are reduced by a growing emphasis on universal rights often enforced by transnational institutions. For example, the European Convention on Human Rights has been incorporated into the laws of member states of the European Union and this acts as an important check on national immigration legislation. Similarly, there is a growing body of international treaties, conventions and charters which govern employment issues, residency requirements, social security and family reunification policies, all of which limit state action.

In the European Union community law enshrines the free movement of labour as a cornerstone of trade policy and it prohibits discrimination based on nationality among workers from different member states in employment, social security and educational provision. The European Commission recommends full political rights in the long run for Community citizens living in other member states, including the right to stand as candidates in elections (Soysal, 1998: 199). The key conflict developing in this area is between a demand for universal rights, on the one hand, and the sovereignty of the nation-state, on the other. In certain key respects these principles are incompatible with each other. A similar process is at work at the sub-national level as Bretons, Catalans, Corsicans, Basques, Scots and Sardinians seek national autonomy within the framework of existing nation-states, reinforcing these tendencies towards multiple identities and therefore a multidimensional conception of citizenship.

The idea of transnational citizenship is an interesting one, but a key problem for writers who welcome this development is that in reality citizens give their allegiance to the nation-state and not to transnational institutions. This point can be seen most easily in the case of the European Union where there is no transnational political culture to support and legitimate the establishment of a United States of Europe. In the Citizen Audit survey examined more fully in later chapters, respondents were asked if they thought of themselves principally as English, Scottish, Welsh, Irish, British or European. Only 2 per cent of respondents to this question chose the European option. While increasing transnational cooperation is occurring and an emerging legal framework exists to support this, it is premature to start arguing that this development portends the growth of a transnational citizenship. Indeed the growth of transnational institutions might easily provoke a backlash if citizens feel that these institutions are remote and unresponsive to their concerns.

Multicultural theorists make a similar point to transnational theorists, except they are principally concerned with the treatment of ethnic minorities who most commonly are already full citizens. Their particular concern is to promote the idea that such minorities should have special *group rights* in addition to their individual rights, which should enable them to sustain their minority identities and cultures within the wider society. Kymlicka puts it as follows:

> In a society that recognizes group-differentiated rights, the members of certain groups are incorporated into the political community not only as individuals, but also through the group, and their rights depend, in part, on their group membership. (1998: 167)

As Kymlicka recognises, however, the concept of group rights poses serious difficulties for liberal conceptions of universal rights. If individual rights are universal and not dependent on ethnic, territorial or cultural identities of the type which defined status and rights in feudal societies, then the call for group rights is a call for the abandonment of modern conceptions of citizenship. If groups claim special treatment based on their distinctive differences, then as Nathan Glazer notes in his analysis of social policy in the United States this represents a retreat from universalism. He writes: 'This retreat from universalism, to my mind, stems from a weakening of commonly held values as to the good society. We once seemed to agree that the same public education for all, limits on abortion, all youth serving in the armed forces, and merit as the test for employment and higher education represented the good society . . . We don't any longer' (1988: 95). Thus it is a weakening of liberal conceptions of citizenship which creates the demand for group rights. In defence of this conception Kymlicka argues that the demand for special rights by disadvantaged groups is really a demand for social inclusion. Thus many of these groups feel excluded and want the recognition of the wider society for their particular cultures and hope to achieve this by group-based representation in the political system.

The political success of this group rights approach to citizenship really depends on whether such rights challenge or complement the values and culture of the wider society. For example, some Muslim groups in Britain want state support for Muslim schools to be operated on the same basis as the state support for Christian schools. This raises issues of social inclusion, that is whether or not a Muslim education will serve to include or exclude children from the wider society, but assuming such problems can be solved this development is not a challenge to the fundamental values of British society. For this reason it may very well succeed. On the other hand, the demand by a few Muslim groups that the medieval laws of blasphemy should be revived so that individuals who criticise Islam can be prosecuted in the courts is acutely at odds with the agnostic values of the wider society, particularly the strong preference for freedom of speech. This is never likely to be accepted by British society and rather than promoting inclusion it is likely to promote division. Clearly there is scope for a group rights approach in any democratic society, but the scope is limited by the risk of destroying the universalistic values of citizenship which are the hallmark of contemporary liberal thinking.

The feminist contribution to the citizenship debate raises similar issues as transnational and multicultural citizenship but it makes an additional point as well. This is the argument that the dominant conceptualisation of citizenship is itself gendered and this discourse needs to be challenged in order to give a feminist account of citizenship. Kathleen Jones (1998) makes this point in the following terms:

unless we directly challenge the dominant gendered political discourse, women's experiences and self-understandings will be fit into existing paradigms that privilege elite men's behaviour and norms, and the relationship between gender and citizenship will be reduced to the 'presence or absence of actual women' among the ranks of citizens. (1998: 222)

Jones makes some suggestions as to what this discourse would look like. It would focus attention on issues of sexuality, reproduction and the physical self, or as she puts it, bring 'a new attention to the "body" in the "body politic"' (1998: 223). It would try to remove the distinction between strong ties, that is family relationships, and weak ties, such as working relationships, in order to bring these together. This supports the idea that 'the personal is the political'. She writes: 'we feminists have returned to descriptions of political action in familial or personal terms: sisters, mothers, lovers, friends are the citizens of a feminist political community' (1998: 225). It would also try to 'search for new forms of organization that are both humane and reflect more open and ambiguous organizational structures and behavioral codes' (1998: 225). Finally, it would shift 'the boundaries of political action away from citizenship as a relationship between the state and its subjects toward a model of politics and public space more consistent with anarchist and communitarian principles' (1998: 226).

In this view changes in contemporary citizenship should go well beyond the task of correcting the discrimination against women in the economy, politics and society and move towards creating a new discourse of political understanding. This is an ambitious programme but its implications for public policy are hard to discern. For example, an emphasis on the body would presumably involve raising issues of reproductive rights, but how will this help to deal with the problem of unequal pay for women? Similarly, if there is no distinction between the private and public spheres, between family ties and relationships based on work, what does this mean for public policy? Does it mean that mothers should be required to treat strangers in the same way as they treat their own children? Equally, if transforming politics involves developing open ambiguous structures, how are the complex policies of a contemporary society in welfare, education and health to be organised and delivered? The risk is that by seeking universalistic changes to the foundations of society and politics the practical problems of dealing with day-to-day discrimination against women will be forgotten.

These are some of the debates arising from transnational citizenship, multiculturalism and feminist perspectives on citizenship. They all face a problem which Marshall's account also faces, and which potentially undermines their claim to provide valid theoretical explanations of citizenship. The problem is that they see citizenship exclusively as a matter of extending or creating rights. In Marshall's case it is social rights, and in Kymlica's it is ethnic minority rights. But as the earlier discussion of the Greek conception of citizenship indicates, rights are only half of the story when it comes to theorising citizenship. Rights cannot be divorced from responsibilities and obligations, because to a significant extent one person's rights are another person's obligations.

Marshall took the problem of enforcing rights for granted, since he was writing at a time when the British state was both highly interventionist and very welfare-orientated. It was pushing through major reforms in health, education and welfare supported by a large Labour parliamentary majority. This majority legitimated the tax rises needed to fund the new social rights created in that government's legislative programme. In contemporary times social rights are easy to extend if tax resistance is limited. But if tax resistance becomes a serious problem, and makes its presence felt via electoral behaviour, then social rights cannot be extended and may even be cut back. Put another way, if there is no support for extending social rights because of a 'culture of contentment' (Galbraith, 1992) on the part of the majority of the voters, then social rights will be curtailed. Rights theorists assume that a disembodied state provides the resources needed to extend social benefits and rights. But in reality it is other citizens who provide these rights by paying their taxes and by supporting such things as legislation outlawing discrimination on the grounds of race and sex. By ignoring this crucial dimension of citizenship, rights-based discourse is in danger of becoming divorced from any political reality.

The balancing act between rights and obligations is seen most acutely in relation to taxation and public expenditure. In 1950 when Marshall was writing, total tax revenue in Britain was just over 30 per cent of Gross Domestic Product (Steinmo, 1993: 27). In 1979 a new Conservative government was elected and led by Margaret Thatcher with an explicit commitment to reducing taxes and limiting the size of the state. In effect the electorate supported a policy of reducing social rights and the government started this process by removing the link between the value of state pensions and average earnings in 1981 (Bradshaw, 1992).

However, by 1989, after ten years of rhetoric from the government about the need to limit the size of the state, tax revenues were nonetheless 36.5 per cent of GDP (Steinmo, 1993: 40). Steinmo (1993: 47) shows that British post-war tax policy has been highly contested, with Labour governments increasing the tax burden on the rich and Conservative governments reducing it, set against a background of a rising overall tax burden. The growing burden of taxation even in the context of a government committed to reducing taxes shows how difficult it is to withdraw social rights once they are established, but it also points to the limits of the expansion of social rights. Prior to the 1997 general election New Labour gave a commitment not to increase income tax in the life of the Parliament, and after they were elected the new government held down public expenditure to the levels promised by the outgoing Conservatives for two years (Toynbee and Walker, 2001). All this was done in order to gain electoral credibility and to win the confidence of financial markets. Thus tax resistance is potentially a serious issue for any government.

This means that a theory of citizenship has to address issues of responsibilities and obligations as well as rights. The latter cannot be taken for granted in a democracy when one person's rights are another person's obligations. On the other hand some rights are easier to introduce than others. Civil rights are easy to enact, since there are few costs and great gains to be made by the average citizen from the introduction of freedom of speech, impartial justice and the freedom to pursue the career of one's choice. Attempts to extend political rights in the nineteenth century ran up against vested interests worried about confiscatory taxation arising from universal adult suffrage, and this is why they were harder to enact. Social rights are even harder to enact, since redistribution means that one person's benefits are another person's taxes. If a majority gain from redistribution, then democracy is likely to ensure that it is introduced, but at some point if the majority starts to lose from further redistribution and begins to oppose it, democracy will move in the opposite direction. Thus social rights differ from civil and political rights in having many of the characteristics of a zero-sum game, rather than a positive-sum gain in which everyone can gain from extending rights further.

In the light of this discussion we examine what we mean by citizenship in a final section of this chapter.

The theory of citizenship

The core problem to be addressed by a theory of citizenship is to explain why a group of people are willing to cooperate with each other to solve common problems when there are real incentives not to do so and to free-ride on the efforts of others. The issue of how a political community is created is an old one, much discussed by philosophers and theorists from the ancient Greeks to Hobbes, Locke, Rousseau and beyond. There have been a number of answers to this question, but it is at the core of debates about the nature and determinants of citizenship.

The language of game theory helps us to see the core problem, although it does not necessarily provide all the answers. This approach does, however, highlight the key issue of promoting cooperation in the face of incentives not to cooperate. To apply this perspective we should imagine a group of individuals debating whether or not to cooperate in order to deliver common security, which is the most basic and fundamental function of government. Common security is a public good, that is a good which has two defining characteristics, jointness of supply and the impossibility of exclusion (Samuelson, 1954).

Jointness of supply means that the consumption of the good by one person does not reduce the amount available to anyone else. If security is provided and one individual benefits from it, this does not reduce the benefits available to his or her neighbours. Impossibility of exclusion means that if an individual does not contribute to common security, he or she will nonetheless benefit from it since it is impractical to provide security only to those who have paid for it. Clearly, if individuals who did not pay their taxes could be murdered with impunity then nobody in a society would be secure. The rule of law must be applied to everyone if it is to be effective.

This means that there is a risk of security being inadequately provided by these individuals because each has an incentive to free-ride on the efforts of others. The problem can of course be solved by establishing a dictatorship which coerces people into providing the public good. But this would not produce citizenship in the sense described above, so we rule this out as a solution to the problem. In this case the task of explaining the emergence of citizenship is the same as the well-known problem of explaining the emergence of cooperation among rational egoists (see Axelrod, 1984, 1997; Taylor, 1987; Knight and Sened, 1995). It can be modelled as a prisoner's dilemma game in which there are incentives to cooperate but also to defect or not cooperate.

The game is illustrated in its simplest form in figure1.1 which contains the payoffs from a two-person version of the game. Each cell of the table

Player B

Player A	COOPERATE	DO NOT COOPERATE
COOPERATE	**10, 10**	5, 15
DO NOT COOPERATE	15, 5	7, 7

Note: cells contain payoffs for players A and B respectively.

Figure 1.1 Providing Collective Security as a Prisoner's Dilemma Game

describes the payoff to players A and B respectively from their joint course of action and it can be seen that they both get a bigger payoff if they cooperate (10) and provide security than if neither of them cooperates to do this (7). On the other hand each has an incentive to free-ride on the efforts of the other person and refuse to cooperate, since there is a bigger payoff to be made by refusing to cooperate (15) when your opponent cooperates (5). As is well known the equilibrium solution to this game, when it is played only once, is for neither player to cooperate, so that common security will not be provided and they both end up worse off as a consequence.[1] As Mueller points out in his review of this literature:

Jointness of supply is the carrot, making cooperative-collective decisions beneficial to all; absence of the exclusion principle is the apple tempting individuals into independent, non-cooperative behavior. (2003: 11)

It turns out that actors can be induced to cooperate in this game if four conditions are met (Axelrod, 1984, 1997). Firstly, individuals should not be too myopic, that is very short-sighted in their desire for payoffs. If people want instant gratification and are not prepared to wait for the benefits to emerge then they are unlikely to cooperate and once again security will not be provided. Secondly, and more importantly, the game should be a repeat game, that is played many times over, illustrating the point that cooperation needs to be based on frequent interaction between actors. It may be rational to rob a stranger whom you will never meet again, but not to rob your neighbour whom you will expect to meet again quite often. A third factor is that individuals should be uncertain about when the game ends – if they are not then the incentives to cooperate collapse.[2] This means that temporary communities where everyone

---

[1] The reason for this is that each individual gets a bigger payoff from not cooperating *regardless of what the other person does*. Thus if A cooperates when B defects he does worse than if he defects at the same time as B. Similarly if A cooperates when B also cooperates he does worse than if he defects and free-rides on the efforts of B. Consequently it is not rational to cooperate.

[2] If A knows he is going to interact with B ten times, then he is rational to defect on the tenth or last interaction, since that will produce a higher payoff. But since both players

expects soon to depart are less likely to cooperate than permanent communities where everyone expects repeated interactions to take place on a continuing basis. Thus hunter–gatherers are less likely to develop cooperative institutions outside the immediate family or tribe than are farmers. Finally, and most importantly, individuals should be able to sanction non-cooperative behaviour by punishing those who attempt to free-ride. If institutions exist to solve collective action problems, then they can be used to sanction non-cooperative behaviour. In the highly simplified world of the two-person game, Axelrod showed that tit-for-tat was the most effective strategy for doing this.[3]

Obviously cooperation between citizens in the real world can be enforced by state action, but to assume that the state will provide the collective good is, in effect, to assume away the problem. The brief historical review of citizenship above shows that from the time of the Greeks citizenship has referred to a relationship between individuals who see themselves as political equals with enough shared values and interests to pursue cooperation. The game theory model is useful since it simultaneously draws attention to the rights and obligations of citizenship. Individuals cooperate, even though their immediate short-term payoffs might be higher if they did not, because the long-term payoffs make it worth it. In other words they accept obligations because they can see it helps to preserve their rights. They are predisposed to cooperate with people like themselves rather than with people who are very different from themselves because they trust such people to reciprocate.

If individuals are given rights without any obligations this upsets the balance, giving the recipients an incentive to free-ride on the efforts of others. Similarly, if power is divided up unequally between people, then exploitation is likely to be a more lucrative strategy for the powerful actor than cooperation. Equally, if actors believe that they have a continuing relationship in the future, this promotes cooperation, which is why cooperation between members of the same ethnic, religious or cultural communities is more likely to occur than cooperation between people from different communities. Similarly, the knowledge that they can sanction other people who refuse to cooperate helps the process, again making

---

know this the problem gets shifted back to the ninth interaction. It then becomes rational to defect on this interaction, and in turn on the eighth and seventh interactions and so on back to the first interaction. Paradoxically, uncertainty about when the interaction will end promotes cooperation.

3 Tit-for-tat means that A starts out by cooperating in the first play of the game and if B reciprocates he continues. If, on the other hand, B defects, then A defects immediately after and continues to do so as long as B plays this strategy. If B then decides to cooperate after several rounds, A immediately forgives the earlier defection and starts to cooperate as well.

it more likely that cooperation will take place between people who know each other than between strangers.

This is of course a very sparse model, ignoring such issues as identity, morality and the law, but the core elements of the theory of cooperation give some guidance as to the circumstances under which citizenship will emerge. Citizenship is more likely to emerge among equals in a permanently settled community who are neighbours and who have a forum in which they can interact and where this institution can impose sanctions. Thus it is no surprise that citizenship emerged in the Greek city state. Obviously, geographical contiguity plays an important role in influencing citizenship, as does cultural, religious and ethnic homogeneity.

Nationalism is very helpful in supporting citizenship because it binds together people who are geographically separated, and who are never likely to meet each other face-to-face, into 'imaginary communities' (Whiteley, 1999). Clearly nationalism can also unite individuals from diverse ethnic, religious and cultural backgrounds and overcome some of the difficulties arising from the heterogeneity which these produce. But if nationalism weakens, and is not replaced by some similar integrating set of values and beliefs, citizenship will very likely break down.

This kind of approach to understanding citizenship has distinct advantages over exclusively rights-based approaches in explaining why individuals cooperate together to provide civil, political and social rights. Exclusively rights-based approaches cannot explain why there is no universal citizenship. If citizenship is such a good thing, why are we not all citizens of the world? The answer is because individuals are more likely to cooperate with people like themselves than with those who are very different, and there are no overarching transnational or multicultural values strong enough to bind together individuals from different nation-states to offset these effects.

Similarly, the rights-based approach cannot explain tax resistance. If social rights are such a good thing, why don't we all live in redistributive states which produce income equality? Societies such as the Scandinavian countries which have gone furthest down the road of providing social rights have relatively small populations and in the past were very homogeneous societies in terms of ethnicity, religion and culture. Since homogeneity promotes cooperation such societies find it easier to provide social rights than do large heterogeneous societies such as the United States. People are willing to extend benefits to others like themselves, but not to those they perceive as radically different. It is also well known that collective action problems are easier to overcome in small groups than they are in large groups (Olson, 1965). So it is not surprising that social rights are most developed in relative small culturally homogeneous societies.

This approach also explains why social security systems have often been sold to the population as a form of insurance rather than as a straight inter-generational transfer of resources which is what they are in reality. As is well known, national insurance in Britain is a tax which is virtually indistinguishable from income tax, but it was promoted originally as a form of insurance. This is because individuals are more willing to support insurance which gives them benefits in exchange for contributions, than straight transfers which are less certain to bring any benefits.

To round off this section we can now define the concept of citizenship as it will be used in this book. *Citizenship is a set of norms, values and practices designed to solve collective action problems which involve the recognition by individuals that they have rights and obligations to each other if they wish to solve such problems.* The state is essentially the transmission mechanism for these values and practices rather than the source of them, although state action can contribute both to their promotion and to their destruction. Both historically and contemporaneously most states are not democracies and this reflects the fact that one powerful solution to the collective action problem is dictatorship, where one individual or group imposes a solution on everyone else. But this is incompatible with democracy and it would be inaccurate to describe such societies as being made up of citizens, when actually they are subjects. So this definition only really applies to democratic societies. Curiously, in Britain individuals are still described as subjects of the crown, rather than as citizens. But this merely reflects the origins of the British state as a feudal dictatorship. The modern state has to balance rights and obligations, and as long as there is an electoral sanction at work to curb the overbearing tendencies of governments, this will continue to be true. The rest of this book will be devoted to spelling out the meaning of rights, obligations and the practices of political participation which underpin citizenship in modern Britain.

An outline of the book

The book begins in part I by empirically mapping out the nature of citizenship in Britain. We have defined it in terms of attitudes, norms and values, on the one hand, and behaviour, on the other. Chapter 2 starts this exercise by exploring individual attitudes and values and investigates whether Britons think that their political system is responsive to their needs and works efficiently or whether it is unresponsive and inefficient. A key issue in investigating attitudes is individual perceptions of efficacy, or the feeling that they can make a difference to politics and their lives if they participate. In our conception, citizenship is defined in terms of rights and obligations and this chapter investigates public perceptions of these aspects of citizenship. An important question is to determine whether there is a significant imbalance between perceptions of rights and obligations, in particular whether people want more rights without acknowledging the obligations which accompany those rights. The chapter concludes by investigating whether the attitudes and values which people share are supportive of governance in Britain or make it more difficult.

Chapter 3 looks at the second important aspect of citizenship, individual behaviour, particularly in relation to political participation. Such participation involves activities such as voting, joining interest groups, contacting public officials and campaigning. But it also includes protesting, taking part in demonstrations and being involved in political strikes. Talking about politics with other people and taking an interest in political matters also constitutes participation, and these are examined as well. In addition, the chapter goes beyond just identifying behaviour to examine potential behaviour, that is a respondent's willingness to undertake various activities in addition to their actual activities. Similarly, citizenship is broader than just involvement in politics, since it takes in voluntary activities of all kinds, some of which comprise informal activities with friends, relatives and neighbours, but others of which involve formal membership in various organisations. Participation in sports, recreational and cultural organisations are important aspects of social life and recent work has suggested that they may be important to the political system as well. So these activities are also examined in this chapter.

The analysis in chapter 3 brings up to date an empirical investigation of participation in Britain which has been going on since the first survey conducted by Almond and Verba in 1959 (Almond and Verba, 1963; see also Parry, Moyser and Day, 1992). However, the average citizen in Britain votes only once every four years, is not a member of a political organisation such as a party and rarely, if ever, goes on a protest demonstration. So most people have contact with the institutions of the state not through these forms of participation, but through the local representatives of the state which they may interact with on a daily basis. Thus patients in hospitals deal with the National Health Service as an arm of the state, parents deal with public-sector professionals in the education system, victims of crime deal with the police, public-sector workers deal with the state as their employer, and so on. It is at this micro level that the state obtrudes into everyday life. Arguably, this is much more important to the average citizen than following parliamentary debates about national issues or voting every four years. Chapter 4 examines this *small-scale* participation or the experiences people have in dealing with these important state institutions in their everyday lives, and their attempts to try to influence policies and services at this level. This chapter is concerned with a form of participation which has not in the past been seen as political participation at all.

Once the activities and attitudes which constitute citizenship have been examined in part I, the task of part II is to explore the determinants of these activities and attitudes. The approach taken is to examine a series of rival theories of citizenship which have been used in the literature to explain political participation and political attitudes. Chapter 5 provides a theoretical overview which sets the scene and spells out the concepts underlying the models which are specified and tested in chapter 6. Chapter 6 focuses on issues of measurement and testing so that the models can be evaluated empirically. The overall aim of the chapter is to determine which of these theoretical accounts provides the best explanation of the determinants of citizen attitudes and behaviour.

One set of theories of citizenship are anchored in sociological accounts which stress the importance of socialisation processes arising from the social structure in inculcating the norms and behaviours which are supportive of citizenship. These socialisation processes are in turn anchored in basic social cleavages such as class, ethnicity, gender and age. This might be referred to as *structural* theories of citizenship. A second set of theories see citizenship as being much more contingently based on a set of implicit and explicit contracts between individuals and the state. This perspective sees citizenship as a matter of individuals choosing to cooperate with each other and with the state. This approach is related to the concept of citizenship discussed earlier and might be described as *choice* theories of citizenship. Such choice theories present a rival perspective to structural theories. Chapters 5 and 6 investigate which of these alternative perspectives gives the most plausible account of the values and behaviours which constitute citizenship.

Given that part II focuses on explaining the determinants of citizenship, part III turns to the task of exploring the consequences of citizenship for the British political system. It has been suggested that communities with strong civic norms and patterns of civic-minded behaviour are more active, healthy, crime-free, educated and even happier than communities which lack these norms and behaviours (Putnam, 1993, 2000). Chapter 7 examines geographical variations in the indicators of citizenship discussed in part I and explores the issue of whether a benign local civic culture improves policy outcomes. In this way the country can be used as a laboratory to test hypotheses about the benefits of good citizenship in the form of civic-minded communities.

Chapter 7 discusses spatial variations in citizenship, whereas chapter 8 examines temporal variations. The Citizens Audit included a panel survey of the adult population in Great Britain which makes it possible to investigate the dynamics of citizenship over the period of a year. The two waves of the surveys were conducted in the autumns of 2000 and 2001, so that the general election occurred between them. Thus it is possible to examine the dynamics of citizenship in the context of a major mobilising event like a general election. The core issue to be addressed in this chapter is whether or not citizenship is malleable and can change significantly over time. This clearly has important implications for public policy, since if citizenship consists of a set of ingrained attitudes and behaviours which cannot significantly be influenced by outside forces, then the prospects for improving the civic culture of Britain are limited. On the other hand, if citizenship changes then there is at least the possibility that it might be induced to change for the better.

Finally, chapter 9 rounds off the book by summarising the findings as a whole and drawing more general conclusions from the research about the future of citizenship in Britain. We begin the task of understanding citizenship in Britain in the next chapter.

Part I

Understanding Citizenship

2   Civic Beliefs and Citizenship

In part I of this book we answer the question 'What is citizenship?' in contemporary Britain by exploring, firstly, people's beliefs about their civic duties and rights and, secondly, their patterns of civic behaviour. In this chapter we look specifically at their beliefs and attitudes, but we do so in very broad terms. This means examining some of the attitudes and beliefs associated with the idea of citizenship in rather general terms. However, for modelling purposes, when we begin to ask the question 'What determines the attitudes which underpin effective citizenship?' we have to refine the analysis and concentrate on certain key issues. These are attitudes to rights and obligations which the discussion in chapter 1 suggested are at the heart of modern citizenship. However, before embarking upon any analysis of attitudes, we need to elaborate on some of the key features of the Citizen Audit from which our findings are drawn.

The Citizen Audit

The Citizen Audit was funded by the Economic and Social Research Council as part of its Democracy and Participation research programme.[1] It was a series of surveys designed to examine citizenship in Britain today. In addition to measuring people's civic attitudes and behaviour, the Citizen Audit was constructed in such a way as to investigate some of the key political concepts which are relevant to citizenship including political knowledge, interest, efficacy, tolerance and participation. The design rationale of the Citizen Audit was, first, that it should be a representative sample of the British population; second, that it should be a large enough sample so that geographical analysis could be carried out; and, third, that it should be able to measure the dynamics of citizenship over time. These objectives mean that the audit had three different components: firstly, a baseline cross-section survey conducted by means of face-to-face

---

[1] For details of the ESRC Democracy and Participation programme, see http//:www.essex.ac.uk/democracy/

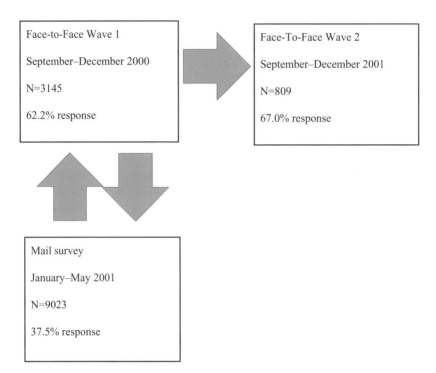

Figure 2.1 Design of the Citizen Audit

interviews; secondly, a large cross-section survey linked to the baseline survey but conducted by mail; and thirdly, a panel survey in which respondents from the baseline survey were re-interviewed a year later. The key features of the Citizen Audit are demonstrated in figure 2.1.

In parts I and II of this book we use the data acquired from the wave 1, face-to-face survey, which provides a representative sample of British citizens. The geographical analysis in chapter 7 requires local samples which are large enough to capture local variations in attitudes and behaviour and which therefore require a much larger overall sample. For this type of analysis we use the data acquired from merging the wave 1, face-to-face survey and from the mail-back survey. This merged data set provides us with this larger sample (N = 12,163) of respondents. Cost constraints made it impossible to undertake such a large survey using face-to-face interviews solely and therefore the Citizen Audit combined both face-to-face interviews and mail-back questionnaires.

The total number of questions asked of our respondents varied according to whether it was the wave 1, face-to-face or mail-back survey. In any survey there is a trade-off between length of questionnaire and response rates and this is particularly true for a mail survey. Whereas in the wave 1, face-to-face survey 62 questions were asked, this was reduced to 40 in the mail-back survey. Pilot work showed that response rates would have plummeted if we had tried to replicate the 62 questions on the mail survey. It is this reduced set of questions which is utilised in the merged data set. In appendix B a copy of the wave 1, face-to-face questionnaire is reproduced along with details of which questions were also used in the mail-back questionnaire.

Finally, to measure the dynamics of people's civic attitudes and behaviour a panel element was added to the Citizen Audit. Again cost restraints necessitated our selecting a smaller sample of respondents for the second wave of the face-to-face survey. Seventy per cent (2,126) of our respondents in the first wave agreed to be reinterviewed in the second wave, and from these 50 per cent were selected for inclusion in the second survey.[2] Analysis of the dynamics of civic attitudes and behaviour in chapter 8 is based upon waves 1 and 2 of the face-to-face surveys. In appendix B details are provided of which questions used in wave 1 were again used in wave 2. In appendix A details are provided on the means by which the individual respondents were selected for interview.

Citizenship: an overall framework

As an introduction to the discussion in this chapter of people's civic attitudes, and as a guide to the remainder of this book, we here discuss the overall framework within which we approach a discussion of citizenship. Our starting point is an overarching, or general meta-theoretical, perspective in which we distinguish between choice-based and structural-based theories. The former see citizenship emerging from the choices that individuals make, and these reflect the costs and benefits of the choice situation, broadly defined. Thus individuals choose their levels of participation as well as their attitudes to the rights and obligations imposed by society. The latter see citizenship as a matter of individuals being socialised into the norms, values and behaviours of the social groups to which they belong and into those of the wider society. In this perspective individuals

---

[2] Since the panel was conducted using face-to-face interviews cost considerations prevented the re-interviewing of all baseline survey respondents.

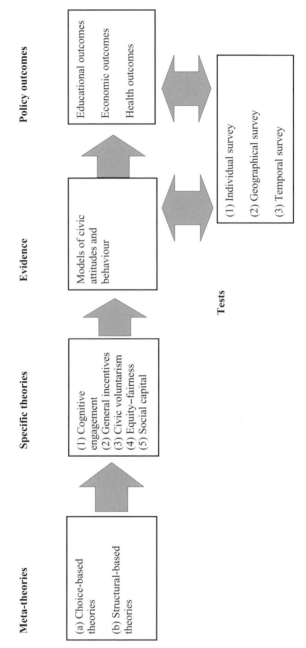

Figure 2.2 Overall Approach to the Study of Citizenship

are seen as being the product of social forces and structures which mould and shape their behaviour and attitudes.

These broad perspectives are useful, but since we intend to test the value of particular theories in explaining citizenship they need to be refined into more specific forms which can be measured and subsequently tested. In the case of choice-theoretic accounts of citizenship, we consider two specific alternatives: cognitive engagement and general incentives theories. In the case of structural accounts of citizenship, we examine three alternatives: civic voluntarism, equity–fairness and social capital theories. A detailed analysis of these alternative theoretical approaches appears in chapter 5, but here we briefly introduce them to the reader.

Cognitive engagement theory stresses people's acquisition and processing of information, and the ways in which these help them to make choices concerning civic rights, duties and engagement. General incentives theory is rooted in rational choice theory, but it adopts a broader perspective than a narrowly defined rational actor model and includes other variables not normally examined in such theory. Unlike cognitive engagement theory, the general incentives theory stresses the importance of various types of incentives which motivate people to get involved. Civic voluntarism theory argues that citizen engagement reflects people's resources which are primarily derived from their socio-economic status. Other factors are involved in this account as well, but civic voluntarism theory sees citizen participation essentially as being the product of the individual's resource endowments. Equity–fairness theory is based upon the notion that citizen attitudes and participation are the product of the comparisons which people make between their own lives and the lives of others. If these comparisons are favourable, this will affect their attitudes and behaviour rather differently from a situation where these comparisons are unfavourable. Finally, social capital theory sees citizenship as being rooted in community-based networks and inter-personal trust; in this account good citizenship derives from places with a strong sense of community where people know and trust each other.

Both the overall and the specific theories contribute to the causal side of our citizenship equation and provide the independent variables for our later models. On the outcomes or consequences side of our equation come the actual measures of civic attitudes and behaviour, or our dependent variables. We will test the relative influence of these independent variables on the dependent variables by using our individual, cross-sectional, our geographical and our temporal data. Our overall approach to citizenship is presented in visual form in figure 2.2. It can be seen that we analyse the attitudes and behaviour associated with citizenship in relation to five alternative models. The aim is to determine which model or combination of models provides the best account of citizen attitudes and behaviour, and this is the focus of chapters 5 and 6. However, once this modelling exercise is complete we then ask the question: 'Do citizen attitudes and behaviour influence outcomes?' This is the 'So what?' question which is the focus of chapters 7 and 8, which look at a variety of outcome measures.

In the light of this road-map, we now return to the task of describing in broad terms some of the key features of people's civic beliefs and attitudes. We begin by examining people's sense of attachment or geographical identity and inter-personal trust.

Personal identity and trust

Identity would seem to be an essential characteristic of citizenship. An ideal citizen is the person who has a sense of belonging to a community and feels a sense of obligation and commitment to other members of that community. The community is most likely to be contained within a territorial unit.[3] But what territorial unit? We asked all our respondents, from those living in city centres to those living in the most rural parts of Britain, how strong their feelings of attachment were to five territorial units starting with their neighbourhood or their village, then proceeding to their municipality or their town, their region and, finally, their country. In addition, we asked them how strongly they felt attached to the European Union. Respondents were required to score their attachment to all five of these units on an 11-point scale, from 0 to 10, with 0 representing 'no attachment at all' and 10 representing 'very strong attachment'. Table 2.1 shows that they feel most strongly attached to their country, and there are weak but statistically significant differences between their levels of attachment to their neighbourhoods, municipalities and regions. Finally, they feel much less attached to the European Union.

If people's identity is primarily with their country then the question is what country. We asked our respondents whether they thought of themselves 'first and foremost' as English, Scottish, Welsh, Irish, British, European, or of another identity and, as we see in figure 2.3, the majority (57 per cent) answered 'English'. The second largest group, made up of 24 per cent of our respondents, identified themselves as 'British'. Who these British identifiers are is something we will discuss later in this chapter. Only a small percentage of our respondents identified themselves as Scottish (8 per cent) or Welsh (4 per cent). This is unsurprising since our sample was nationally representative. Majorities of our respondents

---

[3] There will be some people, however, who identify with others transcending particular territorial state boundaries.

Table 2.1 *Feelings of Attachment*

	Mean	Std Dev	Region t-tests	Neighbourhood/ village t-tests	Municipality/ town t-tests	European Union t-tests
Country	7.72	2.34	17.6*	20.5*	22.3*	58.0*
Region	6.95	2.51	–	6.2*	8.4*	45.0*
Neighbourhood or village	6.68	2.69	–	–	1.3	39.4*
Municipality or town	6.62	2.62	–	–	–	39.4*
European Union	3.96	2.86	–	–	–	–

Source: Weighted 2000 face-to-face survey. N = c3,081. *p < .01
'*How strong are your feelings of attachment to your neighbourhood, town, region, country and the European Union?*' Respondents were asked to give a score ranging from 0 (no attachment at all) to 10 (very strong attachment). Note that the t-tests measure the statistical significance of the different mean attachment scores. For example the t statistic of 17.6 indicates that there is a significant difference between the mean attachment to region and the mean attachment to country.

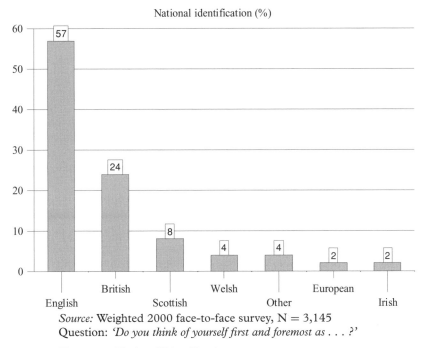

National identification (%)

Source: Weighted 2000 face-to-face survey, N = 3,145
Question: '*Do you think of yourself first and foremost as . . . ?*'

Figure 2.3 National Identification

Table 2.2 *Levels of Personal Trust, Helpfulness and Fairness*

	Mean	Standard deviation
Personal trust	6.59	2.19
Personal helpfulness	6.13	2.23
Personal fairness	6.27	2.10

Source: Weighted 2000 face-to-face survey. N = c3,114
Questions:
'Thinking for a moment about whether people with whom you have contact can be trusted. Please use the 0–10 scale where 10 means definitely can be trusted and 0 means definitely cannot be trusted.'
'Would you say that most of the time people you come into contact with try to be helpful or that they are mostly looking out for themselves?' (0–10 scale, with 0 'looking out for themselves', and 10 'try to be helpful').
'Do you think that most people you come into contact with would try to take advantage of you if they got the chance or would they try to be fair?' (0–10 scale, with 0 'try to take advantage', and 10 'try to be fair').

living in Scotland and Wales identified themselves as Scottish and Welsh (81 and 64 per cent respectively).[4]

What of the people living in Britain? What do they think of each other? Do they trust one another, do they believe that the people they come into contact with will take advantage of them whenever possible? Using a similar 11-point scale to that used already to measure people's sense of attachment to a territorial unit, we asked our respondents whether they could trust the people with whom they had contact, whether they thought such people were helpful and, finally, whether they thought such people would try to take advantage of them. Table 2.2 reveals that people's perceptions of others are relatively positive: the mean scores on all three range from 6.1 to 6.6 and these are closer to the most positive end of the scales. People tend to trust others with whom they have contact. They trust one another marginally more so than they find people that they come into contact with to be fair and helpful. The fact that the British are relatively trusting of one another is an important finding. Its presence makes life easier while its absence makes the task of day-to-day civic management and maintenance almost impossible (O'Neill, 2002). Evidence from the British Social Attitudes surveys (Johnston and Jowell, 2001) suggests that people's trust of others has remained stable over the

[4] Among the people living in England 1 per cent identified themselves as Scottish and another 1 per cent identified themselves as Welsh.

past twenty years.[5] We will examine personal trust in more detail when we consider its possible impact upon policy outcomes in chapter 7.

Does people's inter-personal trust carry over into trusting institutions? It is this question which we now address.

Institutional trust

We asked our respondents for their views on a wide range of institutions, both public and private, and transnational, national and local. Again we asked them to give a score for these various institutions, on an 11-point scale, ranging from 0 ('do not trust at all') to 10 ('trust completely'). Table 2.3 provides the mean scores, and we see that people are more likely to trust the institutions which are not directly associated with elected politicians. They regard the police, the courts, the Civil Service and the banks as more trustworthy than the House of Commons, the Scottish Parliament, the Welsh Assembly, and the various political parties.[6] The public are almost twice as likely to trust the police as they are to trust politicians. In their distrust of both political institutions and the people who are elected to them, the British are no different from people in other advanced industrial democracies (Newton and Norris, 2000; Putnam, Pharr and Dalton, 2000).

Among the elected institutions, it is noteworthy that the public trusts local government more than national government, the House of Commons, or the parties from which government ministers are drawn. Perhaps local government's closer proximity to the people, in the sense that it is involved in the provision of many day-to-day services, accounts for this higher level of trust. There is a paradox here, however, in that while people trust local government more than other elected institutions, they are less likely to vote in local than national government elections. Furthermore, closer proximity to the people doesn't automatically generate greater trust for a political institution. The Welsh suspicion of their newly established, devolved Assembly and of the champion of Welsh separateness, Plaid Cymru, is noteworthy; of all the institutions and parties which we examine in table 2.3 they both attract the lowest levels of trust. As we will see later in this chapter, the Scots feel more positively towards their devolved institutions than do the Welsh.

We have already made the point that our respondents feel relatively good about the people around them. They trust one another and they

---

[5] Johnston and Jowell (2001: 182) report that between 1981 and 2000 four people in every ten agreed with the statement 'Most people can be trusted.'

[6] The public's greater trust of non-elected personnel, such as the police and civil servants, is consistent over time. See, for example, Jowell and Topf, 1988: 112.

Table 2.3 *Levels of Institutional Trust*

	Mean	Standard deviation
Police	6.29	2.42
Banks	5.58	2.58
Civil Service	5.51	2.33
Courts	5.50	2.39
Local government	4.59	2.41
House of Commons	3.83	2.37
Liberal Democrat Party	3.82	2.38
Government	3.72	2.44
Labour Party	3.70	2.56
Scottish Parliament*	3.67	2.59
Scottish National Party*	3.66	2.70
European Union	3.46	2.43
Conservative Party	3.32	2.51
Politicians	3.26	2.25
Welsh Assembly*	3.14	2.59
Plaid Cymru*	2.84	2.62

Source: Weighted 2000 face-to-face survey. N = c2,983; N = c246 (Scotland); N = c130 (Wales).
Statement: '*And now your views on various institutions. Do you trust . . .?*' Respondents were given an 11-point scale ranging from 0 ('do not trust at all') to 10 ('trust completely').
* Asked of respondents residing in Scotland and Wales only.

believe that others are caring and helpful. So to what extent are they tolerant of other people? Are they willing to tolerate other people's opinions and lifestyles?

Tolerance of others

The British are limited in their tolerance of others' free speech or right of abode. When asked whether environmental, animal liberation, religious or neo-nazi and racist groups should have the right to air their views in public, relatively few were committed to unrestricted freedom of speech. Table 2.4 reports that a simple plurality (47 per cent) would definitely grant environmentalists the right to speak out in public, but fewer would grant that right to animal liberationists, religious fundamentalists or neo-nazis and racists.

A previous study of political tolerance (Crewe, Conover and Searing, 1994) reported that the British were intolerant of groups of people of whom they disapproved. Overwhelming majorities were willing to forbid people in such groups to teach in local schools or to form a local branch of

Table 2.4 *Tolerance of the Rights of Other Groups to Speak in Public*

	Definitely not %	Possibly not %	Possibly yes %	Definitely yes %	Don't know %
Neo-nazi & racists	64	11	13	8	5
Religious fundamentalists	34	23	27	10	6
Animal liberationists	14	13	45	24	5
Environmentalists	6	5	38	47	4

Source: Weighted 2000 face-to-face survey. N = 3,145.
Question:
'*To what extent should the following groups be allowed to speak out in public*
• *neo-nazi and racist groups*
• *religious fundamentalists*
• *animal liberation groups*
• *environmental groups?*'
Note that in this table and all those that follow in which percentage responses are recorded, the figures have been rounded and therefore the totals may not always equal 100.

the group. Question wording differences between this earlier study and the Citizen Audit make direct comparisons difficult, but our evidence confirms people's similar limited levels of tolerance. In the Citizen Audit we asked our respondents whether they would tolerate particular groups living in their community. Table 2.5 reveals that the NIMBY (Not In My Back Yard) factor is very powerful. Around one-half or more of our respondents opposed a resettlement home for young offenders, a new age travellers' camp, or a sex offenders' rehabilitation centre in their neighbourhood.

Pride in British citizenship and democracy

Moving now from questions concerning individual tolerance into issues of pride in general, we start by asking how proud people are to be British citizens. Over three-quarters of our respondents expressed a pride in their British citizenship. Figure 2.4 shows that 33 per cent were 'very proud', and a further 48 per cent were 'somewhat proud'; by contrast, only 1 in 33 (3 per cent) felt no pride whatsoever, and a total of 16 per cent had negative feelings.

People are proud to be British citizens, but they are far less enthusiastic about British democracy. When asked how satisfied they are with the way democracy works in Britain we find remarkably that almost as many people express dissatisfaction as satisfaction. In figure 2.5, we see

Table 2.5 *Tolerance of the Rights of Other Groups of People to be Housed in the Community*

	Strongly support %	Support %	Neither support nor oppose %	Oppose %	Strongly oppose %	Don't know %
New school	25	53	13	5	1	3
Retirement home	21	57	14	5	1	2
Young offenders' resettlement home	3	25	22	25	22	4
New age travellers' camp	1	10	14	28	45	2
Sex offenders' unit	1	6	11	23	57	3

Source: Weighted 2000 face-to-face survey. N = 3,145.
Question:
'If one of the following were proposed in your locality or neighbourhood, would you support or oppose it:
- *a new school*
- *a retirement home*
- *a resettlement centre for young offenders*
- *a new age travellers' camp site*
- *a sex offenders' rehabilitation centre?'*

that only 35 per cent are satisfied while 33 per cent are dissatisfied, and a further 29 per cent are neither satisfied nor dissatisfied. The fact that only one in three respondents are satisfied with the workings of British democracy is a strong statement of no confidence in the country's traditional political institutions and procedures. In response to a similar type of question in the 1995 Eurobarometer (Klingemann, 1999: 50), 46 per cent of the British then stated that they were satisfied with the way democracy worked in their country which suggests that a decline in public confidence in democracy has occurred during the past ten years.[7]

Recent changes in the structure of British government, specifically the creation of devolved legislatures in Scotland and Wales, elected by

[7] However, one needs to be careful drawing such a conclusion based upon observations from just two time points. Particularly since, even though the Eurobarometer question was similar to the Citizen Audit question, it provided people with four options – 'very satisfied', 'fairly satisfied', 'not very satisfied' and 'not at all satisfied' – but not with the 'neither satisfied nor dissatisfied' option as in the Citizen Audit. As a consequence, people who did not have an opinion may have opted for the 'fairly satisfied' response, thus artificially boosting the percentage of 'satisfied' respondents in the Eurobarometer study. Additionally, the Eurobarometer had the slightly weaker 'fairly satisfied' option, whereas the Citizen Audit had the stronger 'satisfied' wording which again makes direct comparison very difficult.

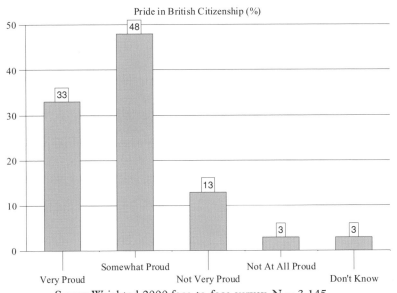

Pride in British Citizenship (%)

Source: Weighted 2000 face-to-face survey. N = 3,145.
Question: *'Thinking what it means to be a citizen of Britain today, would you say that you were very proud, somewhat proud, not very proud or not at all proud to be a British citizen?'*

Figure 2.4 Pride in British Citizenship

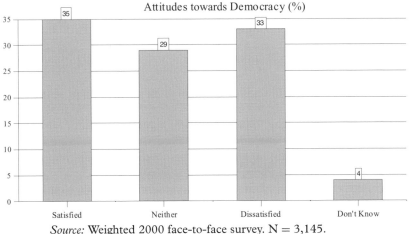

Attitudes towards Democracy (%)

Source: Weighted 2000 face-to-face survey. N = 3,145.
Question: *'Thinking about Britain, how satisfied are you with the way democracy works?'*

Figure 2.5 Attitudes towards Democracy

Attitudes towards Democracy in Scotland and Wales (%)

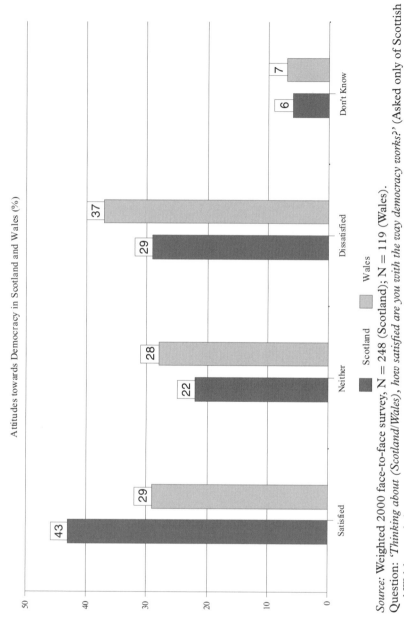

Source: Weighted 2000 face-to-face survey, N = 248 (Scotland); N = 119 (Wales).
Question: *'Thinking about (Scotland/Wales), how satisfied are you with the way democracy works?'* (Asked only of Scottish and Welsh sample.)

Figure 2.6 Attitudes towards Democracy in Scotland and Wales

Table 2.6 *Government Responsiveness to Public Opinion*

	Mean	Standard deviation
Government listens to person's opinions	3.18	2.27
Government takes decisions in accordance with person's wishes	2.85	2.10
Government listens to majority opinion	4.10	2.42
Government takes decisions in accordance with majority wishes	3.81	2.30

Source: Weighted 2000 face-to-face survey. N = c3,016
Question: *'How much do you think the British government (a) listens personally to people like yourself; (b) takes decisions in accordance with your personal wishes; (c) listens to majority opinion; (d) takes decisions in accordance with majority wishes?'* Responses were on an eleven-point scale 0–10, with 0 as 'not at all' and 10 as 'a great deal'.

a more proportionate system than for the British House of Commons, were introduced in response to public disquiet about the prevailing institutional arrangements. However, the impact of these reforms has been mixed. Among the Scots, as figure 2.6 reports, a plurality are satisfied with the way democracy works. In fact, the proportion of Scots satisfied with democracy is greater than among the English. However, among the Welsh there is less satisfaction with democracy; a plurality (37 per cent) in fact is dissatisfied. Among the Scots the difference between the satisfied and the dissatisfied is plus 14 percentage points, whereas among the Welsh it is minus 8 points. So devolved government does not automatically increase people's satisfaction with democracy. The Citizen Audit was conducted only one year after the devolution proposals had been implemented and therefore these are early days to judge their impact, but the Welsh are clearly very sceptical of this political project. As we have already noted in table 2.3, the Welsh are also more distrustful of their Assembly and their nationalist party than are the Scots of their Parliament and nationalist party.

Government responsiveness

Do people believe that governments are responsive to their opinions? We asked our respondents two questions, the first being 'How much do you think the British government listens personally to people like yourself?', and the second, 'How much do you think the British government takes decisions in accordance with your personal wishes?' It is clear, as we see in table 2.6, that there are few people who believe that the government takes any notice of their personal opinions. On an 11-point scale from 0 to 10, the mean scores on these two questions were 3.2 and 2.9 respectively. As far as our respondents' personal influence on government is concerned, they would seem to be taking an eminently realistic and unsurprising view.

When people were then asked two further questions, the first being whether the British government 'listens to majority opinion', and the second whether the government 'takes decisions in accordance with majority wishes', the mean scores rose significantly (4.1 and 3.8 respectively). However, it needs stressing that although contemporary governments make every effort to monitor public opinion very closely, fewer than one in two people believe that their government takes much notice of majority wishes. Even the idea of a government listening to majority opinion, let alone acting in accordance with majority opinion, fails to attract popular endorsement.

The public's view that government is indifferent to their opinions, either individually or collectively, is further confirmed by the fact that a majority (55 per cent) agree with the statement that 'people like me have no say in what the government does'. Table 2.7 reveals that nine times more people 'strongly agree' than 'strongly disagree' with this statement. Comparison of the Citizen Audit's findings with similar British Social Attitudes data over the past two decades suggests a trendless fluctuation of public attitudes on this question.[8]

We also see in table 2.7 that most people do not believe that the government treats them fairly as individuals. Whereas 37 per cent disagree with the statement that 'the government generally treats people like me fairly', only 27 per cent agree; a further 37 per cent are agnostic and neither agree nor disagree. This contrasts starkly with the findings of the Civic Culture study (Almond and Verba, 1963: 107–9), the fieldwork for which was conducted in 1959, in which majorities expected 'equal treatment' from government offices (83 per cent), and 'serious consideration' of the concerns they raised from government officials (59 per cent). Exact comparison with this earlier study of the British is impossible because of question wording differences, but it would seem that a very significant decline in public confidence in government has occurred over the past forty years. Whereas then the British believed that government was judicious, this no longer appears to be the case. When the British were

---

[8] The percentage of respondents 'strongly agreeing' with the statement that 'people like me have no say in what the government does' is

1974	1986	1987	1991	1994	1996	1998	2000
14	23	20	16	28	24	17	25

(Curtice and Jowell, 1995: 93; Bromley, Curtice and Seyd, 2001: 206)

Table 2.7 *Personal Influence on Government*

	Strongly agree %	Agree %	Neither agree nor disagree %	Disagree %	Strongly disagree %
No say in government	19	36	22	20	2
Government treats people fairly	3	24	37	29	8
Matters which party in power	17	38	22	18	5
Vote makes no difference	8	20	19	44	9
Political influence if involved	5	35	26	27	7
Politics so complicated	16	38	20	22	4
People influence local community	10	48	27	13	3
People change Britain	8	35	33	20	5

Source: Weighted 2000 face-to-face survey. N = c3,128.
Statements:
> '*People like me have no say in what the government does.*'
> '*The government generally treats people like me fairly.*'
> '*It really matters which party is in power, because it will affect our lives.*'
> '*My vote makes no difference to the outcome of an election.*'
> '*People like me can have a real influence on politics if they are prepared to get involved.*'
> '*Sometimes politics and government seem so complicated that a person like me cannot really understand what is going on.*'
> '*When people like me all work together we can really make a difference to our local community.*'
> '*If people like me work together we can really change Britain.*'

asked then what they were most proud of in their country their most frequent response was some aspect of the political system (Almond and Verba, 1963: 102). It is very doubtful whether a similar response would be obtained if the same question were repeated in Britain today.

Nevertheless, even though people feel that government takes little note of either personal or majority wishes, a majority (55 per cent) believe that 'it really matters which party is in power'. Three times more people 'strongly agree' than 'strongly disagree' with the statement; just under one in four people (23 per cent) disagree. So even though people feel that they have little impact upon governments, they believe that who governs, in the sense of which party is elected to office, matters to them. Similarly, although our respondents are sceptical of the impact of their views on governmental outcomes, a majority (53 per cent) disagree with the statement that 'my vote makes no difference to the outcome of an election'. The public believes that its vote is important in terms of an

Table 2.8 *The Impact of Voting on Political Institutions*

	Not at all %	Some %	Great deal %	Don't know %
Local authorities	28	57	9	7
Scottish Parliament*	37	51	12	0
Welsh Assembly*	51	43	6	0
House of Commons	36	46	8	10
European Parliament	49	32	5	14

Source: Weighted 2000 face-to-face survey. N = c3,145; N = 231 (Scotland); N = 106 (Wales).
Question: *'Thinking about voters in general to what extent does voting allow people to influence decisions made by . . .?'*
* Asked of respondents residing in Scotland and Wales only

election outcome, just as it believes that whoever is the governing party is important.

Locality is revealed as important when our respondents considered the potential impact of their collective actions. When we compare locality and nation in table 2.7 we see that people are more likely to believe that working together can have an impact upon local communities than upon national outcomes. Whereas over one-half (58 per cent) agree that 'when people like me all work together we can really make a difference to our local community', by contrast, fewer people (43 per cent) agree that by working together they can change Britain. Clearly people feel that it is at the local level that their potential impact is greatest. Similar findings regarding people's greater sense of local rather than national political impact are reported in the USA (Oliver, 2001).

Although people are sceptical that government takes much notice of them personally, we have noted in table 2.7 that an institution's proximity to people makes a difference to their sense of political influence. This is further confirmed in table 2.8. When we asked our respondents whether they believed that voting could influence decisions taken by various elected institutions, two in every three people thought that their votes would have 'some' or 'a great deal' of influence on the decisions taken by local authorities, whereas, by contrast, only just over one in two people felt similarly about the House of Commons. Just over one in three felt that their vote would influence the decisions taken by the European Parliament. We have previously noted that the Scots have a more positive attitude towards democracy than the English or the Welsh, and in table 2.8 we see that more Scots are likely to believe that their votes influence decisions taken by the Scottish Parliament than English or Welsh think that their votes are likely to influence decisions taken by the House

Table 2.9 *The Structure of Political Efficacy Measures*

	External efficacy	Internal: collective	Internal: personal
Government takes decisions in accordance with majority wishes	0.87		
Government takes decisions in accordance with your wishes	0.87		
Government listens personally to you	0.86		
Government listens to majority opinion	0.84		
Government treats people like me fairly	0.52		
If work together can change Britain		0.77	
If work together can make a difference to local community		0.77	
Real influence on politics if willing to get involved		0.67	
Really matters which party in power		0.57	
Politics and government so complicated			0.83
No say in what the government does			0.57
My vote makes no difference to election outcome			0.57
Eigenvalue	4.97	1.47	1.11
Percentage of variance explained	33.2	9.82	7.43

Note: This table indicates the extent to which responses to the different survey questions are correlated with unobserved latent measures of political efficacy (varimax rotated factor matrix).

of Commons or the Welsh Assembly. The Welsh have little to say for their Assembly, with a majority of them (51 per cent) believing that their vote will have no influence upon its decisions.

Can we now devise a measure of political efficacy to summarise these various public attitudes towards government? If we subject the questions and statements used in tables 2.6 and 2.7 to a principal components analysis, we see in table 2.9 that there are three distinct, underlying dimensions. The first is concerned with the individual's relationship to the political system in general and we describe this as external efficacy. In this case it measures the extent to which an individual feels that the government takes any notice of his or her personal opinions, responds to majority opinions, and treats individuals fairly. The second dimension measures the individual's sense of efficacy if he or she acts collectively, and we describe this as internal, collective efficacy. So people who believe that they can have a political impact by working with others are also more likely to believe that which party is in power matters. And the third dimension measures the individual's sense of personal competence and ability, and we describe this as internal, personal efficacy. Accordingly, someone

Table 2.10 *Attitudes towards Civic Obligations*

	Not at all important %	Not very important %	Fairly important %	Very important %	Don't know %
Always to obey the law	1	3	28	66	2
Never to evade tax payments	2	7	30	58	4
To make regular charity donations	5	25	49	17	5
To work for local voluntary organisations	6	32	43	13	6
Questions: *'How important do you feel it is . . .?'*					
How likely is it that you will?	*Not at all likely*	*Not very likely*	*Fairly likely*	*Very likely*	
Turn out and vote in the next general election	*9*	*8*	*14*	*64*	

Source: Weighted 2000 face-to-face survey. N = 3,145.

who feels that politics is complicated is also more likely to believe that his or her personal impact upon government in general, or on election outcomes in particular, is very marginal. These three factors account for 50 per cent of the variance.

So far in this chapter we have been examining people's attitudes towards others around them, towards a range of institutions and, finally, towards democracy in general; with regard to their opinions on the latter topic, we have assessed their sense of influence on political outcomes. We now turn to an examination of their views regarding duties, obligations and rights.

Civic duties and obligations

What do people feel are their civic duties and obligations? In general, we can say that a sense of civic duty runs deep among the British. They have a very strong commitment to obey the law, to pay their taxes, and not to defraud the state. Table 2.10 reports that very few condone disobedience of the law (4 per cent) or the evasion of taxes (9 per cent); an overwhelming number believe in obeying the law and paying their taxes.

We see that two out of every three people believe that it is 'very important' that the law should always be obeyed, and between one in two and two in three believe that it is 'very important' that tax payments should never be evaded. Furthermore, three in every four believe that claiming government benefits to which they are not entitled is unjustified (see table 2.11). In addition there is a strong norm that people have a duty to vote in elections. This was measured in two ways: one was to ask respondents if they would vote in the next election, and the results of this can be seen in table 2.10; the other will be discussed below in connection with figure 2.7.

In addition to these duties reflecting respect for the state, we find that other possible ones, such as giving regularly to charities and working for local voluntary organisations, do not attract the same strong levels of public commitment. Nevertheless pluralities of the population believe that a commitment to regular charitable donations and to local voluntary work is 'fairly important'.

The public's recognition of its duties to the state appears to be longstanding. For example, the British Social Attitudes surveys reveal (Curtice and Jowell, 1995) a consistent public view over the past twenty years that the law should be obeyed.[9] Furthermore, these same surveys (Johnston, 1988) show public support for the view that individuals should pay the income tax that has been levied upon them. However, these surveys reveal that the public is less committed to the payment of indirect taxes, such as value added tax. This is confirmed by the Citizen Audit. When we asked our respondents whether they had ever paid cash in order to avoid the payment of VAT, 29 per cent admitted that they had done so. Furthermore, the Citizen Audit reveals that in other areas of civic life people feel less sense of obligation. So, for example, 76 per cent of our respondents admit to breaking the speed limit when driving a vehicle, and 38 per cent would not admit to the Inland Revenue if it made a mistake in their favour. These findings tend to undermine the frequently voiced criticism that questions about obedience to the law or about norms concerning taxation are invalid because everyone will agree with them. As these results indicate, people are quite willing to admit breaking the law on occasions.

In addition to obeying the law, paying their taxes and not defrauding the state, people also have a very strong sense of their duty to vote. As we see in figure 2.7, almost three-quarters of our respondents agree with

[9] In response to the question 'In general would you say that people should obey the law without exception?', the percentage agreeing is

1983	1984	1986	1989	1991	1994
53	57	55	50	52	41

(Curtice and Jowell, 1995: 158)

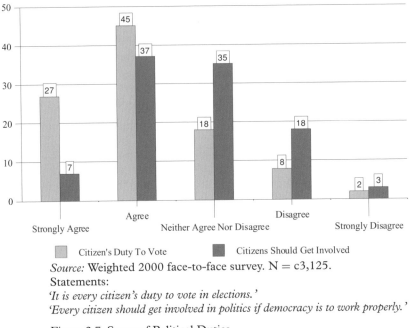

Source: Weighted 2000 face-to-face survey. N = c3,125.
Statements:
'It is every citizen's duty to vote in elections.'
'Every citizen should get involved in politics if democracy is to work properly.'

Figure 2.7 Sense of Political Duties

the statement that 'it is every citizen's duty to vote in elections', while only one in ten disagree. This is the first of our indicators of duty to vote, and more than one in four (27 per cent) 'strongly agree' with the statement. How then does one explain the 59 per cent turnout in the 2001 general election? Are a significant proportion of our respondents liars who will say one thing in a questionnaire but then act differently in everyday life? We will discuss the question of the relationship between beliefs and actions in chapter 3, but here our response is that perhaps the distinctive features of that election – a consistent Labour lead in the public opinion polls, a weak Conservative party in opposition, and no clear ideological distinction between Labour and Conservative parties and evidence of a decline in such civic norms among younger citizens – encouraged non-voting in 2001 (Clarke et al., 2004).

Beyond the act of voting, however, people's sense of a duty to become politically engaged is fairly limited. In response to the statement that 'every citizen should get involved in politics if democracy is to work properly', a plurality (44 per cent) believe that involvement in politics is necessary to maintain democracy. However, one in three people (35 per cent) are indifferent, in the sense that they neither agree nor disagree.

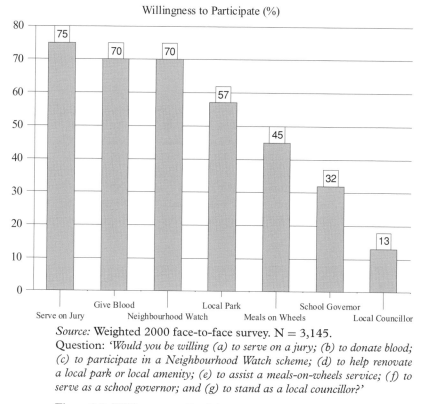

Source: Weighted 2000 face-to-face survey. N = 3,145.
Question: *'Would you be willing (a) to serve on a jury; (b) to donate blood; (c) to participate in a Neighbourhood Watch scheme; (d) to help renovate a local park or local amenity; (e) to assist a meals-on-wheels service; (f) to serve as a school governor; and (g) to stand as a local councillor?'*

Figure 2.8 Willingness to Participate

We are going to examine people's levels of participation in the following chapter, but we refer here to their responses to a battery of questions asking them whether they would participate in a wide range of actions contributing to the public good. We mention them here because we believe that their responses reflect attitudes towards various civic duties and responsibilities that go beyond paying one's taxes and obeying the law. So, for example, trial by jury is an important feature of the British legal system and to act in judgement of others is regarded as obligatory in Britain. Figure 2.8 demonstrates that three-quarters of the population express a willingness to serve on a jury. In addition to obligatory jury service, there are a range of other forms of non-obligatory community engagement in which we asked our respondents whether they would be willing to participate. Seven in ten stated that they are willing to give blood; a similar number are willing to assist in a Neighbourhood Watch scheme; one in two are willing to assist in renovating a local park or amenity; fewer are willing to assist with a meals-on-wheels service or to serve as a school governor; and, finally, only one in eight are willing to consider standing as a local councillor. So although, as we have already noted, people feel a sense of attachment to their local community, they are unwilling to put themselves forward as local councillors.

The problem with these potential participation questions is the halo effect that they can create in which people will agree in theory to what they perceive as good actions, but they will not act on their beliefs in practice. One reason for a mismatch between beliefs and actions may be the costs involved in acting on beliefs. A second reason may be that the opportunities for action do not arise, that is the *opportunity structures* do not support participation. A third reason may be that our respondents are liars who say one thing and do another, although the evidence tends to suggest that people do not do this in large numbers.[10] All three factors may prevail among our respondents. We will return to this question when we discuss participation in chapter 3. At this point, however, we believe that these potential participation questions are of value because, firstly, they reveal a hierarchy of civic attitudes (for example, giving blood is regarded as more laudable than serving as a school governor) and, secondly, they demonstrate whether or not there exists an underlying bedrock of civic values in society. Notwithstanding the fact that more people are willing to participate than actually do so, our findings reveal that individual civic commitment is high (for example, giving blood and participating in neighbourhood activities) but political civic commitment (in this case, standing for election as a local councillor) is low. This latter finding is disturbing in a country in which elected local government has played such an important role in British politics for over 100 years.

We conclude this discussion of civic duties by pointing out that people have clear and distinctive moral codes concerning their own behaviour towards the people around them. We have already reported that three in every four people believe that claiming government benefits to which they are not entitled is unjustified. In addition, table 2.11 reports a very powerful public belief (at least three in every four) that driving under the influence of alcohol, buying goods known to be stolen, or throwing litter down in a public place can never be justified. And people feel almost as strongly that having sex with someone under the legal age of consent, or failing to report accidental damage to a parked car can never be justified. Only with regard to the taking of cannabis or keeping money found in

---

[10] In the 2001 British Election Study it was possible to compare people's claims that they voted in the election with their actual voting record, since the latter can be verified. This comparison showed that only 4 per cent of respondents to the election study survey claimed to have voted when they did not (see Clarke et al., 2004).

Table 2.11 *Attitudes towards Personal Obligations*

	Never justified %	Rarely justified %	Sometimes justified %	Always justified %	Don't know %
Claiming government benefits	77	13	7	1	2
Taking cannabis	49	11	32	5	3
Sex under legal age	70	15	10	1	4
Driving under influence of alcohol	93	4	1	–	1
Buying stolen goods	73	16	9	–	2
Keeping money	36	20	35	6	3
Failing to report vehicle damage	68	20	8	1	4
Throwing litter	75	17	6	1	2

Source: Weighted 2000 face-to-face survey. N = 3,145.

Statements: *'Consider the following: please tell me if you think they can be justified or not?*
* *claiming government benefits which you are not entitled to*
* *taking cannabis*
* *having sex under the legal age of consent*
* *driving under the influence of alcohol*
* *buying something you know is stolen*
* *keeping money that you found in the street*
* *failing to report accidental damage you've done to a parked vehicle*
* *throwing away litter in a public place'*

the street are more than one in three likely to assert that such actions are justified.

Overall then we can summarise that people's sense of civic obligation encompasses obedience to the state, a willingness to undertake voluntary actions, such as participating in a Neighbourhood Watch or a local renovation project, and a willingness to engage in civic service, such as going on a jury or giving blood. But for most people their sense of duty does not extend to more obvious political undertakings, such as becoming a school governor or standing for the local council; on such matters, their commitment is much more limited.

We now turn to the question of rights. If people have a rather restricted, but nevertheless strong sense of their civic obligations, what then do they think are their civic rights? The Citizen Audit included an extensive battery of indicators of citizen rights ranging from individuals' private freedoms of action to their expectations of the role of government in supporting various rights. Rather than ask our questions about topics where universal support would be very likely (for example, freedom to associate), we concentrated upon those issues where rights would be more controversial. We did so in order to be able to examine the variations in attitudes in greater detail.

Civic rights

Conover and Searing (2002) suggest, in a comparative study of citizenship in the USA and Britain, that the British think of citizenship more in terms of membership of a culturally homogeneous community than of legal rights and duties. This is a major reason, they argue, why an individual rights culture has been relatively weak in Great Britain. However, we see in table 2.12 that a majority of our respondents believe that all people should have the right to choose to die, that fathers should have the right to three months' paid paternity leave, and that women should have the right to abortion on demand; but only one in three believe that homosexuals should not be discriminated against, in the sense that they should have the right to the same legal partnership status as heterosexuals.

In addition to these private rights, our respondents also believe that they have certain state-provided rights, such as housing where people cannot afford to pay for it, and the right to live in a society in which the poor do not suffer at the expense of the rich, expressed here in terms of government aiming to reduce the income differences between rich and poor. The majority of our respondents also believe that if tuition fees undermine the right to higher education then they should be abolished. However, there is less public support, albeit a plurality (48 per cent), for the notion that the government should find work for every person requiring it.

Finally, there are the individualistic rights involving the desire to be left alone by the state, to look after oneself, for example, in old age or in ill health. On such questions as these, people are very evenly divided between those believing that individuals should be unfettered by the state and those believing that the state should provide. This is the case, for example, on the question of whether people should have individual or state-provided rights for their retirement. However, a plurality (42 per cent) recognise the individual right to provide their own health care when they are sick. Finally, our respondents are also very evenly divided over whether individuals should or should not possess the right to withdraw their labour by striking.

We will return to the question of rights in chapter 9 when we examine recent trends in both civic duties and rights. However, we now propose to summarise our findings so far on civic attitudes before we examine to

Table 2.12 *Attitudes towards Private, Individualistic and State-provided Rights*

	Strongly agree %	Agree %	Neither agree/ disagree %	Disagree %	Strongly disagree %
Private rights					
Gay relationships	12	24	25	22	17
Choose to die	24	41	21	10	4
Three months' paid paternity leave	26	30	17	21	7
Abortion on demand	16	35	26	16	8
State-provided rights					
Housing for those who can afford it	22	55	16	6	1
Reduce income differences between rich and poor	21	43	22	12	2
Higher education	32	38	17	11	2
Job for everyone	16	32	21	27	4
Individualistic rights					
Provision for retirement	7	30	26	30	8
Meet costs of personal health care	7	28	23	34	9
Strike	10	27	32	26	5

Source: Weighted 2000 face-to-face survey. N = c3,134.
Statements:

> 'Gay relationships should have an equal status to marriage.'
> 'Everyone should have the right to choose to die.'
> 'Fathers should have the right to three months' paternity leave following the birth of a child.'
> 'Women should have the right to abortion on demand.'
> 'Government should provide housing for those who cannot afford it.'
> 'Government should reduce income differences between the rich and poor.'
> 'In order to preserve the right to higher education student tuition fees should be abolished.'
> 'It is the government's responsibility to find a job for everyone who wants one.'
> 'Individuals should not rely on the state to provide for their own retirement.'
> 'Individuals who can afford it should meet the cost of their own health care when they are sick.'
> 'The government should remove present legal restrictions on the right to strike.'

what extent, if any, these attitudes vary among different sections of the British people.

Civic attitudes: a summary

Our initial conclusions are that civic beliefs are robust and in a relatively healthy state in twenty-first-century Britain. Notwithstanding both the external and internal challenges to the British state, people's identification with their country is stronger than with any other territorial formation. Furthermore, they are proud of their British citizenship. They also respect the law, they do not condone tax evasion, they believe that they have a duty to vote, and they feel obliged to act in various ways which contribute to the collective good, such as by giving blood or going to the aid of someone being robbed in the street.[11] The British have a selective approach to rights. So they believe that they have some private rights, such as the right to choose to die, but they are less supportive of homosexuals' rights. Similarly, they adopt a selective approach to state-provided rights; they are more likely to think that governments have a duty to look after the poor, but less likely to believe that governments should provide a job for everyone. This selective approach to rights, combined with a strong sense of civic identity, must make the task of governing slightly easier.

In the mid-twentieth century the British were most proud of their political institutions and practices (Almond and Verba, 1963), but this is now no longer the case. Only one in three are satisfied with British democracy, and the government is regarded as insensitive to majority opinion. People's sense of their own collective political impact is low; however, they are more likely to feel that they have greater political influence at the local than at the national level. Public esteem for politicians is very low, and traditional political engagement, such as offering to be a local councillor, attracts little public enthusiasm. Nevertheless, people regard their vote in elections as important and they also believe that it matters which party wins elections.

Overall, if one feature of good citizenship is people's awareness of their rights and duties, then we conclude this section by stating that there is a good deal of evidence of such awareness in contemporary Britain. In chapter 3 we will examine another feature of good citizenship: participation in society; but beforehand we need to consider how people's civic attitudes vary and who might be regarded as good and bad citizens.

---

[11] 59 per cent of our respondents stated that they would intervene if they saw a person being robbed in the street.

Variations in levels of citizenship

So far in this chapter we have been engaged in a simple description of people's attitudes towards their country, their fellow countrymen and women, and some of the key institutions, and of people's perceptions of their rights and duties. In the remainder of this chapter we discuss civic attitudes in the context of people's social and economic backgrounds. Later, in chapters 5 and 6, when we examine alternative theoretical accounts of civic attitudes and behaviour, we will consider the variations in citizenship more extensively and consider other factors than purely the socioeconomic. Here, however, we want to examine whether civic attitudes vary according to a person's social and economic background.

In Britain a person's class background has historically been a powerful factor in explaining their political attitudes and behaviour. We therefore examine our respondents' occupational status as an indicator of social class. In addition, we include their household income and their length of time in full-time education, both useful additions to the simple occupational classification. As we will see in chapter 6, there is evidence that an individual's resources – money, time and skills, in particular – have a significant impact upon their political behaviour.

As the influence of class has waned as a major factor in determining political attitudes and behaviour in the late twentieth century, people's age, gender and ethnic background have assumed greater relative importance. We therefore include these three in our analysis of variations in civic attitudes. Two further categories are also used: firstly, religiosity, defined as the extent to which a person regards himself or herself as belonging to a particular religion; and, secondly, where people live. Notwithstanding the decline in church attendance in contemporary Britain, there is evidence that people with religious commitments adopt distinctive political views. For example, among Conservative Party members in the 1990s, attitudes towards the Thatcherite political project varied significantly depending upon their religious commitments (Whiteley, Seyd and Richardson, 1994). And as far as where people live is concerned, it became increasingly apparent in the 1990s that geographical location affects political behaviour (Johnston, 1991; Johnston et al., 1998). So we will now examine whether people's civic attitudes vary according to their age, gender, occupational status, income, education, ethnicity, religiosity and regional location.

We begin by examining people's sense of national identity. Who are our British, English, Scottish and Welsh identifiers, and do they differ significantly from one another? In table 2.13, and in the remainder of the tables in this chapter, we start by reminding our readers of the overall

Table 2.13 *Variations in National Identity*
'Do you think of yourself first and foremost as . . .?'

	English %	British %	Scottish %	Welsh %
All	57	24	8	4
Age				
24 and under	59	24	6	4
25–44	55	24	8	3
45–64	56	24	7	4
65 and over	60	23	9	4
(V = .063; p = .017)				
Gender				
Male	58	23	7	3
Female	55	25	8	4
(V = .056; p = .206)				
*Class**				
Professional and managerial	53	27	7	4
Intermediate	60	24	7	3
Manual	58	22	9	4
(V = .071; p = .000)				
*Religiosity***				
Religious	55	26	7	4
Non-religious	59	22	8	4
(V = .118; p = .000)				
Household income				
Under £10,000	59	19	10	5
£10,000 up to £19,999	61	23	7	4
£20,000 up to £29,999	52	24	7	4
£30,000 up to £39,999	50	34	6	5
£40,000 up to £49,999	52	33	5	3
£50,000 and above	56	23	7	1
(V = .090; p = .000)				
*Education****				
15 years and under	60	21	9	4
16–18	58	24	8	3
19 years and over	45	29	5	4
(V = .114; p = .000)				
*Ethnicity*****				
White/European	59	23	8	4
Black/Asian/ Caribbean/Other	12	42	1	1
(V = .233; p = .000)				

Table 2.13 (*cont.*)

	English %	British %	Scottish %	Welsh %
Location*****				
Greater London	50	24	1	1
South West	60	29	1	2
East/West Midlands	72	19	1	2
North West/North/Yorkshire	68	25	3	1
South East/East Anglia	60	28	2	2
Scotland	6	12	81	0
Wales	11	16	0	64
(V = .404; p = .000)				

* Respondents were classified into 7 Standard Economic Categories as follows: (1) Professional or technical; (2) Manager or administrator; (3) Clerical; (4) Sales; (5) Foreman; (6) Skilled manual; (7) Semi-skilled or unskilled manual; and (8) Other. Categories (1) and (2) = Professional and Managerial; (3) and (4) = Intermediate; (5), (6) and (7) = Manual.

** Respondents were asked whether they regarded themselves as belonging to any particular religion with a yes/no response.

*** Respondents were asked at what age they finished full-time education.

**** Respondents were asked whether their ethnic origin was White/European, Asian (e.g. Indian or Pakistani), East Asian (e.g. Chinese, Japanese or Malaysian), Black (e.g. West Indian or African) and Other. The Asian, East Asian, Black and Other categories have been merged.

***** Apart from the South West and Greater London regions, England's other seven standard government regions were merged into three as detailed.

attitudinal distributions and then we examine the distribution among the various categories of people that we have selected for analysis. Table 2.13 reports that the most significant variations[12] depend upon a person's place of residence and colour of their skin. English identifiers are more likely to be living in the Midlands and, not surprisingly, least likely to be living in Scotland and Wales. Black people are also much less likely to identify themselves as English. We also find that English identifiers are more likely to be found among intermediate workers (in other words, those primarily in clerical occupations), and among the less well-off. In stark contrast, British identifiers are concentrated among black people[13] and among

[12] In this table, and the following ones in chapters 2 and 3 where we are examining variations in attitudes and behaviour, we report Cramer's V statistics. Cramer's V is a measure of association based upon the chi-squared statistic. It varies from 0 (no association) to 1 (perfect association) and measures the association between variables in cross-tabulations.

[13] Among the ethnic groupings used in the questionnaire (White/Europeans, Asians, East Asians and Black) it is the Asians and East Asians who most strongly identify themselves as British.

those with higher household incomes (although not the richest house-holds). Professional and managerial workers, and those who remained in full-time education beyond the age of 19 have a slightly greater tendency to identify themselves as British. It is noteworthy that neither the age nor the gender of the respondent has any significant impact upon their sense of identity. Predictably our Welsh and Scottish identifiers are overwhelmingly concentrated among those living in these two parts of the country. It is noticeable, however, that the richer the households of those living in Wales and Scotland then the less likely they are to identify themselves as Welsh and Scottish.

We argued earlier that people's trust of one another is of fundamental importance in providing the basic glue which holds a society together. In table 2.14 we contrast the overall mean score for personal trust with the scores of our particular categories of respondent. We see that it is among the elderly, the religious, the richest households, white people, and the Scots that the most personally trusting people are concentrated. The least personally trusting are found among the very young (24 years old and under) and among black people.

Our earlier discussion of institutional trust revealed the public's greater confidence in non-elected than elected institutions. Here we select public trust of the police and politicians for consideration and comparison and, as in the previous table, we again contrast the overall mean scores. Table 2.15 demonstrates that it is the elderly, the religious, and women who are more likely to trust the police, and the young and black people who are less likely to trust them. As far as the public's trust of politicians is concerned, it is almost uniformly low across all the types of people we are considering. What variation there is reveals that again it is the elderly who are more likely to be trusting and, in addition, so are the more highly educated. Those aged between 25 and 45, and the non-religious, are less likely to trust politicians.

We have already made the point that the British may have a relatively high degree of personal trust of other people, but their tolerance of others' opinions and lifestyles is limited. Are there any significant variations in their levels of political tolerance, in particular, their commitment to freedom of speech? In the Citizen Audit we asked our respondents whether they were willing to accord this freedom to neo-nazi and racist, religious fundamentalist, animal liberation, and environmental groups. From these various groups we select here public attitudes towards the most unpopular of the groups, neo-nazi and racists, in order to examine in more detail the characteristics of those who would defend such people's right to speak out openly in public. In table 2.16 we report that the libertarians are more likely to be found among men, among households with an annual income

Table 2.14 *Variations in Inter-personal Trust*
'*Thinking for a moment about whether people with whom you have contact can be trusted. Please use the 0–10 scale where 10 means definitely can be trusted and 0 means definitely cannot be trusted.*'

	Mean	Standard deviation
All	**6.59**	**2.19**
Age		
24 and under	5.91	2.19
25–44	6.31	2.42
45–64	6.78	2.14
65 and over	7.26	2.00
(V = .136; p = .000)		
Gender		
Male	6.49	2.16
Female	6.66	2.22
(V = .072; p = .099)		
Class		
Professional and managerial	6.79	2.00
Intermediate	6.69	2.14
Manual	6.47	2.30
(V = .082; p = .000)		
Religiosity		
Religious	6.82	2.00
Non-religious	6.31	2.29
(V = .130; p = .000)		
Household income		
Under £10,000	6.42	2.44
£10,000 up to £19,999	6.45	2.15
£20,000 up to £29,999	6.70	2.05
£30,000 up to £39,999	6.83	1.88
£40,000 up to £49,999	6.70	1.82
£50,000 and above	6.94	1.81
(V = .090; p = .000)		
Education		
15 years and under	6.78	2.26
16–18	6.32	2.25
19 years and over	6.91	1.84
(V = .106; p = .000)		
Ethnicity		
White/European	6.63	2.20
Black/Asian/Caribbean/Other	5.82	2.12
(V = .083; p = .000)		
Location		
Greater London	6.16	2.16
South West	6.46	2.06
East/West Midlands	6.47	2.26
North West/North/Yorkshire	6.55	2.37
South East/East Anglia	6.73	1.97
Scotland	7.18	2.16
Wales	6.49	2.58
(V = .084; p = .000)		

Demographic characteristics as in table 2.13.

Table 2.15 *Variations in Public Trust of the Police and Politicians*
'*Do you trust the police/politicians?*'

	Police		Politicians	
	Mean	Standard deviation	Mean	Standard deviation
All	**6.29**	**2.41**	**3.26**	**2.25**
Age				
24 and under	5.94	2.78	3.27	2.27
25–44	6.15	2.37	3.01	2.13
45–64	6.21	2.39	3.20	2.25
65 and over	6.94	2.16	3.88	2.35
	(V = .113; p = .000)		(V = .108; p = .000)	
Gender				
Male	6.01	2.50	3.07	2.23
Female	6.49	2.33	3.40	2.27
	(V = .135; p = .000)		(V = .091; p = .005)	
Class				
Professional and managerial	6.41	2.20	3.42	2.15
Intermediate	6.29	2.27	3.35	2.20
Manual	6.22	2.58	3.11	2.32
	(V = .083; p = .000)		(V = .076; p = .006)	
Religiosity				
Religious	6.66	2.25	3.23	2.28
Non-religious	5.85	2.52	2.94	2.18
	(V = .174; p = .000)		(V = .143; p = .000)	
Household income				
Under £10,000	6.39	2.61	3.23	2.43
£10,000 up to £19,999	6.19	2.40	3.23	2.25
£20,000 up to £29,999	6.19	2.40	3.16	2.17
£30,000 up to £39,999	6.22	2.08	3.35	1.95
£40,000 up to £49,999	6.01	2.38	3.27	2.08
£50,000 and above	6.45	2.24	3.49	2.29
	(V = .077; p = .006)		(V = .083; p = .000)	
Education				
15 years and under	6.46	2.48	3.31	2.40
16–18	6.20	2.49	3.06	2.20
19 years and over	6.19	2.08	3.65	2.05
	(V = .093; p = .000)		(V = .105; p = .000)	

Table 2.15 (*cont.*)

	Police		Politicians	
	Mean	Standard deviation	Mean	Standard deviation
Ethnicity				
White/European	6.34	2.40	3.26	2.25
Black/Asian/ Caribbean/Other	5.59	2.48	3.28	2.29
	(V = .085; p = .000)		(V = .061; p = .288)	
Location				
Greater London	6.04	2.51	3.39	2.23
South West	6.14	2.61	3.10	2.22
East/West Midlands	6.23	2.39	3.22	2.19
North West/North/ Yorkshire	6.26	2.46	3.18	2.21
South East/East Anglia	6.44	2.49	3.38	2.24
Scotland	6.54	2.39	3.21	2.47
Wales	6.28	2.64	3.19	2.38
	(V = .063; p = .570)		(V = .065; p = .039)	

Demographic characteristics as in table 2.13.

of £30,000 and upwards, and among those living in the south-west or the north of England. The elderly, those who left school at 15 (of whom 40 per cent are aged 65 or over), and those living in Scotland are less likely to support freedom of speech for neo-nazis and racists.

The British, as we noted earlier, are pretty evenly divided between those satisfied and those dissatisfied with the workings of British democracy. We see in table 2.17 that the satisfied are more likely to come from the black community in Britain, and also from the richest households, those whose full-time education continued up to the age of 19 or beyond, and the elderly. It is also noticeable that there are more contented among the Scots than among the Welsh. The one in three who are dissatisfied are pretty evenly distributed among the population, but the discontented are more likely to be found among the non-religious and those households with an annual income of around £40,000.

It is clear that people believe government to be unresponsive to their opinions. To what extent is their sense of political efficacy affected by their background? We have previously distinguished three underlying dimensions to political efficacy: external, internal collective, and internal

Table 2.16 *Variations in Freedom of Speech: Neo-Nazis and Racists*
'To what extent should . . . (neo-nazi and racist groups) be allowed to speak out in public?'

	No %	Yes %
All	**64**	**8**
Age		
24 and under	58	9
25–44	63	8
45–64	62	9
65 and over	69	6
(V = .065; p = .025)		
Gender		
Male	60	13
Female	66	5
(V = .172; p = .000)		
Class		
Professional and managerial	60	10
Intermediate	65	7
Manual	65	7
(V = .114; p = .000)		
Religiosity		
Religious	64	7
Non-religious	62	9
(V = .060; p = .005)		
Household income		
Under £10,000	65	8
£10,000 up to £19,999	64	6
£20,000 up to £29,999	63	5
£30,000 up to £39,999	58	11
£40,000 up to £49,999	62	13
£50,000 and above	56	13
(V = .117; p = .001)		
Education		
15 years and under	68	6
16–18	62	9
19 years and over	59	9
(V = .075; p = .014)		
Ethnicity		
White/European	63	8
Black/Asian/Caribbean/Other	66	2
(V = .060; p = .097)		
Location		
Greater London	63	7
South West	65	10
East/West Midlands	62	4
North West/North/Yorkshire	59	11
South East/East Anglia	65	8
Scotland	74	3
Wales	66	8
(V = .132; p = .000)		

Note that only the 'definitely not' and the 'definitely yes' responses have been included. Both the 'possibly not', and the 'possibly yes' responses and the 'don't knows' have been excluded.
Demographic characteristics as in table 2.13.

Table 2.17 *Variations in Attitudes to Democracy*
'Thinking about Britain, how satisfied are you with the way democracy works?'

	Very satisfied/ satisfied %	Neither satisfied nor dissatisfied %	Very dissatisfied/ dissatisfied %
All	**35**	**29**	**33**
Age			
24 and under	31	33	29
25–44	33	28	35
45–64	34	28	36
65 and over	43	29	25
(V = .075; p = .000)			
Gender			
Male	38	25	35
Female	33	32	31
(V = .104; p = .000)			
Class			
Professional and managerial	39	26	33
Intermediate	35	30	32
Manual	32	30	33
(V = .086; p = .000)			
Religiosity			
Religious	39	29	29
Non-religious	29	29	38
(V = .117; p = .000)			
Household income			
Under £10,000	33	28	34
£10,000 up to £19,999	33	31	32
£20,000 up to £29,999	36	31	32
£30,000 up to £39,999	33	33	35
£40,000 up to £49,999	34	26	39
£50,000 and above	46	19	35
(V = .082; p = .000)			
Education			
15 years and under	34	29	32
16–18	32	30	34
19 years and over	44	25	31
(V = .086; p = .000)			
Ethnicity			
White/European	34	29	33
Black/Asian/Caribbean/Other	49	23	26
(V = .061; p = .001)			
Location			
Greater London	40	29	28
South West	33	29	35
East/West Midlands	36	32	27
North West/North/Yorkshire	34	29	34
South East/East Anglia	33	28	36
Scotland	40	22	34
Wales	33	30	34
(V = .074; p = .001)			

Demographic characteristics as in table 2.13.

personal. Rather than examine all three forms of political efficacy, we here examine the internal personal dimension since this reveals the greatest amount of variation among our socio-demographic categories.[14] We choose for analysis the question with the highest factor loading on this measure of efficacy (see table 2.9), namely, 'Sometimes politics and government seem so complicated that a person like me cannot really understand what is going on': one in two of our respondents agreed with this statement. Who are the people who lack a sense of personal efficacy? Table 2.18 reports that they are concentrated among the very elderly, women, manual workers, the poorest in society, those who left full-time education at 15 years of age, and the Scots. Some of the contrasts are most striking. For example, the rich, those in professional and managerial occupations, and the highly educated are between two and three times more likely than the poor, manual workers, and the least educated to disagree with the statement.

What now of people's views regarding their civic duties and rights? It is clear from our earlier comments that the British have a strong sense of civic duty to obey laws and pay taxes. To what extent are these citizenship values spread equally across the entire population? In fact, the variations in people's beliefs on these two subjects are very similar, and so we will just report, in table 2.19, the figures for obedience to the law. As the Cramer's V statistics show, large and very striking variations in attitudes to the law occur between the religious and non-religious, men and women, and young and old. Those most respectful of the law are concentrated among the religious, women, and the elderly. In addition, we see that Scots, the poor,[15] and those with the minimum number of years in full-time education are also more likely to be respectful of the law. The fact that those who remained in full-time education until the age of 19 or beyond are far less likely than those who left at the age of 15 to respect the law deserves notice. It is often claimed that education makes better citizens, but with regard to these duties to obey the law and pay taxes it appears that education reduces people's commitment to the state. Also, among the 18–24 age group, in other words those who are either still in full-time education, or who have most recently finished, there is the lowest commitment to the state. Finally, there is less attachment to these civic duties among those living in the south-west of England.

---

[14] As far as both the external political and internal collective dimensions are concerned, the most efficacious are concentrated among those working in professional and managerial occupations, the better educated, and the richer households.

[15] The only category in which attitudes towards the payment of taxes do not replicate attitudes towards the law is that of household income. The poor do not differ from richer households.

Table 2.18 *Variations in Internal, Personal Political Efficacy*
'Sometimes politics and government seem so complicated that a person like me cannot really understand what is going on.'

	Strongly agree/ agree %	Neither agree nor disagree %	Strongly disagree/ disagree %
All	**54**	**20**	**26**
Age			
24 and under	56	24	20
25–44	52	21	27
45–64	51	19	30
65 and over	61	16	23
(V = .065; p = .000)			
Gender			
Male	46	20	35
Female	60	20	21
(V = .175; p = .000)			
Class			
Professional and managerial	39	19	42
Intermediate	53	19	28
Manual	65	20	15
(V = .159; p = .000)			
Religiosity			
Religious	56	18	26
Non-religious	52	22	27
(V = .061; p = .023)			
Household income			
Under £10,000	65	18	17
£10,000 up to £19,999	57	20	23
£20,000 up to £29,999	51	20	29
£30,000 up to £39,999	46	21	33
£40,000 up to £49,999	34	22	45
£50,000 and above	32	12	56
(V = .146; p = .000)			
Education			
15 years and under	63	18	19
16–18	55	21	24
19 years and over	37	19	45
(V = .133; p = .000)			
Ethnicity			
White/European	54	19	27
Black/Asian/Caribbean/Other	57	20	23
(V = .039; p = .272)			
Location			
Greater London	48	21	31
South West	51	15	33
East/West Midlands	59	21	19
North West/North/Yorkshire	54	19	27
South East/East Anglia	50	21	29
Scotland	66	16	19
Wales	56	23	21
(V = .095; p = .000)			

Demographic characteristics as in table 2.13.

Table 2.19 *Variations in Attitudes to the Law*
'*How important do you feel it is always to obey the law?*'

	Not at all important %	Not very important %	Fairly important %	Very important %	Don't know %
All	1	3	28	66	2
Age					
24 and under	2	9	35	52	2
25–44	1	3	35	60	1
45–64	1	2	26	69	2
65 and over	0	2	12	85	2
(V = .142; p = .000)					
Gender					
Male	1	6	33	58	2
Female	1	2	24	72	2
(V = .167; p = .000)					
Class					
Professional and managerial	1	3	31	65	1
Intermediate	1	3	28	67	1
Manual	1	3	26	68	2
(V = .063; p = .009)					
Religiosity					
Religious	1	2	22	74	1
Non-religious	1	5	35	57	2
(V = .196; p = .000)					
Household income					
Under £10,000	1	4	24	69	2
£10,000 up to £19,999	1	3	27	68	1
£20,000 up to £29,999	2	3	34	61	1
£30,000 up to £39,999	1	4	33	62	0
£40,000 up to £49,999	2	3	40	54	1
£50,000 and above	0	4	35	61	1
(V = .073; p = .002)					
Education					
15 years and under	1	3	20	75	1
16–18	1	3	29	64	2
19 years and over	1	5	38	56	1
V = .089; p = .000)					
Ethnicity					
White/European	1	3	28	67	2
Black/Asian/ Caribbean/Other	0	2	28	65	5
(V = .051; p = .009)					
Location					
Greater London	1	2	30	66	2
South West	2	6	29	60	3
East/West Midlands	1	3	27	68	1
North West/North/ Yorkshire	1	4	29	65	2
South East/East Anglia	1	3	29	64	2
Scotland	0	1	17	80	1
Wales	0	5	25	71	0
(V = .085; p = .000)					

Demographic characteristics as in table 2.13.

Moving now to a more obvious civic political duty, namely to vote in an election, we have already noted that people's sense of citizenship is strong. As with our analysis of previous forms of civic duty, religiosity and age are the categories in which the strongest variations occur. Those who feel most strongly that their citizen duty is to vote are concentrated among the religious and the elderly. By contrast, the very young, the non-religious, and also men are less likely to possess this sense of civic duty. The occupation status and household income of the respondent also reveals significant differences of attitude. Table 2.20 reports a linear relationship with regard to age, occupational status, and household income; namely, that the older a respondent, the higher a respondent's occupational status, and the greater a respondent's household income then the more that he or she will believe that there is a duty to vote in an election. Finally, it is worth noting that, notwithstanding the Welsh people's dissatisfaction with the working of democracy in their part of the country, and their lack of trust in the Welsh Assembly, they possess the strongest commitment to this civic duty.

As far as people's rights are concerned, we will contrast attitudes with regard to private, state-provided and individualistic rights. On the first of these types of rights, we select the issue which most divided our respondents, namely whether homosexual partnerships should have the same legal rights as heterosexual partnerships. From table 2.21 it is apparent that age, religiosity, gender and education are the most important factors in examining the variations in attitudes. There is a clear linear relationship between the age of our respondent and his or her attitudes; the younger the person the greater likelihood that he or she supports gay relationships having equal status to marriage, and the older the person the more likely the contrary viewpoint will be held. Similarly, there are more likely to be religious people, men, and those with less full-time schooling among those who disagree with the normalisation of gay relationships.

With regard to state-provided rights, we examine people's attitudes to the question of income redistribution, and whether people have the right to live in a society where the poor do not suffer at the expense of the rich. In specific terms, we asked our respondents whether government should reduce the income differences between rich and poor. Table 2.22 reports that it is among manual workers, the poorest households, and the Scots and Welsh that we find more people who are committed to such a state-provided right, whereas, on the contrary, there are fewer committed to such a right among those classified in intermediate occupations (primarily clerical workers and the self-employed), the richest households, and those living in the south-east and East Anglia.

Finally, we compare people's attitudes on individualistic rights, namely those areas where people believe they should be free to act unfettered

Table 2.20 *Variations in Duty to Vote*
'It is a citizen's duty to vote in an election'

	Strongly agree/agree %	Neither agree nor disagree %	Strongly disagree/disagree %
All	**72**	**18**	**11**
Age			
24 and under	49	28	23
25–44	67	21	13
45–64	80	13	8
65 and over	84	12	5
(V = .156; p = .000)			
Gender			
Male	69	17	14
Female	73	18	9
(V = .091; p = .000)			
Class			
Professional and managerial	80	12	8
Intermediate	75	16	9
Manual	67	20	13
(V = .082; p = .000)			
Religiosity			
Religious	78	15	7
Non-religious	65	21	15
(V = .157; p = .000)			
Household income			
Under £10,000	68	21	11
£10,000 up to £19,999	71	17	13
£20,000 up to £29,999	70	20	11
£30,000 up to £39,999	75	18	6
£40,000 up to £49,999	78	15	7
£50,000 and above	78	9	13
(V = .066; p = .032)			
Education			
15 years and under	75	16	9
16–18	67	20	12
19 years and over	78	12	10
(V = .074; p = .000)			
Ethnicity			
White/European	72	17	11
Black/Asian/Caribbean/ Other	63	22	15
(V = .041; p = .194)			
Location			
Greater London	70	18	12
South West	75	13	12
East/West Midlands	67	22	11
North West/North/Yorkshire	71	18	11
South East/East Anglia	74	15	11
Scotland	72	19	9
Wales	77	15	8
(V = .073; p = .005)			

Demographic characteristics as in table 2.13.

Table 2.21 *Variations in Homosexual Rights*
'Gay relationships should have an equal status to marriage.'

	Strongly agree/agree %	Neither agree nor disagree %	Strongly disagree/disagree %
All	**36**	**25**	**39**
Age			
24 and under	59	23	28
25–44	43	27	30
45–64	29	25	46
65 and over	18	22	59
(V = .187; p = .000)			
Gender			
Male	31	25	44
Female	39	26	35
(V = .113; p = .000)			
Class			
Professional and managerial	39	23	38
Intermediate	33	25	42
Manual	35	27	39
(V = .059; p = .032)			
Religiosity			
Religious	29	25	46
Non-religious	44	25	31
(V = .185; p = .000)			
Household income			
Under £10,000	34	25	42
£10,000 up to £19,999	35	26	40
£20,000 up to £29,999	38	28	34
£30,000 up to £39,999	45	26	29
£40,000 up to £49,999	43	25	31
£50,000 and above	42	23	35
(V = .067; p = .023)			
Education			
15 years and under	25	25	51
16–18	39	26	36
19 years and over	46	24	30
(V = .102; p = .000)			
Ethnicity			
White/European	36	25	39
Black/Asian/Caribbean/ Other	26	26	48
(V = .056; p = .001)			
Location			
Greater London	31	23	36
South West	38	20	32
East/West Midlands	35	27	38
North West/North/Yorkshire	36	25	39
South East/East Anglia	33	26	41
Scotland	38	24	38
Wales	27	30	43
(V = .091; p = .000)			

Demographic characteristics as in table 2.13.

Table 2.22 *Variations in Income Differences*
'Government should reduce income differences between rich and poor.'

	Strongly agree/agree %	Neither agree nor disagree %	Strongly disagree/disagree %
All	**64**	**22**	**14**
Age			
24 and under	63	23	14
25–44	66	21	13
45–64	64	21	15
65 and over	59	26	16
(V = .052; p = .013)			
Gender			
Male	62	21	17
Female	64	23	13
(V = .068; p = .006)			
Class			
Professional and managerial	60	24	17
Intermediate	58	24	18
Manual	69	20	11
(V = .073; p = .000)			
Religiosity			
Religious	62	24	15
Non-religious	66	20	13
(V = .095; p = .000)			
Household income			
Under £10,000	66	22	10
£10,000 up to £19,999	69	17	14
£20,000 up to £29,999	64	24	11
£30,000 up to £39,999	55	29	17
£40,000 up to £49,999	62	26	13
£50,000 and above	51	20	30
(V = .097; p = .000)			
Education			
15 years and under	66	22	13
16–18	64	22	14
19 years and over	63	24	17
(V = .052; p = .006)			
Ethnicity			
White/European	64	23	14
Black/Asian/Caribbean/Other	70	21	10
(V = .041; p = .206)			
Location			
Greater London	69	22	10
South West	65	20	14
East/West Midlands	63	24	14
North West/North/Yorkshire	67	22	11
South East/East Anglia	56	25	20
Scotland	75	18	6
Wales	74	15	11
(V = .111; p = .000)			

Demographic characteristics as in table 2.13.

Table 2.23 *Variations in Health Care*
'Individuals who can afford it should meet the cost of their own health care when they are sick.'

	Strongly agree/agree	Neither agree nor disagree	Strongly disagree/disagree
	%	%	%
All	**35**	**23**	**43**
Age			
24 and under	40	24	36
25–44	33	24	45
45–64	35	21	44
65 and over	39	22	40
(V = .058; p = .002)			
Gender			
Male	29	21	43
Female	35	24	42
(V = .073; p = .003)			
Class			
Professional and managerial	29	22	49
Intermediate	35	23	43
Manual	39	23	39
(V = .078; p = .000)			
Religiosity			
Religious	37	22	41
Non-religious	34	23	43
(V = .047; p = .146)			
Household income			
Under £10,000	43	24	33
£10,000 up to £19,999	35	23	43
£20,000 up to £29,999	32	22	46
£30,000 up to £39,999	25	24	51
£40,000 up to £49,999	38	19	44
£50,000 and above	35	14	51
(V = .087; p = .000)			
Education			
15 years and under	37	22	41
16–18	36	23	40
19 years and over	30	21	50
(V = .047; p = .037)			
Ethnicity			
White/European	35	22	42
Black/Asian/Caribbean/Other	37	27	36
(V = .036; p = .441)			
Location			
Greater London	46	23	32
South West	36	16	47
East/West Midlands	34	24	42
North West/North/Yorkshire	34	20	46
South East/East Anglia	32	27	41
Scotland	33	21	46
Wales	47	16	36
(V = .106; p = .000)			

Demographic characteristics as in table 2.13.

Table 2.24 *Summary of the Impact of Particular Variables on Citizenship Attitudes*

	Age	Gender	Occupation	Religion	Income	Education	Ethnicity	Place
National identity	no	no	**yes**	**yes**	**yes**	**yes**	**yes**	**yes**
Trust of other people	**yes**	yes	**yes**	**yes**	**yes**	**yes**	**yes**	**yes**
Trust of police	**yes**	**yes**	**yes**	**yes**	yes	**yes**	**yes**	no
Trust of politicians	**yes**	yes	yes	**yes**	**yes**	**yes**	no	no
Freedom of speech	no	**yes**	**yes**	yes	**yes**	yes	no	**yes**
British democracy	**yes**	**yes**	**yes**	**yes**	**yes**	**yes**	**yes**	**yes**
Political efficacy	**yes**	**yes**	**yes**	no	**yes**	**yes**	no	**yes**
Obedience of law	**yes**	**yes**	yes	**yes**	**yes**	**yes**	yes	**yes**
Duty to vote	**yes**	**yes**	**yes**	**yes**	no	**yes**	no	yes
Homosexual rights	**yes**	**yes**	no	**yes**	no	**yes**	**yes**	**yes**
Income differences	yes	yes	**yes**	**yes**	**yes**	yes	no	**yes**
Provision of health care	**yes**	**yes**	**yes**	no	**yes**	no	no	**yes**

yes, bold: significant at 0.01 level; yes, non-bold: significant at 0.05 level.

by the state. In particular, on the issue of individuals providing for themselves, we select the issue of health care, and the question of whether individuals who can afford it should meet the cost of their own health care when they are sick. In table 2.23 we see that individualists are more likely to be found among the young, manual workers, the poor, and people living in either Greater London or Wales.

Conclusions

In this second part of the chapter we have examined whether civic attitudes vary according to the demographic characteristics of our respondents. Table 2.24 highlights the most significant variations. We see that, overall, all eight of the factors we have considered are highly significant; but one, ethnic background, has less importance than the others. So civic beliefs will vary according to a person's age, gender, occupational status, extent of religious commitment, income, education, ethnic background and place of residence. However, their particular importance varies from one attitude to another. The extent to which these characteristics, and others, play a significant, independent role in explaining variations in civic attitudes is something we consider in chapters 5 and 6.

We now turn in the following chapter to the second part of our discussion of citizenship in contemporary Britain and examine civic behaviour.

3 Civic Behaviour and Citizenship: Macro Politics

In addition to measuring people's civic beliefs, the Citizen Audit is also a census of people's participation in Britain at the beginning of the twenty-first century. It tells us what they are getting up to. It maps out the broad range of activities, both formal and informal, that people engage in outside of their families and beyond their work, and for which they do not get paid. It details their political activities, their associational life, and the way they behave when dealing with the problems arising in their daily lives over their children's education, their own health, or their working conditions. We begin this chapter by examining people's political behaviour. We then consider their associational activities. Then in the following chapter we discuss people's attempts to influence day-to-day practical matters, such as schooling, medical care or work conditions, which we describe as micro level political behaviour.

Repertoires of political behaviour

In order to learn more about the range of political activities in which people get involved, we asked our respondents whether, over the previous twelve months, they had engaged in any of a listed seventeen activities while attempting to 'influence rules, laws or policies'. Our list was devised after extensive piloting of the survey in which people's perceptions of politics were closely observed, and the final questionnaire reflected this preliminary analysis. The list is deliberately wide-ranging and covers activities which are not captured by studies that concentrate upon the more traditional forms of politics.[1]

---

[1] Critics of this methodology often claim that it imposes a narrow and normative definition of politics. A research team (Marsh 2002: 16) studying young people's political attitudes and behaviour by using qualitative research suggest that the young define politics as 'anything to do with government, including the running of schools, hospitals and the police', and that their political behaviour is broader than an activity engaged in periodically, but is rather 'a lived experience'. While we do not disagree with the point that politics to most people is broadly defined (and our later discussion in chapter 4 of people's behaviour in

In response to our question asking people what actions they had taken during the previous twelve months, we see in table 3.1 that the most common form of political action had been to donate money or to vote in a local government election. Almost two-thirds of our respondents claimed to have donated money to an organisation and one-half claimed to have voted in a local government election. The fact that the actual electoral turnout in the 2000 local government elections in England, Wales, and Scotland was 28 per cent confirms what previous research has revealed (Swaddle and Heath, 1989), namely that people over-report their voting. However, as we pointed out in the previous chapter, research based upon the most recent British Election Study (Clarke et al., 2004) reveals that the exaggeration is not that large (4 per cent). Furthermore, as we will see in table 3.2, the trend figures of claimed voting over the past twenty years are downwards in line with the trend in actual turnout. So while some exaggeration may prevail, surveys of people's participation are not seriously distorting reality. Also, as with our previous discussion of civic attitudes in chapter 2, it is people's ranking of their various political activities which is of great interest. In this hierarchy of behaviour, giving money to an organisation ranks higher than voting in a local government election.

The third most popular action was the signing of a petition; almost one-half of our respondents claimed to have done so in the previous twelve months. Taking these three most popular actions, three in four people had engaged in at least one of them in order to influence political outcomes. It is clear from table 3.1 that people use their purchasing powers as a means of political influence; 31 per cent of our respondents had boycotted certain products and 28 per cent had bought particular goods 'for political, ethical or environmental reasons'. In today's world many campaigning organisations recommend people to use their purchasing powers to influence global corporations, and clearly a large number of people, whether as a consequence of such prompts or on their own initiative, are taking such action. In other words, in their day-to-day consumption behaviour they are acting politically.

Whereas almost two in three of our respondents had given money to organisations, an action which might be regarded as a fairly simple one that passed political responsibility to others, almost one in three had also raised funds for organisations, a far more onerous form of commitment.

relation to questions of schooling, health and work reflects this approach), nevertheless Marsh and his colleagues do not suggest any new, alternative forms of political participation which were excluded by our methodology. A research project on citizenship which combines both quantitative and qualitative methodologies to great effect can be seen in Crewe, Conover and Searing (1994) and Conover and Searing (2002).

Table 3.1 *Acts of Political Participation*

	Actual	Potential
	% yes	% yes
Donated money to an organisation	62	75
Voted in a local government election	50	71
Signed a petition	42	76
Boycotted certain products	31	59
Raised funds for an organisation	30	55
Bought certain products for political, ethical or environmental reasons	28	49
Contacted a public official	25	59
Worn or displayed a campaign badge or sticker	22	49
Contacted a solicitor or judicial body	20	60
Contacted a politician	13	53
Contacted an organisation	11	50
Contacted the media	9	43
Attended a political meeting or rally	5	26
Taken part in a public demonstration	5	34
Formed a group of like-minded people	5	23
Taken part in a strike	2	27
Participated in illegal protest activities	2	13

Source: Weighted 2000 face-to-face survey. Actual: N = c3,120; Potential: N = c3,005.

Questions: *'During the last twelve months have you done any of the following to influence rules, laws or policies?' 'Would you do any of the following to influence rules, laws or policies?'*

Then came a range of actions involving contact with public officials, legal personnel, national or local politicians, organisations, or the media. Just over one in four had contacted a public official, one in eight a politician, and one in ten had contacted an organisation or the media. The least common forms of political action among our respondents were attending a political meeting, demonstrating, forming a group, taking part in a strike, or engaging in an illegal protest; one in twenty had taken part in a demonstration and one in fifty had participated in an illegal protest.

What these data reveal is that political participation most commonly takes the form of individualistic, rather than collectively organised, action. For example, the giving of money, voting, the signing of a petition or the display of a poster, the purchase or non-purchase of goods while shopping, or the contacting of an organisation or person in a professional position are the most common forms of action in people's political

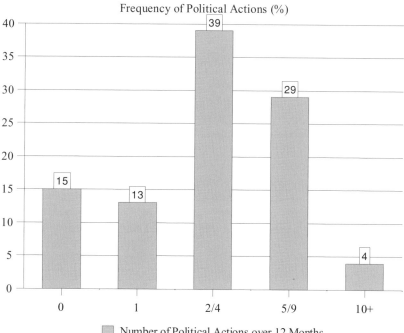

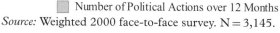 Number of Political Actions over 12 Months

Source: Weighted 2000 face-to-face survey. N = 3,145.

Figure 3.1 Frequency of Political Actions

repertoire. Acting together in a political meeting, a demonstration, a strike, or an illegal protest is much less common. Perhaps this is unsurprising. On the one hand, we have seen the development of a marketised society in which emphasis is placed upon the optimisation of individual needs in the market (Lane, 1991). On the other hand, some previously large collective organisations, such as the trade unions, political parties, and the cooperative movement, have declined (Whiteley and Seyd, 2002). Traditional representative, collectively organised politics is being steadily replaced by individualistic, consumerist politics. This has significant implications for the social character of political behaviour. A good deal of working-class political activity was collectively channelled through trade unions and the Labour Party. The individualisation of political action tends, as we will see later in the chapter, to reinforce the trend towards a middle-class profile.

Not only is the repertoire of people's political behaviour broad, but so is its frequency. We see in figure 3.1 that more than three-quarters of our respondents had engaged in one or more of these political actions over the previous twelve months, and one in three had taken five or more actions.[2] The mean number of actions that individuals had taken in the year was 3.6. If we delete donating money from the political repertoire, since some claim that this is a surrogate form of political participation, we still find that the mean remains high at 2.7. We conclude, therefore, that contrary to the claims of political apathy, people frequently participate in activities designed to influence political outcomes. Dalton's (2002: 55) assertion that 'British patterns of participation focus on voting, with modest involvement beyond the ballot box' is wide of the mark.

Beyond the act of voting, for which we have past figures, it is difficult to make firm statements regarding trends. Our comparisons over time are dependent, firstly, upon the nature of questions asked about political participation in previous surveys and, secondly, upon whether question wordings enable meaningful comparisons to be drawn. The previous large-scale, national study of political participation, carried out during 1984 and 1985 (Parry, Moyser and Day, 1992), asked respondents whether they had engaged in twenty-three distinct political actions ranging through voting, party campaigning, group activities, contacting and protesting (Parry, Moyser and Day, 1992: 43). We should be aware of the wording differences between this survey and the Citizen Audit which entail some caution in drawing comparisons. So when Parry, Moyser and Day (1992: 48) report a mean of 4.2 political actions, as compared with 3.6 in the Citizen Audit, we need to be wary of the conclusion that political activity has declined, because the earlier study measured this over a five-year period rather than our one-year period. However, what is very clear is that between the two time points of 1984 and 2001 little variation in the hierarchy of political behaviour has occurred. This is demonstrated in table 3.2. Individualistic actions (for example, voting and petition signing) rank higher than contacting and then collectively organised actions (for example, attending a political meeting or taking part in a demonstration). These earlier data reveal that a majority of the public had voted and signed a petition, but other forms of participation were limited to small minorities. Between one in five and one in ten had contacted various people in official positions, while fewer than one in ten had engaged in various forms of direct action. What is very noticeable is the considerable rise in the use of the boycott as a political action between the two time points; whereas only one in twenty acted in such a manner

---

[2] A Home Office Citizenship Survey, conducted in 2001, found that 38 per cent had participated in political actions in the previous twelve months. However, respondents had the choice of only five political actions, and voting was one activity excluded from the listing (Prime, Zimmeck and Zurawan, 2002: 5).

Table 3.2 *Changes in Political Participation 1984–2000 (percentages saying 'yes')*

	1984	2000
Voted in general election	83	72
Voted in local election	69	50
Signed a petition	63	42
Boycotted products*	4	31
Contacted a public official	25	25
Contacted a politician+	30	13
Contacted the media	4	9
Attended a political meeting/rally	9	6
Attended a demonstration^	5	5
Taken part in a strike¬	7	2
Taken part in an illegal protest~	1	2

Sources: Parry, Moyser and Day, 1992: 44; Citizen Audit 2000 weighted face-to-face survey.

* In 1984 the question was 'taken part in a boycott about a political issue'; in 2000 it was 'boycotted certain products'.

+ In 1984 the questions were 'contacted a Department of Central Government, or a civil servant' and 'contacted a Town Hall or County Hall official' and the responses to these two have been merged; in 2000 the question was 'contacted a public official'.

^ In 1984 the question was 'taken part in a protest march which had not been banned by the police'; in 2000 the question was 'taken part in a public demonstration'.

¬ In 1984 the question was 'taken part in a strike about an issue which you feel is political'; in 2000 the question was 'taken part in a strike'.

~ In 1984 the question was 'blocked traffic with a street demonstration'; in 2000 the question was 'participated in illegal protest activities'.

in the 1980s, now one in three take such action. Neither donating money nor selective purchasing of goods for political reasons, which are important forms of political participation in 2001, were asked of respondents in 1984.

How do people come to engage in these political activities? Is it as a result of their own initiatives or by being mobilised by others? We asked our respondents whether they had received direct personal requests to engage in these various forms of political action, and from their responses it is clear that the overwhelming majority are self-starters. Three-quarters (73 per cent) of political participants had *not* received a request to engage in political action. Among the 25 per cent who had received a personal request to engage in political action, figure 3.2 reports that the majority of requests (51 per cent) came from strangers. Another one in three requests

Requests to Act (%)

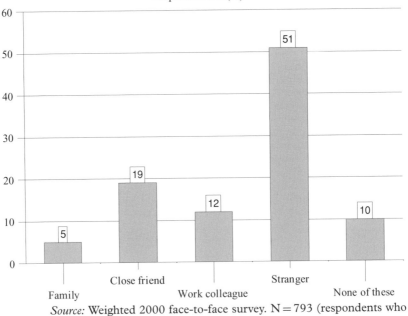

Source: Weighted 2000 face-to-face survey. N = 793 (respondents who had been asked to participate).

Question: *'Thinking about the last occasion this happened (i.e. received a personal request to take action to influence rules, laws or policies) was the person who asked you family, a close friend, a work colleague, someone you didn't know or none of these?'*

Figure 3.2 Requests to Act

came from close friends or work colleagues. Only one in twenty came from within the family. It appears, therefore, that among the minority of people who do take some form of political action, as a consequence of a specific request, it is more likely to be as a result of a cold-call from the political entrepreneurs in society.

In addition to measuring people's actual participation over the previous twelve months, we also measured their *potential* participation. In other words, we asked them what they *would* do to influence rules, laws or policies. The measurement of participation potential is important for two reasons (Barnes and Kaase, 1979). Firstly, it is a valuable normative guide to the way in which people rank various forms of political behaviour. Secondly, it provides us with a measure of what people would become engaged in if the opportunities arose. Given the opportunities,

Table 3.3 *Changes in Participation Potential 1979–2000 (percentages saying very likely or quite likely (1979) and yes (2000))*

	1979	2000
Would contact an MP	31	53
Would sign or collect a petition	44	75
Would contact the media	31	42
Would attend a political meeting	44	25
Would go on a demonstration	20	33
Would take part in an illegal protest	10	12

Sources: British Election Study survey, 1979; Citizen Audit 2000 weighted face-to-face survey.

we would expect people's political participation to be higher than it actually is, and this is confirmed by the evidence. Whereas the mean number of actual political acts in a year is 3.6, the comparative figure for potential acts is almost double (6.6). We see in table 3.1 that people's rank ordering of their potential activity is very similar to their actual behaviour except that they give slightly greater priority to contacting legal personnel and politicians than in practice. Interestingly, around one in three of our respondents are willing to consider taking part in a demonstration or strike and one in eight in illegal protests, which suggests that protest potential in Britain is relatively high. As was the case following the introduction of the poll tax in 1990, the proposal to ban fox hunting in 1998, fuel tax on lorries in 2000, and the US/British invasion of Iraq in 2003, when some people feel aggrieved they are willing to take their protests to the streets.

Again it is possible to make some limited comparisons over time which reveal some trends in potential action. Similar potential political action questions were asked in both the 1979 British Election Study and the Citizen Audit. In table 3.3 it is apparent that people's potential for political participation has risen significantly. Most people would now sign a petition, contact an MP, contact the media, and go on a demonstration. Similar numbers of people (one in ten) would participate in an illegal protest. Only the prospect of attending a political meeting dampens enthusiasm. Whereas twenty years ago almost one in two would have considered attending a political meeting, now that proportion has dropped to one in four.

So far we have examined people's political behaviour as separate, distinct acts on a single continuum of activities. But are there underlying structures to this political behaviour? What we find is that, rather than people engaging in political activities in some random or haphazard manner, there is a structure to their actions. We examine this issue more fully in chapter 5, but for now it is apparent that there are clear repertoires of political participation. First, there is what we describe as individualistic behaviour. In other words, people who purchase or boycott particular goods for political and ethical reasons are also more likely to give money to, or raise money for, an organisation, sign a petition, display a poster or campaign badge, and vote in a local government election in order to influence political outcomes. Second, people who contact a politician are also more likely to engage in other forms of contact with public officials, legal personnel, organisations, or the media, and we categorise this as contact behaviour. Finally, people who take part in demonstrations are more likely to attend party meetings, participate in an illegal protest, form a group of like-minded people, or take part in a strike; in other words, they engage in some form of collectively organised behaviour. The same point applies to potential political action, which has a rather similar underlying structure to that of actual political action. We return to these issues in chapter 5.

Research on political participation since the 1970s has often distinguished conventional and unconventional political actions (Marsh, 1977; McAllister, 1992; Dalton, 2002). Conventional, or orthodox, political behaviour has included voting, contacting, and lobbying through formal interest groups. Unconventional, or unorthodox, behaviour has ranged from the legal, such as signing petitions, and participating in lawful strikes or demonstrations, to the semi-legal, such as boycotts, to the illegal, but non-violent, such as mass-trespass occupations, and finally to the illegal and violent, such as sabotage and terrorism. We believe that the distinction between conventional and unconventional political behaviour is less appropriate in Britain today. We have noted that signing a petition is a mainstream and popular activity for the British and, therefore, the term 'unconventional' to describe it is inappropriate. Furthermore, whereas boycotts were regarded as semi-legal and unorthodox in this earlier literature this is no longer the case and we now see that one in three shop selectively in order to influence political outcomes. Hardly unorthodox political behaviour!

In the previous chapter we examined whether people's civic attitudes varied according to their particular demographic characteristics. We now repeat this exercise for political participation; in particular, we examine whether, firstly, we can distinguish political participants from non-participants and, secondly, whether individualistic, contact, and collectively organised political participants are distinguishable.

Variations in political participation

In order to distinguish the non-participant from the active participant, we classify our respondents into those who engaged in no political actions whatsoever, those who took between one and four, and those who took five or more. We see in table 3.4 that gender and ethnic background are statistically non-significant; all of the other characteristics that we have selected reveal interesting differences. People are more likely to be active political participants, in other words to have taken five or more political actions, in middle age; both young and old are more likely to be completely disengaged or to have taken fewer political actions. In addition, the poorest members of society, manual workers, and those with fewer years in full-time education are more likely to be politically inactive, and the richest, those in professional and managerial occupations, and the best educated are more likely to be politically active. For example, those with an annual household income of £50,000 or more are twice as likely as those with an annual household income of less than £10,000 to have taken five or more political actions. And manual workers are two times more likely to have taken no political actions than professional and managerial workers.

So far we have examined the distinguishing characteristics of the nil, medium and multiple political participants. What of those who do participate but do so in different manners? We have demonstrated that people engage in three distinct forms of political participation: individualistic, contact and collectively organised acts. Can we also distinguish three forms of political actor? Do different types of people become involved in these different types of action?

If we take the behaviours which have the highest factor loadings on these three dimensions, in other words the purchase of goods for ethical reasons, the contact of a politician, and the taking part in a public demonstration, we discover in table 3.5 that the types of people who engage in individualistic, contact, or collectively organised actions do differ somewhat, although the highly educated person is common among all of them. The political participants engaging in individualistic actions are concentrated among the middle-aged, those in professional and managerial occupations, the rich, the highly educated and those living in London and the southern counties. They are less likely to be found among the old, manual workers, the poor, and those living in Scotland and Wales. The contrasts are most marked in educational background, where the

Table 3.4 *Variations in Political Participation*

Number of political actions	0 %	1–4 %	5+ %
All	**15**	**52**	**33**
Age			
24 and under	17	55	29
25–44	15	49	37
45–64	13	50	37
65 and over	16	60	24
(V = .100; p = .000)			
Gender			
Male	15	53	33
Female	15	51	34
(V = .063; p = .726)			
Class			
Professional and managerial	8	45	47
Intermediate	14	51	36
Manual	18	58	24
(V = .133; p = .000)			
Religiosity			
Religious	12	52	36
Non-religious	17	52	31
(V = .106; p = .004)			
Household income			
Under £10,000	19	56	25
£10,000 up to £19,999	15	54	31
£20,000 up to £29,999	10	51	39
£30,000 up to £39,999	10	47	44
£40,000 up to £49,999	9	41	50
£50,000 and above	3	43	54
(V = .115; p = .000)			
Education			
15 years and under	19	57	24
16–18	15	52	33
19 years and over	7	43	50
(V = .145; p = .000)			
Ethnicity			
White/European	15	52	34
Black/Asian/Caribbean/Other	18	56	26
(V = .071; p = .524)			
Location			
Greater London	11	51	38
South West	16	50	34
East/West Midlands	21	54	25
North West/North/Yorkshire	14	54	31
South East/East Anglia	13	47	40
Scotland	17	54	29
Wales	6	73	21
(V = .090; p = .000)			

Demographic characteristics as defined in table 2.3.

Table 3.5 *Variations in Individual, Contact and Collective Actors*

	Individual % yes*	Contact % yes**	Collective % yes***
All	**28**	**13**	**5**
Age			
24 and under	28	6	10
25–44	33	11	5
45–64	29	17	4
65 and over	16	13	3
	V = .114;	V = .098;	V = .143;
	p = .001	p = .000	p = .000
Gender			
Male	27	14	6
Female	29	12	4
	V = .054;	V = .022;	V = .059;
	p = .049	p = .219	p = .032
Class			
Professional and managerial	43	19	7
Intermediate	31	13	4
Manual	18	9	4
	V = .291;	V = .132;	V = .087;
	p = .000	p = .000	p = .177
Religiosity			
Religious	28	14	4
Non-religious	28	11	6
	V = .020;	V = .049;	V = .052;
	p = .472	p = .006	p = .060
Household income			
Under £10,000	18	11	4
£10,000 up to £19,999	24	14	5
£20,000 up to £29,999	34	12	7
£30,000 up to £39,999	41	15	4
£40,000 up to £49,999	57	13	8
£50,000 and above	56	18	7
	V = .321;	V = .067;	V = .081;
	p = .000	p = .126	p = .379
Education			
15 years and under	17	11	2
16–18	27	12	5
19 years and over	52	19	10
	V = .270;	V = .089;	V = .116;
	p = .000	p = .000	p = .001

(cont.)

Table 3.5 (*cont.*)

	Individual % yes*	Contact % yes**	Collective % yes***
Ethnicity			
White/European	28	13	5
Black/Asian/Caribbean/ Other	27	13	5
	V = .049; p = .539	V = .018; p = .908	V = .025; p = .938
Location			
Greater London	38	14	6
South West	28	13	6
East/West Midlands	22	10	4
North West/North/ Yorkshire	25	14	5
South East/East Anglia	34	14	4
Scotland	20	13	6
Wales	14	7	4
	V = .239; p = .000	V = .063; p = .253	V = .135; p = .018

Demographic characteristics as defined in table 2.13.
* percentage who had 'bought certain products for political, ethical, or environmental reasons'.
** percentage who had 'contacted a politician (for example, a member of parliament or a local councillor)'.
*** percentage who had 'taken part in a public demonstration'.

highly educated are three times more likely to be engaged in this form of individualistic action than those who left full-time education at the age of 15, and in occupation, where professionals and managers are twice as likely as manual workers to act in this manner.

The contacting political participant is more likely to be found among the professional and managerial ranks, among the highly educated, and among the middle-aged. A person's gender, income, ethnicity, religiosity, and place of living will not make any significant difference to whether or not they are contacters.

Finally, among the relatively small number of people who engage in collectively organised political action, the distinguishing characteristics are very limited. The only two are age and education; so those aged 24 and under, and those who remained in full-time education until the age of 19 or beyond, are much more likely to be engaged in collectively organised actions. There are five times more highly educated than less educated,

Table 3.6 *Political Knowledge*

	% providing correct answer
Minimum voting age is 21	91
Separate elections for European and British parliaments	75
House of Lords has equal powers to House of Commons	62
The number of MPs is about 100	60
No one may stand for Parliament unless they pay a deposit	59
Electoral system for Westminster is based upon proportional representation	43
The European Union is composed of 15 states	35

Source: Weighted 2000 face-to-face survey. N = 3,145.
The seven statements required a yes or no answer.

and three times more young than elderly, among the collective political activists. The implications of these variations in political engagement are something that we discuss in the concluding comments to this chapter.

So far we have examined whether variations in people's levels of political participation might be linked to their distinct demographic characteristics. However, another important contextual factor could be the extent of a person's political knowledge, political interest, or engagement in political discussions (Verba and Nie, 1972; Verba, Schlozman and Brady, 1995; Zaller, 1992). We examine this issue more fully in chapters 5 and 6, but for now it is interesting to examine aggregate levels of political knowledge, interest in politics and political discussion in order to assess whether political participation might be linked to these three factors.

Political knowledge, interest and discussions

We asked our respondents a range of questions about some of the key institutions and procedures of the British state in order to determine their levels of political knowledge. Table 3.6 reports that their knowledge of the rules and procedures regarding parliamentary elections is relatively high. Ninety-one per cent know the age when one can first vote in Britain, and majorities of over 50 per cent know that separate elections are held to elect MPs and MEPs to the British and European parliaments respectively, that the two Houses of Parliament do not share equal powers, that the House of Commons is made up of more than 100 MPs, and that candidates have to pay a deposit in order to contest parliamentary elections. It is only on questions regarding the British electoral system and the make-up of the European Union that fewer than one-half of respondents are able

Table 3.7 *Variations in the Politically Knowledgeable and Less Knowledgeable*

	5–7 correct answers	5–7 incorrect answers
All	**50**	**22**
Age		
24 and under	29	37
25–44	46	24
45–64	60	15
65 and over	52	21
(V = .225; p = .000)		
Gender		
Male	63	14
Female	40	28
(V = .254; p = .000)		
Class		
Professional and managerial	70	10
Intermediate	53	17
Manual	36	30
(V = .371; p = .000)		
Religiosity		
Religious	51	20
Non-religious	48	25
(V = .060; p = .004)		
Household income		
Under £10,000	37	32
£10,000 up to £19,999	48	21
£20,000 up to £29,999	55	17
£30,000 up to £39,999	66	16
£40,000 up to £49,999	66	8
£50,000 and above	72	6
(V = .275; p = .000)		
Education		
15 years and under	42	26
16–18	46	24
19 years and over	71	11
(V = .226; p = .000)		
Ethnicity		
White/European	50	22
Black/Asian/Caribbean/Other	40	18
(V = .063; p = .071)		
Location		
Greater London	52	19
South West	54	20
East/West Midlands	41	28
North West/North/ Yorkshire	54	19
South East/East Anglia	52	21
Scotland	41	27
Wales	44	29
(V = .153; p = .000)		

Demographic characteristics as in table 2.13.

Table 3.8 *Personal Interest in Politics*

	Very %	Fairly %	Not very %	Not at all %	Don't know %
Local	4	31	33	31	1
Regional	4	29	35	32	1
National	13	35	24	28	1
European	6	20	33	41	1
International	7	25	29	38	1

Source: Weighted 2000 face-to-face survey. N = 3,145.
Question: *'How interested are you personally in each of the following levels . . .?'*

to give the correct answers. Overall, 13 per cent of respondents answered all seven questions correctly and 6 per cent answered all of the questions incorrectly.

Can we distinguish the politically knowledgeable from the less knowledgeable? In table 3.7 we discover that there are very significant differences between the politically knowledgeable (defined as those answering five or more of the questions correctly) and the politically less knowledgeable (defined as those answering five or more questions incorrectly). The politically knowledgeable are concentrated among the middle-aged, men, professional and managerial workers, the rich, and the highly educated. It is among the young, manual workers, and the poor that the less politically knowledgeable are most concentrated. Professional and managerial workers and the rich are twice as likely to be among the politically knowledgeable than manual workers and the poor.

To what extent are people interested in politics and to what extent do they engage in political discussions? Table 3.8 reports that a solid core of people, ranging from one in four to more than one in three, have no interest whatsoever in either domestic politics, whether it is local, regional or national, or European or international politics. On the other hand, a small core of people, ranging from one in twenty-five to one in twelve, are 'very interested' in local, regional, European or international politics, and one in eight (13 per cent) are 'very interested' in national politics. If we exclude both the hard-core interested ('very') and non-interested ('not at all') groups of people, there are majorities who admit to a modicum of interest in politics ('fairly' or 'not very') at all levels. Not surprisingly given the current public hostility towards the European Union, European politics attract the least interest among the British public.[3]

---

[3] Peter Hall (2002: 50) reports that the percentage of people expressing some interest in politics has fluctuated over recent decades, but was higher in 1990 than in 1963.

Table 3.9 *Variations in Political Interest in National Politics*

	Very interested %	Fairly interested %	Not very interested %	Not at all interested %
All	**13**	**35**	**24**	**28**
Age				
24 and under	8	29	28	35
25–44	11	35	23	31
45–64	15	38	24	23
65 and over	18	35	23	24
(V = .078; p = .000)				
Gender				
Male	17	37	22	24
Female	11	33	25	31
(V = .121; p = .000)				
Class				
Professional and managerial	22	42	20	16
Intermediate	14	37	24	25
Manual	7	30	26	36
(V = .149; p = .000)				
Religiosity				
Religious	13	38	24	25
Non-religious	13	32	24	31
(V = .105; p = .000)				
Household income				
Under £10,000	10	27	25	37
£10,000 up to £19,999	12	36	24	28
£20,000 up to £29,999	13	39	23	24
£30,000 up to £39,999	18	42	20	20
£40,000 up to £49,999	16	49	23	12
£50,000 and above	22	43	22	14
(V = .113; p = .000)				
Education				
15 years and under	10	31	26	32
16–18	10	34	25	31
19 years and over	24	45	17	13
(V = .125; p = .000)				
Ethnicity				
White/European	13	36	23	28
Black/Asian/Caribbean/ Other	13	28	26	32
(V = .044; p = .097)				
Location				
Greater London	14	36	20	29
South West	12	34	27	27
East/West Midlands	10	37	19	34
North West/North/ Yorkshire	15	32	28	25
South East/East Anglia	14	39	23	23
Scotland	9	28	25	38
Wales	12	29	25	34
(V = .092; p = .000)				

Demographic characteristics as in table 2.13. Don't knows excluded.

Table 3.10 *Political Discussions*

	Often %	Sometimes %	Rarely %	Never %	Don't know %
Friends	13	29	26	32	0
Family	12	28	26	33	0
Neighbours	3	13	24	60	1
Fellow workers	5	18	16	47	15

Source: Weighted 2000 face-to-face survey. N = 3,145.
Question: '*How often would you say you discuss political matters when you get together with the following groups . . .?*'

Who are the politically interested and non-interested? In table 3.9 we select the levels of interest in national politics and again examine our respondents' characteristics. We see significant variations. The elderly, males, those in professional and managerial occupations, the rich, and the highly educated are more likely to be 'very interested' in national politics than the young, women, manual workers, the poor, and less well-educated people. Some of the contrasts are very striking. For example, professional and managerial workers are three times more likely to be 'very interested' in national politics than manual workers. It is also worth noting that those people who remained in full-time education beyond the age of 19 reveal a far higher interest in national politics than those who left at the age of 18 or earlier. In other words, perhaps not surprisingly, higher education appears to boost an interest in politics.

If we describe people's interest in politics as being generally slight, how about their engagement in political discussions? Do they talk to others about politics? Table 3.10 reveals that, when we combine the 'often' and 'sometimes' responses, four in every ten people discuss politics among their family and friends; one in ten 'often' talk about politics with their family or friends. By contrast, the numbers who 'never' talk politics range from one in three to one in two according to the nature of the potential discussant group. Very few of our respondents talk with their neighbours about political matters; a majority (60 per cent) 'never' discuss political matters with them. It is very clear that talking politics over the garden fence is not a common activity! Verbal political communication where it occurs is more likely to take place within family and friendship networks.[4]

---

[4] Bennett, Flickinger and Rhine (2000: 111), using the 1992 British Election Study data, confirm that political talk-mates are overwhelmingly family members and friends. Peter Hall (2002: 50) reports that the proportion of the population who frequently discuss politics with friends remained stable between 15 and 19 per cent from 1970 to 1990.

Table 3.11 *Variations in Political Discussions with Friends*

	Often %	Sometimes %	Rarely %	Never %
All	**13**	**29**	**26**	**32**
Age				
24 and under	10	27	23	40
25–44	10	29	31	32
45–64	16	32	26	27
65 and over	17	28	22	33
(V = .079; p = .000)				
Gender				
Male	17	32	26	24
Female	10	28	26	37
(V = .163; p = .000)				
Class				
Professional and managerial	21	36	27	17
Intermediate	13	31	30	27
Manual	8	25	26	42
(V = .157; p = .000)				
Religiosity				
Religious	12	31	26	30
Non-religious	14	27	26	33
(V = .067; p = .032)				
Household income				
Under £10,000	11	24	22	44
£10,000 up to £19,999	13	29	28	30
£20,000 up to £29,999	12	34	30	23
£30,000 up to £39,999	16	32	26	26
£40,000 up to £49,999	22	31	30	17
£50,000 and above	21	40	27	11
(V = .131; p = .000)				
Education				
15 years and under	12	26	22	40
16–18	10	28	29	33
19 years and over	23	39	25	13
(V = .131; p = .000)				
Ethnicity				
White/European	13	29	26	32
Black/Asian/Caribbean/ Other	13	32	25	31
(V = .034; p = .559)				
Location				
Greater London	17	35	22	26
South West	9	24	36	31
East/West Midlands	9	26	26	38
North West/North/ Yorkshire	13	32	24	31
South East/East Anglia	16	31	26	27
Scotland	8	29	25	39
Wales	15	21	19	46
(V = .101; p = .000)				

Demographic characteristics as in table 2.13.

Table 3.12 *The Relationship between Political Participation and Political Knowledge, Political Interest and Political Discussion*

Number of political actions	0 %	1–4 %	5+ %
All	15	52	33
Political knowledge			
5–7 correct answers	8	48	45
5–7 incorrect answers	29	54	17
(V = .282; p = .000)			
Political interest			
Very interested	5	36	59
Not interested	27	58	15
(V = .469; p = .000)			
Political discussion			
Often discuss	5	40	56
Never discuss	26	56	19
(V = .393; p = .000)			

Can we distinguish those who often talk about politics with friends from those who never talk about politics? Table 3.11 shows that, as with other comparisons in this chapter, political discussants are more likely to be aged 45 and over, men, professional and managerial workers, richer people, and the higher educated. In order to stress the variation in levels of political discussion, we select one noticeable difference. The poor – those with an annual household income of less than £10,000 – are four times more likely to be among those who never discuss politics with friends than the rich – those with an annual household income of £50,000 or more.

In our earlier discussion of political participation, we examined the extent to which people's political engagement varied according to their demographic make-up. We now return to this discussion by examining whether their political participation varies according to their levels of political knowledge, political interest and political discussion. Table 3.12 reports that people's levels of political action vary significantly according to their political knowledge and interest and the extent to which they discuss politics. The politically very active, in other words those who engaged in five or more actions, are concentrated among those who are politically knowledgeable and interested, and who 'often' engage in political discussions with their friends. By contrast, the totally politically inactive are less knowledgeable, less interested and less engaged in discussion. They are three to five times more likely to be politically inactive than those more knowledgeable, interested, and engaged in discussions.

To summarise our findings so far, we see that people's repertoire of political activities is broad, and that their level of political activity is greater than might be assumed from some of the contemporary discussions of traditional political behaviour, such as voting in elections and party membership. Furthermore, people do have a basic political knowledge, but their interest in politics is limited. However, they do engage in some political discussions with close friends and family. What is more difficult to judge is the extent to which people's political actions and discourse have changed over time. But we can be confident in stating that they now make greater use of their consumption powers for political ends.

Up to this point in this chapter we have been examining quite specific forms of *political* action. What about people's civic participation more generally? We now turn to a discussion of their engagement in organised groups.

Repertoires of organisational participation

To what extent do people join organisations? Furthermore, if they do join, what and how many organisations do they belong to? And beyond formal organisational life, do people get together informally with others?

We asked our respondents, firstly, whether they had been a member of one or more of twenty-six types of organisations during the previous twelve months.[5] We defined a member as someone paying a membership fee to the organisation. We see in figure 3.3 that the majority of the public are not members of any organisation.[6] Just four in every ten people pay a fee to an organisation. Among these joiners, the mean number of types of organisation to which they belong is two. The multiple members, in other words, those who are members of five or more organisations, number 3 per cent. Of course these figures underestimate the extent of people's

---

[5] Almond and Verba (1963: 302) itemised ten types of organisations (Trade union, Business, Professional, Farm, Social, Charitable, Religious, Civic-Political, Cooperative and Veterans) plus an Other category. Verba and Nie (1972: 41) itemised sixteen types of organisations. The Citizen Audit finalised its typology of twenty-six organisations plus an Other category after discussions with colleagues in the European Science Foundation Network on Citizenship, Involvement and Democracy. Embarrassingly for the authors, between the piloting of the questionnaires and their final printing one organisational type (Party Organisations) was inadvertently dropped from the listing. It was restored to the questionnaires administered in the second wave of the panel survey.

[6] Wuthnow (2002: 69) and Worms (2002: 145) report that 71 per cent of Americans and 46 per cent of French were members of at least one type of association in 1994. Other research on French associational life (Mayer, 2001) reports that 66 per cent of the French adult population belong to one or more voluntary association.

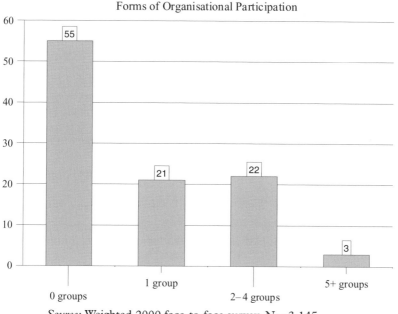

Source: Weighted 2000 face-to-face survey. N = 3,145.
Question: *'In the last twelve months, have you been a member of this type of organisation (in other words have you paid a membership fee if it is required)?'*

Figure 3.3 Members of Organisations

organisational involvement and support because our survey distinguishes *types* of organisations, and people may be members of more than one *group* within any particular type of organisation.

What types of organisations do people belong to as members? Table 3.13 reveals that people are most likely to join a motoring organisation (for example, the Automobile Association or the Royal Automobile Club), followed by sports, fitness and work organisations.[7] Other types of organisations which attract relatively large numbers of members are the residential and neighbourhood, social, conservation, religious, and hobby groups and clubs. Some organisations representing contemporary *post-material* issues (for example, women's rights, human rights, protection of the environment and the treatment of animals), and particular constituencies (for example, the disabled and consumers), attract 1 per cent of our respondents as members. The 2001 Census reports an adult

---

[7] Mayer (2001) classified nine types of organisations, and reports that by far the most popular type of organisation that the French belong to is in the sports and leisure category.

Table 3.13 *Types of Organisational Membership*

	%		%
Motoring	29	Youth	1
Trade union	9	Environmental	1
Sports/Outdoor activities	8	Animal rights	1
Gymnasium	6	Business/Employers	1
Residents/Housing/Neighbourhood	6	Women	1
Professional	5	Humanitarian aid/Human rights	1
Social	5	Medical patients/Illnesses	1
Conservation	4	Consumer	1
Religious/Church	3	Parents and teachers	1
Hobby	3	Disabled	1
Cultural/Music/Dancing/Theatre	2	Other	5
Ex-service	2		

Source: Weighted 2000 face-to-face survey. N = c3,036.

population of 44 million in Great Britain, so these Citizen Audit figures suggest that memberships range from almost 13 million belonging to a motoring organisation, 3 million to a sports or outdoor activities organisation, 2 million to a gymnasium, down to between a quarter- and a half-million belonging to a range of organisations, including animal rights, women's and consumer groups.

Many would argue that joining a motoring organisation is nothing more than taking out an insurance policy against a vehicle breakdown. If we therefore exclude this category of membership from our data, we find that almost one in three people (31 per cent) are members of an organisation. Membership was specified in the Citizen Audit as meaning specifically the payment of a subscription to an organisation. However, we were interested to discover whether the payment of a subscription was the sum total of their commitment or whether they participated and interacted with their fellow members within the organisation. To what extent, in other words, is group membership nothing more than a cheque-book or credit-card commitment? It was not possible in the Citizen Audit to ask our respondents to itemise their activities in all the groups to which they belonged, and so we asked members to choose the one organisation which was most important to them and then to tell us something more about their activities within it. Not surprisingly table 3.14 reveals that membership for a large number of people involves neither participation in the organisation's activities nor interaction with their fellow members. But one in three 'often' attend meetings and one in five 'often' participate in decision-making at meetings. Furthermore, outside of the meeting place

Table 3.14 *Participatory Activities in Organisations*

	Often %	Sometimes %	Rarely %	Never %	Don't know %
Attend meetings	32	14	10	41	3
Participate in decision-making at meetings	22	13	11	51	4
Speak at meetings	16	13	11	57	4
Plan/chair meetings	8	6	5	77	4
Write report about meetings	6	6	6	78	4
Talk about organisation problems/goals	25	22	10	39	4
Call upon fellow members for practical help	18	21	12	45	4
Disagree about organisation problems/goals	12	24	14	47	4
Meet socially	24	22	12	38	4

Source: Weighted 2000 face-to-face survey. N = 1,409.
Questions: *'Thinking about the one organisation which is most important to you, how often do you . . .?' 'Again, thinking about the one organisation which is most important to you, how often do you do any of the following with other members of the organisation?'*

one in four 'often' talk with other members of their group about its affairs, and a similar proportion will 'often' meet socially with their fellow members. In total, around four in ten group members are involved in personal interchange with their fellow members at some time. One can see therefore that associational life provides a meeting point and melting pot for their ideas and their social relationships.

In addition to examining people's repertoire of formal, organisational activities we also examine their more informal, less organised activities. We asked our respondents whether they belonged to either an informal network of friends or acquaintances which met regularly, such as a pub quiz team, a book-reading or a children's group, or provided some support beyond their own family for people in the community, such as shopping for neighbours or visiting old people, without doing it through an organisation. Figure 3.4 reveals that one in three (33 per cent) of our respondents provide some support in the community,[8] and one in five (21 per cent) belong to an informal network. One question which arises

[8] The Home Office Citizenship Survey reports that 67 per cent volunteered informally within their communities. But the list of activities is much broader than those in the Citizen Audit, and includes giving advice to someone, looking after property or pets for someone absent from home, babysitting, and keeping in touch with someone (Prime, Zimmeck and Zurawan, 2002: 6).

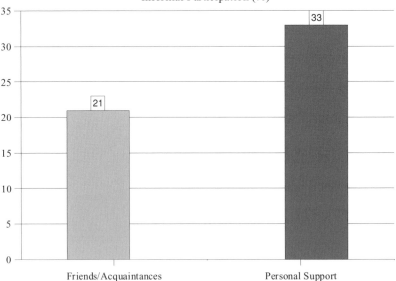

Source: Weighted 2000 face-to-face survey. N = 3,145.

Questions: (a) *'Apart from these organisations we have talked about do you belong to an informal network of friends or acquaintances with whom you have contact on a regular basis (for example, pub quiz team, book-reading group, parent/toddler group, child care group)?'*

(b) *'Do you actively provide any support beyond your immediate family for ill people, elderly neighbours or acquaintances without doing it through an organisation (for example, shopping for neighbours, visiting old people)?'*

Figure 3.4 Informal Participation

is whether these informal activities are distinct in the sense that people prefer to engage in informal rather than formal activities. The answer is that the two worlds of formal and informal engagement are distinct; almost one in two (45 per cent) of those engaged in either of these two types of informal activity are not members of an organisation.

Our audit reveals a very extensive repertoire of associational life, both formal and informal. How much time do individuals give to all these forms of engagement, both formal and informal, organised and less organised? Figure 3.5 reports that more than one in three (39 per cent) spent no time at all in the previous month in any form of participation; by contrast, one in five (22 per cent) spent up to four hours per month,

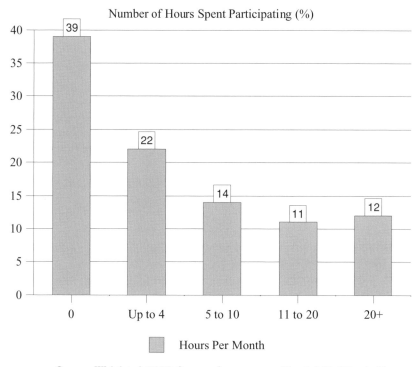

Source: Weighted 2000 face-to-face survey. N = 3,048 (Don't Knows excluded).
'During the last month, approximately how much time in total did you spend on activities, in clubs, associations, groups, networks or in supporting other people?'

Figure 3.5 Number of Hours Spent Participating

one in eight (14 per cent) spent between five and ten hours per month, and another one in ten (11 per cent) spent between eleven and twenty hours per month engaged in such participation. Finally, there exists a small group of hard-core participants (12 per cent) who gave more than twenty hours of their time in the previous month, or an average of more than five hours per week.

Earlier in this chapter we commented upon the difficulties involved in comparing political participation over time. Similar problems arise when examining trend figures for people's associational activities. Earlier surveys have asked people to itemise their organisational membership, but the number and range of organisations has varied. So the Civic

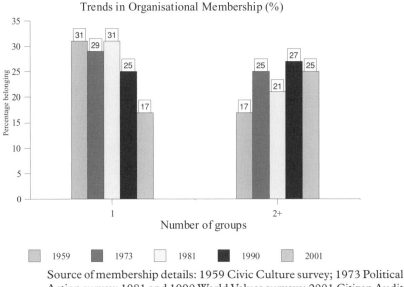

Source of membership details: 1959 Civic Culture survey; 1973 Political
Action survey; 1981 and 1990 World Values surveys; 2001 Citizen Audit
(Weighted 2000 face-to-face survey). See Hall (2002: 421) for pre-2001
figures.

Figure 3.6 Trends in Organisational Membership

Culture survey of 1959 (Almond and Verba, 1963) asked British respondents whether they were a member of eleven listed types of organisations,
whereas the 1981 World Values survey listed ten types of association and
then the 1991 World Values survey added a further six types to the list
(Inglehart, 1997). Some of these categories are coterminous with those
used in the Citizen Audit; however, eleven that are used in the Citizen
Audit are not included in the World Values surveys.[9] Whatever the definition of membership, and whatever the typology used to classify groups,
figure 3.6 reports that fewer people are now joining just a single organisation but there is an upward trend in the number of people belonging
to two or more groups.

We now repeat the same exercise as in chapter 2 and earlier in this chapter and examine the variations in people's organisational participation and
support. Who are the organisational joiners and how do they compare
with the non-joiners?

[9] Types of organisation included in the Citizen Audit and not in the 1981/91
World Values surveys were: conservation, humanitarian, pensioners, ex-service clubs,
business/employers, consumers, cultural, hobby, motoring, ethnic and social.

Characteristics of the organisational participants

In table 3.15 we distinguish members and non-members; furthermore, among the members we examine to what extent those who are members of a single organisation differ from those who belong to two or more types of organisation. It is apparent that both the young and old, women, manual workers, the poor, the less well-educated, and the Scots are less likely to belong to groups than the middle-aged, men, those employed in professional and managerial occupations, the rich, the well-educated, and those living in the south-east of England. Among those belonging to just one group the variations are limited, but among those belonging to two or more groups the contrasts become most noticeable. In particular, among the multiple members, in other words, those belonging to five or more organisations, there is a concentration of professionals and managers, the rich, and the well-educated.

Some of the contrasts are most striking. For example, someone with a household income of £50,000 or more per annum is eleven times more likely to be a member of five or more groups than is the person with a household income of £10,000 or less per annum. Similarly, the person who remained in full-time education to the age of 19 is seven times more likely to belong to five or more groups than the person whose full-time education ceased at the age of 15.

The above comparisons are of *organisational* membership and activism. But, as we have already pointed out, the Citizen Audit also measures informal activities, such as pub quiz teams or shopping for an elderly neighbour, in which people participate. Do we find that these informal activities attract a different type of person? Or are the rich, the well-educated, and the higher-ranked occupations over-represented here as well? In table 3.16 we see that the demographic profile of informal participants is partially similar to that of group members. We still find the professional and managerial workers and the highly educated more heavily involved in both forms of informal activity than manual workers or the least educated. However, there are some noticeable differences. The young are more likely to be found in informal networks than are all other age groups. And in personal support activities the middle-aged, women, the religious, and mid-income households are more prominent.

Finally, by examining the hours people give to all activities, both formal and informal, organised and non-organised, we can draw up a picture in table 3.17 of both the time misers and the time donors. We see that the time misers (in other words, those who devote no time to any of these activities) are more likely to be found among the elderly and the

Table 3.15 *Variations in Group Membership*

Number of groups	0 %	1 %	2–4 %	5+ %
All	**55**	**21**	**22**	**3**
Age				
24 and under	69	13	16	2
25 to 44	52	22	23	3
45 to 64	48	24	26	3
65 and over	64	18	15	2
(V = .090; p = .000)				
Gender				
Male	49	22	26	3
Female	60	20	18	3
(V = .113; p = .000)				
Class				
Professional and managerial	36	24	34	6
Intermediate	57	21	20	2
Manual	67	19	14	1
(V = .183; p = .000)				
Religiosity				
Religious	52	21	24	3
Non-religious	58	20	19	2
(V = .066; p = .004)				
Household income				
Under £10,000	76	15	9	1
£10,000 and under £19,999	56	22	21	1
£20,000 and under £29,999	42	27	28	3
£30,000 and under £39,999	36	28	32	5
£40,000 and under £49,999	35	20	40	5
£50,000 and over	28	16	46	11
(V = .232; p = .000)				
Education				
15 years and under	65	20	15	1
16 to 18	56	21	21	2
19 years and over	36	21	36	7
(V = .156; p = .000)				
Ethnicity				
White/European	55	21	22	3
Black/Asian/Caribbean/Other	57	22	16	5
(V = .040; p = .233)				
Location				
Greater London	55	21	19	5
South West	53	21	21	4
East/West Midlands	58	21	19	2
North West/North/Yorkshire	61	16	22	7
South East/East Anglia	47	23	26	3
Scotland	68	20	11	0
Wales	53	27	17	3
(V = .135; p = .000)				

Demographic characteristics as defined in table 2.13.

Table 3.16 *Variations in Informal Participation*

Engaged in informal activities	Informal network % yes*	Personal support % yes**
All	**21**	**33**
Age		
24 and under	27	21
25 to 44	23	32
45 to 64	21	41
65 and over	15	31
	V = .129; p = .000	V = .118; p = .000
Gender		
Male	21	27
Female	21	37
	V = .092; p = .004	V = .120; p = .000
Class		
Professional and managerial	29	37
Intermediate	26	34
Manual	15	31
	V = .152; p = .000	V = .106; p = .001
Religiosity		
Religious	22	39
Non-religious	20	26
	V = .100; p = .001	V = .154; p = .000
Household income		
Under £10,000	13	31
£10,000 and under £19,999	22	34
£20,000 and under £29,999	24	41
£30,000 and under £39,999	27	37
£40,000 and under £49,999	33	29
£50,000 and above	42	33
	V = .176; p = .000	V = .133; p = .000
Education		
15 and under	13	31
16 to 18	22	33
19 and over	35	37
	V = .156; p = .000	V = .099; p = .000
Ethnicity		
White/European	21	33
Black/Asian/Caribbean/Other	23	35
	V = .031; p = .956	V = .032; p = .982
Location		
Greater London	24	38
South West	20	31
East/West Midlands	18	30
North West/North/ Yorkshire	18	30
South East/East Anglia	26	38
Scotland	19	28
Wales	14	28
	V = .121; p = .006	V = .082; p = .612

Demographic characteristics as defined in table 2.13
* per cent belonging to 'an informal network of friends or acquaintances with whom you have contact on a regular basis'; ** per cent actively providing 'any support beyond your immediate family for ill people, elderly neighbours, or acquaintances without doing it through an organisation'.

Table 3.17 *Variations in Time Misers and Time Donors*

Number of hours per month	0 %	Up to 5 %	5+ %
All	**40**	**22**	**37**
Age			
24 and under	46	20	34
25–44	38	24	38
45–64	37	23	40
65 and over	47	21	33
(V = .056; p = .006)			
Gender			
Male	41	20	39
Female	40	24	36
(V = .051; p = .022)			
Class			
Professional and managerial	27	24	49
Intermediate	41	23	36
Manual	48	21	31
(V = .103; p = .000)			
Religiosity			
Religious	36	24	41
Non-religious	46	21	33
(V = .103; p = .000)			
Household income			
Under £10,000	52	19	29
£10,000 up to £19,999	41	22	38
£20,000 up to £29,999	32	22	45
£30,000 up to £39,999	28	28	44
£40,000 up to £49,999	34	25	42
£50,000 and above	20	32	48
(V = .156; p = .000)			
Education			
15 years and under	48	20	32
16–18	42	23	36
19 years and over	25	25	50
(V = .145; p = .000)			
Ethnicity			
White/European	41	23	37
Black/Asian/Caribbean/Other	41	21	38
(V = .035; p = .512)			
Location			
Greater London	41	25	33
South West	42	23	36
East/West Midlands	44	20	36
North West/North/Yorkshire	42	22	35
South East/East Anglia	32	26	43
Scotland	56	11	33
Wales	41	22	37
(V = .118; p = .000)			

Demographic characteristics as in table 2.13. Don't knows have been excluded.

young, manual workers, the non-religious, the poor, the least educated, and Scots while, on the other hand, the time donors (in other words, those who spend five hours or more per month on any of these activities) are professional and managerial workers, the middle-income and the richest households, and the well-educated.

In table 3.18 we repeat the summary exercise that concluded chapter 2 by displaying the impact that these demographic characteristics have upon civic behaviour. We see that the levels of education, household income and occupational status are the three most significant characteristics in distinguishing between the active, engaged citizen and the inactive. After examining the contours of civic participation one would conclude, as have observers of civic participation in the USA (Verba, Schlozman and Brady, 1995), that it is the well-educated and the well-heeled who are more likely to be engaged in politics and voluntary activities.

Conclusions

Concern is often expressed that people are now participating less in various orthodox forms of political behaviour, such as voting in general or local elections, or joining political parties. Political apathy and abstention are both regarded as major problems in contemporary Britain. For example, the Home Secretary, David Blunkett (2003), writes of 'worrying signs that people are retreating from active citizenship'. However, without wanting to minimise the significance of public disillusion with long-established political institutions and practices, we would suggest that by concentrating upon just a few of these political institutions and practices the public exit from civic behaviour has been exaggerated. We believe that the Citizen Audit reveals that citizens have not contracted out, but are engaged in a multiplicity of political activities beyond the traditional; three in every four people are engaged in political activity, defined as attempting to influence rules, laws or policies. The most common forms of political activities tend to be ones that an individual takes on his or her own, like giving money, signing a petition, or purchasing particular types of goods, without the need to interact with other people.[10] But political engagement does not lie upon one single continuum. Rather, there are distinct individualistic, contact and collectively organised forms of political engagement.

[10] However, the fact that an individual does decide to donate money, sign a petition, or purchase a particular product is the result of organised, collective action on the part of other individuals, that is to say political activists and entrepreneurs.

Table 3.18 *Summary of the Impact of Particular Variables on Citizenship Behaviour*

	Age	Gender	Occupation	Religion	Income	Education	Ethnicity	Place
Political engagement	**yes**	no	**yes**	**yes**	**yes**	**yes**	no	**yes**
Individualistic actor	**yes**	no	**yes**	**yes**	**yes**	**yes**	no	**yes**
Contacting actor	no	no	**yes**	no	no	**yes**	no	**yes**
Collectivist actor	**yes**	no	no	no	no	**yes**	no	no
Politically knowledgeable	**yes**	**yes**	**yes**	**yes**	**yes**	**yes**	no	**yes**
Politically interested	**yes**	**yes**	**yes**	**yes**	**yes**	**yes**	no	**yes**
Political discussant	**yes**	**yes**	**yes**	no	**yes**	**yes**	no	**yes**
Group membership	**yes**	**yes**	**yes**	**yes**	**yes**	**yes**	no	**yes**
Informal participant	**yes**	**yes**	**yes**	**yes**	**yes**	**yes**	no	**yes**
Personal support participant	**yes**	**yes**	**yes**	**yes**	**yes**	**yes**	no	**yes**
Time commitment	yes	no	**yes**	**yes**	**yes**	**yes**	no	**yes**

yes, bold: significant at 0.01 level; yes, non-bold: significant at 0.05 level.

What is clear, however, is that this political engagement is very much dominated by the already well-resourced; in other words, the most highly educated, the rich, and those from the top occupational echelons. Political voice, therefore, must inevitably take on the sound of protecting the interests of those who already possess the greatest resources.

Not only are people politically engaged, but people are also extensively networked into various forms of associational life and informal activities.[11] Two in every three people either belong to an organisation, or participate in an informal group or a neighbourhood support network, and a similar proportion devote some time each month to an organisation, an informal group, or a personal support network. As with political engagement, much of this diverse and rich associational activity is dominated by the rich, the well-educated, and those from professional and managerial backgrounds. A very similar demographic profile is apparent when examining people's participation in informal associations and personal support networks. What the consequences might be of this social distortion of civic behaviour is something that we discuss in our concluding comments in chapter 9.

We now turn in the next chapter to a consideration of people's micro political behaviour, namely their actions to influence the quality of their children's schooling, their or their family's medical treatment, or their own working environment.

---

[11] The Home Office Citizenship Survey, to which we have already referred, utilises different measures of people's participation in the community, but it concludes that their engagement is substantial (Prime, Zimmeck and Zurawan, 2002: 7).

4   Civic Behaviour and Citizenship: Micro Politics

We suggested in chapter 3 that people's civic engagement is more diverse than traditional approaches to the study of politics often recognise. People's political activities extend well beyond the traditional ones associated with elections and Parliament. We may safely assume that their conception of politics is also broader than one which concentrates upon governments, whether national, state, regional or local. For individuals concerned with the daily essentials of life, such as food, income, health, habitation, knowledge and security, their experience of politics will not be with the formal institutions of government such as Parliament or ministries, but rather with a range of bodies and people who are continuously mediating their daily lives: for example, the hospital, the surgery, the school, the old people's home, the benefits agency, the social services department, the police station, and the place of work. Within these organisations such people as the doctor, the nurse, the teacher, the care worker, the policeman, and the employer will be their contact point with the state. Furthermore, politics in this sense is not episodic, like voting which takes place at periodic intervals, but ever-present and continuous.

Day by day people interact with the state as they conduct their lives. Increasingly over recent decades, however, the state has devolved its responsibilities to a range of other authorities. There has been a retreat from the post-1945 universal, collective provision of many services to the selective, private provision of the twenty-first century. Nowadays a broad range of agencies – public and private, national and local, elected and appointed – are responsible for service delivery. The state is becoming less of a provider and more of a regulator, establishing targets and then monitoring the extent to which these are met.

Since 1945 the tendency of all British governments has been to remove powers from locally elected authorities. So local government's historic responsibilities for major services, such as hospitals, schools, transport and urban planning, to name but a few, have been either removed completely or substantially reduced. The centralising tendencies of national government were particularly apparent during the 1980s and early 1990s.

In 1997 the newly elected Labour government was committed to greater decentralisation of powers, but its commitment to targets for the delivery of all public services has resulted in considerable central intervention in, and direction of, policies. The balance of powers, therefore, between central and local government remains very much at the centre. Although the point of delivery for most services is the locality, the nature of the services is determined centrally.[1]

We have previously noted in chapter 2 that although people feel most strongly attached to their country, their attachment to the locality (region, town and village) is also strong. We also noted that they feel a greater sense of political efficacy within their local community than in society at large. Whereas 60 per cent agreed with the statement that 'when people like me all work together we can really make a difference to our local community', only 40 per cent agreed with the statement that 'people like me can have a real influence on politics if they are prepared to get involved'. Furthermore, people trust local government more than any other political institution, and they feel that their vote has more chance of influencing decisions taken by local authorities than those taken by the House of Commons.[2] The paradox, however, is that turnout in local elections is much lower than in general elections. Partially this might be explained by the fact that the sense of duty to vote, which, as we have already seen, is very strong, extends no further than general elections. Another explanation may be that the voter is aware that local authorities have less power to make policies themselves and therefore there is less reason to vote when the impact upon policy outcomes is only marginal.[3] Furthermore, it is clear that our respondents are acutely aware that it is government at the centre which is the most important influence on their standard of living. When asked which one institution most affected their standard of living, 61 per cent of our respondents said the British government and only 10 per cent said local government. And our respondents in Scotland and Wales were almost as certain that it was the national rather than any devolved government which most affected them: 46 per cent of Scots and 51 per cent of Welsh said the British government, with only 16 per

---

[1] With the creation of a devolved Parliament and Assembly in Scotland and Wales the delivery of some major services is beginning to show signs of local variation.

[2] In response to the question 'Thinking about voters in general to what extent does voting allow people to influence decisions made by local authorities/House of Commons?', the responses were 'not at all', 'some', 'a great deal', and 'don't know'. Merging the 'some' and 'a great deal' responses produces 65 per cent for local authorities and 54 per cent for the House of Commons; 28 per cent responded 'not at all' for local authorities and 36 per cent for the House of Commons.

[3] However, elections for the newly devolved, and more powerful, executives in Scotland and Wales have not significantly boosted turnout.

Table 4.1 *Levels of Satisfaction with Local and National Services*

	Very satisfied %	Satisfied %	Neither %	Dissatisfied %	Very dissatisfied %	Don't know %
Libraries	14	56	11	6	2	11
Street cleaning	5	49	14	21	10	2
Parks + sports facilities	6	46	16	17	6	9
Schools	9	40	14	9	3	25
Care for elderly	5	31	18	20	4	21
Social services	3	32	23	13	5	24
Roads	2	29	17	34	16	3

N = 3,145. Question: *'Are you satisfied or dissatisfied with the delivery of the following services provided by your local authority? Care for the elderly, road maintenance, street cleaning, social services, parks and sports facilities, libraries.'*

	Strongly agree %	Agree %	Neither %	Disagree %	Strongly disagree %
(a) Managing public services	3	21	28	34	15
(b) Managing economy	10	27	35	24	4

N = c3,127. Citizen Audit 2000 weighted face-to-face survey.
(a) *'The government is doing a good job in managing public services like health care and education.'*
(b) *'The government is doing a bad job in managing the economy.'*

cent of Scots and 13 per cent of Welsh believing it was the government of Scotland or Wales.

Our final introductory point is that people are more likely to be satisfied than dissatisfied with the delivery of services by local authorities. Almost three in every four people are satisfied with library services, and one in two with street cleaning, parks and sports facilities, and schools. We asked our respondents for their views on seven local services in total and, as can be seen in table 4.1, only one, road maintenance, produced a critical majority. By contrast, people were more critical of service delivery from the centre. We asked our respondents for their views on the government's management of public services in general and of the economy in particular. In both cases they were more dissatisfied than satisfied. We conclude, therefore, that while governments have been constantly centralising their service delivery powers, ironically using the argument that this would make them more efficient, the public is sceptical of the centre's ability to manage things. The public prefers service providers to be local rather than national.

The extent of political engagement

As we outlined in chapter 2, our initial approach in the Citizen Audit to the measurement of political action and engagement was to provide our respondents with a wide-ranging list of actions to influence rules, laws or policies and then to ask them to tell us which, if any of these, they had undertaken. This list of actions might be described as macro political activities. A second approach was then to ask our respondents to tell us about their experiences on issues to do with their daily lives. We asked them whether they had taken any actions in order to try and influence their children's education (if they had children in school), their or their family's medical treatment (if they had received some form of medical treatment), or their working conditions (if they were in paid employment), and, if so, how they had acted. These actions might be described as micro political activities. They are designed to give us a picture of public experience of politics at this micro level.

In this chapter, we will, firstly, examine how many people get involved in this form of micro, personal political activity, what they do, and how pleased or otherwise they are with the outcomes, how influential they think they are in this activity and, finally, who gets involved in this form of action. Then, secondly, we will examine what relationship there is, if any, between macro and micro politics. It may be that there is no relationship at all between the two; namely, those who engage in macro political actions do not engage in micro political actions, or vice versa. Alternatively, there may be a positive relationship, in the sense that people who are active in one form of political action are also active in the other. And, finally, there may be a negative relationship, with one form of activity substituting for the other. If this is the case, it might be that the opportunities for access, or the opportunity structures in politics (Tarrow, 1998), are greater at the micro than at the macro levels.

We see, firstly, in figure 4.1 the extent to which people attempt to influence the education that their children receive, the medical treatment that they or their relatives receive, or the working conditions in which they earn their living. The analysis started by asking people if they had children in school, had sought or obtained medical treatment in the previous twelve months, or were in paid employment. Almost one in two of our respondents in paid employment had taken action to try and improve

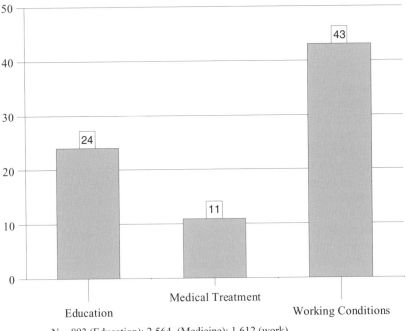

Attempts to Influence Education, Medicine or Work (% yes)

N = 893 (Education); 2,564, (Medicine); 1,612 (work)

Question: *'During the last twelve months have you done anything to try and change the way education is provided at any of your children's schools/the way medical treatment was provided/to improve your working conditions?'*

Figure 4.1 Attempts to Influence Educational or Medical Provision, or Working Conditions

their working conditions, one in four with children in school had taken action to try and change the way their children's education was provided, and one in ten who had sought medical treatment had taken action to try and change the way the treatment was provided.

The differences in the numbers of people trying to influence outcomes in these three areas of day-to-day life are striking and might be explained by the quality of the service provided or by the opportunities available to take such actions. In other words, people only take action when they are dissatisfied or when the opportunities to become involved are available. As far as satisfaction levels are concerned, we see in table 4.1 that people's overall satisfaction levels with their children's schooling and their, or their relative's, medical treatment are high. In both cases three in four are satisfied, with one in three being very satisfied. People are slightly less

Table 4.2 *Levels of Satisfaction with Schooling, Medical Treatment and Working Conditions*

	Very satisfied %	Satisfied %	Neither %	Dissatisfied %	Very dissatisfied %	Don't know %	Total N
Schooling	32	46	8	9	3	2	893
Medicine	35	46	6	9	4	0	2572
Work	20	48	11	15	6	1	1636

Citizen Audit 2000 weighted face-to-face survey.
Questions:
(a) *'During the last 12 months to what extent have you been satisfied or dissatisfied with any of your children's education at school?'*
(b) *'During the last 12 months to what extent have you felt satisfied or dissatisfied with your medical treatment?'*
(c) *'During the last 12 months to what extent have you felt satisfied or dissatisfied with your working conditions?'*

satisfied about their working conditions; nevertheless two in every three recorded a positive view. So there are not such great differences in levels of satisfaction in these rather different areas of day-to-day life.

Nevertheless, table 4.2 confirms the fact that personal dissatisfaction with educational provision or with the working environment does act as a stimulus to micro political action. Among those satisfied with their children's education only one in six became involved in action to try and change the way education, was provided in these schools. By contrast, two in three among those dissatisfied had become involved in action. And as far as the working environment was concerned, three in every four among those dissatisfied with their working conditions acted to try and improve them. However, as far as medical care is concerned, it is clear that people who are dissatisfied with their medical treatment are less likely to do something about it. Only just over one in three among the dissatisfied take action while the remainder of the dissatisfied remain passive.

Clearly the opportunity structures that are available to people would seem to be an important explanation of micro political actions. Parents of school children are likely to be drawn into the day-to-day activities in schools. Beyond the organised parent evenings teachers will often encourage parents to become involved in informal ways in their children's education. The opportunity structures exist enabling parents to try and influence the way education is provided at their children's schools. As far as the working environment is concerned, there is a legal framework of rights and working conditions, and bargaining and negotiation over these

Table 4.3 *Levels of Satisfaction and Micro Political Action*

	Satisfied %	Neither satisfied nor dissatisfied %	Dissatisfied %
Education			
Yes	16	38	64
No	83	59	36
Don't know	1	3	0
Total	100	100	100
Medicine			
Yes	6	14	38
No	94	86	62
Don't know	0	0	0
Total	100	100	100
Work			
Yes	30	56	77
No	70	44	23
Don't know	0	0	0
Total	100	100	100

Citizen Audit 2000 weighted face-to-face survey.

rights and conditions is a normal feature of everyday life. In addition, often trade unions, works councils, and other institutions and procedures exist to articulate people's concerns in the working environment. Again opportunity structures exist for participation in this form of micro politics.

By contrast with schools and work, there are fewer opportunities for patient involvement in hospitals or doctors' surgeries. Furthermore, the nature of the service lends itself to a professionalism which excludes the amateur (in other words, the patient). Hospital consultants and doctors often encourage a degree of patient deference and a distance between the service provider and the service user which restricts the opportunities for engagement in discussions over medical treatment.

Whom do people approach in attempting to influence their children's education, their medical treatment, or their working conditions? We provided our respondents with a wide-ranging list of relevant personnel and figure 4.2 reports that, with regard to education, they overwhelmingly contacted the school professionals, in other words, the teachers at the school. Other parents with children at the same school were also approached. So, by contrast with macro political activity, where we saw in chapter 3 that people do not talk with their neighbours about political

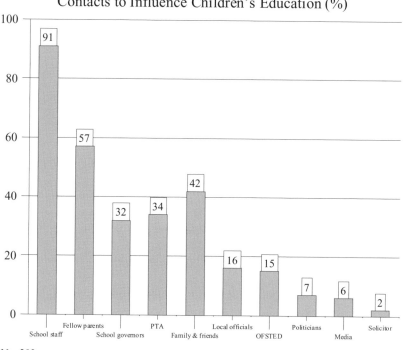

Contacts to Influence Children's Education (%)

N=c203

Question: 'Which of the following did you do to change the way education is provided at any of your children's schools?' (Note that multiple responses were possible.)

Figure 4.2 Contacts to Influence Children's Education

matters, clearly parents do discuss their children's education with fellow parents at the school gates and elsewhere. Apart from fellow parents, people also approached those involved either directly or indirectly in the management of the school, that is to say the school governors and the parent–teacher association. People also turned for help in influencing their children's schooling to their own family and friends. People were less likely to engage in what might be regarded as a more traditional form of contact, namely with officials from the local council or OFSTED, or politicians, solicitors or the media.

As with education so with medicine. We see in figure 4.3 that people overwhelmingly turned first to the service professionals, that is to say the medical staff, to try and influence their medical treatment. The other two groups they turned to were their own family and friends, or health

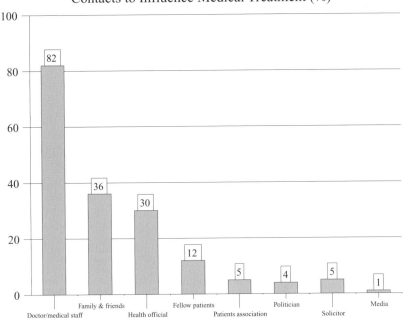

Contacts to Influence Medical Treatment (%)

N=c258

Question: '*Which of the following did you do to try and influence the way medical treatment was provided?*' (Note that multiple responses were possible.)

Figure 4.3 Contacts to Influence Medical Treatment

service officials. Whereas parents would approach fellow school parents for help over educational matters, by contrast our respondents were less likely to approach their fellow patients for assistance on medical matters. However, in general, people acted similarly on medical and on educational matters, in making few contacts with politicians, solicitors and the media.

As far as our respondents' attempts to influence their working conditions were concerned, people go directly to their employer. They also turn to work colleagues for help. Again, as with schools and medicine, people talk with family and friends about their problems. Finally, in this area of micro politics, one in five (18 per cent) of our respondents approached a trade union for help.

What we have seen so far, therefore, in our examination of these three forms of micro political activity is that there is a good deal going on. People

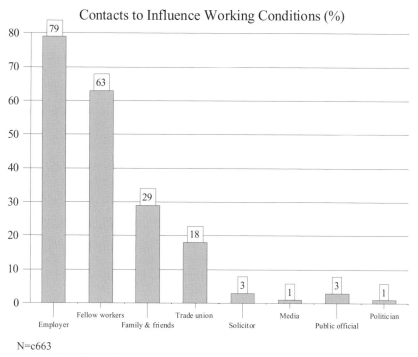

N=c663

Question: *'Which of the following did you do to try and improve your working conditions?'* (Note that multiple responses were possible.)

Figure 4.4 Contacts to Influence Working Conditions

are active in trying to improve the quality of their daily lives as far as the services they receive and their own working conditions are concerned. Their actions, however, are less likely to be channelled through the orthodox, and perhaps traditional, route of contacting a politician and more likely to involve contacting the professionals, in other words, the teachers, doctors or employers, fellow parents, patients or workers and, finally, others immediately around them, in other words, friends or family members. Micro political activities are more likely to be conducted through personal contact and individualised forms of action. The one exception to this is that some employees make contact with a collective organisation, namely a trade union, in order to resolve problems regarding their working conditions.

Asked to say whether they were successful or not in their approaches, one in two said that they were successful in changing the way education was provided at their children's school (59 per cent) and in influencing

Table 4.4 *Fair Treatment and Micro Political Action*

	Low (0–3) %	Medium (4–6) %	High (7–10) %	Mean %	Standard deviation %	Total N %
School	17	36	46	5.9	2.7	207
Medicine	24	31	46	5.6	2.8	254
Work	18	26	56	6.3	2.8	661

Citizen Audit 2000 weighted face-to-face survey.
Question: '*Do you think you were treated fairly in your attempt to change the way education is provided at any of your children's schools/to influence the medical treatment/to try and improve your working conditions?*'

the way medical treatment was provided (50 per cent), and almost two in three said that they were successful in improving their work conditions (62 per cent).[4] So in this micro form of politics a large number of people feel that their intervention was successful.

Furthermore, among those who tried to influence their children's schooling, their medical treatment, or their working conditions, the majority of our respondents felt that they were treated fairly in their attempts to improve things. Table 4.4 reports that, on an 11-point scale running from 0–10, where 0 meant 'not treated at all fairly', to 10, which meant 'treated very fairly', only between one in five and one in four ranked their attempts negatively. By contrast, almost one in two believed that they had been treated in a very positive manner.

In order to assess people's overall sense of political efficacy in these areas of micro politics, we asked our respondents a range of questions regarding their influence on education, health and work matters. We asked parents how much they felt able to influence the choice of school for their children, the teaching within the school, and the running of the school. Table 4.5 reveals that the majority of our respondents felt able to have some influence on the choice of school, but were unable to influence either the teaching or the running of the school. Nonetheless, on these two latter issues, one in three felt that they had influence on both the teaching and the running of the school.

On medical matters, we asked our respondents whether they had influenced the medical treatment of themselves or their family, whether they had obtained adequate medical information about the treatment, whether they had been able to choose their preferred doctor, whether they had

---

[4] A larger proportion of professional and managerial workers (69 per cent) than of manual workers (52 per cent) stated that they were successful in their attempt to improve their working conditions.

Table 4.5 *Parental Influence on Educational Matters*

	Not at all %	Some %	Great deal %	Don't know %
Choice of school	33	44	17	6
Teaching in school	58	31	4	8
Running of school	56	34	3	8

Citizen Audit 2000 weighted face-to-face survey. N = 893.
Question: *'More generally with regard to any of your children's schooling, do you think you are able to influence the choice of school, influence the teaching in the school, influence the running of the school?'*

Table 4.6 *Patients' Influence on Medical Matters*

	Yes %	No %	Don't know %
Prompt treatment	81	18	2
Influence medical treatment	19	78	4
Adequate information	77	20	2
Choose doctor	50	48	2
Second opinion	12	86	2
Private sector	7	91	2
Refuse treatment	3	96	2

Citizen Audit 2000 weighted face-to-face survey. N = 2572.
Question: *'With regard to the medical treatment that you or your relative received during the last 12 months, did you: influence the medical treatment; obtain adequate medical information about your treatment; choose the doctor you wanted; obtain a second opinion?'*

obtained a second opinion, and whether they had refused treatment. We see in table 4.6 that three in every four (78 per cent) felt that they had no influence on medical treatment, but one in two (50 per cent) had chosen the doctor that they wanted; three in four (77 per cent) felt that they had obtained adequate medical information about their treatment. Just over one in ten (12 per cent) had obtained a second opinion. Finally, an often-made claim is that when patients pay for their medical treatment they will obtain more choice and influence; however, fewer than one in ten (7 per cent) of our respondents changed from the public to the private sector in response to the treatment they had received.

We asked people in paid employment whether they felt able to influence their working time, the organisation of their work, or their working conditions. We see in table 4.7 that a majority felt that they had 'some' or

Table 4.7 *Influence in the Work Environment*

	Not at all %	Some %	Great deal %	Don't know %
Work time	43	28	28	1
Work organisation	27	29	42	1
Work conditions	33	35	31	2

Citizen Audit 2000 weighted face-to-face survey. N = 1,636.
Question: *'With regards to your work, can you: influence the time when your work will begin or end for the day; influence how your own daily work will be organised; influence your working conditions (e.g. rest periods, safety conditions)?'*

a 'great deal' of influence on all three of these issues. People felt they had most influence on their work organisation and least influence on their work time. Whether this prevailing sense of influence on working matters is common among all in work, or varies according to the nature of the work, is an important question. The degree of control people have over their working lives has traditionally been an important factor in distinguishing manual from white-collar workers. Among our respondents we find significant differences in their perception of their workplace influence. On all three issues of work time, work organisation, and work conditions there are twice as many manual workers than professionals and managers stating that they have no influence. Almost two-thirds of manual workers state that they have no influence over their work time, and almost one-half state that they have no influence over work organisation and work conditions.

We have already noted that parents of school children often talk to their fellow parents when attempting to have an impact upon their children's education, but patients are less likely to talk to their fellow patients in any endeavours to influence medical treatment. The working environment offers opportunities for interchange of ideas and opinions between colleagues and therefore we asked our respondents whether they had attended meetings as part of their job, and if so whether they had spoken, or participated in decision-making, whether they had planned or chaired them, and whether they had written a report of them. Furthermore, we asked them how much they contacted their fellow workers to talk about work problems, to ask for practical help or assistance, to express disagreement about work issues or, finally, to meet with them socially.

Table 4.8 shows that around one in two had 'often' or 'sometimes' attended, spoken, or participated in decision-making meetings with their

Table 4.8 *Interchange in the Workplace*

	Often %	Sometimes %	Rarely %	Never %	Don't know %
Meetings					
Attend meeting	38	21	12	27	2
Participate in decision-making	31	22	11	35	2
Speak at meeting	32	21	10	35	2
Plan/chair meeting	14	10	10	64	2
Write report on meeting	15	13	9	61	2
Inter-personal links					
Talk about work problems	59	25	6	8	1
Call for practical help/assistance	45	34	9	11	1
Express disagreement about work issues	36	35	15	13	1
Meet socially	25	36	21	17	1

Citizen Audit 2000 weighted face-to-face survey. N = 1,636.
Questions: *'Here are a few things that people sometimes do as part of their job. As part of your work how often do you: attend a meeting; participate in decision-making at a meeting; speak at a meeting; plan or chair a meeting; write a report on a meeting?' 'Some people have a lot of contact with their fellow workers or colleagues, and others have only limited contact. How about you? How often do you: talk with your fellow workers about problems at work; call upon fellow workers to give practical help or assistance; express disagreement about work issues with fellow workers; meet fellow workers socially?'*

colleagues. And three in four had 'often' or 'sometimes' talked about work problems or disagreed about work issues with, and called for help from, work colleagues. Finally, almost two in three had 'often' or 'sometimes' met with their work colleagues socially. So work provides a collective environment in which people network formally and informally, organisationally and socially. In chapter 3 we pointed out that talking about political matters with other people is not common; even among fellow workers only one in four said that they did so. However, taking politics in this broader sense that we have been using in this chapter, we see that workers do have conversations about issues and problems arising in the workplace. Within a specific social context, in this case the workplace, information will be shared and opinions voiced, which are of major significance to civic attitudes and engagement in general (Huckfeldt and Sprague, 1995).

When we examined in the previous chapter the characteristics of the people who engaged in macro political actions we concluded that the

Table 4.9 *Variations in Micro Political Actions*

Took action in past year	Education %	Medical %	Work %
All	**24**	**11**	**43**
Age			
24 and under	12	7	42
25–44	22	13	46
45–64	31	12	39
65 and over	0	7	10
	V = .094: p = .014	V = .076; p = .002	V = .093; p = .003
Gender			
Male	25	10	50
Female	23	11	36
	V = .091; p = .027	V = .015; p = .460	V = .136; p = .000
Class			
Professional and managerial	35	16	56
Intermediate	19	9	34
Manual	17	7	34
	V = .159; p = .000	V = .135; p = .000	V = .256; p = .000
Religiosity			
Religious	24	10	41
Non-religious	24	11	45
	V = .025; p = .764	V = .008; p = .676	V = .041; p = .103
Household income			
Under £10,000	19	8	29
£10,000 up to £19,999	21	10	39
£20,000 up to £29,999	26	14	45
£30,000 up to £39,999	36	14	50
£40,000 up to £49,999	28	13	56
£50,000 and above	26	18	56
	V = .114; p = .163	V = .101; p = .003	V = .159; p = .000
Education			
15 years and under	28	8	31
16–18	19	10	43
19 years and over	39	15	54
	V = .148; p = .000	V = .093; p = .000	V = .179; p = .000
Ethnicity			
White/European	23	10	43
Black/Asian/Afro-Caribbean/Other	32	17	42
	V = .056; p = .699	V = .051; p = .158	V = .046; p = .517
Location			
Greater London	25	17	45
South West	26	10	52
East/West Midlands	23	7	37
North West/North/Yorkshire	27	9	43
South East/East Anglia	25	12	48
Scotland	11	9	34
Wales	23	7	33
	V = .104; p = .517	V = .098; p = .007	V = .137; p = .001

Citizen Audit 2000 weighted face-to-face survey. Demographic characteristics as in table 2.13.

well-educated, the relatively prosperous, and the professionally and man-
agerially employed were more likely to participate. Is there a similar profile
when we consider micro political action? Table 4.9 reveals that as far as
schooling is concerned, the highly educated, professionals and managers,
and those with a household income in the £30,000 range are most likely
to be pressurising the teachers and others about their children's education. But black people are more likely than their white counterparts to
be engaged in this form of micro politics. Intriguingly, the Scots are less
likely to engage in school politics than their English and Welsh compa-
triots. Is schooling so much better in Scotland that parents are rarely
prompted into action, or are the Scots far more deferential towards the
teaching professionals? We note that the Scots are not so prominent as
the English and Welsh in articulating concerns about medical treatment
and working conditions either, which suggests either a deference towards
those in authority or a distinct weakness in the opportunity structures
north of the border.

Again, as with schools, it is the professionals and managers, and the
most highly educated, who are involved in attempts to influence their
medical treatment. The middle-aged and the richest households are also
more prominent in making demands of this service. Noticeably black
people are again more prominent than white people in demanding better
services. For some time now governments have attempted to distribute
the money for medical services equally across England. This task must
be made difficult, however, by the fact that more demands on medical
treatment come from London and the south-east than from the Midlands
and the north of England.

Gender appears to be of no significant importance as far as schooling and medicine are concerned, in the sense that men and women
are equally likely to be involved in attempting to improve the provision
of these services. However, gender does assume greater significance at
work. Men are more likely than women to be involved, as are professionals and managers, and also the most highly educated in attempting to
influence their working conditions. In addition, what is most striking is
the linear relationship between household income and voice in this area
of micro politics. The richer people are, the more likely they are to be
engaged.

The answer to our question about the social profiles of macro and
micro political activists, therefore, is that the two are very similar, with
one notable exception. When it comes to the provision of educational
and health services, black people are far more prominent than their white
counterparts. Furthermore, while black people's voice is relatively weak
in macro politics, in micro politics it is relatively strong.

Conclusions

We have already made the point in chapter 3 that people's political behaviour is broad and diverse. People are engaged in politics in ways which many commentators might not recognise because these activities go beyond the more orthodox and traditional. In this chapter we have extended our concept of politics to examine people's behaviour on issues in which agents of the state affect their daily lives because we believe that for very many of them this is real politics. People respond to the decisions taken on a continuing basis by a wide range of professionals and institutions in their locality which determine important aspects of their life. In responding to these decisions, they deal primarily with the professionals, in other words, the teacher, the doctor or the employer. At this level they feel that they have an impact upon the outcomes, they are generally satisfied with the way they are treated and with the outcome of their actions. However, as with macro political engagement so also with the micro variant, it is the well-heeled who are more prominent. Any notion that at the point of service delivery the down-at-heel might be more involved is not the case. Furthermore, any notion that service delivery might prompt more extensive civic engagement is only partially true. Only one in four of those who abstain from any form of macro engagement become involved in micro politics.

We now turn in part II of this book to consider how we might explain citizen attitudes and behaviour.

Part II

Modelling Citizenship

5   Alternative Theories of Citizenship

In earlier chapters we have examined the attitudinal and behavioural foundations of citizenship in Britain. As we have seen, there is a lot of voluntary activity, both formal and informal, which underpins citizenship and a broad set of attitudes and values which support the democratic system. In common usage, the term 'citizenship' is a very broad concept and it encompasses questions of identity, ethnicity, gender, participation, attitudes and values as well as perceptions of rights and obligations. Unfortunately, such a broad concept is not very useful for purposes of empirical analysis, since it encompasses too many issues. In chapter 1 we suggested that citizenship is at root a set of norms, values and practices which evolve so that individuals can solve collective action problems. Accordingly, we focus on just two key dimensions which are linked to this idea, one being attitudinal and the other behavioural. The attitudinal dimension relates to the balance between the individual's sense of their rights and their obligations to the wider society. The behavioural dimension relates to whether or not they participate in a way which supports civil society and democratic politics.

The key task of this chapter is to provide alternative theoretical accounts of the determinants of citizenship in the sense defined earlier. We shall consider different theoretical explanations of why people vary both in their civic attitudes and in their behaviour. The starting point of the analysis, however, is to clarify how the concept of citizenship should be measured. This is a preliminary exercise to that of examining the factors which influence it. Modelling variations in citizenship among our survey respondents means explaining why some people score highly on the citizenship scales discussed below, whereas others score poorly on them. The former might be described as 'good' citizens and the latter 'bad' citizens.

In this sense a 'good' citizen would be someone who is aware of their rights, but also of their obligations to other people and the wider society. In addition, good citizens participate in voluntary activities of various kinds as well as in politics more generally, although they may not necessarily be high-intensity participants (Whiteley and Seyd, 2002). By implication a 'bad' citizen is an individual who demands their rights, but is reluctant to acknowledge their obligations to the rest of society. Moreover, they are unlikely to participate either in voluntary activity or in politics more generally.

To organise ideas, we structure the discussion around two overarching meta-theories, each of which encompasses alternative models of citizenship. Within these meta-theories there are a total of five models of citizenship to be examined, and the task of the present chapter is to set out the theoretical ideas behind each of these models. In a subsequent chapter we will examine evidence which explores which of the models provides the best empirical account of citizenship in the survey. But we begin with the task of measuring citizenship.

Measuring citizenship

We have suggested that the attitudinal dimension of citizenship involves the recognition by individuals that they have both rights and obligations to each other, and also to the state if democracy is to work properly. We shall translate this idea into practice by developing measurement scales of both rights and obligations, which are designed to capture the values underpinning citizenship. Secondly, the behavioural dimension of citizenship will be measured using indicators of participation and voluntary activity which have been examined already in previous chapters.

If there is an imbalance between the individual's perceptions of their rights and of their obligations, then society and the state will face great difficulties in delivering the benefits and services which individuals expect. This is because to a large extent one person's rights are another's obligations; a social benefit for one person is a tax for another. As we suggested in chapter 1, a purely rights-based definition of citizenship ignores this important point. So the starting point of the measurement of citizenship is to examine the balance between perceptions of rights and obligations among the respondents in the survey.

It will be recalled that we examined indicators of attitudes to rights in table 2.12. The measures were classified into three groups: private rights relating to issues like paternity leave, gay rights and abortion; state-provided rights relating to housing, jobs and income inequalities; and finally, individualistic rights, relating to private health care and retirement costs. Some of these indicators relate to the individual's private freedom of action, and others to their expectations concerning the role of government in supporting rights. As table 2.12 showed, many of the rights included are controversial, and this was the reason for including them. Since there is near unanimity about the desirability of basic human rights like freedom of speech and the independence of the judiciary from political interference, there is little point in trying to measure variations in public attitudes to such widely accepted rights. It is at the margins of rights discourse where we find debates and disagreements. Despite this point, there was a good deal of support in table 2.12 for the right to paternity leave and also the right to die, with a majority of respondents supporting both rights. On the other hand, gay rights are more controversial, with quite a lot of opposition to the recognition of gay marriages.

Looking at state-provided rights in table 2.12, there is strong support for government action in relation to the right to work, the right to housing, and support for greater income equality and a reduction in poverty. Responses to these indicators show that citizens have a strong preference in favour of the state intervening to guarantee such rights. At the same time there is an awareness that individuals may not be able to rely exclusively on the state for their retirement income, and there is also support for the idea that wealthy people should pay for their own health care. Thus support for state action to provide for the basic needs is apparent in the survey, but there is also a willingness amongst respondents to consider private alternatives as well.

If the demand for rights is fairly strong, the sense of citizen obligations is also quite strong, as can be seen in tables 2.10 and 2.11. In table 2.10 there is very strong support for the idea that citizens should pay their taxes, obey the law and not claim benefits when they are not entitled to them. There is also considerable support for the idea that individuals should be willing to participate in voluntary activity. Moreover, nearly two-thirds of people think that they are very likely to vote at the next general election. So there is considerable evidence of a strong social norm operating which suggests that participation is desirable. This is further reinforced by the evidence on attitudes to specific types of voluntary activities in figure 2.8. Almost three-quarters of citizens are willing to serve on a jury, and seven out of ten are willing to give blood or to participate in a Neighbourhood Watch scheme. The recognition of obligations only declines somewhat when individuals are considering high-cost activities like assisting in a meals-on-wheels service and helping volunteers to renovate a local park.

There are many indicators of rights and obligations in chapter 2 and so before we can use them in a modelling exercise it is important to examine the extent to which these attitudes are structured in the minds of respondents. Clearly if individuals saw no particular links between different rights, for example, favouring some and opposing others more or less at random, then little underlying structure to attitudes would exist. On the other hand, if relationships existed between perceptions of

Table 5.1 *The Structure of Attitudes to Rights*

	State-provided rights	Private rights	Individualistic rights
Government find job	0.65		
Government reduce income differences	0.73		
Government provide housing	0.65		
Spend money on poverty	0.59		
Paternity leave		0.54	
Gay relationships		0.82	
Right to die		0.65	
Not rely on state for retirement			0.65
Individuals meet cost of health care			0.67
Encourage private medicine			0.62
—	—	—	—
Eigen values	1.96	1.44	1.28
Variance explained	20	14	13

Weighted 2000 face-to-face survey.
Note: This table shows the strength of the correlations between the responses to the questions in the survey and three underlying latent measures of rights (varimax rotated factor matrix).

different rights, with citizens favouring one also supporting others, this would imply that rights were grouped together. In this case, attitude structures would exist which underlie these perceptions. The principal components analysis in table 5.1 confirms that there are three separate dimensions to the rights indicators in table 2.12.[1] The first dimension relates to state-provided rights such as employment, housing and income equality. Thus individuals who support employment rights, for example, tend also to support housing rights. These are described as 'state-provided rights'. The second, independent dimension relates to private rights such as paternity leave and the right to die. These are rights which involve tolerance of others rather than subsidies from the state, although state action may be involved to enforce them. For that reason they are described as 'private rights'. The third dimension are rights which value individualistic action unfettered by the state and which support the idea

[1] Not all of the indicators in table 2.12 appear in table 5.1. The principal components analysis revealed that there was a dominant three-factor solution and some of the indicators were unrelated to this and so were excluded.

Table 5.2 *The Structure of Attitudes to Obligations*

	Voluntary action	Obedience to the law	Civic service
Help renovate a local park	0.72		
Help with meals on wheels	0.74		
Help with Neighbourhood Watch	0.58		
Work for voluntary organisation	0.50		
Never evade taxes		0.79	
Always obey the law		0.79	
Claim benefits without entitlement		−0.58	
Serve on a jury			0.68
Give blood			0.50
Vote in the next election			0.68
—	—	—	—
Eigen values	1.9	1.9	1.3
Variance explained	19	19	13

Weighted 2000 face-to-face survey.
Note: This table shows the strength of the correlations between the responses to the questions in the survey and three underlying latent measures of obligations (varimax rotated factor matrix).

that individuals should provide for themselves. It is clear that citizens who feel that the state should not provide for their retirement are also quite likely to favour private medicine, so this dimension is described as an 'individualistic rights' dimension.

Table 5.2 examines the structure of attitudes to obligations indicators examined in chapter 2, and much like perceptions of rights this involves three dimensions.[2] Firstly, there is a voluntary action dimension in which individuals who support participation in a Neighbourhood Watch scheme are also quite likely to support working for a voluntary organisation or helping with the renovation of a local park. These are relatively high-cost types of activities from the point of view of the average citizen. The second dimension relates to obedience to the law, so that individuals who oppose tax evasion also have strong views which oppose individuals claiming benefits to which they are not entitled. Clearly, this is a lower-cost set of activities than is measured by the voluntary action dimension. Finally, the

---

[2] Again, we have extracted the dominant three principal components in an analysis of the measures of obligations in chapter 2.

Table 5.3 *The Structure of Political Participation*

	Individual	Contact	Collective
Bought goods for political or ethical reasons	0.70		
Boycotted certain products	0.69		
Given money to an organisation	0.64		
Raised money for an organisation	0.48		
Signed a petition	0.61		
Worn or displayed a campaign badge	0.51		
Voted in a local government election	0.45		
Contacted a public official		0.68	
Contacted a politician		0.61	
Contacted an organisation		0.59	
Contacted the media		0.54	
Contacted a solicitor or judicial body		0.52	
Taken part in a public demonstration			0.74
Attended a political rally or meeting			0.66
Participated in an illegal protest			0.62
Formed a group of like-minded people			0.39
—	—	—	—
Percentage of variance explained	22	9	8

Weighted 2000 face-to-face survey.
Note: This table shows the strength of the correlations between the responses to the questions in the survey and three underlying latent measures of participation (varimax rotated factor matrix).

third dimension relates to civic service, or the belief that citizens should be willing to serve on a jury, donate blood and to participate in a general election. These are also slightly higher-cost activities than obedience to the law.

Citizenship can be seen in terms of norms and values, but as the discussion in chapter 3 indicates it is also a matter of civic behaviour, that is, a willingness to participate in politics and public affairs in a way which supports democracy. We observed in table 3.1 that there were wide variations in the willingness of individuals to undertake different types of activities. Roughly two-thirds of respondents had given money to an organisation in the previous twelve months and about half had signed a petition. On the other hand, few had formed a group of like-minded people or had taken part in a demonstration.

The dimensions of participation in Britain are set out in table 5.3 based on a principal components analysis of the indicators in chapter 3, and it can be seen that these are fairly clear-cut. There is an individualistic dimension which consists of forms of participation which can be undertaken without the cooperation of other people. Thus citizens can vote or they can boycott goods for political reasons or donate money to an organisation on their own initiative without the help of others. This is the dominant factor in table 5.3, which indicates how important individualistic participation is in Britain today.

The second factor is a contact dimension of participation, which is also an individualistic type of participation from the perspective of the respondent. However, it also involves the participation of elected representatives or public officials. Very often when individuals undertake these types of activities they are pursuing private goals of various kinds; they may go to see their MP in order to seek welfare benefits, or write to the press about a planning decision which affects them. However, it is also the case that people contact officials and the media about national issues which they care about, so this is not all private in character. Thus the contact dimension can be individualistic or collectivist in character.

The third factor is clearly a collective action dimension of participation. In this case citizens must join together with others in formal or informal organisations in order to participate. The evidence shows that individuals who have taken part in demonstrations are also quite likely to have attended a political meeting and some of them will have taken part in an illegal protest, since all of these items are significantly correlated with this factor. This dimension explains the least variance of all the factors, but it is clearly an important part of the structure of participation in Britain.

In chapter 3 we examined participation potential as well as actual participation, and the structure of this is set out in table 5.4. It can be seen that the participation potential scales are very similar to the actual participation scales. Thus there is no great difference between the underlying dimensions of what people might do and what they actually do in the way of political participation. Again there are individualistic, contact and collective dimensions to participation potential.

In chapter 4 we examined micro level participation and this is clearly another aspect of participation which needs to be considered in any model. Table 5.5 cumulates participation activities in relation to education, health and the workplace into an overall participation scale. The scale measures the extent to which individuals tried to change their service provision in health and education, or their working conditions during the previous year. In the year 2000 some 73 per cent of citizens did not participate at all in the sense of trying to influence service delivery in health or education, or in relation to their workplace conditions. On the other hand, some 22 per cent of respondents did participate in at least one of these activities, and 5 per cent participated in two or more. So

Table 5.4 *The Structure of Potential Political Participation*

	Individual	Contact	Collective
Donate money to an organisation	0.78		
Sign a petition	0.70		
Raise funds for an organisation	0.62		
Boycott certain products	0.66		
Vote in a local government election	0.63		
Buy certain products	0.61		
Wear or display a campaign badge or sticker	0.49		
Contact a public official		0.73	
Contact a politician (for example, a member of parliament or local councillor)		0.75	
Contact an organisation		0.72	
Contact a solicitor or judicial body		0.68	
Contact the media		0.66	
Participate in an illegal protest			0.76
Take part in a public demonstration			0.69
Attend a political meeting or rally			0.69
Form a group of like-minded people			0.68
Variance explained	42.3	9.0	6.6

Weighted 2000 face-to-face survey.
Question: *'Would you do any of the following to influence rules, laws or policies?'*
Note: This table shows the strength of the correlations between the responses to the questions in the survey and three underlying latent measures of participation potential (varimax rotated factor matrix).

Table 5.5 *The Small-Scale Democracy Participation Scale*

Attempts to influence education, health or work conditions	%
None	73
One	22
Two	4
Three	1

Weighted 2000 face-to-face survey.

although small-scale participation was a minority activity, it nonetheless involved large numbers of people.

Given that we have defined the macro and micro political participation scales, this raises the question as to whether there is a relationship between them. One possibility is that macro participation complements micro participation – individuals who get involved in one are also likely to get involved in the other. Another possibility is that macro participation is a substitute for micro participation – individuals who engage in macro politics are less likely to engage in micro politics or vice versa. The third possibility is that these forms of participation are simply unrelated to each other. We can investigate these possibilities by examining the correlations between these scales.

The correlation between the micro participation scale and the individual participation scale defined in table 5.3 was 0.25, indicating that a modest positive relationship existed between the two variables. Thus there is a weak tendency for those who undertake individualistic macro political actions to also undertake micro political actions, making the relationship complementary rather than one of substitution. This is not really surprising since the two forms of participation are individualistic in character. It is, however, important to recall that this relationship does not apply to the whole sample, since only those eligible to take micro actions, in other words, those with children of school age, those who had sought or obtained medical treatment, and those in paid employment are included in our analysis. The correlation between micro participation and contact participation scales was rather weaker at 0.15, and the correlation between micro participation and collective action scales was weakest of all at 0.06. Overall then, it appears that these types of participation are complements to each other, or in the case of collective action close to being unrelated.

Up to this point we have been examining measures of citizenship in Britain, which constitute the dependent variables in subsequent models. As we have seen, there are both attitudinal and behavioural dimensions of citizenship. The next step is to examine alternative theoretical accounts of citizenship which can be used to explain variations in these measures.

Theories of citizenship

The discussion in chapter 1 pointed out that citizenship has been analysed according to three alternative models: the liberal, the republican and the communitarian models. Each of these provides a framework for understanding the concept of citizenship. But there is a more general metatheoretical perspective which can be applied to the analysis of citizenship which underlies these models and which pervades social theory. This is the distinction between choice-based and structural-based approaches to social analysis. Choice-based theories are exemplified in their purest form by economics, and in this perspective actors are seen as operating in a world of constrained optimisation. In this world individuals seek to maximise their utility by obtaining the highest return at the minimum cost from any course of action which they undertake. Such utilitarian theories are rooted in liberal conceptions of society. Applied to the task of understanding citizenship, this type of theory sees citizenship emerging from the choices which agents make, and these reflect the costs and benefits of the choice situation. Thus individuals choose their levels of participation as well as their attitudes to the rights and obligations imposed by society.

An alternative perspective sees citizenship as a matter of individuals being socialised into the norms, values and behaviours of the social groups to which they belong and into those of the wider society. In this perspective, the individual citizen is seen as being the product of social forces and structures which mould and shape their behaviour and attitudes. Individual choice has only a limited influence on this system of ideas since the key determinants of attitudes and behaviour are thought to be found at the societal level. It is apparent that communitarian theories with their emphasis on the group and also republican theories with their emphasis on the nation-state are heavily influenced by this tradition of social analysis.

These broad distinctions are useful, but for the purpose of understanding citizenship they need to be refined into a more specific form which can be measured and subsequently tested. In the case of choice theoretic accounts of citizenship we consider two alternative models: the cognitive engagement and general incentives models. In the case of structural theories we examine three alternatives: the civic voluntarism, equity–fairness and social capital models. Each of these was developed in order to explain different forms of political participation, but they can be readily adapted to the task of explaining the determinants of the attitudes and behaviours which constitute citizenship. We begin this account by spelling out the theoretical ideas behind each of the models in more detail.

Choice theories of citizenship

Cognitive engagement theory

The first of the choice theories is the cognitive engagement model. The core idea of cognitive engagement theory is that participation depends on the individual's access to information and on their ability and willingness to use that information to make informed choices. Two developments in society help to explain the growth of interest in cognitive engagement theories of participation (Dalton, 2002). One is the growth of education, particularly higher education, which has been very significant in Britain. Participation in higher education increased from about 800,000 students in 1980/81 to more than 1,600,000 in 1996/97 (see *Times Higher Education Supplement*, 26 September 1997). In addition, the Labour government has committed itself to the goal of ensuring that 50 per cent of the young participate in higher education in the future. Education is important to this type of theory because it helps people to acquire, and more importantly to process, large amounts of information. It provides skills, for example, in the area of information technology, while at the same time increasing the individual's ability to analyse information by placing it into a meaningful context – to make sense of information.

Another important development is the declining cost of acquiring information due to its increased availability in print, electronic and web-based forms. Thus a growth of education on the one hand, and decline in the costs of acquiring and processing information on the other, produces a process of cognitive mobilisation (Barnes and Kaase, 1979). Media consumption is a key factor in this process, since the cognitively engaged are likely to follow politics and public affairs in the media. Similarly, political knowledge is also important since the engaged are quite likely to be knowledgeable about how the system works.

Viewed from the perspective of the history of citizenship, cognitively engaged individuals are close to the classical Greek conceptions of the good citizen. As we saw in chapter 1, the classical citizen is an informed member of the *polis* who fully participates in politics and understands the issues and complexities of government. Cognitive mobilisation produces individuals who have an interest in politics and civic affairs, are politically knowledgeable and have a clear understanding of the norms and principles of democracy. In addition, the cognitively engaged citizen is likely to be influenced by the performance of the state in delivering the benefits of citizenship. This means that cognitively engaged citizens are critical citizens (Norris et al., 1999). By implication, a perception that the state may be failing to deliver in terms of services is likely to mobilise them to participate in unorthodox ways, for example, by protesting. It may also reduce their willingness to acknowledge the obligations of citizenship, if they feel that they are not receiving benefits. This is why cognitive engagement theory is at root a choice-based theory of citizenship, since the performance of the system is a key factor in explaining why some people are good citizens when others are not.

The core concepts or key variables in the cognitive engagement model are education, media consumption, interest in politics, political knowledge and policy satisfaction/dissatisfaction. Education is typically measured in terms of whether individuals have more than the minimum levels of education, in particular whether they have higher education. Media consumption refers to their use of the media to acquire information about politics and public affairs. Political interest is defined in terms of their motivation to follow the activities of government and to understand policy-making. Political knowledge is about their understanding of the way the system works and about policy information which is relevant to making a decision to participate. Finally, policy satisfaction relates to attitudes to the performance of the system in delivering the benefits of citizenship.

The cognitive engagement model has been used to provide an account of certain types of participation, notably voting (Dalton and Wattenberg, 2000; Clarke et al., 2004), but it needs to be generalised to a wider conception of citizenship. One implication might be that uneducated individuals who lack an interest in politics and who do not follow the media are 'poor' citizens. Another might be that the disengaged are likely to want rights while failing to acknowledge their obligations. A third is that the engaged are likely to participate in voluntary activity whilst the disengaged are likely to be apathetic. We will investigate these possibilities further, but for the moment the theory implies that the good citizen is educated, interested in politics and media-conscious. Of course it may not be necessary to have these characteristics in order for an individual to participate in informal voluntary activity such as helping out friends and neighbours. But wider participation and the civic values which go with it should involve such characteristics.

All theories can be criticised and the cognitive engagement theory is no exception. One criticism of the theory is that while it is clearly choice-based and involves information processing, it is not clear why individuals should be willing to act on this information once they have acquired it. Citizens may be able to process and understand information about politics and society, but in the absence of incentives to act on this information it is not clear why this should encourage them to participate. It is easy to imagine an individual who is educated, interested in politics, follows current affairs in the media and is knowledgeable about how the system works, but who does not participate in voluntary activity. Thus acquiring and processing information seems an incomplete mechanism for explaining participation in the absence of a theory of incentives to use that information. Having made that point, however, cognitive engagement theory may capture an important dimension of citizenship.

The general incentives theory

The general incentives model of participation was introduced specifically to explain the incidence of high-intensity types of participation involving party activists (see Seyd and Whiteley, 1992, 2002a; Whiteley, Seyd and

Richardson, 1994; Whiteley and Seyd, 2002). The theory is a synthesis of rational choice and social psychological accounts of participation, and the core idea behind it is that actors need incentives if they are to participate and have positive civic values. The emphasis on incentives for action means that the theory has many similarities with rational choice accounts of political action. However, it postulates that actors take into account a wider array of incentives when they are considering participation rather than the narrowly defined individual incentives which appear in standard rational choice models. The incentives to participate in the theory are classified into five types: *collective, selective, group, social* and *expressive*. In addition, perceptions of the costs of participation have to be taken into account when citizens are deciding whether or not to get involved.

To consider each of these in turn, collective incentives refer to the benefits of citizenship which accrue to all individuals whether they participate or not. These benefits are referred to by economists as public goods (Samuelson, 1954; Olson, 1965). The theoretical concept of public goods was discussed briefly in chapter 1, and it refers to goods having the characteristics of jointness of supply and impossibility of exclusion. Basic security, that is, freedom from invasion and freedom from crime, are goods of this type, and these are provided by the state. They are available to all citizens and their use cannot be limited to only specific individuals or groups. In the absence of compulsory taxation these goods would be inadequately provided, because individuals have an incentive to free-ride on the efforts of others and not to contribute to their provision. The state also provides many other goods such as health care, welfare, education and infrastructure, many of which are not public goods in the formal sense of the definition, since free-riding can be avoided by selling them in private markets. But the state nonetheless supplies such goods where there is a strong argument that their provision would be inadequate in the absence of state intervention.

Applied to the task of explaining citizenship, collective incentives refer to the policy outputs of government, particularly in relation to individual security and economic performance, which are the most salient issues for voters (see Clarke et al., 2004). If individuals think that policy delivery is effective then that should motivate them to participate. If, on the other hand, they think that policy delivery is failing and that government has a problem delivering on its promises, this should act as a disincentive to participate. This perception might also produce a gap between the individual's sense of rights and obligations.

In the general incentives model the individual's sense of personal efficacy, or their perception that they can make a difference to outcomes, plays an important role. The reasoning behind this is simple: if individuals think that the system works well, but at the same time they believe that their own participation has little or no influence on outcomes, then they have no incentive to get involved. But if they feel that the system can deliver and that they can make a difference to outcomes, then it will be rational for them to participate to try to improve its performance. The model can be specified in terms of an interaction between benefits and efficacy, or it can be specified in terms of benefits and efficacy acting as separate determinants of participation and civic values.

Selective incentives refer to the benefits which individuals receive from the exercise of participating itself, so that non-participants do not receive these benefits. In this sense they are the private returns from being a good citizen, and they may be important for understanding why some people are active citizens when others are not. Selective incentives are of two types: process and outcome incentives.[3] Process incentives refer to motives for participating which derive from the process of participation itself. Different writers have referred to a number of different motives which might be counted under this heading. Tullock (1971) has written of the 'entertainment' value of being involved in revolution; Opp (1990) writes about the 'catharsis' value of involvement in political protest. For some people, the political process is interesting and stimulating in itself, regardless of the outcomes or goals. Participation is a way of meeting like-minded and interesting people, and for some this is motive enough for getting involved.

Outcome incentives refer to motives concerned with achieving certain goals in the political process, but goals which are private rather than collective. An active citizen might harbour ambitions to become a local councillor, for example, or the local mayor, or even to be elected to the House of Commons. Others may want to become a school governor, or a local magistrate. Yet others might be interested in voluntary activity for its own sake because they enjoy such activities, or because they are retired and want to occupy their time. These incentives for involvement will ensure that some people participate and are good citizens for private reasons.

Group incentives refer to the individual's perception that group benefits are a good reason to participate and to support civic values. When people

[3] When the model is applied to the task of explaining party activism, ideology is also included as a selective incentive. Thus left-wing beliefs will motivate Labour Party members to be active in Labour Party politics (Seyd and Whiteley, 2002a). This type of incentive is not appropriate for a wider conception of citizenship participation, however, since individuals do not have to be left-wing or right-wing to participate in voluntary activity.

consider collective action to solve social problems, they may often think about the welfare of the group rather than their own personal welfare. So there is a type of group consciousness at work with individuals still calculating the costs and benefits of collective action, but at the level of the group rather than at the level of the individual. If this idea is applied to the question of explaining what motivates individuals to be good citizens, then it implies that one reason why some people participate is because they believe that it is important to get benefits for groups that they care about.

Another motive for involvement in the general incentives model derives from social norms, or people's perceptions that the attitudes and beliefs of people close to them support participation and civic values. If individuals perceive themselves to be surrounded by people who think that rights are important but who ignore their obligations, or who think that someone else should look after the interests of the wider society other than themselves, this is likely to inhibit their own participation. Since individuals are embedded in networks of relationships with others, then social norms which recognise the views of other people should have an important influence on their own behaviour.

Finally, within the general incentives model there are motives for engagement based on emotional or affective attachments to society. These motives lie outside the standard cost–benefit model of decision-making, with its emphasis on cognitive calculations, and are rooted very much in the social-psychological research tradition. Such motives have long been discussed in the literature on party identification, since the early theorists saw partisanship as an affective orientation towards a significant social or political group in the individual's environment (Campbell et al., 1960). Similarly, Frank (1988) has developed what he terms a *commitment* model in which actors' emotional predispositions override their short-run calculations of self-interest and allow them to cooperate with each other. This means that some people will be motivated to become good citizens by an affective attachment to their country, in other words a sense of pride in being British. This has little to do with the benefits they might receive from being an active citizen, either at the individual or collective levels. Rather, such motives for involvement are grounded in a sense of loyalty and affection for their country.

Clearly the general incentives model does not have the problems of the cognitive engagement model in ignoring the incentives for action. But it can be criticised for over-emphasising the importance of choice behaviour. Arguably, socialisation processes play a very important role in explaining why some people are good citizens and others are not. There is evidence to suggest that people get involved in voluntary activity because their parents were involved in such activity (Barnes and Kaase, 1979: 449–522). We know that partisanship is often inherited from parents and the same may be true of patriotism. It seems plausible that individuals who are strongly embedded in their communities with friends and relatives living locally are more likely to be good citizens than individuals with few such ties. Thus the emphasis on individual choice and incentives in the theory may neglect structural determinants of citizenship emanating from the wider society rather than from individual choices. We examine these in the context of structural theories next.

Structural theories of citizenship

To reiterate the earlier point, structural theories of citizenship differ from choice-based theories in that they suggest that citizenship is the product of macro level social forces rather than being the product of choices by individuals.

The civic voluntarism model

The most well-known and widely applied model of political participation in political science, the civic voluntarism model has its origins in the work of Sidney Verba and Norman Nie in their influential research on participation in the United States (Verba and Nie, 1972). It was subsequently applied by them and by others to explain participation in a number of countries, including Britain (Verba, Nie and Jae-On Kim, 1978; Barnes and Kaase, 1979; Parry, Moyser and Day, 1992; Verba, Schlozman and Brady, 1995). The central ideas of the civic voluntarism model of participation are captured in the following quote:

> We focus on three factors to account for political activity. We suggested earlier that one helpful way to understand the three factors is to invert the usual question and ask instead why people do not become political activists. Three answers come to mind: because they can't; because they don't want to; or because nobody asked. In other words people may be inactive because they lack resources, because they lack psychological engagement with politics, or because they are outside of the recruitment networks that bring people into politics. (Verba, Schlozman and Brady, 1995: 269)

The authors define the resources aspect of this in terms of 'time, money and civic skills' (Verba, Schlozman and Brady, 1995: 271). The psychological engagements aspect is defined principally in terms of the individual's sense of political efficacy (Verba, Schlozman and Brady, 1995: 272), and finally, the recruitment networks aspect is defined as 'requests for participation that come to individuals at work, in church, or in organizations – especially those that come from friends, relatives, or acquaintances' (Verba, Schlozman and Brady, 1995: 272).

The core idea of this model is that individuals with resources will participate, where these resources are the product of social structures, inherited characteristics from parents and education. As the authors explained in an earlier version of the theory:

> According to this model, the social status of an individual – his job, education, and income – determines to a large extent how much he participates. It does this through the intervening effects of a variety of 'civic attitudes' conducive to participation: attitudes such as a sense of efficacy, of psychological involvement in politics and a feeling of obligation to participate. (Verba and Nie, 1972: 13)

Thus resources were paramount in the original version of the model, and since these are not the product of specific choices, but often the product of birth and family upbringing, this makes the model a structural theory of citizenship. Psychological engagement is obviously more subject to individual choice, but in the model it is seen as being both derivative and less important than resources.

Verba and his colleagues developed the first empirical typology of different modes of participation, and classified citizens into six different groups on the basis of the types of activities they undertook (Verba and Nie, 1972: 118–19). There are, firstly, the *inactives*, who as the name suggests do little or nothing; secondly, the *voting specialists*, who vote regularly, but do nothing else; thirdly, the *parochial participants*, who contact officials in relation to specific problems, but are otherwise inactive; fourthly, the *communalists*, who intermittently engage in political action on broad social issues, but are not highly involved; fifthly, *campaigners*, who are heavily involved in campaigns of various kinds; and finally, the *complete activists*, who participate in all kinds of activities.

This theoretical model has been widely cited and replicated; however, it does face problems. The first problem relates to the use of socio-economic status as a predictor of participation and civic values. It is well established that participants are generally higher-status individuals than non-participants; for example, Verba and his collaborators show that high-status individuals are over-represented in the category of very active participants and under-represented in the category of inactives (Verba and Nie, 1972: 131–3). What the model fails to explain, however, is why large numbers of high-status individuals do not participate in politics. In other words, while participation is associated with social status, the latter is nonetheless a relatively weak predictor of participation, because many high-status individuals do not get involved in politics. This problem for the model can be seen in Verba's recent work on participation in the United States (Verba, Schlozman and Brady, 1995). In the theory, family income is treated as a good proxy measure of socio-economic status in the American context, but nonetheless it has a very weak influence on participation.[4]

This latter point explains a paradox which is apparent to students of participation in advanced industrial societies. If socio-economic status is such an important determinant of political participation, then societies which are gradually becoming more middle-class and better educated over time should experience increased rates of participation. The increase in white-collar occupations at the expense of blue-collar occupations, and the tremendous growth in higher education in many advanced industrial countries is now well documented (see Dalton, Flanagan and Beck, 1984; Abramson and Inglehart, 1995). However, there is no evidence of increased political participation in these countries, and in the case of the United States both voting turnout and participation in voluntary organisations have actually declined rather than increased (Brody, 1978; Miller and Shanks, 1996).[5]

If we apply the model to Britain there is clearly a problem in explaining why participation in the 2001 British general election was significantly lower than, for example, in the 1979 election, when a massive expansion had occurred in higher education during the intervening years.[6] Again, it would have to explain the trends in party membership, which with the sole exception of the Labour Party between 1994 and 1997 are downwards, not upwards (Katz and Mair, 1992; Seyd and Whiteley, 2002a).

A second problem with the socio-economic model is identified by Verba and his colleagues themselves. They write:

[T]he SES model is weak in its theoretical underpinnings. It fails to provide a coherent rationale for the connection between the explanatory socio-economic variables and participation. Numerous intervening factors are invoked – resources, norms, stake in the outcome, psychological involvement in politics, greater opportunities, favorable legal status, and so forth. But there is no clearly specified mechanism linking social statuses to activity. (Verba, Schlozman and Brady, 1995: 281)

---

[4] In their model of participation, the beta coefficient of the family income predictor variable is only 0.11, and is the weakest of seven predictors of participation used in this model (see Verba, Schlozman and Brady, 1995: 342).

[5] Turnout in presidential elections has declined by more than a fifth between the 1950s and 1980s. See Miller and Shanks, 1996: 39–69.

[6] Turnout in the 1979 election was 76 per cent (see figure 1.2). Participation in higher education has more than doubled from about 800,000 students in 1980/81 to more than 1,600,000 in 1996/97 (see *Times Higher Education Supplement*, 1,299, 26 September 1997).

They go on to suggest that a focus on broader resources, such as the amount of spare time the individual has available in the average week and his or her financial resources, helps to deal with this problem. However, it is difficult to see why this should be true, since if individuals are rich and have plenty of leisure time, there is still no reason why they should spend their money or free time on political activities, rather than on vacationing, playing sports or watching TV.[7]

The key problem with the resources model is that it focuses exclusively on the 'supply' side of the equation and neglects 'demand' side aspects. Thus individuals supply more participation if they have the resources or a psychological sense of efficacy. What is missing is any understanding of why individuals have a demand for participation – what incentives they have to get involved in politics. Many high-status individuals have no such incentives, which explains why they do not participate. Just as the general incentives theory neglected structural factors so the civic voluntarism theory neglects incentives. The theory may contribute to explaining citizenship, but it is unlikely to provide the sole explanation of what makes a good citizen.

The equity–fairness theory

The equity–fairness model provides an alternative perspective on participation but one which is still centred on the sociological tradition of analysis. The starting point is that society is divided into various competing groups which vie with each other for resources. The core idea of the theory is that individuals compare themselves with various peer groups, and if these comparisons reflect unfavourably on themselves that can produce frustration and/or aggression. This in turn can be manifested in aggressive political participation (Runciman, 1966; Gurr, 1970; Muller, 1979; Dalton, 2002). The basic mechanism at work here is relative deprivation in which individuals compare and contrast their life situation with their expectations of that situation. These expectations are commonly defined by these comparisons with peer groups. If there is a significant gap between expectations and reality then relative deprivation is likely to result and this in turn will have political consequences. Clearly, this is more likely to occur among groups who are objectively deprived in some way, such as ethnic minorities or the low-paid.

Reference groups or peer groups are very important to this theory, since individuals do not usually compare themselves with groups which are far

---

[7] Putnam (1995) actually attributes the decline in civic voluntarism in the United States to the spread of television.

removed from their own situation. If a well-known millionaire becomes even richer, this is not likely to engender relative deprivation in the average individual because they do not compare themselves with such a person. But if a colleague at work gets a pay rise and they do not, this is likely to create a sense of deprivation. The bigger the gap between expectations and reality, the larger the sense of deprivation and potentially the bigger the political consequences.

The model has been used to explain the incidence of 'unorthodox' political participation, involving such activities as attending protest rallies, blocking traffic, supporting strike action and even participating in illegal protest activities. (Gurr, 1970; Muller, 1979). It provides a theoretical explanation of the well-known phenomenon of 'NIMBYism', or protest against planning proposals and road schemes likely to adversely affect the individual's property values. From this perspective, it is the relative deprivation caused by such proposals which triggers the protest action.

There is good evidence to suggest that the equity–fairness model provides an explanation for certain types of political participation. But there is a real question about its relevance for explaining participation more generally, particularly orthodox types of participation such as voting in elections and joining political parties. It is theoretically possible that a sense of deprivation will make people more likely to vote against a governing party, if they blame that party for their perceived deprivation. However, there is also evidence to suggest that relative deprivation inhibits orthodox forms of participation such as voting, since deprived people can become apathetic (Clarke et al., 2004). So relative deprivation can have different effects in different contexts, making the theoretical predictions from the theory unclear.

The relationship between perceptions of equity–fairness and attitudes to rights and obligations has not been clarified either. One hypothesis would be that a sense of relative deprivation makes individuals more likely to demand rights and less likely to accept obligations, but it is equally possible that it makes people apathetic and less willing to demand their rights as well as to acknowledge their obligations. These possibilities will be explored further in chapter 6.

The criticism of the civic voluntarism model, that it does not take into account incentives, cannot be made about the equity–fairness theory. Incentives are at the heart of the theory, since individuals are reacting to a sense of disadvantage and are motivated to do something about it. On the other hand, it has little to say about the precise calculations of the costs and benefits of political participation, other than the argument that a greater sense of deprivation should engender greater participation in certain contexts. Clearly, it is possible for an individual to feel a strong

sense of deprivation, but at the same time to conclude that they can do little about it to change their life, which explains why deprivation can cause apathy. Thus although the theory is concerned with incentives, it does not have a clear understanding of the nature and significance of these incentives. Additional assumptions are needed about the individual's sense of political efficacy if deprivation is to be translated into political action.

Another problem from the perspective of the civic voluntarism model is that in the equity–fairness model resources inhibit rather than promote participation. In this theory it is the absence of resources relative to one's peers which motivates participation. Since a well-resourced individual is unlikely to feel a sense of deprivation, they are unlikely to participate as a consequence. Obviously, this is precisely the opposite prediction to that made by the civic voluntarism model. On the other hand, this difference in the predictions from the theories is an advantage since it provides a clear empirical test of these rival models.

The social capital model

The social capital model is also a structural model of participation. There is some debate about the definition and meaning of social capital in the literature, but Putnam defines it as 'features of social organization, such as trust, norms and networks, that can improve the efficiency of society by facilitating co-ordinated actions' (1993: 167). Coleman, however, sees social capital as a set of obligations and expectations on the one hand, and a set of information channels linking citizens with each other on the other hand (1988). For him social interaction generates 'credit slips' of obligations and norms of reciprocation, and in an environment in which individuals can trust others, these credit slips can be utilised by third parties to solve collective action problems.

The core idea of social capital theory is that if individuals can be persuaded to trust each other and to work together to solve common problems then society will be much better off as a consequence. In this sense social capital is like other types of capital and can be used to make society more productive and the economy more efficient. Just as financial capital can be invested in order to promote economic growth, and human capital or education can be used to promote productivity, then social capital can be used to achieve similar objectives.

For most writers trust is the key indicator of social capital (Fukuyama, 1995; Putnam, 1993, 2000; Brehm and Rahn, 1997; Van Deth et al., 1999). Trust is important because it allows individuals to move beyond their own immediate family or communities and engage in cooperative activities with others whom they do not know. There is a debate about the origins of social capital (Whiteley, 1999) but the dominant model which explains this is the de Tocqueville model, named after the French philosopher who studied American society in the early nineteenth century. Writing in 1832 de Tocqueville noted that:

> In no country in the world has the principle of association been more successfully used or applied to a greater multitude of objects than in America. Besides the permanent associations which are established by law under the names of townships, cities and counties, a vast number of others are formed and maintained by the agency of private individuals. (1990: 191)

In de Tocqueville's theory interactions between individuals in voluntary associations generate interpersonal trust or social capital. Communities characterised by high levels of social capital have dense networks of civic engagement and appear to have better health and education, less crime and higher rates of political participation (Putnam, 1993, 2000). Trust in this model refers to generalised reciprocity or the willingness of individuals to trust strangers. This is important since it represents 'bridging' social capital rather than 'bonding' social capital, terms originally introduced by Putnam. Bridging social capital, or the willingness to trust strangers, creates benign effects, whereas bonding social capital, a willingness to trust only members of one's immediate group, can bring malign effects because it fragments society.

There has been an interesting debate about the causes of a decline in social capital in the United States. Putnam has claimed that television viewing may account for this apparent decline (2000), although this has been challenged (Norris, 1996). The evidence on trends in social capital in Britain is not as extensive as in the United States, but it suggests that social capital may not have declined in Britain in the same way (Hall, 1999).

The social capital model has received a lot of attention, but like the other theories we have considered it does face some problems. One such problem is the danger of circularity when it is applied to the task of explaining wide forms of political participation; it comes close to saying that participation in voluntary activity creates further participation and so on. This is not such a problem when one is trying to explain specialist types of participation such as voting, but it is a potential problem when broad measures of participation in effect become both independent and dependent variables in explanatory models.

A second point about the social capital model reiterates the point made earlier about the civic voluntarism model, in that it neglects incentives for participation. If society is characterised by high levels of social capital, which make cooperative behaviour easy, there is still the problem of explaining why some people should cooperate when others do not. From a rational choice perspective there are even stronger incentives to free-ride on the efforts of others is such societies. This is because when social capital is abundant, big gains can be made by individuals who cheat their fellow citizens. More generally, while it is true that choice theories should not neglect structural explanations, it is also true that structural models should not neglect choice explanations.

Conclusions

We have reviewed both choice theories and structural theories which might be used to explain variations in both participation and in civic attitudes in Britain. The starting point of the analysis was to define what is meant by citizenship and then subsequently to examine how it can be measured in terms of attitudes and behaviour. It is clear from an initial look at the data in the tables that there are significant variations in both civic values and attitudes and participation among citizens in Britain. It is evident that there are 'good' citizens who participate and have attitudes which support civic society and enhance governance. At the same time there are also 'bad' citizens, or people who do not participate and who have attitudes which undermine civic society and inhibit good governance. The explanation for these variations should lie in one or more of the theoretical models examined in this chapter. The task of the next chapter is to test these rival accounts in order to discover which one provides the most plausible account of citizenship in modern Britain.

6   Testing Rival Theories of Citizenship

Introduction

In the previous chapter we examined alternative theories of citizenship, defining this in terms of both attitudes and behaviour. In this chapter we focus on testing these theories to see which one gives the most plausible account of citizenship using the empirical evidence from the Citizen Audit. The analysis in the chapter begins by translating the five rival theories discussed in chapter 5 into testable models, so that we can then determine which model or combination of models provides the best explanation of attitudes and behaviour in relation to citizenship. The aim is not merely to identify the best model, but to draw conclusions about the relevance of structural and choice theories as explanations of citizenship in contemporary Britain. The identification of the best model will show that choice theories are particularly important in explaining citizenship. We begin by specifying the alternative models of citizenship in a form that can be estimated from the survey data. The analysis concludes with a discussion of the findings and their relevance to debates about the nature of citizenship in contemporary Britain.

Modelling citizenship in contemporary Britain

The examination of theories of citizenship in chapter 5 began by examining choice theories and this was followed by a discussion of structural theories. We repeat this sequence in the present chapter, by examining the two choice models first and subsequently the three structural models. It will be recalled that the first of the choice models was the cognitive engagement model, which can be specified as follows.

The cognitive engagement model

$Citizenship_i = a_i + b_{i1} Education + b_{i2} Political\ Knowledge$
$\qquad + b_{i3} Media\ Exposure + b_{i4} Interest\ in\ Politics$
$\qquad + b_{i5} Policy\ Dissatisfaction + u_i$

where:

Citizenship$_i$ are the citizenship dependent variables, measuring participation and attitudes to rights and obligations;

Education measures the respondent's educational attainment;

Political Knowledge is an index of knowledge which is relevant to citizenship;

Media Exposure is an index of the individual's exposure to media coverage of politics;

Interest in Politics measures the extent to which individuals are motivated to follow politics;

Policy Dissatisfaction is an index of dissatisfaction with the government's performance in relation to the most salient issues in politics;

u_i is an error term in which $E(u_i) = 0$, and σ_u^2 is constant.[1]

As the discussion in chapter 5 indicated, cognitive engagement theories of citizenship focus on individuals' exposure to information about politics and government, on their ability and willingness to respond to that information, and on their reactions to the content of that information. Media exposure captures the first of these ideas; education and political knowledge capture their ability to respond to information; and interest in politics and policy dissatisfaction measure their reactions to the content of information.

Prior expectations are that all of these variables should be positive predictors of participation and of attitudes to rights and obligations. Individuals who are educated, knowledgeable, interested in politics and exposed to the media should be more willing to participate in politics than their less engaged counterparts. In addition they should have a solid sense of their rights while at the same time acknowledging their obligations to society.

Some of the variables in the cognitive engagement model have already been examined in previous chapters, but for ease of comparison they are repeated in table 6.1. Some are constructed from combinations of variables which appeared earlier. Education is measured using two indicators, the first being the age respondents finished full-time education, and the second graduate status. With regard to the latter, only 10 per cent of respondents were graduates despite the fact that higher education has expanded rapidly in recent years. Clearly, it will be some time before the effects of the recent expansion of higher education are felt in all age groups. In addition, as table 6.1 shows, less than a fifth of the population

---

[1] This is the error term in the regression equation, and with an expected value of zero and homoscedastic errors, it is assumed to be well-behaved.

Table 6.1 *Indicators in the Cognitive Engagement Model*

'At what age did you finish full-time education?'

Age	%
15 and under	37
16	28
17	8
18	8
19 and over	18

Graduate	%
Yes	10
No	90

Political Knowledge Scale (see table 3.7)

Number of correct answers	% getting correct answers
0	6
1	8
2	10
3	12
4	15
5	16
6	21
7	13

'In the average week how often do you. . . . .'

	Read a newspaper for political news %	Listen to the radio or watch TV for political news %
Every day	17	36
4 to 6 days	6	10
1 to 3 days	17	13
Less than once	17	13
Never	42	29

Interest in politics at different levels – percentages	Very %	Fairly %	Not very %	Not at all %
Local politics	5	31	33	31
Regional politics	4	29	34	32

Table 6.1 (*cont.*)

Interest in politics at different levels – percentages	Very	Fairly	Not very	Not at all	
National politics	14	35	23	27	
European politics	6	20	33	40	
International politics	8	25	29	38	
	Strongly agree	Agree	Neither	Disagree	Strongly disagree
Policy dissatisfaction	%	%	%	%	%
Managing public services*	3	22	28	33	15
Managing the economy**	11	27	34	24	4

* 'The government is doing a good job in managing public services like health care and education'.
** 'The government is doing a bad job in managing the economy' (wave one of the weighted face-to-face survey).

have been educated beyond the age of 19. Education provides the most basic measure of the individual's ability to process political information.

The second such measure is provided by the political knowledge quiz, the results of which were described in table 3.7. Table 6.1 combines the information from that table into a single scale and it shows that only 13 per cent of the respondents got all seven answers correct. Surprisingly enough 6 per cent got all the answers wrong, despite the fact that this was quite difficult to do if they were just guessing.[2] Clearly, levels of political knowledge in Britain are not that high. The third measure in table 6.1 is an indicator of the individual's exposure to political information in the media. It shows that while most people follow politics in the media, a sizeable minority do not. More people get political information from television than from reading newspapers, suggesting that the electronic media are particularly important. The fourth variable is interest in politics, and this is measured by means of a cumulative index of the responses to questions on levels of interest in politics set out in table 3.9.[3]

[2] Given that random guessing is likely to produce between three and four correct answers to True/False statements of this type it is actually difficult to get all seven answers wrong.
[3] Each respondent is given 4 points for being very interested, 3 points for being fairly interested, and so on. Thus the scale varies from 20 where someone is very interested in all five levels of politics, to 5 where they are not at all interested in any of them.

The responses in that table are repeated in table 6.1 for ease of presentation, and they show that while most people take an interest in politics, particularly national politics, a sizeable minority do not. It appears that interest in national politics comes before interest in international politics, and that in turn comes before interest in regional and local politics.

The policy dissatisfaction measures in the cognitive engagement model appear in the final section of table 6.1. This is the key measure of individuals' reaction to the content of the information they receive. It can be seen that there was a considerable amount of dissatisfaction with the government's management of public services and only a relatively modest level of satisfaction with its handling of the economy. The scales are combined in the estimating equations and coded so that a high score represents a high level of dissatisfaction with these policies.[4]

As mentioned earlier, cognitive engagement theory suggests that educated, knowledgeable and interested individuals are more likely to have values which promote good citizenship and they are also likely to participate more than the uneducated and the uninterested. Moreover, given a widespread level of discontent with the government's performance in managing the public services (Toynbee and Walker, 2001), attentive and informed citizens are quite likely to be among the ranks of those dissatisfied with the government's performance. So the prediction is that all of the variables in this model will have a positive impact on citizen attitudes and participation.

The general incentives model

The general incentives model is the second of our choice-based models and it can be specified as follows:

$$
\begin{aligned}
Citizenship_i = {} & \beta_0 + \beta_1 Efficacy + \beta_2 Collective\ Benefits - \beta_3 Costs \\
& + \beta_4 Process\ Incentives + \beta_5 Outcome\ Incentives \\
& + \beta_6 Group\ Incentives + \beta_7 Altruistic\ Motives \\
& + \beta_8 Social\ Norms + \beta_9 Expressive\ Benefits + u_i
\end{aligned}
$$

where:

$Citizenship_i$ are the citizenship dependent variables, measuring participation and attitudes to rights and obligations;

---

[4] Individuals who strongly agree that 'the government has done a bad job in managing the economy' score 5, and those who strongly disagree with this statement score 1. Individuals who strongly agree that 'the government is doing a good job in managing the public services' score 1, and those who strongly disagree with this statement score 5. The dissatisfaction scale is the sum of these questions and therefore varies from 2 to 10.

Efficacy measures the perception that the individual can influence government and politics;

Collective Benefits measure the perception that the system as a whole works well and can provide benefits for the individual;

Costs measure the extent to which the individual perceives that participation is costly and time consuming;

Process Incentives measure the benefits to the individual provided by the process of participation itself;

Outcome Incentives measure the benefits to the individual of achieving political status;

Group Incentives measure the individual's sense that participation brings benefits to groups which they support;

Altruistic Motives measure the individual's sense of duty that citizens should participate in order to support democracy;

Social Norms measure the effects of other people's attitudes to participation on the individual's own attitudes;

Expressive Benefits measure the effect of the individual's affective attachments to the political system which may influence his or her values and can motivate participation;

u_i is an error term in which $E(u_i) = 0$, and σ_u^2 is constant.

The core idea of the general incentives model is that individuals are motivated to participate and to have positive civic values by various types of incentives. At the centre of this model is a rational choice theory of citizenship which hypothesises that individuals will participate or hold civic values if the benefits of doing so outweigh the costs (Riker and Ordeshook, 1968).

The collective benefits variable in the general incentives model measures levels of satisfaction with the performance of the political system, using three indicators. These are: satisfaction with medical treatment, satisfaction with work conditions and, more generally, satisfaction with democracy. The first two are deliberately policy-specific, relating to the individual's everyday experiences, and the third is a more general indicator of satisfaction with the performance of the system as a whole. Theoretically, it is possible that these measures might be completely unrelated to each other, but in practice they scale together quite effectively.[5] This indicates that personal experience in two key areas of day-to-day life which are both significantly influenced by state action is associated with the effectiveness of the political system as a whole.

---

[5] When subject to a principal components analysis one component was significant and explained 38 per cent of the variance. The loadings on the three variables are 0.47 for satisfaction with medical treatment, 0.61 for satisfaction with working conditions and 0.75 for satisfaction with democracy.

Table 6.2 *Indicators in the General Incentives Model*

	Very satisfied %	Satisfied %	Neither %	Dissatisfied %	Very dissatisfied %	Don't know %
Democracy	3	32	28	25	8	4
Medical treatment	36	46	5	8	4	0
Workplace conditions	19	48	11	15	6	1

	Yes %	No %	Don't know %			
Efficacy						
Can you influence your medical treatment?	18	78	4			

Can you influence your working conditions?	Not at all %	Some %	Great deal %	Don't know %
	32	34	32	2

	Strongly agree %	Agree %	Neither %	Disagree %	Strongly disagree %
Costs					
Getting involved in politics can be tiring after a hard day	16	49	28	6	1
Being involved in politics takes time away from one's family	20	56	19	5	1
People are so busy these days that they don't have time to vote	5	14	21	43	18
Process incentives					
Participating is a good way to meet interesting people	3	27	40	24	6
Participating in politics is not much fun	15	41	29	14	2
Outcome incentives					
A person like me could do a good job as a local councillor	4	17	28	37	14

Table 6.2 (*cont.*)

	Strongly agree	Agree	Neither	Disagree	Strongly disagree
Politics would be more effective if people like me were elected to Parliament	6	24	37	27	7
Group incentives					
Being active is a good way to get benefits for one's family	5	35	38	18	4
Being active is a good way to get benefits for groups I care about	4	22	38	30	6
Altruistic motives					
Every citizen should get involved if democracy is to work properly	8	37	34	18	3
If a person is dissatisfied with government he/she has a duty to do something about it	9	50	31	9	1
*Social norms**					
People who get involved in politics are often a bit odd	6	30	27	34	4
The only way to change anything is to get involved	7	50	28	13	1
MPs are respected figures in the community	4	31	29	31	5

	Very proud %	Somewhat proud %	Not very proud %	Not at all proud %
Expressive incentives				
Proud to be a British citizen?	33	45	12	9

* *Note:* Respondents are asked to indicate their perceptions of the replies of a significant other such as a spouse or friend. (Wave one of the weighted face-to-face survey.)

The collective benefits variable captures the idea that satisfaction with the performance of the system should motivate individuals to participate. If citizens believe that the system works well and is able to deliver benefits, this should motivate them to get involved. It should also make them willing to acknowledge both rights and obligations. If they do not see the system in this light then they will be deterred from participating or having supportive civic values. If people perceive great benefits from participating but at the same time feel that they cannot influence outcomes, then they have little incentive to get involved. So efficacy has to be taken into account when evaluating the benefits of citizen participation.[6] This is done by examining medical treatment and workplace conditions once again. In relation to the former, respondents were asked if they were able to influence their medical treatment. In the case of workplace conditions, they were asked if they were able to influence their working conditions (e.g. rest periods, safety conditions). Exercising influence over these key areas of life means that individuals have a sense of efficacy and so responses to these questions are aggregated into a single scale.[7] The data indicate that, not surprisingly, less than a fifth of respondents had tried to influence their medical treatment in the previous year. However, a much larger proportion felt that they had influence over their working conditions.

In addition to collective benefits and efficacy there are other types of incentives which can contribute to citizen attitudes and behaviour. These are process, outcome, group, altruistic incentives, and incentives provided by social norms.[8] Finally, there are incentives arising from affective feelings, which are not directly linked to calculations of costs and benefits. The additional indicators used to measure these concepts in the general incentives model also appear in table 6.2. Also there are three indicators of costs in the model, and these show that individuals are acutely aware of the costs of participation. The implication is that awareness of costs will deter participation as well as inhibit

---

[6] In the standard specification of rational choice models collective benefits and efficacy interact with each other to influence outcomes. But an exploratory analysis showed that an additive specification of the general incentives model works better than an interactive version, so this is used in all subsequent modelling.

[7] A respondent trying to influence their medical treatment scores 1, and one who is able to influence their work conditions to some extent also scores 1. A respondent who is able to influence their work conditions a great deal scores 2. These items are summed so that the scale varies from 0 to 3.

[8] These scales are all constructed from the Likert statements in table 6.2, so that strongly agree scores 5, agree scores 4, neither agree nor disagree scores 3, disagree scores 2 and strongly disagree scores 1. The respondent scores on the different statements are then summed. Don't know responses are coded 3.

individuals from accepting their obligations and possibly even asserting their rights.[9]

There are two indicators of process incentives and two of outcome incentives in table 6.2. Both process and outcome incentives are measures of selective incentives or the private returns from participation. In the case of process incentives, some people enjoy participation because of the friendships this might bring or because they see volunteering and participation as enjoyable activities in their own right. One of the process incentives measures is positively worded and the other is negatively worded. Thus many people see participation as a good way of meeting interesting people, while others are put off by the idea of politics. With regard to outcome incentives, only a minority show evidence of a willingness to engage in political activities as elected representatives. On the other hand, research has shown that such incentives can be a powerful motivator to encourage some citizens to engage in high-intensity forms of participation (see Whiteley and Seyd, 2002).

There are two indicators of group incentives in table 6.2, which measure motives for engagement grounded in the desire to get benefits for groups rather than just for oneself as an individual. Again there is evidence that a sizeable minority of the population are motivated to participate in order to obtain these types of benefits. The two indicators of altruistic incentives suggest that there is strong support for the idea that individuals have a duty to participate in order to support democracy, although again a minority do not take this view. The social norms questions asked respondents to indicate their perceptions of the views of significant others whose opinions they respect and who might be expected to influence their attitudes. Respondents perceive that some people are sceptical about the value of political involvement, but there are also many people who are thought to agree with the idea that participation is the only way to change things.

Finally, expressive incentives are measured by an indicator of the respondent's sense of pride in being a British citizen. The idea here is that individuals who are proud to be British are also likely to have a strong sense of rights and obligations, and are also likely to participate in a way which supports the political system. They do this, however, not out of a sense that it will bring immediate benefits, but rather out of a sense of affective attachments to the political system. Overall, the expectation with the general incentives model is that individuals who have strong incentives to participate are more likely to be active and to have positive civic values which support the political system in comparison with people

---

[9] The costs scale is coded in the same way as the other scales discussed in note 8.

who lack such incentives. In the next section we start to examine the first of the structural models of citizenship, the civic voluntarism model.

The civic voluntarism model

It will be recalled from the previous chapter that the core idea behind the civic voluntarism model is that individuals with resources will participate and have good civic values. Thus social class, income and educational attainment should all help to promote participation and develop supportive values. Participation and civic attitudes will also be influenced by the mobilising activities of other people, and by the degree to which the respondent is psychologically engaged with politics. The civic voluntarism model can be specified as follows:

$$Citizenship_i = \beta_0 + \beta_1 Efficacy + \beta_2 Resources + \beta_3 Mobilisation$$
$$+ \beta_4 Psychological\ Engagement + \beta_5 Partisanship + u_i$$

where:

> $Citizenship_i$ are the citizenship dependent variables, measuring participation and attitudes to rights and obligations;
>
> $Resources$ measure the resources that individuals bring to the exercise of participation; including their occupational status, income, educational attainment and the amount of time they have available;
>
> $Efficacy$ is an index of the respondents' judgements that they are able to influence politics;
>
> $Mobilisation$ is a measure of whether or not the individual has been asked to participate by others;
>
> $Psychological\ Engagement$ measures interest in politics at different levels;
>
> $Partisanship$ measures strength of partisanship;
>
> u_i is an error term in which $E(u_i) = 0$, and σ_u^2 is constant.

The resources concept in the civic voluntarism model is measured by five items. These are: educational attainment; graduate status; occupational status; household income; and time resources. The educational attainment variable measures the age at which the respondent left full-time education and this together with graduate status also appears in the cognitive engagement model described in table 6.1. In table 6.3 the occupational status variable is a self-coded measure with professionals at the top of the scale and the semi-skilled and unskilled manual workers at the bottom. The household income variable classifies respondents into six categories varying from incomes of under £10,000 to over £50,000

Table 6.3 *Indicators in the Civic Voluntarism Model*

Resources	%
Occupational status	
Professional or technical work	15
Manager or administrator	13
Clerical	12
Sales	6
Foreman	2
Skilled manual	15
Semi-skilled or unskilled manual	27
Household income	
Under £10,000	37
£10,000 up to £19,999	27
£20,000 up to £29,999	16
£30,000 up to £39,999	9
£40,000 up to £49,999	5
£50,000 up to £59,999	3
£60,000 up to £69,999	1
£70,000 plus	2

Time spent on activities other than work, studying, sports or work in the home	%
None	22
Up to 3 hours	34
From 3 up to 6 hours	24
From 6 up to 9 hours	12
More than 9 hours	7

	Strongly agree %	Agree %	Neither %	Disagree %	Strongly disagree %
Efficacy					
People like me can have no say in what the government does	20	37	21	20	2
Sometimes politics seems so complicated that a person like me cannot understand it	16	38	19	22	5

Table 6.3 (*cont.*)

	Strongly agree %	Agree %	Neither %	Disagree %	Strongly disagree %
People like me can have a real influence on politics if they get involved	5	35	26	27	7
It really matters which party is in power because it will affect our lives	18	38	22	18	5

Mobilisation – Asked to Participate	%
Not asked	75
Asked by a stranger	15
Asked by a work colleague	3
Asked by a close friend	5
Asked by a member of the family	1

Strength of attachment to parties	%
Very strongly attached	18
Fairly strongly attached	42
Not very strongly attached	38
Don't know	2

(Wave one of the weighted face-to-face survey.)

per annum. Finally, the time resource variable is based on a set of questions asking respondents to indicate the number of hours they devote to various activities such as working, leisure and sleeping. This captures the idea that individuals who are time-poor are unlikely to participate in comparison with the time-rich.

The second concept in the civic voluntarism model, efficacy, is measured by an index of responses to a set of items about their perceptions of the political system. This is a different measure of political efficacy from the one used in the general incentives model. In the general incentives model we focused on very specific perceptions of efficacy derived from everyday experience. This is in line with rational choice theory in which individuals are required to evaluate the costs and benefits of specific actions. In this rather different model, efficacy is defined in more general terms linked to perceptions of the responsiveness of the political system as a whole. It can be seen that majorities of respondents think that they have no say in the political system and furthermore that the system is often too complicated to understand. At the same time there are significant minorities of respondents who think that they can influence politics if they are prepared to get involved. In addition, most people think that it matters which party is in power. These four items scaled effectively and the combined efficacy scale is used in the subsequent analysis.[10]

The mobilisation scale in table 6.3 provides a measure of whether or not the respondent had been asked by someone else to participate in the previous year, but it also takes into account who asked them. The idea is that individuals asked to participate by close relatives or friends are more likely to do so than individuals asked to participate by strangers. Equally, individuals asked to participate by strangers are more likely to do so than individuals who were not asked to participate at all. The highest score went to individuals asked to participate by a family member, and the lowest to individuals not asked to participate by anyone. The scale makes it possible to test this hypothesis.

Psychological engagement is measured by interest in politics, which is the same scale appearing in the cognitive engagement model. In this respect the civic voluntarism model overlaps with the cognitive engagement model, although the terminology used to describe this phenomenon in the two models is rather different. Despite this, both assume that individuals' civic values and their participation rates are influenced by levels of interest in politics.

The final measure in the civic voluntarism model is an indicator of the individual's strength of attachment to one of the political parties. Political parties are the most important civic organisations outside the institutions of the state, and it is well known that party identification motivates participation (Clarke et al., 2004). A lot of participation and voluntary activity does not involve political parties, but parties are nonetheless very important to the political system and this is why the measure is included (Verba, Schlozman and Brady, 1995: 477–80).

Overall, in the civic voluntarism model the expectation is that individuals who have high levels of resources, who are psychologically engaged, feel a sense of efficacy or who have been mobilised by others are more likely to participate and to have positive civic values than individuals who lack these characteristics. In the next section we examine the second of the structural models of citizenship, the equity–fairness model.

---

[10] When subject to a principal components analysis the items produced one significant factor which explained 41 per cent of the variance. All factor loadings exceeded 0.50. The factor scores from this component were used to define the scale.

The equity–fairness model

The equity–fairness or relative deprivation model is based on the idea that individuals who perceive a gap between what they expect out of life and what they actually experience are likely to suffer from psychological deprivation. As the discussion in chapter 5 indicates, this perception of relative deprivation may in turn mobilise them to participate, particularly in protest activities. The idea is captured in the following model:

$$Citizenship_i = \beta_0 + \beta_1 Perceptions\ of\ Outcomes\ and\ Expectations$$
$$+ \beta_2 Economic\ Deprivation$$
$$+ \beta_3 Membership\ of\ a\ Deprived\ Group + u_i$$

where:

> *Citizenship*$_i$ are the citizenship dependent variables, measuring participation and attitudes to rights and obligations;
> *Perceptions of Outcomes and Expectations* measures the individual's generalised sense of deprivation;
> *Economic Deprivation* measures the individual's sense of economic deprivation;
> *Membership of a Deprived Group* measures if the respondent is unemployed, a member of an ethnic minority group, retired or female;
> u_i is an error term in which $E(u_i) = 0$, and σ_u^2 is constant.

Perceptions of outcomes and expectations are measured using five Likert-scaled statements designed to capture the gap between expectations and experiences. Three of the indicators specifically name the government, politicians or parties and so feelings of deprivation are linked directly to the performance of the political system.

It can be seen in table 6.4 that almost two-thirds of respondents feel that there is a gap between their expectations and what they experience of life. In addition, clear majorities feel that members of Parliament soon lose touch with the people, and that politicians only look out for themselves. There is also considerable scepticism about the idea that the government treats people like themselves fairly, so there is clear evidence of a sense of deprivation among respondents. These five indicators scaled quite well and so their combined scale is used in the subsequent analysis.[11]

The indicators of economic deprivation ask people to pass judgement on the state of the national economy as well as on the economic position

---

[11] A principal components analysis explained 50 per cent of the variance with the first factor and all variables had loadings of 0.55 or more on this factor. The factor scores from this component were used to define the scale.

Table 6.4 *Indicators in the Equity–Fairness Model*

Expectations and outcomes	Strongly agree %	Agree %	Neither %	Disagree %	Strongly disagree %
There is a big difference between what we expect and what we get	15	41	27	15	1
The government generally treats people like me fairly	3	23	38	28	8
It doesn't matter which party is in power	16	38	19	21	5
Politicians only look after themselves	23	32	29	15	1
MPs soon lose touch with people	22	44	24	9	1

Economic deprivation	A lot better %	A little better %	Stayed same %	A little worse %	A lot worse %
Economic situation in country over last year	4	24	36	22	9
Financial situation of household over last year	5	18	47	21	9
Economic situation in country over next year	2	21	39	20	8
Financial situation of household over next year	4	22	50	13	6

Don't knows not shown.
Wave one of the weighted face-to-face survey.

of their own households. They are asked to comment on the retrospective economic record over the previous year as well as the prospects for the next year. The responses tell a similar story to the general expectations measures, with feelings of pessimism outweighing feelings of optimism on all but one of the indicators. The exception was in relation to the prospects for the financial situation of their households over the next year; slightly more people thought that these would get better than thought they would deteriorate. Again, these indicators scaled very well, and this is used in the subsequent analysis.[12]

In addition to the indicators of deprivation, the model contains measures of membership of potentially deprived groups, which are not shown in table 6.3. Altogether, some 5 per cent of the respondents were from ethnic minorities, and 54 per cent were female. In addition, 28 per cent of the respondents were retired, in some cases having taken early retirement, and 11 per cent were unemployed. These social characteristics are included in the model in the form of dummy variables in the estimating equations.[13] The expectation is that individuals with a high sense of deprivation or who are members of a potentially deprived group are more likely to participate, and possibly have a stronger sense of their civic rights than individuals who lack these characteristics.

The social capital model

The third structural model is the social capital model. Again, the earlier discussion indicates that in this model inter-personal trust is the key factor which promotes cooperation between individuals when they attempt to solve collective action problems. Chapter 5 pointed out that the most influential analysis of the origins of such trust is associated with the work of Alexis de Tocqueville, particularly his analysis of democracy in America. His idea is that trust derives from face-to-face interactions between individuals participating in voluntary activity. Such participation is thought to engender trust and a willingness to cooperate with others in addition to developing participatory skills. Voluntary activity and trust will then in turn promote civic values and broader forms of political participation. In addition, community ties are also likely to engender trust and foster participation, so we can specify the social capital model as follows:

$$Citizenship_i = \beta_0 + \beta_1 Inter\text{-}personal\ Trust + \beta_2 Trust\ in\ Institutions$$
$$+ \beta_3 Membership\ of\ Groups$$
$$+ \beta_4 Membership\ of\ an\ Informal\ Network$$
$$+ \beta_5 Exposure\ to\ TV + \beta_6 Ties\ to\ the\ Local\ Community + u_i$$

[12] The first principal component explained 54 per cent of the variance and all the variables loaded on this factor with factor loadings of 0.68 or greater. Again, factor scores were used to define the scale.
[13] A dummy variable means that respondents with these characteristics score 1, and those without 0.

where:

Citizenship$_i$ are the citizenship dependent variables, measuring participation and attitudes to rights and obligations;

Inter-personal Trust measures the extent to which individuals trust other people;

Trust in Institutions measures the extent to which individuals trust the institutions of the state;

Membership of Groups measures individual membership of interest groups;

Membership of an Informal Network measures individual membership of informal groups;

Exposure to TV is the number of hours respondents watch TV in the average day;

Ties to the Local Community measures the length of residence and family ties in the community;

u_i is an error term in which $E(u_i) = 0$, and σ_u^2 is constant.

Indicators used in the social capital model appear in table 6.5, starting with the measures of trust.[14]

It can be seen in table 6.5 that respondents generally are much more likely to trust other people than they are to trust the institutions of the state. The first three items in table 6.5 were combined into an overall scale.[15] Within the group of indicators of institutional trust there are significant differences depending on the institution under consideration. Individuals are much more likely to trust the courts and the police, that is, the unelected institutions of the state, than they are to trust the government or politicians, or the elected representatives. Again these items were combined into an overall institutional trust scale.[16]

The group membership scale is based on the responses given in table 3.14. It indicates that most people are not members of any organised groups, although about 40 per cent of the population are members of at least one group.[17] In addition, although this does not appear in the table,

[14] The trust variables are measured along an 11-point scale varying from 0 to 10. They are recoded in table 6.5 for presentational purposes, so that scores of 0 to 3 are 'low trust', 4 to 6 'medium trust' and 7 to 10 'high trust'.

[15] Three 11-point scales varying from 0 to 10 were used to measure inter-personal trust and all three indicators were loaded strongly on a principal component which explained 74 per cent of the variance. All factor loadings exceeded 0.84 and the factor scores were used to measure the scale.

[16] The seven institutional trust items loaded strongly on the first principal component which explained 56 per cent of the variance. All loadings on this component exceeded 0.63, and the factor scores from this exercise were used to define the scale.

[17] The scale was constructed by adding together the number of groups which an individual reported belonging to in table 3.15. In response to a suggestion by Robert Putnam we excluded motoring organisations in subsequent analysis on the grounds that they are merely insurance providers for the vast majority of people.

Table 6.5 *Indicators in the Social Capital Model*

	Low trust %	Medium trust %	High trust %
Interpersonal trust			
Trust in other people	10	50	41
Trust in people to be helpful	14	55	31
Trust in people to be fair	10	57	32
Institutional trust			
Government	47	47	6
House of Commons	43	51	6
The courts	20	58	22
The Civil Service	18	60	22
Politicians	54	42	3
The police	13	49	37
Local government	31	58	11

Number of groups which respondents are members of	%		
None	58		
One	20		
Two	11		
Three or more	12		

Number of hours watching TV in the average day	Up to 2 hours %	2 to 4 hours %	More than 4 hours %
	31	41	29

Number of years the respondent has lived at the present address	%		
Under 1 year	13		
From 1 to 5 years	25		
From 5 to 10 years	15		
10 or more years	48		

Wave one of the weighted face-to-face survey.

about one person in five is a member of an informal group such as a book-reading group, a pub quiz team or a childcare network. According to the social capital model both types of membership should boost participation and strengthen civic attitudes. On the other hand, exposure to TV should inhibit both. This follows from Putnam's argument that television may be one of the key causes of declining social capital in the United States (Putnam, 2000). On average, respondents watched about two hours of television a day, so this has significant potential to inhibit their civic values and activities.

Finally, ties to the local community are also important influences in the social capital model. These are measured in two ways: firstly, by the number of years which respondents had lived at their present address. This is clearly likely to influence their ties to the community, since the geographically mobile have less opportunity to develop local social capital. The table shows that nearly half of the respondents had lived in their present address for ten or more years. The second indicator of community ties measured whether they had family living nearby, and some 65 per cent reported that they did. This should promote social solidarity and community ties and thus enhance social capital and trust. Overall, the expectation is that all of the variables in the social capital model, except television viewing, should have a positive impact on participation and civic values.

Having set out the detailed specification of the models in the next section we begin to investigate the empirical evidence for their validity. We begin with a discussion of the methodological strategy to be used in estimating the models.

Estimating the rival models

The standard approach in political science for evaluating alternative models has been to use a goodness of fit measure such as R-squared or the t-statistics associated with a particular estimate. However, applied econometricians are increasingly sceptical of the value of this approach in the absence of clearly specified alternative models (Charemza and Deadman, 1992: 14–30). In an influential article Leamer pointed out that evidence can be found in favour of any theory, if the researcher privileges that theory by ignoring its rivals. He writes:

Diagnostic tests such as goodness of fit tests, without explicit alternative hypotheses, are useless since, if the sample size is large enough, any maintained hypothesis will be rejected . . . Such tests therefore degenerate into elaborate rituals for measuring the sample size. (1983: 39)

Recent work has created an alternative 'encompassing methodology' that is explicitly designed to test rival theories and avoid this criticism (Granger, 1988; Hendry, 1995). Encompassing methodology involves the idea that the best theory should be able to account for, or incorporate, the results of rival theories by out-performing them in various diagnostic tests.

The approach starts with the data generating process (DGP), which is the theoretical mechanism underlying the observed relationships in the data. This is usually very complex and can only be approximated in practice by the models that are estimated. In this case the best methodological strategy involves testing rival models against each other to see which provides the best approximation to the DGP. If one model is better than another it should encompass the alternative; that is, it should account for the results of the alternative model as well as for phenomena that the rival model is unable to account for. No single model is likely to give a perfect representation of the DGP, but the aim of empirical research should be to try and identify the best of a set of alternative models. In this type of exercise, one model may encompass another, or none of the models may encompass each other. In the latter case the individual models represent components of a more general model which encompasses them all.

One complication with the exercise of testing these rival models, as the discussion in chapter 5 indicates, is that there are a total of ten different dependent variables in these models.[18] This fact, coupled with the point that there are five rival models, means that a full test of all the alternatives would involve estimating and comparing fifty different models. To avoid this problem and to ensure that the estimation exercise is manageable we will examine only the first factor extracted in the analyses in table 5.1 through table 5.3, which in each case is the most important factor. The one exception to this relates to the collective action variable which is the third factor in table 5.3. Since this is a particularly important dimension of citizenship we include tests of this factor separately. Overall, the estimation exercise involves using the state rights factor from table 5.1, the volunteering obligations factor from table 5.2, the individualistic and collective participation factors from table 5.3 and the small-scale democracy participation scale from table 5.5, as dependent variables in the various models.

The investigation begins by estimating each of the different models described above separately, starting with the cognitive engagement model, and the results of this exercise appear in table 6.6. Each of the models contains a control for age, and it can be seen that they provide only relatively modest fits to the data but they all explain variance. The

---

[18] That is three indicators of rights from table 5.1, three of obligations from table 5.2, three of participation from table 5.3 and one of participation in small-scale democracy in table 5.5.

Table 6.6 *The Cognitive Engagement Model*

	Rights to state action	Obligation to volunteer	Individual action	Collective action	Small-scale democracy
Years education	−0.14***	0.02	0.09***	0.07***	0.06***
Graduate status	0.01	−0.03	0.02	0.01	0.09***
Political knowledge	−0.05***	0.12***	0.20***	−0.02	0.11***
Media exposure	−0.01	0.07***	0.04**	0.04*	0.03
Interest in politics	−0.04*	0.13***	0.22***	0.10***	0.11***
Dissatisfaction with policy	−0.03*	0.04**	0.05***	0.02	0.05***
Age	−0.11***	−0.24***	−0.08***	−0.07***	−0.24***
R-squared	0.03	0.10	0.16	0.03	0.12

Wave one of the weighted face-to-face survey.
Note: The table contains the standardised regression coefficients obtained from regressing the row variables on the column variables. Asterisks indicate the statistical significance of the coefficients with $p < 0.10^*$; $p < 0.05^{**}$; $p < 0.01^{***}$.

control for age is included since it is well known that there are age-related differences in participation and civic values, something which can be observed in earlier chapters. The theoretical explanation is that young people (under the age of 20) have less of a stake in the system than their older counterparts and therefore are less likely to participate and have civic values which support participation than their older counterparts.

It appears that education, political knowledge and political interest all have negative impacts on the demand for state-provided rights, which is the first dependent variable. Clearly, individuals who lack education, have little political knowledge and are not very interested in politics favour state action to provide jobs, housing and to fight against poverty. On the other hand, the educated, informed and knowledgeable do not favour such action. This is a counter-intuitive finding, since it indicates that disengagement is associated with the demand for rights. Similarly, policy dissatisfaction reduces the demand for state action while policy satisfaction increases it. Clearly, the failure to deliver on policies means that citizens lose confidence in the ability of the state to deliver on their concerns and they become less likely to demand these rights. With regard to the individual's sense of obligation to volunteer, the politically informed, the politically interested and those exposed to media coverage of politics all feel an obligation to volunteer. In contrast, the politically uninformed and the uninterested feel no such obligation. Thus cognitive engagement motivates a sense of obligation to volunteer while at the same time inhibiting the demand for state action to support economic rights.

The pattern of findings for the indicators of participation in table 6.6 are similar to those of the obligations model. In this case education, knowledge, media exposure and interest in politics all stimulate individualistic, collectivist and small-scale democratic participation. In addition, policy dissatisfaction provides a positive motivation for individuals to participate although it appears to have no influence on collective action. In all of these participation models, age inhibits involvement.

The findings are all consistent with expectations, except in relation to the demand for rights model. Despite this, the findings in the rights model nonetheless make perfect sense. The state is the core agency which provides for the needs of all its citizens, but the uninformed and the uneducated demand extensive state intervention to provide jobs and to redistribute income in their favour. In simple terms the losers in the market economy look to the state to compensate them, whereas the winners are wary of excessive state action. When the rights and obligations models are linked, we can see that the uneducated and ill-informed want the state to take action to provide these important economic rights, but they feel no obligation to do anything themselves to bring this about. In contrast, the informed and educated are wary of state action on redistribution while at the same time believing that they should volunteer and participate in order to bring about change. It is important to remember that the state rights scale is not measuring relatively uncontroversial rights such as freedom of speech or the right to demonstrate, but rather policies involving massive redistribution of income. In this narrow sense, there is a gap between expectations of rights and individual obligations to participate. From this perspective it is easy to understand the results.

Table 6.7 contains the estimates of the general incentives model of civic values and participation. It can be seen that collective benefits have a significant positive influence on perceptions of rights, on volunteering obligations as well as on individualistic, collective and small-scale democratic participation. Thus satisfaction with policy delivery in relation to health care and the workplace, but also in relation to the democratic performance of the political system as a whole, stimulates perceptions of rights, obligations and participation. The effects of efficacy show a similar pattern, except in this case efficacy inhibits the demand for redistributive rights; this is consistent with the earlier finding that those who lack a sense of efficacy are likely to demand redistributive rights.

Table 6.7 *The General Incentives Model*

	Rights to state action	Obligation to volunteer	Individual action	Collective action	Small-scale democracy
Specific efficacy	−0.08***	0.08***	0.16***	0.00	0.31***
Benefits	0.05***	0.04**	0.05***	0.02	0.21***
Costs	0.13***	−0.00	−0.06***	−0.02	−0.00
Process incentives	−0.09***	0.05***	0.06***	0.04**	0.05***
Outcome incentives	−0.04**	0.11***	0.05***	0.04**	0.05***
Group incentives	0.07***	0.03	−0.03	−0.01	−0.04*
Altruistic motives	0.12***	0.12***	0.14***	0.07***	0.06***
Social norms	0.02	0.07**	−0.02	0.04**	−0.01
Expressive incentives	0.01	0.01	−0.02	−0.03*	−0.04**
Age	−0.07***	−0.20***	−0.04**	−0.09***	−0.17***
R-squared	0.05	0.10	0.06	0.02	0.18

Wave one of the weighted face-to-face survey.
Note: The table contains the standardised regression coefficients obtained from regressing the row variables on the column variables. Asterisks indicate the statistical significance of the coefficients with $p < 0.10^*$; $p < 0.05^{**}$; $p < 0.01^{***}$.

Perceptions of costs have a positive impact on the demand for rights and no impact at all on perceptions of obligations. Respondents who perceive that participation is costly are likely to favour state intervention to redistribute income, but this perception has no influence on their willingness to volunteer. Such perceptions do, however, inhibit individual participation, although they do not influence collective participation or small-scale democratic participation. Selective incentives to participate appear to be quite important in all of the models. They stimulate a sense of obligations and influence all of the different measures of participation, while inhibiting the demand for redistributive rights. The group incentive measures appear to be important only in relation to rights and small-scale democratic participation, in that they stimulate a sense of rights, but they inhibit small-scale democratic participation. Altruistic incentives positively influence all of the dependent variables, but social norms influence only obligations and collective participation. Finally, expressive incentives have a modest impact on collective participation and small-scale participation. The control variable, age, inhibits all forms of civic values

Table 6.8 *The Civic Voluntarism Model*

	Rights to state action	Obligation to volunteer	Individual action	Collective action	Small-scale democracy
General efficacy	−0.04***	0.04**	0.07***	−0.02	−0.02
Occupational status	−0.11***	−0.00	0.07***	−0.03	0.05***
Years education	−0.05**	0.01	0.05***	0.08***	0.04*
Time available	−0.01	−0.03	−0.01	−0.01	−0.02
Household income	−0.12***	0.05**	0.11***	0.04*	0.18***
Mobilisation	0.05***	0.07***	0.19***	0.17***	0.10***
Psychological engagement (interest in politics)	−0.03*	0.16***	0.22***	0.10***	0.12***
Strength of partisanship	0.04**	0.04	0.03	0.02	−0.00
Age	−0.13***	−0.20***	−0.03	−0.07***	−0.19***
R-squared	0.06	0.10	0.19	0.06	0.15

Wave one of the weighted face-to-face survey.
Note: The table contains the standardised regression coefficients obtained from regressing the row variables on the column variables. Asterisks indicate the statistical significance of the coefficients with $p < 0.10^*$; $p < 0.05^{**}$; $p < 0.01^{***}$.

and participation. Thus the elderly are less likely to demand rights, to recognise their obligations and to participate.

Overall, the results in table 6.7 indicate that the general incentives model behaves much as expected when it comes to explaining citizen obligations and participation. The exception relates to the demand for state action on rights. Again, there is a clear logic behind the findings. When it comes to the demand for state intervention to promote economic rights, those who see participation as costly and who recognise few benefits from involvement want the state to intervene on their behalf even if they themselves do not want to get involved. Thus the desire to free-ride goes alongside the desire for the state to provide collective rights.

Table 6.8 contains the estimates of the civic voluntarism model, the first of the structural models of citizenship. In this case general efficacy promotes perceptions of obligations and individualistic participation and

Table 6.9 *The Equity–Fairness Model*

	Rights to state action	Obligation to volunteer	Individual action	Collective action	Small-scale democracy
Expectations & outcomes	0.19***	−0.04**	−0.10***	−0.01	−0.04**
Economic expectations	−0.05**	−0.07***	−0.06***	−0.03	0.01
Unemployed	0.10***	−0.01	0.08***	−0.00	−0.17***
Retired	−0.00	−0.11***	0.05**	0.04	−0.26***
Female	0.07***	0.04***	0.06***	−0.04*	−0.08***
Ethnic minority	0.07***	−0.03*	−0.06***	0.00	0.02
Age	−0.04	−0.13***	−0.04*	−0.11***	−0.07
R-squared	0.06	0.06	0.04	0.01	0.12

Wave one of the weighted face-to-face survey.

Note: The table contains the standardised regression coefficients obtained from regressing the row variables on the column variables. Asterisks indicate the statistical significance of the coefficients with p < 0.10*; p < 0.05**; p < 0.01***.

inhibits perceptions of state rights. Occupational status, income and education all inhibit perceptions of rights while at the same time promoting participation. Psychological engagement inhibits rights and promotes participation, while partisanship has no effect on any of the dependent variables, apart from rights. The pattern which emerges in this table is that resources clearly promote participation and also a sense of obligation to participate, but they inhibit the demand for state redistribution. This is a similar pattern to that found in the earlier models. Again, those who lack resources want the state to provide redistribution, jobs and housing, but they do not want to participate themselves. The sole exception to this relates to mobilisation, which serves to promote both civic values and participation.

The equity–fairness model appears in table 6.9 and again there are significant differences between perceptions of rights and the other dependent variables in these models. Essentially, relative deprivation stimulates the demand for state rights, while inhibiting feelings of obligations to volunteer and also to participate. Economic pessimism also has an inhibiting effect on obligations and participation and in this case the demand for state rights as well. In relation to membership of a potentially deprived group, being unemployed, female or a member of an ethnic minority promotes the demand for state rights, but ethnic minorities are inhibited both from individualistic forms of participation and the obligation to volunteer.

Table 6.10 *The Social Capital Model*

	Rights to state action	Obligation to volunteer	Individual participation	Collective action	Small-scale democracy
Inter-personal trust	−0.04*	0.03*	0.02	−0.04*	−0.07***
Institutional trust	−0.02	−0.01	0.03	0.01	−0.00
Membership of groups	−0.07***	0.13***	0.26***	0.01	0.21***
Informal group member	−0.03*	0.09***	0.10***	0.07***	0.05***
TV exposure	0.15***	−0.05***	−0.09***	−0.03	−0.10***
Years in current home	−0.01	−0.02	0.04***	−0.02	−0.01
Family in community	0.02	0.05***	−0.01	−0.03	0.02
Age	−0.07***	−0.19***	−0.07***	−0.06***	−0.20***
R-squared	0.05	0.08	0.11	0.02	0.13

Wave one of the weighted face-to-face survey.
Note: The table contains the standardised regression coefficients obtained from regressing the row variables on the column variables. Asterisks indicate the statistical significance of the coefficients with $p < 0.10^*$; $p < 0.05^{**}$; $p < 0.01^{***}$.

Females are more likely to want state action on rights than males, but they are also more likely to feel a sense of obligation to participate and less likely to get involved in collective action. Being unemployed, retired or female appears to stimulate individualistic participation although it inhibits participation in small-scale democracy. Membership of such groups appears to have no influence on collective action, except in the case of females where the evidence suggests that it inhibits participation.

Overall, the equity–fairness model suggests that a sense of deprivation creates apathy rather than stimulating participation, and at the same time promotes a desire for state redistribution. The evidence in relation to membership of a potentially deprived group is more equivocal, but the pattern suggests that such membership promotes a demand for state action while inhibiting a sense of obligations and all types of participation except individualistic action.

The estimates of the social capital model appear in table 6.10, and it can be seen that membership of groups, both informal and formal, promotes obligations to volunteer as well as all types of participation. In this sense, the social capital model is supported. However, inter-personal trust only has a weak positive influence on obligations and it appears to inhibit the demand for state action as well as collective action and small-scale democratic participation. These effects are not compatible with the social capital model. Moreover, institutional trust appears to have no influence at all on participation or civic values. Having community roots promotes volunteering and individualistic participation, but has no other effects. TV exposure promotes the demand for state rights and inhibits obligations and participation, so in that respect Putnam's argument is supported. Overall though, these results suggest that social capital has a weak influence on participation and volunteering if it is defined in terms of membership of formal and informal groups. But there is little evidence to suggest that trust promotes such participation.

Having examined the pattern of results for each of the individual models, we next examine which of these models or groups of models provides the best explanation of civic attitudes and participation.

Testing rival models

To test the rivals we incorporate all the predictor variables into one global model and use this to determine which are significant factors in explaining behaviour and civic attitudes. With this approach, if one of the models dominates the picture then many of its variables will be significant predictors of participation and attitudes to rights and obligations. If this occurs, then rival models will have very little explanatory power in the global model, since they will be encompassed by the dominant model. On the other hand, if two models dominate the picture then their variables will account for the variations in citizenship, but neither model will dominate the other. A third possibility is that there are no dominant models, and in this case variables from all of the models will appear as equally important predictors of citizenship. In this way, we can identify which of these models, if any, provides the best account of citizenship. The results of this exercise appear in tables 6.11 and 6.12, which include the statistically significant effects only.

Table 6.11 contains the best models of attitudes to rights and obligations. It is apparent that no single model dominates the picture, but it is also clear that some models are more important than others. In relation to attitudes to rights, two models in particular are important: the equity–fairness and the civic voluntarism models. From the former, expectations and outcomes together with membership of disadvantaged groups have a significant impact on perceptions of rights. Thus individuals who feel deprived, who are unemployed, female and members of an ethnic minority are more likely to support state intervention to maintain rights than

Table 6.11 *Best Models of Rights and Obligations*

	Rights	Obligations
Political knowledge		0.11***
Media exposure		0.05***
Interest in politics		0.07***
Years education	−0.06***	
Graduate status	0.04**	
Dissatisfaction with policy	−0.10***	0.04**
Expectations & outcomes	0.17***	
Economic expectations		−0.03*
Unemployed	0.06***	
Female	0.06***	0.09***
Ethnic minority	0.07***	
Retired		−0.08***
Specific efficacy		0.03*
Costs	0.10***	
Outcome incentives		0.07***
Process incentives	−0.05***	
Group incentives		0.05***
Altruistic motives	0.13***	0.08***
Social norms		0.06***
Occupational status	−0.10***	−0.04**
Household income	−0.09***	
Time available		0.06***
General efficacy	0.07***	
Mobilisation	0.06***	0.04***
TV exposure	0.10***	
Trust in institutions		−0.04*
Membership of groups		0.08***
Informal group member		0.05***
Family in community		0.05***
Age	−0.09***	−0.18***
R-squared	0.14	0.16

Wave one of the weighted face-to-face survey.
Note: The table contains the standardised regression coefficients obtained from regressing the row variables on the column variables. Asterisks indicate the statistical significance of the coefficients with $p < 0.10^*$; $p < 0.05^{**}$; $p < 0.01^{***}$.

people in general. In the case of the civic voluntarism model there are four variables which are significant predictors of rights. Occupational status and income are the resources indicators and general efficacy and mobilisation are also relevant. In line with the equity–fairness model, a lack of resources encourages individuals to demand rights. Thus the uneducated, the low-status and those at the bottom of the income distribution are more likely to demand redistributive rights than the educated and high-status individuals. In addition to these two models, the general incentives model also plays a role in explaining the demand for rights. Specifically, perceptions of costs, process incentives and altruistic motives are important variables in explaining the demand for rights. Perceptions of costs and altruistic motives stimulate the desire for rights, while process incentives inhibit that desire. The effects are very similar to those discussed in table 6.7.

The obligation to volunteer model is rather different from the rights model. In this case the general incentives and social capital models appear to be most important. Altogether five variables in the general incentives and a further five in the social capital model influence obligations to volunteer. Of the incentive variables, altruistic motives appear to have marginally the strongest influence on obligations, but outcome incentives and social norms also play a positive role. In relation to the social capital model, membership of groups has the biggest impact on obligations, with informal group membership and community ties being relevant also for promoting a sense of obligations. Other models make a contribution to explaining obligations as well. From the cognitive engagement model, the politically knowledgeable, those who are interested in politics, and individuals who are exposed to politics in the media all have a stronger sense of obligations to volunteer than the population in general. It is also apparent that policy dissatisfaction motivates individuals to volunteer. From the social capital model, community roots and membership of informal and formal groups promote a sense of obligations to volunteer, while institutional trust appears to have an inhibiting effect. It appears that individuals who trust the institutions of the state are less likely to volunteer, perhaps because they are content to let the state run things.

The biggest contrast between the rights and obligations models is that a lack of resources creates a demand for rights, whereas obligations to participate are much more about being interested in politics and being rooted in the community. Putting this the other way round, those with a strong sense of obligations are inclined to take political action, whereas supporters of rights are more likely to want the state to act on their behalf.

Table 6.12 contains the models of individual and collective participation. It can be seen that in the case of individual participation while all five models contribute to explaining variations in participation, the general incentives model appears to be more important than its rivals. Thus perceptions of benefits, specific efficacy, costs, altruistic motives and social norms all play a role in explaining individualistic participation. In the latter case perceptions of social norms inhibit participation, but this reflects

Table 6.12 *Best Models of Individual and Collective Participation*

	Individual action	Collective action	Small-scale action
Interest in politics	0.16***	0.09***	0.09***
Years education		0.07***	
Graduate status			0.06***
Political knowledge	0.17***	−0.04**	
Media exposure	0.04***		
Expectations & outcomes		0.05**	
Unemployed			−0.11***
Retired			−0.18***
Female	0.15***	−0.04**	
Ethnic minority	−0.05***		
Benefits	0.05***		0.24***
Specific efficacy	0.07***		0.20***
Costs	−0.03**		
Process incentives		0.03*	
Altruistic motives	0.06***	0.04***	
Social norms	−0.04**	0.03*	
Time available	0.05***		
Household income	0.07***		0.09***
Mobilisation	0.17***	0.16***	0.07***
Interpersonal trust		−0.04**	−0.03*
Institutional trust			0.03*
Membership of groups	0.14***	−0.04**	0.10***
Informal group member		0.03*	
TV exposure	−0.03**		−0.03*
Years in current home	0.03*		
Age	−0.10***	−0.04**	−0.06**
R-squared	0.26	0.06	0.27

Wave one of the weighted face-to-face survey.
Note: The table contains the standardised regression coefficients obtained from regressing the row variables on the column variables. Asterisks indicate the statistical significance of the coefficients with $p < 0.10*$; $p < 0.05**$; $p < 0.01***$.

the fact that the measure relates primarily to collective action as can be seen in table 6.2. So it is not surprising that social norms promoting collective action have a different effect on individualistic participation. Other models contribute to the explanation of individualistic action as well. The political interest and knowledge variables from the cognitive engagement model, and the community and group attachments variables from the social capital model, all promote individualistic forms of participation. On the other hand, with the exception of the mobilisation measure, the civic voluntarism model makes very little contribution to explaining individualistic action. A similar point can be made about the equity–fairness model.

Turning next to collective action, the general incentives model plays a rather less important role in explaining collective participation than it does individualistic participation. Process incentives, altruistic incentives and social norms all appear to motivate collective action, but several of the other variables in this model do not. From the cognitive engagement model, respondents who are interested in politics and who are educated beyond secondary school are more likely to participate in collective action. From the equity–fairness model a gap between individuals' expectations and their experiences of life motivates them to participate in collective action. Equally, mobilisation is an important factor in explaining collective action, but apart from that the civic voluntarism model plays no role in explaining this type of participation. Finally, inter-personal trust and group membership from the social capital model appear to be important, but the signs on these effects are inconsistent with the theory.

In the case of small-scale democratic political action, the social capital model appears to be quite important; inter-personal and institutional trust influence participation as does membership of groups. TV exposure appears to inhibit participation as it does in the individualistic participation model. The general incentives, cognitive engagement and equity–fairness models play modest roles in explaining small-scale participation, while once again the civic voluntarism model appears to be largely irrelevant except in relation to mobilisation.

Looking at the results in tables 6.11 and 6.12 as a whole, there is clearly no one dominant model for explaining political attitudes and behaviour which encompasses all the rest. Perhaps this is not really surprising, since these are rather different aspects of citizenship. But there are nonetheless clear patterns in the models of citizenship in these tables. In chapter 5 we introduced the distinction between choice-based and structural-based models of citizenship, with cognitive engagement and the general incentives model being examples of the former, and the equity–fairness, civic voluntarism and social capital models being examples of the latter. It is clear from the findings that choice-based models are more important than structural-based models for explaining certain aspects of citizenship, particularly participation, while the reverse is true for key aspects of attitudes.

In the case of the rights model a clear majority of the important effects come from structural-based models, with equity–fairness and civic voluntarism being particularly important. It is a lack of resources and status and a sense of relative deprivation which motivate individuals to demand state-enforced redistribution. For obligations, however, the choice-based models appear to be much more important, with the cognitive engagement and general incentives models dominating the picture. Unlike rights, perceptions of obligations are linked closely to political knowledge and interests as well as to incentives of various kinds.

This is also true in the case of the participation measures. Individualistic participation is much more influenced by incentives, knowledge and interest than by status and community attachments. The strength of choice-based models is also apparent in relation to collective action as well. Apart from mobilisation, which we have classified as a structure-based measure, collective action is mostly about incentives and engagement. Indeed, several of the structure-based models of collective action have the wrong signs from the point of view of theory. The only qualification to this point relates to small-scale democratic political action where indicators of status, such as being unemployed or retired, and attachments to groups do influence participation in the predicted direction. In this case structure-based theories of participation seem to be more important than is true in the individualistic and collective participation models.

Discussion and conclusions

The findings in this chapter have important implications for our understanding of the concept of citizenship. Citizenship has all too often been seen as a permanent fixture of the political landscape, something which can be taken for granted as a stable feature of reality against which political conflicts are played out. In fact, citizenship is malleable as individuals make choices about their participation and their perceptions of rights and obligations. In effect, their relationship with the state is subject to a continuing negotiation and can change in response to shifting incentives and circumstances. Community ties and resources certainly play an important role in the story, but choice-based theories are dominant in many of these models.

In the earlier discussion we suggested that one source of problems for the contemporary nation-state is the existence of a gap between individuals' sense of obligations and their sense of rights. The models of rights and obligations show that there is evidence to support this conjecture, since many low-status and poorly motivated individuals want the state to enforce rights on their behalf, while at the same time they do not want to participate. However, as table 5.3 showed, the desire for state-provided rights is only one aspect of the demand for rights. Alongside those is the demand for individualistic rights which stress the importance of the state, in effect, leaving people alone to provide for themselves. So while this argument has force, it can be taken too far.

Perceptions of obligations are also quite varied as well. We have focused on the obligation to volunteer in the later analysis, but there are strong norms implying that individuals should obey the law and be civic-minded in their relationships with others. When these complexities are taken into account it is hard to argue that the state is being overburdened by a demand for benefits which is not balanced by a recognition of obligations.

With regard to participation, it is clear that no one theory dominates the picture and all have something to contribute in explaining individual and collective participation. At the same time, it is also clear that some theories are much weaker than others. Social capital, for example, contributes group membership to the explanation of participation, but the trust variable is either absent from the models or wrongly signed, so it is not clear that trust plays the role assigned by theory in explaining participation. The equity–fairness model is similarly weak as an explanation of participation, though it appears to have more relevance for collective action than it does for individual participation. Cognitive engagement theory is particularly important in explaining collective participation, and the general incentives model plays a key role in explaining both individual and collective participation. In general terms, choice-based theories are more important than structural-based theories, which again points to the malleability of citizenship. The civic voluntarism model contributes mobilisation to the picture, but apart from that, the model has little to contribute when it comes to explaining participation in general, and collective action in particular.

This concludes our examination of these rival models of citizenship attitudes and participation. Up to this point, we have been concerned with describing and analysing the nature and causes of citizenship in Britain. In part III, we go on to examine what might be described as the 'So what?' question: Do participation and civic values have consequences for the political system?

Part III

The Consequences of Citizenship

7   So What? The Consequences

The preceding chapters have examined the nature of citizenship in modern Britain. The British public are, as we have seen, still active members of their communities, engaged in a wide range of both formal and informal activities. Contrary to the widespread view that citizenship is in crisis (Putnam, 2000), Britain at the start of the twenty-first century still enjoys a civic culture, albeit rather different from that outlined by Almond and Verba (1963) forty years ago.

There is a hidden assumption in all this, however, that citizenship 'matters'. As well as being assumed to be good in its own right, a strong civic tradition, it is argued, will also be reflected in better lives: better government, more concern for one's fellow citizens, and so on. But is this really the case? In this chapter, we examine variations in citizenship in Great Britain across communities. Do communities with strong local civic cultures fare better than communities where the civic tradition is weaker? Does being good citizens mean we live better lives?

Citizenship and government

Much of the current interest in the putative effects of good citizenship on the quality of life can be traced back to Putnam's (1993) now classic analysis of Italian regional government. The Italian regions were reformed in the early 1970s with the aim of creating relatively powerful, democratically accountable, administratively efficient regional political institutions that would contribute positively to social and economic development in their areas. Twenty years on, however, there were still substantial variations in the quality of regional government and in social and economic living standards across the Italian regions. The northern regions seemed to have been successful: they had achieved a relatively high amount of legitimacy, local economies were strong, and living standards were rising. In the south, however, things were not so hopeful: the regional governments there had not achieved public legitimacy, the economy remained relatively stagnant, and so on. But why should this be so?

Putnam's answer was to look at variations in social capital across the Italian regions. The main difference between the successful north and the stagnating south, he claimed, was in the way people interacted with each other. In the north, people were socially active, joining and taking part in a wide variety of activities, both formal and informal, which put them in close contact with their fellow citizens. Much associational life was horizontal, rather than vertical, that is between equals working together for a shared purpose, pooling their skills, ideas and expertise, and working cooperatively. People had to collaborate to solve their own problems, rather than looking to a hierarchical leadership to offer solutions for them. By singing in local choirs, or getting involved with the local tenants' group, and so on, they came to know a cross-section of their fellow residents well, and came to like and trust them. This, Putnam argued, built a reservoir of social capital in these active communities. The combination of the experience of working together towards a common goal (whether or not that goal was a political one did not matter), and the feeling that one's fellow residents on the whole were decent, trustworthy people, he claimed, helped oil the wheels of regional government. Feeling able to trust one's fellows most of the time on most issues helped reduce the costs of political interaction and helped develop 'norms of reciprocity'. People came to expect broadly fair dealing, both from their fellows and from government.

By contrast, in the Italian south, civic life was not conducive to building social capital. A strong client–patron tradition and the relative absence of the horizontal associational structures of the type which featured in the north, meant that southern Italians did not have the same opportunities as their northern counterparts to interact on equal terms with their fellow residents. Norms of reciprocity and trust were therefore relatively poorly developed in the south, Putnam claimed. And the outcome, he argued, was less effective government in the south than in the north, a less efficient regional economy because of the additional costs incurred by the lack of trust, and a poorer living standard . More recently Putnam (2000) reports similar patterns in the United States. Things work better, he reports, in states like Minnesota which are rich in social capital than in states like Mississippi where social capital is low – schools produce better results on the whole, the murder rate is considerably lower, people are healthier, and so on.

The moral seems simple, therefore. Communities with abundant social capital, where residents are busily engaged in a range of associational activities, from good works, through hobby groups, to helping their neighbours, will prosper; communities lacking in social capital will not. In this more recent work, Putnam has turned his attention to a perceived decline in citizen activism in the United States since the 1960s (Putnam, 1995,

2000). Why do fewer Americans seem to become politically active at the dawn of the twenty-first century than was the case in the 1950s? Once again, social capital is held to be crucial, and television is painted as the villain of the piece. Television now constitutes the main leisure pursuit for increasing numbers of Americans and, it might be added, citizens of other Western societies. The trend towards privatised television watching has grown rapidly over time, isolating people in their own homes, and reducing the time available for precisely the various kinds of social networking and associational activity which are claimed to be conducive to developing social capital (though see e.g. Norris, 1996). Americans (and others), Putnam argues, need to get out more!

The social capital thesis has been subject to considerable scrutiny, not all of it favourable (Tarrow, 1996; Newton, 1999; Milner, 2002). Not only is the relationship between social capital and trust theoretically rather tautological (Milner, 2002), but there is some indication that it does not stand up empirically (Newton, 1999; Claibourn and Martin, 2000).

However, for our purposes here, the key issue is whether good citizenship actually delivers in terms of better living standards. Much of the research effort has been geared towards cross-national analyses. There seems to be general agreement in the literature that trust in one's fellow residents does indeed contribute to economic well-being. Trusting societies tend to perform better on a range of economic and political indicators than do societies where trust is lacking (Knack and Keefer, 1997; Inglehart, 1999a; Whiteley, 2000; though see Newton and Norris, 2000; Norris, 2002). However, membership in associational organisations, a key element of Putnam's social capital model, does not seem to have an influence on economic performance (Knack and Keefer, 1997). Recent work on variations in government performance between American states suggests similar results: performance is positively associated with social trust, volunteering and the proportion of households completing the Census, but not with 'connectedness' – associational membership, informal socializing, and so on (Knack, 2002). This begs the question of causal direction, of course. Does living in a trusting society engender economic and political success? Or, vice versa, is it, for instance, economic affluence which creates the conditions under which trust in others, and trust in public institutions can flourish (McAllister, 1999; Miller and Listhaug, 1999)? Even so, it does appear that, at the cross-national level at least, trust, if not associational membership, on the one hand, and economic and political performance, on the other, are related. In addition, recent European work suggests that levels of trust in government, especially local government, vary according to the size of the municipality in which people live: the smaller the authority, the more the people living there trust their local government (Denters, 2002).

Other factors besides social capital are implicated in the health of civic life, however, as Eric Oliver's recent work has shown (Oliver, 1999, 2000, 2001). His analysis of the impacts of rapid suburbanisation on the health of grassroots democracy in the Unites States combines evidence from Verba, Schlozman and Brady's (1995) data on public participation in politics with census data on US cities. The results suggest that the health of citizenship varies systematically across different types of community. Even after controlling for individual-level factors, people living in less populous communities are more likely, other things being equal, to participate in politics than are people living in larger urban centres (results that also hold outside North America: Frandsen, 2002; Rose, 2002). This, it is claimed, reflects the relatively smaller prospects of free-riding in a small community than in a large one. At the same time, political participation is greater, *ceteris paribus*, in economically mixed communities than in very poor or very rich communities. And it is also greater in racially mixed than in near all-black or all-white communities. Both, Oliver claims, reflect the greater political stakes in mixed than in homogeneous communities: while politics in the former involves a battle between potential winners and losers, in the latter, all residents start off in the same basic situation, and hence both the risks of non-participation and the potential gains are not so great. In a sense individuals do not need to participate in homogeneous communities, since their interests will be protected by the very fact that their fellow citizens are like themselves with the same basic interests. In heterogeneous communites, by contrast, individuals need to participate if they are to protect their interests from the demands of others who have a different agenda.

Oliver's findings concerning the geography of citizenship raise an intriguing question regarding its impact on local living standards. If good citizenship itself correlates with the local social context, then the apparent relationship between citizenship measures and policy outputs may well be spurious. In other words, social structural variables such as the social homogeneity of a community may be responsible for the apparent relationship between measures of citizenship and performance. The implications of Oliver's suburban democracy argument are at odds with those of Putnam's social capital model. In particular, Putnam would predict high participation rates in homogeneous suburbs with high levels of social capital. In contrast, Oliver predicts, with some convincing evidence, that such suburbs have lower participation rates than less homogeneous, more mixed communities. At the very least, there is a case to be investigated.

Nor do Putnam and Oliver exhaust the possible range of explanatory models. In the United Kingdom, for instance, there is copious evidence that community socio-economic status is a key explanation of variations

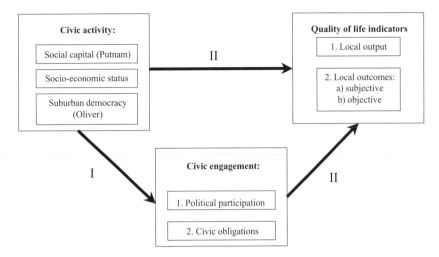

Figure 7.1 The Analytical Strategy to Account for Inter-Community Variations in the Quality of Life

in the quality of life. Rich communities are healthier, happier and better served than poor ones (Dorling, 1997). We therefore need to include adequate controls for the socio-economic composition of communities, not just social capital and suburban democracy. The remainder of this chapter takes up that investigation through an analysis of citizenship in Britain at the start of the twenty-first century. In particular, we are interested in variations in quality of life across communities: to what extent do they depend on the health of the local civic culture?

The chapter compares the ability of Putnam's social capital thesis and Oliver's (civic voluntarism-based) suburban democracy thesis to account for inter-community variations in the quality of life. In addition, it is possible that the quality of life measures are simply the product of affluence. On a variety of indicators, richer communities tend to fare better than poorer ones, so we also control for socio-economic status in order to investigate this possibility. It is also possible that social capital, socio-economic status and suburban democracy might all affect the quality of life directly. But they may also have indirect effects, through, for instance, their impacts on political participation and people's sense of civic duty. Our analytical strategy, shown schematically in figure 7.1, takes this into account by modelling the relationship between civic activity and quality of life in two stages. The first stage of the analysis, indicated by the arrow labelled I in the figure, looks at the influence of community civic activity, as measured by social capital, suburban democracy and socio-economic status on two measures of civic engagement: political participation and sense of civic obligations. The second stage, indicated by the arrows marked II, models variations in a number of quality of life indicators in terms of both civic activity and civic engagement across communities. In examining local quality of life indicators, we draw on a longstanding distinction in the literature on public services between *outputs*, or how much of a service is provided, and *outcomes*, or how well or how effective a service appears to be (Levy, Melttsner and Wildavsky, 1974). The amount spent per capita on a particular service such as education is a classic output measure. By contrast, examination results are classic outcome indicators. We further divide service outcomes into two categories: subjective and objective outcomes. The former reflect public perceptions of their quality of life: do they feel they receive a good deal? The latter are based on measurable outcomes of particular services or processes. While outputs and outcomes may be correlated in some instances, there is no necessary relationship between them: throwing money at a problem is not always the best way of solving it. Large outputs do not necessarily lead to good outcomes, especially if the level of output reflects inefficiencies in delivery.

Broadly, we expect that service *outputs* will be influenced mainly by socio-economic and demographic factors. For instance, spending on social services should correlate with local socio-economic status, since poorer communities are likely to make more demands on social services. It is less clear, for the reasons outlined above, that service outputs should be correlated with other measures of the health of local civic life. However, we expect that service *outcomes* should be influenced to some extent by the quality of local civic life. If active citizenship does have a positive impact on the quality of life locally, communities where civic life is rich should, *ceteris paribus*, receive more efficient, effective services than communities where people are relatively disengaged from civic life. Our quality of life measures include both subjective and objective indicators: while the former are based on local people's self-reported assessments of their quality of life, the latter draw on a range of independent measures of public service delivery and quality, local entrepreneurialism and public health. We start, in the next section, by examining inter-community variations in civic activity and civic engagement. What sorts of community are rich in civic resources, and which are poor?

Stage 1: measuring the geography of citizenship

Before we embark on the detail of that story, however, we need to say a little about our units of analysis. So far in the book, we have focused largely on individual members of the public, their views and their activities. In this chapter, however, we are interested in variations between communities rather than between individuals. The communities we concentrate on are local government areas. Local authorities provide many of the public services used by the British public on a day-to-day basis, including state education, social services, libraries and museums, parks and amenities, and environmental services. As such, they are important influences on people's local quality of life. However, different local authorities provide different mixes of services, depending on their place within the local government hierarchy. Following local government reform in the 1990s, the structure of British local government is now rather complicated, and this has implications for which authorities do what (Chisholm, 2000). Unitary authorities were established throughout Scotland and Wales, and in some parts of England, especially in the larger cities. These councils are responsible for the provision of all local government services within their areas. In other parts of England, a two-tier system was retained. Lower tier district authorities are responsible for services such as environmental health and housing, while larger, upper tier counties retain responsibility for services such as education.

As indicated in the introduction, we focus here on three explanatory models of civic activism: Putnam's social capital model, Oliver's suburban democracy model, and a community socio-economic status model. Key indicators have been derived from each model. Some indicators have been derived from official reports on local authority conditions, mainly from the 2001 Census. Others have been derived from the Citizen Audit. This was possible because of the way in which the Audit was designed. At the same time as the first wave of the face-to-face panel was conducted, a much larger mail survey was also carried out.

Both surveys[1] were conducted in the same 101 district and unitary local district and unitary authorities in late 2000 and early 2001. Taken together, they give us a sample of 12,182 individuals, around 120 selected at random in each of our 101 local authorities. This is considerably larger than the numbers interviewed in particular local authorities typically associated with most national sample surveys, and gives us a reasonable base from which to estimate inter-authority variations in a range of measures of citizenship. By aggregating information for all individuals within each local authority, therefore, we obtain an overall picture of community-level activity (Oliver, 2001).

Putnam's social capital model suggests we should investigate inter-authority variations in two factors: trust in fellow residents and

---

[1] The mail survey repeated many, though not all, of the questions in the face-to-face survey, albeit with a much larger sample size. For details of the questions asked, see appendix B.

Table 7.1 *The Structure of Variations in Social Capital across District Authorities*

	Trust in others	Associational activity
Average how helpful are others	0.95	
Average how fair are others	0.94	
Average trust in others	0.93	
Average number of groups member of		0.90
Average hours watching TV		−0.82
% in an informal network		0.70
—	—	—
Eigen value	2.90	1.79
% variance accounted for	48	30
Cronbach's alpha	0.94	0.74
N	101	

Citizen Audit 2000 face-to-face and mail survey, aggregated to district authorities: N = 101.

Note: This table shows the correlations between community characteristics obtained from the surveys and two underlying latent measures of Social Capital (varimax rotated factor loadings).

associational activity. These measures of community social capital are taken from the Citizen Audit. They are: the number of types of groups individuals had joined, had participated in or had carried out voluntary work for; percentage of respondents in informal networks; and scores on the 11-point scales measuring respondents' trust in others, and their assessments of how helpful and fair others are. Finally, we include time spent viewing television, since this plays a prominent role in Putnam's work in explaining the decline of social capital. Local authority averages were calculated for each of these six social capital measures.

A principal components analysis of the local authority average scores on the six, reported in table 7.1, suggests we need two distinct scales to capture the inter-authority variations in these aspects of social capital. The first scale is a summary measure of associational activity, based on local authority averages for the number of associational groups joined, time spent watching television (the less TV watching, the higher the social capital), and the percentage of local respondents in informal networks. The second scale is a trust scale, with average scores for trust in others, helpfulness of others and fairness of others loading heavily on the component.

On the basis of these component structures, a summary scale was created for associational activity by summing the local authority z-scores for each variable loading strongly on that dimension.

We employ z-scores[2] here as the original variables are measured on a variety of different scales. Z-scores allow us to standardise each scale into a common rubric. Because it loaded negatively on the component, the z-score for TV viewing was subtracted from, rather than added to, the associational activity scale: TV viewing detracts from social capital; it does not add to it. Both scales are extremely robust, with large scores on Cronbach's alpha.[3]

Levels of associational activity are furthest below average in East Ayrshire, with a score of −5.19, Derwentside (−4.87) and Liverpool (−4.48), and highest in Huntingdonshire (4.73), Rutland (5.16) and Harrogate (5.23). An analysis of variance test for regional variations in community-level associational activity reveals a statistically significant north–south divide.[4] As can be seen in figure 7.2, associational life is, on average, more active in the south and the English Midlands than in the north of Britain.

The social capital scale for trust in others is constructed from the sum of the z-scores for the three average trust scores which form the first component in the principal components analysis reported in table 7.1. Local authority average levels of trust in others are lowest in Great Yarmouth (−7.24), Fylde (−7.12) and Havering (−5.72), and highest in Cardiff (4.88), Harrogate (5.00) and Ryedale (5.67). Figure 7.3 shows the distribution of local authority average scores on the trust in others scale. The bars show the actual number of authorities at each level of trust, with low trust on the left of the graph and high trust on the right. And the smooth curve shows an idealised normal distribution. As can be seen, the basic pattern is near normal, but there is a slight skew. Trust in others is particularly low in a few local authorities. Average community scores on the trust in others scale do not vary regionally, however, so that an analysis of variance test for regional differences in community levels of trust in others was insignificant. While there were

[2] A z-score is a standardised measure of deviation from the overall average. It is calculated by first obtaining the overall mean and standard deviation for a variable. Each value can then be expressed as a z-score by obtaining the difference between it and the overall mean and dividing by the standard deviation. In other words, the z-score tells us how many standard deviates above or below the overall mean a particular value is. Negative z-scores indicate values below the overall mean, while positive z-scores indicate values above the mean. The further from 0 the z-score, the further from the overall average is the particular value we are interested in.

[3] Cronbach's alpha is a measure of the average correlation between each pair of items in a scale. It varies between 0 (where the items used to build the scale are not correlated at all with one another, and hence are not really suitable for inclusion in a common scale) and 1 (in which case the items making up the scale are perfectly correlated with each other). The closer Cronbach's alpha is to 1.0, the more robust and reliable the scale is.

[4] The analysis of variance produced an F-ratio of 3.12, and an associated p-value of 0.003.

Figure 7.2 Associational Activity: Regional Patterns

community-level variations in trust, therefore, this did not translate to the level of the region.[5]

The resources, both economic and social, on which a community can draw will be influenced by its socio-economic conditions. More affluent communities have access to a range of skills and capital which might not be so easily available in poorer communities. And as we have already seen in chapter 5, socio-economic factors play a part in several of the theories of civic participation analysed in this book. Education plays a part in the cognitive engagement and civic voluntarism models, for instance;

[5] The test produced an F-ratio of just 0.974, and a p-value of 0.467.

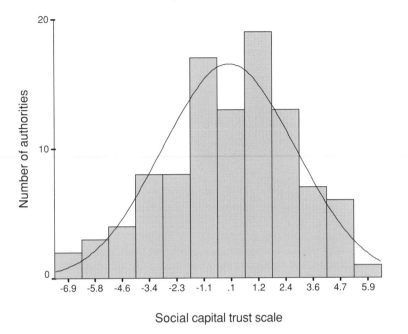

Social capital trust scale

Figure 7.3 The Distribution of Trust in Others across Communities

unemployment is a factor in the equity–fairness model; and occupational status is a factor in civic voluntarism. In part, therefore, variations in good citizenship across local authorities might be a function of variations in local social structure. Individual-level analyses of civic participation repeatedly show a correlation between personal affluence and education on the one hand and civic engagement on the other (Crewe, 1981; Parry, Moyser and Day, 1992; Brady, Verba and Schlozman, 1995; Verba, Schlozman and Brady, 1995; Franklin, 1996; Johnston, 1988; Johnston and Jowell 2001; Whiteley et al., 2001). For each local authority, therefore, we have 2001 Census data on two aspects of local socio-economic conditions, related to the participation theories: the percentage employed in middle-class jobs, and the percentage with a degree.

Though it was conducted some months after the Citizen Audit survey, the 2001 Census[6] is a good guide to Britain's social geography at the time

---

[6] The Census is conducted every ten years, and provides the most complete and accurate available snapshot of Britain's population. Every household in the country is issued with a Census form and completing it is a legal requirement. The Census provides a wealth of information on a wide range of demographic, social and economic factors, including: population counts; housing conditions; employment information; health; ethnic background; and family structures.

Table 7.2 *The Structure of Variations in Socio-Economic Status across District Authorities*

Principal components analysis	Varimax rotated loadings
	Socio-economic status
% middle class jobs, 2001 Census	0.97
% with degree, 2001 Census	0.87
% unemployed, November 2000	−0.68
—	—
Eigen value	2.16
% variance accounted for	72.02
Cronbach's alpha	0.80
N	101

2001 Census, local authority data.
Note: This table shows the correlations between community characteristics obtained from the Census and an underlying latent measure of socio-economic status (varimax rotated factor loadings).

of the survey: very little of real substance will have changed between 2000 and 2001. In addition, Benefits Agency figures give us information on the percentage of economically active adults in each authority on unemployment benefit in November 2000, roughly the time when the Audit survey began. A principal components analysis of these data, the results of which can be seen in table 7.2, reveals that there is one clear socio-economic component to the geography of our 101 local authorities. The component summarises the three original variables extremely well, accounting for 72 per cent of the original variation. The component is strongly and positively associated with the percentage of economically active adults in middle-class jobs and the percentage of degree holders, and is negatively related to the percentage unemployed in November 2000.

Because they are so highly inter-correlated as the principal components analysis reveals, to include all three of the original socio-economic measures in our analysis would create problems of multi-collinearity. We have therefore built a socio-economic status scale which captures their joint pattern, by adding each local authority's z-score for percentage middle-class and percentage with degrees, and subtracting the z-score for unemployment. Once again, the scale is very robust: Cronbach's alpha is 0.8. Areas with high positive scores on the scale are middle-class authorities with high proportions of graduates and low unemployment rates: South Buckinghamshire, Waverley, Guildford, Merton, Wandsworth and much gentrified Camden are among the most middle-class. By contrast, areas with large negative scores, headed by places like Kingston-upon-Hull,

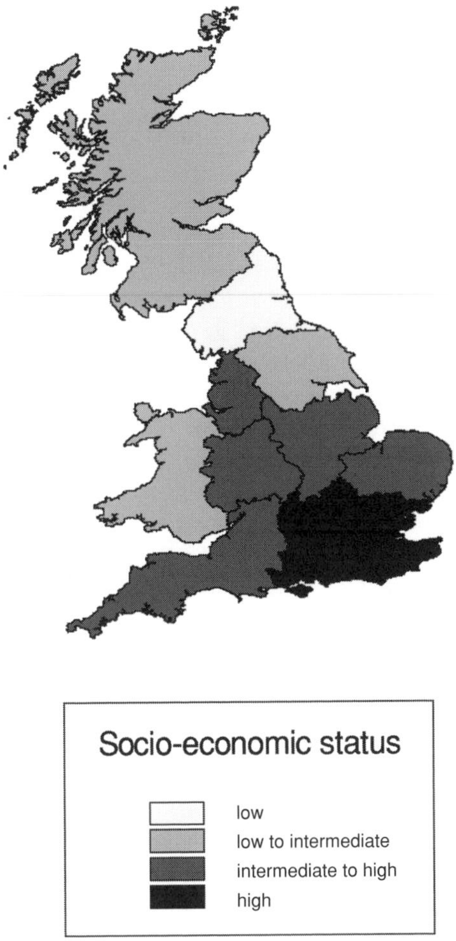

Figure 7.4 Socio-Economic Status: Regional Patterns

Great Yarmouth, East Ayrshire, Redcar and Cleveland, and Bolsover, have relatively few middle-class residents, few graduates, and high unemployment. Although there are pockets of affluence and poverty throughout the country, there is a well-documented and clear north–south divide in socio-economic status, as shown by figure 7.4.

The map is based on our 101 local authorities, averaging the socio-economic status score for each authority in each region.[7] It illustrates

---

[7] Not surprisingly, an analysis of variance test for regional differences in community socio-economic status proved highly significant: $F = 4.719$, $p = 0.000$.

that the well-known pattern of generally affluent communities in the south and especially south-east, and less affluent communities in the north, is still an important feature of British society at the start of the twenty-first century.

Finally, what of Oliver's (2001) study of suburban democracy? In his work, he points to the impact of three factors: population size; economic diversity; and ethnic diversity. To a large extent, economic diversity is already captured by our socio-economic status measure, discussed above. Local ethnic diversity is measured by the percentage of local people reporting a non-white ethnicity at the 2001 Census. The least ethnically diverse areas of the United Kingdom in 2001 were primarily relatively remote rural areas, such as Allerdale, Ryedale and Dumfries and Galloway: in all these areas, only just over 0.5 per cent of the local population claimed a non-white ethnicity in 2001. By contrast, the most ethnically diverse local authorities were in large major metropolitan authorities like Birmingham, where around 30 per cent of the population said they were not white, and in London, where over a third of the populations of Haringey, Hounslow, Waltham Forest and Harrow were from a non-white ethnic group (41 per cent in the case of Harrow). Finally, and following Oliver (2001, 2002), we include a measure reflecting local authority population and area: population density per hectare, calculated from the 2001 Census. This is a rough indicator of how urban an authority is, since population densities are lower in rural areas than in cities.

As indicated in figure 7.1, we are interested in how the above factors influence levels of community civic engagement, as measured by average levels of political activity and the sense of civic obligation. Firstly, we are interested in how political activity varied from place to place: are the residents of a community active citizens who engage in civic life, or not? Typically this has been assessed on the basis of electoral turnout (see Putnam, 2000). However, we are interested in a wider range of citizen involvement than just voting, so we use the Audit questions employed in chapters 5 and 6 asking respondents which of a wide range of civic activities they had taken part in over the previous twelve months. Our measure of political activity is based on how many of these activities each individual claimed to have taken part in, again averaged across each local authority. The average citizen in the average local authority claimed to have taken part in 3.64 different forms of civic engagement. The lowest average levels of political involvement were in Portsmouth, where the average person undertook 2.28 activities over the year, Derwentside (2.30 activities), Northampton (2.81) and Fylde (2.84). The most politically active communities, on average, were Brighton and

Hove (4.38 activities), the Isle of Wight (4.44), South Hams (4.46), Harrogate (4.93) and Wandsworth, where the average citizen claimed to have taken part in 5.19 different civic activities during the previous year. Regional variations in average levels of political activity were less dramatic than variations between individuals or between local authorities, but they were still (just) statistically significant.[8] Thus there is a clear geography to participation in Britain. As can be seen in figure 7.5, average levels of political activity are highest in the south of Britain and in Yorkshire and Humberside, and are lowest in the north of England. However, this is not a simple north–south pattern. Average activity levels are also relatively high in East Anglia, the north-west of England and in Scotland. But they are relatively low throughout the English Midlands and in Wales.

As we have argued in earlier chapters, however, political activity is only one aspect of citizenship. Of at least equal importance are people's attitudes to citizenship, their sense of civic rights, duties and obligations. Our second focus in this section, therefore, is on inter-community variations in those attitudes. Rights and obligations scales were developed for individual Citizen Audit respondents in chapter 5, and analysed in chapter 6. We cannot fully replicate them here for communities, as many of the relevant questions were not asked in the mail survey.[9] In particular, we are unable to reproduce a community-level version of the rights scales. However, we can look at community-level variations in the sense of civic obligation. Respondents to both the Citizen Audit face-to-face and mail surveys were asked whether they would be willing to carry out a range of civic activities: serving on a jury; renovating a local park or amenity; donating blood; providing a meals-on-wheels service; or joining a Neighbourhood Watch scheme. As discussed in chapter 5, these questions do not, of course, indicate actual levels of activity in any of the areas mentioned. Rather, they do tell us something about whether people see each activity as normatively expected of the good citizen. We have calculated from the Citizen Audit the percentage of respondents in each local authority saying they were willing to carry out each activity. A principal components analysis of these authority level percentages, reported in table 7.3, indicates that all five measures scale together well into one overarching sense of obligations. We have therefore calculated a civic obligations score for each authority by summing the authority's z-scores on each of the willingness measures: with a Cronbach's alpha of

[8] An analysis of variance test for regional variations in local authority average levels of political activity is just significant, with $F = 2.064$, and $p = 0.041$.

[9] Piloting showed the mail survey had to be significantly shorter than the face-to-face survey to gain an adequate response rate. This necessitated dropping a number of indicators.

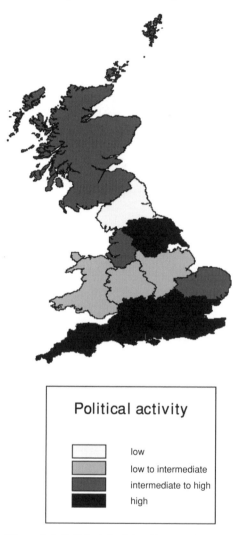

Figure 7.5 Political Activity: Regional Patterns

0.72, this is a robust scale. The civic obligation scale varies substantially from local authority to local authority. The most negative scores, indicating places where the average local sense of civic obligations is below the national average, are found in places as diverse as Cardiff, Wellingborough and Plymouth. The most positive scores, which pick out places where the sense of civic obligation is higher than the national average,

Table 7.3 *The Structure of Variations in Sense of*
Obligations across District Authorities

Principal components analysis	Varimax rotated loadings
% willing to:	Sense of obligations
Serve on jury	0.76
Renovate local park	0.76
Donate blood	0.71
Provide meals on wheels	0.70
Join Neighbourhood Watch	0.53
—	—
Eigen value	2.42
% variance accounted for	48.42
Cronbach's alpha	0.72
N	101

Citizen Audit 2000 face-to-face and mail survey, aggregated to district authorities: N = 101.
Note: This table shows the correlations between community character-istics obtained from the surveys and an underlying latent measure of obligations (varimax rotated factor loadings).

include authorities like Salford, Hertsmere and Rutland. As with trust in others, however, there are no significant inter-regional variations in the community-level sense of civic obligation.[10]

The above figures reveal substantial variations between local authorities in average levels of social capital, political participation and civic obliga-tion. However, within each authority there are also substantial variations between citizens in all of these things. Even in the authorities with the highest average levels of associational activity, for instance, some indi-viduals are almost entirely inactive. And in authorities with low average levels of activity, some people are very active indeed. This begs an impor-tant question. Are our 101 communities really distinct from each other in terms of citizen activity? If the variation in social capital, political par-ticipation or civic obligation is greater between individuals than between local authorities, then citizens in different authorities may be more alike than citizens in the same authority. On the other hand, if there are dis-tinct 'civic cultures' within each local authority, then individuals living there should be generally similar to other people in the same authority in their levels of civic participation, and should have different levels of citizen activity compared to residents of other authorities. To find out

[10] The relevant analysis of variance has an F-ratio of 0.95 and a p-value of 0.486.

Table 7.4 *Being an Active Citizen: Variations across Local Authorities*

	Authority-level descriptives				Individual-level analysis of variance		
	Mean	St. Dev	Min	Max	F	p	N
Social capital measures							
Associational life scale	*0.00*	*2.43*	*−5.19*	*5.23*			
N groups joined	2.36	0.45	1.42	3.59	3.43	0.00	101
TV watching	3.83	0.41	2.85	4.78	4.29	0.00	101
% in an informal network	26.84	5.30	14.20	40.50	1.64	0.00	101
Trust in others scale	*0.00*	*2.84*	*−7.24*	*5.67*			
How helpful are others	6.42	0.33	5.52	7.14	2.59	0.00	101
How fair are others	6.35	0.31	5.64	7.03	2.30	0.00	101
Trust in others	6.67	0.33	5.70	7.41	2.79	0.00	101
Civic obligation measures							
% willing to:							
Civic obligations scale	*0.00*	*3.46*	*−13.11*	*8.08*			
Serve on jury	69.65	4.99	55.40	80.20	1.35	0.01	101
Renovate local park	48.07	6.15	32.30	60.50	1.72	0.00	101
Donate blood	65.00	5.81	50.10	76.10	1.62	0.00	101
Provide meals on wheels	35.62	6.22	13.70	48.70	1.93	0.00	101
Join Neighbourhood Watch	63.05	5.58	44.00	77.20	2.15	0.00	101
N of political activities	3.64	0.51	2.28	5.19	3.68	0.00	101

Citizen Audit 2000 face-to-face and mail survey, aggregated to district authorities: N = 101.

Note: This table shows that there are significant differences in measures of social capital, obligations and political activities across the local authorities.

which is true, we conducted a series of analysis of variance (ANOVA) tests for each of the variables used to construct our scales of civic involvement. The ANOVA tests use the individual level survey data, and compare the variation on each measure within each local authority to the variation across all local authorities. The results, shown in table 7.4, are all significant, showing that there is a substantial degree of homogeneity within each local authority, and considerable heterogeneity between authorities. In other words, people living in the same place exhibit roughly similar levels of citizenship and trust. But individuals living in different places are likely to differ from each other. There are inter-authority variations on all these dimensions – some contain more trusting residents, and some do not. People in one authority might be active in civic life, while in another they are quiescent.

But what is it about each authority that might account for these variations in good citizenship? We start by evaluating the stage I models outlined in figure 7.1. To what extent do variations in social capital, socio-economic status, ethnicity and population density account for variations in levels of political activity or sense of civic obligations across local authorities? Several writers, including Putnam and Oliver, suggest that a healthy civic life also encourages participation in conventional politics. It is argued that communities where people tend to be active citizens are also areas where people take part in elections. Given recent concerns about falling turnout in Western societies, it is worth investigating not only the relationship between local civic life and political activity in the wide sense analysed throughout this book, but also in the narrower sense of whether there is a link between local civic life and local electoral participation. To do so, we analyse turnout in district council elections in the 1999 and 2000 local elections, as these were the competitions nearest in time to the conduct of the Citizen Audit.[11] Given the cycle of local authority elections, most, though not all, of our 101 local authorities had a local election in one or other of these years. Twelve authorities, mainly in London, were on a different electoral cycle, and did not hold local elections in either year, and for this reason they are excluded from the analysis.

The regression analyses reported in table 7.5 suggest both social capital and the suburban democracy model help to account for the variations across authorities. The regression equations on the whole fit the data only moderately well, accounting for between 15 per cent and 32 per cent of the variance in the dependent variables. The average number of political activities, defined in the wide sense, carried out by the citizens of each local authority is positively related to one aspect of social capital: associational activity. The more groups local individuals joined, other things being equal, the more political activities they undertook. From the

[11] The local election turnout data were kindly supplied by Professor Michael Thrasher of the Local Government Chronicle Elections Centre, University of Plymouth.

Table 7.5 *Modelling Variations in Political Activism across District Authorities*

	Average number of political activities	% Turnout in local government elections	Sense of civic obligations
Constant	3.58	40.88	0.39
Socio-economic status	0.02	0.84	−0.08
Putnam model			
Associational activity	0.11***	−1.78***	0.63***
Average trust in others	0.01	0.80**	−0.08
Oliver model			
Population density per ha, 2001	0.01***	−0.45***	−0.02
% non white, 2001	−0.01	0.09	−0.01
—	—	—	—
R^2	0.32	0.31	0.15
N	101[1]	89[2]	101[1]

1. All unitary and district authorities.
2. Authorities holding local elections in 1999 or 2000.
Citizen Audit 2000 face-to-face and mail survey, aggregated to district authorities: N = 101.
Note: The table contains the unstandardised regression coefficients obtained from regressing the row variables on the column variables. Asterisks indicate the statistical significance of the coefficients with $p < 0.10^*$; $p < 0.05^{**}$; $p < 0.01^{***}$.

Oliver model, population density was also positively associated with the average number of political activities undertaken: the more urban the local authority (that is, the higher its population density), the more politically active were its citizens.

The same factors also played a part in the model for political activity narrowly conceived as local election turnout, though interestingly the signs were reversed. Turnout is in general lower in urban than in rural and suburban authorities, as shown by the significant, negative coefficient for population density. But it is also affected by local variations in social capital. Particularly worthy of note is the significant and negative coefficient for associational social capital. The greater the local level of associational activity, therefore, the lower the level of participation in local elections, other things being equal. This is clearly very different from the pattern we would expect from Putnam's social capital model. More in keeping with the theoretical expectations of the social capital model, the relationship between trust in others and turnout is significant and positive. Communities where individuals trust their fellows are also communities in which people are more likely to show up to vote in local elections. The community-wide level of trust in others boosts electoral participation, therefore. But richer associational social capital actually discourages it – perhaps by providing alternative channels for achieving goals. On closer investigation, the apparently anomalous relationship between associational social capital and turnout can be explained in part by the structure of our model. Associational social capital is itself positively related to community socio-economic status (affluent communities have more active residents) and negatively related to population density (rural communities are more active than urban). If socio-economic status and population density are excluded in the relevant model, associational social capital is not related to turnout. It only becomes significant – and negative – when they are included. In other words, the negative relationship between associational social capital and turnout is in part a consequence of controlling for socio-economic status and population density. The difference between the models for political activity in the wide sense, and for participation in the narrow sense of electoral participation, is striking. The two measures are not correlated with each other, suggesting that they are tapping into rather different repertoires of political activity, one formal, the other in large part informal. Social capital appears to inhibit the former and stimulate the latter, a strikingly different finding from Putnam's analysis for the United States.

Finally, social capital provides the best account of the three models analysed here for variations across authorities in the sense of civic obligations, though the model accounts for only 15 per cent of the variance. Again, it is associational activity which matters, and as with political activity broadly defined, the relationship is in the theoretically expected positive direction. The more associational activity there is in a local authority, the greater the sense of civic obligation among its citizens.

The effects of citizenship: service outputs

Turning next to the second link in figure 7.1, does good citizenship have an impact on the quality of public life? One way of finding out is to look at local government performance indicators. If Putnam's claims are correct, for instance, local authorities with abundant social capital should, other things being equal, have better public services than local authorities where social capital is weak. We have therefore compiled a database of performance indicators for English and Welsh local authorities, mainly for the year 1999/2000. Data were drawn, for the most part, from Audit Commission reports: comparable data for Scottish local authorities were not available, and they have been omitted from most analyses.[12] In addition,

---

[12] The Audit Commission is an independent public body charged with ensuring public funds are used efficiently and effectively. As part of that remit, it monitors local government performance in England and Wales, publishing regular reports on all councils.

we have also investigated information on local business activity, public health, and satisfaction with local services. All give insights into how well – or badly – particular communities perform. That said, we would not necessarily expect every measure of local service provision to be equally responsive to the quality of local civic life. Some things can be changed by concerted citizen activity and some probably cannot. Questions of the quantity of provision – for instance, how much is spent on a service – are not totally amenable to citizen influence. The level of service provided by an authority is in large part a function of the sort of place it serves, rather than a function of whether its residents are good or bad citizens. Secondly, British local authorities work in a tightly constrained environment. Their funding is to a large extent controlled by central government, which provides core funding and can limit the extra funding which can be raised by local taxation: central government funding of local councils follows a 'needs' formula which reflects both the size and affluence of the authority. Not only that, but councils' activities are circumscribed by *ultra vires* considerations: in other words, they are not able to stray far from their legally defined functions. Both are powerful constraints on local authorities' ability to exercise discretion in the amount of resources dedicated to particular services, or to services in general. In any case, as we suggested earlier, the absolute level of service delivery alone may not tell us whether a community is served well or badly. A council can spend a great deal on a service because it is excellent and state-of-the-art. But equally, high spending might reflect considerable inefficiency and waste. While the former is desirable, the latter clearly is not.

In this section, we begin the investigation by concentrating on a range of service output measures – how much does each community receive? In later sections we go on to examine variations in service outcomes – how effective are local services?

We look first at three output indicators for services provided by English and Welsh local authorities. For the eighty-nine English and Welsh unitary and district authorities covered by the Citizen Audit, we look at total local government expenditure per capita in 1999/2000. For the sixty-six unitary and county authorities included in the Audit, we also look at expenditure per pupil on secondary education, and at spending per capita on social services. Education and social services are the two largest-spending areas in English and Welsh local government, and dominate the budgets of the authorities charged with providing them. Both services are provided only by the unitary or the county authorities in England and Wales. We regress each performance indicator against our measures of inter-local authority variations in: average number of political actions; average sense of civic obligations; local socio-economic status; social capital (the Putnam model); and population density and ethnicity (the Oliver model).

Our measures of civic-mindedness may have an impact upon service outputs, though as we argued earlier, there are grounds for doubting this. But local authority performance depends on a range of other factors over and above our citizenship measures. A voluminous literature points to the importance of considerations such as local social structure, whether the authority is urban or rural, and so on (Sharpe and Newton, 1984; Boyne, 1984; Pinch, 1985; Hoggart, 1991). In general, poorer authorities have higher levels of need for a range of local authority services than do more affluent authorities. And the costs of, for example, street cleaning and environmental health are likely to be greater in a large metropolis than in a small rural council. We would therefore expect clear relationships between outputs and local socio-demographic conditions: local population density, percentage non-white, and the socio-economic status index. The results of the regression models are shown in table 7.6.[13]

All three models provide good explanations of their respective output measures, with explained variance (R^2) values ranging from 65 to 84 per cent. Not surprisingly, socio-demographic factors have an influence on local spending. Population density is positively related to per capita spending in all three areas. The denser its local population, the more the authority spends overall per capita, and the more it spends on secondary education and social services. Cities are expensive places to live. Compared to rural areas, they have extensive road networks needing cleaning, large numbers of food retailers to be checked by environmental health officers, and a wider range of demands on local resources. Schools tend to be larger. Demands on local social services departments tend to be greater. Indeed, in some cases, services provided by urban authorities serve not only their own populations, but may also provide amenities for residents living in other areas who might travel to the city to make use of particular facilities. Thus, urban parks, municipal museums and central public libraries can all be used by non-residents. The daily commuter flows into and out of major cities, and the wear and tear this entails for urban transport networks all impose extra costs. Total per capita council spending and spending on social services are also negatively related to local socio-economic status. Per pupil expenditure on secondary schools, meanwhile, is positively related to the proportion of the local population reporting a non-white ethnicity in the 2001 Census. Other things being equal, councils serving affluent areas spend less per capita on all services,

---

[13] We have conducted similar analyses for a wide range of local output measures, not reported here: the results are broadly similar.

Table 7.6 *Modelling Variations in Objective Outputs across District Authorities, 1999–2000*

	Total spending per capita	Spending per pupil on secondary schools	Spending per head on social services
Constant	253.21	2521.42	130.68
Average number of political actions	−31.83	−43.30	5.58
Sense of obligations	25.74***	10.84	0.81
Socio-economic status	−57.99***	−4.75	−5.86***
Putnam model			
Associational activity	−7.27	0.05	1.37
Average trust in others	20.25	−1.00	−2.03
Oliver model			
Population density per ha, 2001	15.63***	5.71***	3.17***
% non white, 2001	5.80	7.53***	−0.63
	—	—	—
R^2	0.69	0.65	0.84
N	89+	63++	66++

+ English and Welsh district authorities.
++ English and Welsh county authorities.
Citizen Audit 2000 face-to-face and mail survey, aggregated to district authorities, the Audit Commission, and the 2001 Census: N = 101.
Note: The table contains the unstandardised regression coefficients obtained from regressing the row variables on the column variables. Asterisks indicate the statistical significance of the coefficients with $p < 0.10$*; $p < 0.05$**; $p < 0.01$***.

and less on social services, than do councils serving poorer communities. Social need is an important driver of demand for a range of public services. Thus Oliver's 'suburban democracy' model provides a generally good account of variations in service outputs across local authorities.

In general, however, once these socio-demographic factors are taken into account, little else proves to be a significant influence on the output measures. As we expected, social capital has no direct influence in any of the service output equations: none of the social capital indicators is significant. The only non-socio-demographic factor to have any influence is variations in the sense of civic obligations, which is significant and positively signed in the equation for total per capita local government expenditure in district and unitary authorities. High levels of civic obligation go with high levels of spending, other things being equal. This does imply at least an indirect influence for social capital, since as table 7.5 shows, variations in associational activity are positively related to the sense of civic obligation. That said, social capital does not have much bearing on these output measures. Given the tight constraints within which British local authorities operate, it is, perhaps, hardly surprising that output measures seem to be dominated by socio-economic considerations, with little scope left for local social capital to have an influence.

The effects of citizenship: service outcomes

Thus far, therefore, it seems as though the health of local social capital in English and Welsh local authorities has only a limited impact on the performance of their local authorities, after controlling for other possible determinants of public service provision. But as discussed above, there is a real question as to how one should interpret high levels of public spending. Does spending a large amount per capita indicate a generous, well-provided service? Or does high per capita spending suggest profligate and poorly administered services? Service *outputs* (the quantity of provision) are not necessarily the best indicators of service *outcomes* (the quality and effects of provision). In this section, therefore, we look at measures of service outcomes rather than service outputs.

We begin by looking at subjective outcome measures. How satisfied or dissatisfied are local people with their quality of life? We assess community levels of satisfaction using data from the Citizen Audit. All respondents were asked how satisfied they were with: schools; services for the elderly; street cleaning in their area; social services; parks; libraries; and the state of local roads. Responses were coded on an 11-point scale, with total dissatisfaction coded as 0 and total satisfaction coded as 10. We have derived aggregate measures of satisfaction in each of our areas by taking the local authority average for each measure of satisfaction. Because these variables are based on Audit data, it is possible to estimate averages for all 101 Scottish, English and Welsh unitary and district authorities included in the survey. A principal components analysis of these scales, reported in table 7.7, shows that they form two distinct dimensions. The first, loading strongly and positively on average rates of satisfaction with schools, services for the elderly and social services, clearly reflects levels of satisfaction with public services. The second, loading positively on satisfaction with street cleaning, local parks, the condition of local roads and libraries, reflects levels of satisfaction with the local environment. We have therefore created summary scales for satisfaction with both public services and the local environment by summing local authority average scores on the relevant variables. In the analyses which follow, however, we will focus on the 'satisfaction with services' scale which reflects judgements of local schools, social services, and services for the elderly. In

Table 7.7 *Constructing Local Satisfaction Scales: Principal Components Analysis across Authorities*

	Services	Environment
Satisfied with schools	0.90	
Satisfied with services for elderly	0.90	
Satisfied with social services	0.75	
Satisfied with street cleaning		0.80
Satisfied with parks		0.74
Satisfied with state of roads		0.74
Satisfied with libraries		0.53
—	—	—
Eigen value	2.89	1.66
% variance accounted for	41.27	23.70
Cronbach's alpha	0.82	0.69
N	101	101

Citizen Audit 2000 face-to-face and mail survey, aggregated to district authorities: N = 101.

Note: This table shows the correlations between satisfaction scores for different services obtained from the surveys and two underlying latent measures of policy satisfaction (varimax rotated factor loadings).

addition, we also examine people's satisfaction with democracy and with life in general. Both are based on similar 11-point Citizen Audit questions, and we have calculated average local authority scores on each for all 101 district and unitary authorities covered by the Audit.

As can be seen from table 7.8, satisfaction levels varied substantially from one local authority to another. For instance, while only around 19 per cent of respondents in Islington were satisfied with their schools, over two-thirds were satisfied in Allerdale. These inter-authority variations were substantial in most cases, and for all bar one satisfaction measure, they were larger than the equivalent variations between individuals. Analysis of variance tests were conducted to investigate whether there were inter-authority variations in satisfaction at the level of individual respondents. With the exception of satisfaction with democracy, all the tests proved significant, suggesting that people were more likely to share the views of others living in the same authority than they were to agree with people living in different authorities. The sole exception, satisfaction with democracy, is telling. While most of the issues addressed by the satisfaction questions were at least in part influenced either by local government or by community conditions, satisfaction with democracy is more systemic in its origins, stemming from evaluations of Britain's political system as a whole. It is, therefore, perhaps unsurprising that

Table 7.8 *Variations across Authorities in Satisfaction Scales*

	Authority-level descriptives				Individual-level analysis of variance		
	Mean	St. Dev	Min	Max	F	p	N
% Satisfied with:							
Service satisfaction scale	*98.23*	*19.19*	*50.24*	*156.97*			
Schools	45.43	9.23	19.42	68.58	3.22	0.00	101
Services for elderly	28.67	7.07	8.52	50.41	2.77	0.00	101
Social services	24.13	5.66	9.62	38.11	2.22	0.00	101
Environment satisfaction scale	*172.39*	*24.34*	*91.94*	*232.87*			
Street cleaning	40.23	9.01	12.88	62.92	4.99	0.00	101
Parks	44.28	9.36	21.66	76.90	3.85	0.00	101
State of roads	22.67	7.23	6.62	43.29	5.57	0.00	101
Libraries	65.21	7.95	41.02	80.99	3.45	0.00	101
Democracy	27.59	4.57	13.76	38.37	1.12	0.15	101
Life	68.04	5.64	52.59	82.84	1.72	0.00	101

Citizen Audit 2000 face-to-face and mail survey, aggregated to district authorities: N = 101.

Note: This table shows that there are significant differences in satisfaction scores across the local authorities.

individuals in different local authorities tend to agree with each other on this issue.

How does local civic life influence aggregate levels of satisfaction within communities? To find out, in table 7.9 we regress our measures of satisfaction with services, democracy and life in general on our local authority measures of political activity, civic obligations, socio-economic status, social capital, population density and ethnicity. The equation for inter-authority differences in satisfaction with local services is reasonably well predicted: we are able to account for 43 per cent of the variance in this variable. However, it is much harder to predict inter-authority variations in satisfaction with democracy or life: only around 15 per cent of the variance is accounted for by these equations. At the beginning of the chapter, we argued that social capital should have a clearer effect on local outcomes than on local output. And that is certainly the case with these subjective outcome measures. A social capital variable is significant in all three equations. That said, the direction of the relationship is not always as expected by theory. The social capital literature would lead us

Table 7.9 *Modelling Variations in Satisfaction with Services across District Authorities*

	Satisfaction with		
	Services	Democracy	Life
Constant	98.12	26.85	67.10
Average number of political actions	1.39	−0.09	0.55
Sense of obligations	0.69	0.23	−0.01
Socio-economic status	−2.01*	0.43	0.22
Putnam model			
Associational activity	−2.70**	−0.27	−0.18
Average trust in others	1.04	0.48***	0.64***
Oliver model			
Population density per ha, 2001	−0.43***	−0.01	−0.06
% non white, 2001	0.24	0.19**	−0.03
—	—	—	—
R^2	0.43	0.15	0.17
N	101	101	101

Citizen Audit 2000 face-to-face and mail survey, aggregated to district authorities; and the 2001 Census: N = 101.
Note: The table contains the unstandardised regression coefficients obtained from regressing the row variables on the column variables. Asterisks indicate the statistical significance of the coefficients with $p < 0.10^*$; $p < 0.05^{**}$; $p < 0.01^{***}$.

to expect that encouraging trust in others is beneficial for a community, but this does not seem to be the case. The greater the average level of trust in others in a community, other things being equal, the more satisfied its residents are on the whole with democracy and with life in general. And trust in others is positively related to satisfaction with services, though the coefficient narrowly misses standard levels of statistical significance.[14] Satisfaction with services is affected by local social capital, at least in the form of associational activity. Intriguingly, however, the relationship runs counter to Putnam's claim that communities rich in social capital should also be communities in which local government should be effective. Putnam's argument would lead us to expect a positive relationship between community levels of social capital, as measured by associational activity, and satisfaction with local services. In fact, the relationship, while significant, is negative. If anything, communities with high levels of associational activity are *less* satisfied with local services than are communities where citizens are less active. Why? In part, we suspect the answer has

[14] p = 0.085.

to do with the roots of citizen mobilisation. As the results on small-scale democracy reported in chapter 4 indicate, individuals often become active in an attempt to improve an unsatisfactory state of affairs (see table 4.1). It may be the case, therefore, that causation runs from levels of satisfaction to engagement and not vice versa. It is possible, though difficult, to model two-way causal links with this type of cross-sectional survey data, but we postpone that issue until chapter 8, where such links can be examined much more effectively using panel data.[15] In fact the logic of the small-scale democracy analyses implies that greater dissatisfaction should be a goad to activism. People get involved when there is something they dislike and wish to change.

Oliver's suburban democracy model fares less well in accounting for inter-authority variations in public satisfaction than it did when applied to variations in output measures, though it does still have some bearing. Satisfaction with services is lower in densely populated urban areas than in less densely populated ones. Urban communities are relatively dissatisfied with their services. It is also negatively related to community affluence, as measured by the socio-economic status scale: dissatisfaction is higher in rich than in poor areas, other things being equal. And aggregate levels of satisfaction with democracy are higher the more ethnically diverse is the local community.

Two objections can be raised against the use of average levels of satisfaction with various public goods, however. First, the satisfaction scores measure public perceptions rather than concrete outcomes. In itself, this is not a major objection: after all, satisfaction with a service is an important measure of its success. The second objection is more important, however. Since the satisfaction measures and the measures of community social capital are all derived from the Citizen Audit, the former are not entirely independent of the latter.

To deal with the second objection, we need variables of local outcomes which are not derived from Audit data. Tables 7.10 and 7.11 therefore look at five very different objective outcome measures. Our first measure looks at local tax collection. The property-based council tax is the main discretionary source of income for local government but it can be difficult to collect. The Audit Commission collects data from each English

---

[15] Such two-way causation can only be satisfactorily modelled in cross-sectional data if there are instruments which can be used to stand in for the variables under consideration. However, this estimation strategy, involving non-recursive modelling, is only viable if the instruments are quite good measures of the variables, which really means that the model has a high fit to begin with. In the absence of such a fit, the instruments will be a poor guide to effects, making this strategy questionable. For a full discussion of this issue see Greene, 2003: 74–83.

Table 7.10 *Modelling Variations in Objective Outcomes across Local Authorities I (1999–2001)*

	Tax efficiency	Entrepreneurial activity	Complaints about services
Constant	99.03	2.48	−0.03
Average number of political actions	−0.48	0.29	0.02
Sense of obligations	−0.02	−0.06	0.00
Socio-economic status	0.38***	0.45***	−0.02**
Putnam model			
Associational activity	0.09	−0.03	0.02
Average trust in others	0.09	0.01	0.00
Oliver model			
Population density per ha, 2001	−0.07***	0.02**	−0.01
% non white, 2001	−0.05	0.0	0.0
R^2	0.68	0.63	0.71
N	89[1]	101	66[1]

[1] English and Welsh district and unitary authorities only.
Citizen Audit 2000 face-to-face and mail survey, aggregated to district authorities, Audit Commission, and the 2001 Census. N = 101.
Tax efficiency: % of council tax collected.
Entrepreneurial activity: new VAT registrations per 1000.
Complaints about services: complaints determined by ombudsman per 1000.
Note: The table contains the unstandardised regression coefficients obtained from regressing the row variables on the column variables. Asterisks indicate the statistical significance of the coefficients with $p < 0.10$*; $p < 0.05$**; $p < 0.01$***.

and Welsh local authority on the proportion of each year's council tax the council has been able to collect during the year: we look here at collection rates in the 1999/2000 financial year. This tax efficiency measure therefore provides an indicator both of the civic-mindedness of local people (do they pay their taxes?) and of the relative efficiency of their local authority (can it collect its taxes promptly?). Good citizens, we expect, do not free-ride on the public purse and hence pay their taxes on time. As we might expect, local tax receipts are strongly related to local socio-economic conditions: the more affluent the authority's population, the greater the proportion of its tax income it is able to collect in a year. Population density also has an influence: the significant negative coefficient indicates that urban authorities were less successful at collecting their taxes, other things being equal, than were suburban and rural authorities. Both community affluence and population density are related to Oliver's

Table 7.11 *Modelling Variations in Objective Outcomes across Local Authorities II (1999–2001)*

	Educational outcomes	Health outcomes
Constant	30.56	10.14
Average number of political actions	6.03***	0.67
Sense of obligations	−0.48**	−0.02
Socio-economic status	1.58***	−0.88***
Putnam model		
Associational activity	−0.34	−0.29***
Average trust in others	0.00	−0.04
Oliver model		
Population density per ha, 2001	−0.33***	0.04***
% non white, 2001	−0.01	−0.06
R^2	0.68	0.72
N	66[1]	101

[1] English and Welsh county and unitary authorities.
Citizen Audit 2000 face-to-face and mail survey, aggregated to district authorities; Audit Commission; 2001 Census: N = 101.
Educational outcomes: % 15-year-olds with A–C GCSEs.
Health outcomes: % with long-term illness.
Note: The table contains the unstandardised regression coefficients obtained from regressing the row variables on the column variables. Asterisks indicate the statistical significance of the coefficients with $p < 0.10^*$; $p < 0.05^{**}$; $p < 0.01^{***}$.

suburban democracy model. However, community levels of social capital do not affect the local authorities' tax-raising powers, either directly or indirectly through local variations in political activity or sense of civic obligations.

Our analyses thus far have concentrated largely on public sector outputs and outcomes. However, Putnam's arguments regarding the beneficial effects of social capital extend beyond the public sector to take in the private sector too. Communities rich in social capital, he argues, not only enjoy effective local government, they also have vibrant local economies. Our second objective outcome measure therefore employs government value added tax (VAT) registration records to provide measures of the vibrancy of local economies. New firms are under a legal obligation to register for VAT. Aggregate data are available for all British local authorities on the number of new VAT registrations each year and on the total number of registrations. We have employed these data to provide measures of local entrepreneurialism. VAT registrations per 1000 resident adults in each local authority have been used to standardise for inter-authority variations in population. Other things being equal, more populous local authorities should have higher rates of new firm start-ups than less populous areas, just because of the larger pool of potential entrepreneurs in the former as opposed to the latter areas. Standardising per 1000 population takes this into account.

The geography of new firm start-ups, as indicated by the VAT registration data, is similar to that of council tax collection discussed above. Socio-economic status is clearly related to entrepreneurial activity. The more affluent the area, the more firms are founded there. Population density is also important here, though it does not work in the same direction as for council tax collection. Entrepreneurialism is more likely in an urban than in a rural setting, other things being equal: the higher the local authority population density, the more new firm start-ups there are per 1000 residents. However, as with the geography of council tax receipts, social capital has neither a direct nor an indirect effect on entrepreneurial activity. None of the other civic activity measures is significant once we take local social conditions into account. Local entrepreneurialism seems to be a function of local economic resources, rather than of local civic activity.

We looked earlier at how satisfied local people were with their services, a subjective outcome measure. But there are objective corollaries of this, which allow us to assess the extent to which either satisfaction or dissatisfaction becomes a spur to action. One such measure is whether members of the public are moved to object to the actions of their local authority. In England and Wales, serious complaints against local authority decisions can be referred to the local government ombudsman, a figure who adjudicates between public and authorities in situations where normal channels of communication have not provided adequate redress. Complaints to the ombudsman, therefore, provide a rough measure of general public satisfaction with a local authority's decisions. The more satisfied members of the public are with their council, the less often they should contact the ombudsman. Our measure of contact with the ombudsman is available for English and Welsh unitary and county authorities, and measures the total number of complaints to the ombudsman in 1999/2000 per 1000 population. The relevant model in table 7.10 shows that complaints to the ombudsman are more frequent in more urban than in more rural local authorities (the population density measure is significant and positive). They are also negatively related to local socio-economic conditions: the more affluent the local authority, the fewer complaints its residents make to the ombudsman. However, once again, social capital has no significant impact, direct or indirect, on this outcome measure.

Another important area for which we have useful local authority outcome measures is education. As noted above, education is the largest area of local authority spending for English and Welsh unitary and county councils and it is a policy area that generates considerable public concern. Exam results, perhaps the most charged aspects of education, provide a prime outcome measure. Schools and local education authorities (LEAs) with good reputations are in high demand and parents will often pay heavily inflated prices to buy homes within the catchment areas of the 'best' schools, that is, those with the best exam results. Schools and LEAs seen as 'failing', with poor exam results, are relatively shunned. There is considerable debate around 'value added' in education (Gray, Jesson and Jones, 1984; Gray, Jesson and Sime, 1990; Goldstein, 2001; Yang et al., 2002). A school or LEA with an affluent, middle-class intake may produce better results in total than a school or LEA with a less affluent, more working-class pupil base. But in part this only reflects the different starting positions of pupils as they embark on education: once social background is controlled for, the apparent variation between service providers and exam results may be reversed. It may, in fact, be the school with the less affluent intake which does most to improve its pupils' exam performance. Even so, exam results provide a rough and ready indicator of LEA education outcomes, particularly when we control for local social structure.

Our measure of exam performance is the percentage of 15–16-year-olds in each of the sixty-six English and Welsh LEAs covered by the Citizen Audit who obtained an A–C grade pass at GCSE in the 2000/01 school year.[16] The GCSE is the main school examination for this age group and is attempted by most pupils. An A, B or C pass at GCSE is generally considered a good result. As can be seen in table 7.11, the story is straightforward. Examination results tend to be better in more affluent areas than in poorer ones. They also tend to be better, other things being equal, in rural and suburban than in urban areas, as indicated by the coefficients for population density. Again, these are measures most associated with Oliver's suburban democracy model. The social capital variables do not have a direct impact upon exam performance. But, *pace* the value-added debate discussed above, they do have indirect effects, through inter-authority variations in political activity and the sense of civic obligations measure, both of which are significantly related to variations in exam performance. The more politically active local people are, the better children living in their LEA tend to do in school examinations – even after we control for local social structure and population. But,

---

[16] We have also examined average exam results for a series of other national examinations: GCSEs in 1999/2000; Key Stage 3 (KS 3) exams, which are taken in secondary school at age 14; and A-levels, taken at age 18. The results are generally very similar to those reported in table 7.10.

intriguingly, the greater the local sense of civic obligations, other things being equal, the lower the percentage of 15–16-year-olds gaining good GCSE passes.

Of course, the positive relationship between local levels of political engagement and local average exam performance may reflect a degree of citizen activism. It is likely, for instance, that areas with civic-minded residents will also be areas where parents both help their own children to study at home, and at the same time help local schools, whether by volunteering as classroom assistants or helping with school fundraising activities, or in a variety of other ways.

Finally, what of the effects of local civic culture on other aspects of local life? In his analysis of social capital in the United States, Putnam (2000: ch. 20) demonstrates that the higher the state level of social capital, the healthier are the state's residents. We investigate this at the level of British district councils using data available from the 2001 Census on population health. The data are derived from self-report questions in the Census survey itself, and so do not give us clinical judgements of health and well-being. But they do indicate how local people feel about their own health, and they do correlate, broadly, with the geography of actual ill health. The Census recorded, for each local authority, the percentages of residents self-reporting a long-term illness which limited their ability to work. The model is reported in table 7.10. There is now a very large literature indeed showing that general levels of health and illness in communities are a function of local socio-economic conditions. People living in affluent communities tend to be much healthier, on the whole, than those in poor areas (e.g. Dorling, 1997; Dorling and Shaw, 2001). Not surprisingly, therefore, the socio-demographic variables have a strong influence. As we would expect, given the existing literature on the geography of health and illness, the more affluent an area, the healthier people living there tend to be, with lower numbers reporting a long-term debilitating illness. Residents of communities with high population densities tend to suffer poorer health than those living in areas with lower densities. But even when the socio-demographic controls are taken into account, the better a community scores on the associational activity scale, the lower is the percentage of local people reporting a long-term debilitating illness. Thus social capital appears to have a positive impact on health in Britain.

Conclusions

It does seem that 'good citizenship' can have a community-wide payoff. Levels of service outputs are not particularly influenced by levels of citizenship in communities, once we control for other relevant factors. But this is partly due to the fact that British local authorities are actually quite constrained in terms of what they can do, compared with their continental and American counterparts. Much of their service provision is subject to needs-based or nationally defined targets, and their main income sources are increasingly under the direct and indirect control of central government. In addition, they operate within a constraining *ultra vires* culture which tends to limit their freedom for manoeuvre. Local variations in cultures of citizenship do exist, but they seem to have little purchase on this constrained world of local government service outputs. By and large, it is Oliver's suburban democracy model which provides the greatest purchase on geographies of public service outputs, and social capital does not have much of an influence.

But it is a different story when we consider levels of some service outcomes. Where we can measure the quality as opposed to the quantity of local service provision and quality of life we find that they are affected – in generally positive ways – by local cultures of citizenship. As Putnam (1993) suggested, areas where 'good citizenship' prevails do get a better quality of service than do areas where good citizenship is in short supply. Both the social capital and the suburban democracy models help us to understand why some places are better communities to live in than others. This is especially true when we look at factors such as education performance, illness and satisfaction with life and with democracy. What is striking here is that these are all issues where individuals can make a difference to outcomes. And, in general, the more active local people are in politics and in associational life, the more trusting they feel, and the more affluent they are, the better their lives are. Being good citizens may not influence the *quantity* of community life, therefore. But it does have a generally positive bearing on the *quality* of life.

As this chapter has shown, therefore, citizenship matters. Making better citizens can improve the quality of life. The implication is that improving civic skills and resources will also improve life chances. But how can good citizenship be encouraged? Which factors increase people's civic engagement, and which discourage it? We turn to these questions in the next chapter.

8 The Dynamics of Citizenship

As we have seen in earlier chapters, a frequent claim in recent academic and popular discussions of civic life in Western democracies has been that public involvement in politics is on the decline and democracy is in crisis (Norris, 1999; Pharr and Putnam, 1999). But the evidence for such claims is sometimes weak, not least because the relative absence of time-series data makes it difficult to generalise accurately about trends in many aspects of civic engagement. Nevertheless, where we can measure change over time, indicators are not always encouraging (Norris, 2002). For instance, United Kingdom general election turnout data reveal a trendless fluctuation in the thirteen post-war elections between 1945 and 1992, but then in the most recent two a significant decline (Pattie and Johnston, 2001a; Clarke et al., 2004). In addition, there is evidence of declining participation in political parties (Seyd and Whiteley, 2002a; Whiteley and Seyd, 2002), and declining trust in political leaders and institutions (Bromley, Curtice and Seyd, 2001). Similar patterns of declining civic engagement are apparent in other advanced industrialised countries (Norris, 1999). Explanations of these developments vary, but most commonly they include a discussion of dwindling social capital (Putnam, 2000), weakening networks of civic engagement (Verba, Schlozman and Brady, 1995), and declining cognitive engagement (Huckfeldt and Sprague, 1995).

The apparent evidence of malaise in the Western body politic also extends to worries about public attitudes towards the political system. Scandals and government failure are felt to have eroded popular trust in politicians and state institutions. Where once societies like the United Kingdom and the United States had a rich civic culture, typified by both a willingness of people to get involved in society and a widespread sense of trust in government (Almond and Verba, 1963), there is now, it seems, cynicism and distrust (Kavanagh, 1980; Jowell and Topf, 1988; Mortimore, 1995; Dalton, 1999; Pattie and Johnston, 2001b). That said, there is some debate over how inexorable these trends are (Norris, 2002) and about whether they really indicate a collapse of support for democracy

per se. Some would argue that while respect for and trust in government have declined in the advanced societies, support for democracy
has increased (Inglehart, 1999b; Clarke et al., 2004). Clearly, therefore,
trends in civic engagement – and in attitudes towards civic life – are both
important and debated.

One factor, however, which has been neglected in these discussions is
the role of electoral participation itself as a trigger for encouraging wider
political engagement. Elections are most commonly seen as dependent
variables in these discussions, the outcomes of which need to be explained
by other factors. But elections can be regarded as independent political factors which mobilise or demobilise individuals to participate more
widely beyond the electoral arena. There has been some limited work on
the mobilising effect of elections (Finkel, 1985; Clarke and Kornberg,
1992; Rahn, Brehm and Carlson, 1999), but this issue has rarely been
examined in Britain (Banducci and Karp, 2003). The aim of this chapter
is, firstly, to describe, and, secondly, to model the extent to which citizenship in Britain is renewed or reinvigorated by electoral participation.
The broad question is to what extent does electoral participation sustain
or diminish wider citizen engagement and the norms and values which
support the democratic polity?

This question will be investigated by using the panel element of the
Citizen Audit, which re-interviewed a group of respondents to the original
2000 survey twelve months after their original interviews. Just over 800
individuals were interviewed in 2000 and again in 2001. We can therefore
look not only at net change, but also at how particular individuals' views
and actions change.[1] A well-known feature of panel surveys is that it
is easier to re-interview those who are relatively interested in the topic
being investigated than those who are not interested. And that is what has
happened here. Panel respondents were indeed more civically minded on
most measures than were all respondents to the 2000 survey, many of
whom did not take part in the panel. However, our main interest here
is in explaining how individuals change over time rather than examining
their responses at one point of time. And as we will see, even among our
relatively active group of panel respondents, there was significant change
between 2000 and 2001.

We acknowledge that the general election of 2001 was only one of
a number of significant political events which occurred between waves
one and two of the panel survey. In September 2000 Britain experienced

[1] Because we know what they said in 2000, we know that the results of the 2001 panel
reflect real change, not just sampling error, a potential problem if we had relied on two
distinct cross-section surveys with completely different respondents in each. There is, in
other words, no selection bias in our estimates.

severe disruption to oil and food supplies for a short period of time arising from farmers' and hauliers' demonstrations and blockades in protest at the level of fuel taxes. Then in September 2001 the World Trade Center and the Pentagon were attacked by terrorists. So there were a number of major events, of which the general election was only one, which might impact upon democratic norms and political participation. Nevertheless, the general election was probably the dominant event in British political life over the year, as it did the most to mobilise the population and it lasted longer than the other events. During a short period of between four and six weeks in April and May 2001, political debate and controversy intensified. General election campaigns are multifaceted and multidirectional as parties attempt to ensure popular support at national, regional and local levels (Seyd and Whiteley, 2002b). All forms of media – television, radio and newspapers – increase their coverage of politics. For example, television news broadcasts were dominated by the election campaign during the four weeks prior to the 1997 general election (Norris et al., 1999). In addition, limited though it remains, there is a greater likelihood of direct personal contact with politicians during an election campaign. It is, therefore, reasonable to assume that this major domestic political event will affect civic engagement.

Turnout in the 2001 general election was the lowest in any national contest in contemporary British history. This raises the possibility that electoral participation, or lack of it, demobilised individuals and contributed to a decline in civic engagement rather than the opposite. There may therefore be a spiral of demobilisation at work in which declining electoral participation triggers declining citizen engagement which in turn suppresses electoral participation further. In the campaign monitoring survey run by the British Election Study team in 2001 there was evidence of demobilisation at work during the four-week official campaign (Clarke et al., 2004). But we are going to examine a longer time frame than the relatively short official campaign. This chapter will first examine the shifts in civic attitudes and behaviour which occurred between waves 1 and 2 of the Citizen Audit and then will model the relationships between campaign exposure, electoral participation and civic engagement.

The dynamics of civic attitudes

Over this period of twelve months the public's satisfaction with a wide range of local services decreased; nevertheless the percentage of people satisfied with 'the way democracy works' increased.[2] Figure 8.1 reveals

[2] For example, in the Citizen Audit we asked our respondents whether they were satisfied or dissatisfied with the delivery of a range of local authority services, including schools,

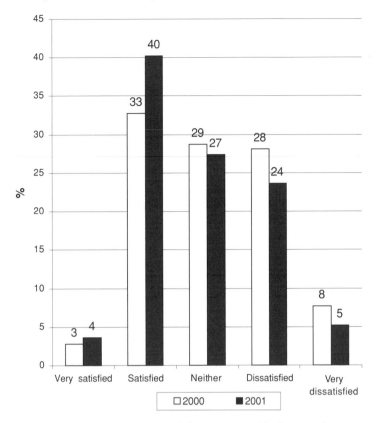

'Thinking about Britain, how satisfied are you with the way democracy works?'
Source: Waves 1 and 2, 2000–2001 Citizen Audit panel study, N = 809.

Figure 8.1 Changes in Satisfaction with Democracy

that an overall rise of 8 per cent occurred in the number of people satisfied with democracy. Whereas in 2000 people had been fairly evenly divided into three groups of satisfied, dissatisfied and no strong opinion, by 2001 a plurality were satisfied.

In chapter 2 we highlighted the fact that people regard their vote as important in determining the outcome of an election and, furthermore, they believe it matters which party is in power. So what impact might this opportunity to choose an MP, and indirectly a government, have had

care for the elderly, social services, road maintenance and street cleaning, and on all these the percentages of dissatisfied had increased.

Table 8.1 *Change in Political Efficacy*

Year	Mean	Standard deviation	t	sig
2000	4.25	2.44	6.04	0.00
2001	4.79		2.24	

'*How much do you think the British government listens to majority opinion?*'
Waves 1 and 2, 2000–2001 Citizen Audit panel study, N = 809.
Note: This table shows that there was a statistically significant change in the respondents' sense of political efficacy over time.

upon people's sense of external political efficacy? Efficacy relates to their views concerning the responsiveness of the political system as a whole and was discussed in chapter 2. Respondents were asked 'How much do you think the British government listens to majority opinion?', and were given an 11-point scale from 0 ('not at all') to 10 ('a great deal'). We see in table 8.1 that the mean score on this scale rose significantly from 4.25 in 2000 to 4.79 in 2001, indicating an increase in external political efficacy.

A general election is likely to be the single most important domestic event in providing the average person with an incentive to both think about and discuss politics. Did our respondents find politics more interesting, and did they become more involved in political discussions? Or was Labour's constant lead in public opinion polls during the campaign and for the four years before enough to depress political interest and political discussion? We find that interest in all forms of politics – local, regional, national, European and international – rose. In figure 8.2 we have merged the 'very interested' and 'fairly interested' categories and we see that interest in international politics rose by twelve percentage points from 34 per cent to 46 per cent and in national politics from 54 per cent to 58 per cent.

We have already noted that during the four-week run-up to the 1997 general election television news was dominated by the campaign. Radio and newspapers similarly gave prominence to it. Media coverage of the 2001 election was similar and, as we see in figure 8.3, our respondents increased their consumption of political news. Over this twelve-month period those watching television or listening to the radio every day for political news rose by nineteen percentage points, from 41 per cent to 60 per cent, and the numbers reading a newspaper every day for political news rose by eight percentage points from 21 per cent to 29 per cent.

Did our respondents discuss politics more or less during this twelve-month period? Very few talk politics with their neighbours: even with the

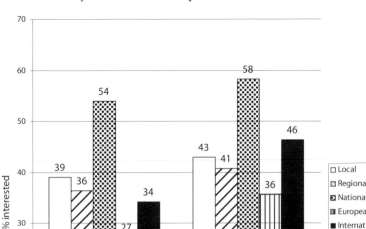

'*How interested are you personally in each of the following . . . ?*'
Source: Waves 1 and 2, 2000–2001 Citizen Audit panel study, N = 809.

Figure 8.2 Changes in Levels of Political Interest

heightened political interest generated by the general election few people were prompted to talk politics over the garden fence. However, as we see in figure 8.4, the numbers 'often' discussing political matters with their family, friends, or fellow workers increased. Twelve months after our original survey, one in five talked politics with their family or friends, and one in ten with their fellow workers.

In our earlier discussions of political trust in chapter 2, we made the point that the public distrusted political institutions more than other state institutions which were not directly associated with politicians. However, we note in table 8.2 that while these non-political institutions – the police, banks, courts and Civil Service – continue to be trusted by the public, only very slight, and generally insignificant, increases in trust occurred

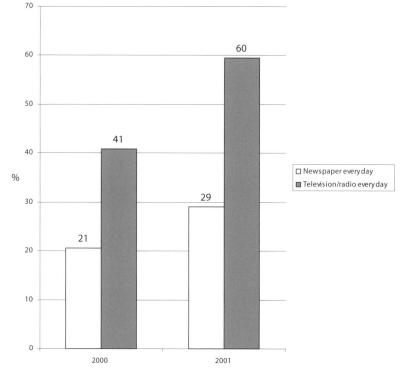

'*In an average day, how often do you read a newspaper/listen to radio/watch television for political news?'*
Source: Waves 1 and 2, 2000–2001 Citizen Audit panel study, N = 809.

Figure 8.3 Changes in the Use of the Media for Political News

over twelve months. By contrast, the public's trust of political institutions, political parties and politicians rose, very strikingly in the case of the new, devolved Scottish and Welsh institutions. For example, the mean score of the Scots' trust of their Parliament rose by 1.4 points. Among the Welsh, the mean trust score in the assembly rose by 1.2 points. Among all respondents trust of the government, the Labour Party, the House of Commons, and politicians rose substantially. Overall, people's trust in twelve of the sixteen institutions listed rose significantly during this period. In the context of an election, this is no surprise. These findings reinforce our assumption that the general election was the main political event in Britain in the 2000–01 period. And there is little evidence here of a media malaise effect (Norris, 2002): people were not disillusioned by media coverage.

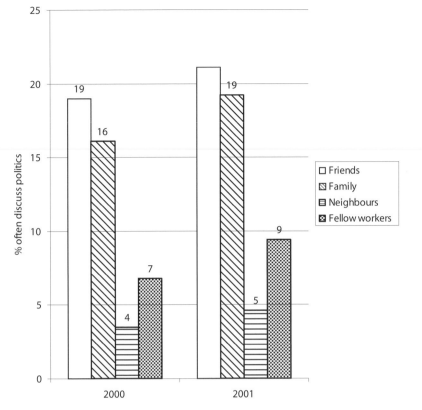

'How often would you say you discuss political matters when you get together with the following groups of people . . . ?' (figures represent those responding 'often').

Source: Waves 1 and 2, 2000–2001 Citizen Audit panel study, N = 809.

Figure 8.4 Changes in Levels of Political Discussions

The dynamics of civic behaviour

In 2000 our panel respondents engaged on average in 4.0 political actions, defined as attempting 'to influence rules, laws or policies', in the twelve months before their interview.[3] Average levels of political activity did not change much over the ensuing year: when we asked the same people a

---

[3] This is somewhat higher than the average reported earlier for all respondents to the 2000 survey. The apparent discrepancy is a function of the nature of panel studies. It tends to be those most interested in the subject of the study who are most likely to remain in panels over time. Inevitably, given the subject matter of our study, our panel contains a higher than normal number of politically active people.

Table 8.2 *Changes in Levels of Institutional Trust*

	Means				
	2000	2001	change	t	sig
Police	6.35	6.36	0.01	0.47	0.64
Courts	5.61	5.72	0.11	2.30	0.02
Banks	5.59	5.93	0.34	4.74	0.00
Civil Service	5.56	5.75	0.19	3.14	0.00
Local government	4.66	4.91	0.25	3.57	0.00
Liberal Democrat Party	3.92	4.42	0.50	7.36	0.00
House of Commons	3.97	4.69	0.72	9.32	0.00
Scottish Parliament*	3.91	5.27	1.36	2.75	0.01
Government	3.84	4.67	0.83	9.30	0.00
Scottish National Party*	3.84	4.57	0.73	2.47	0.00
Labour Party	3.80	4.72	0.92	10.41	0.00
Conservative Party	3.35	3.72	0.37	5.17	0.00
Politicians	3.33	4.08	0.72	9.54	0.00
European Union	3.30	4.17	0.87	11.87	0.00
Welsh Assembly*	3.23	4.42	1.19	2.84	0.01
Plaid Cymru*	3.04	4.06	1.02	1.56	0.13

'And now your views on various institutions: Do you trust . . . ?' Respondents were given an 11-point scale ranging from 0 ('do not trust at all') to 10 ('trust completely').
* Asked of respondents residing in Scotland or Wales only.
Waves 1 and 2, 2000–2001 Citizen Audit panel study, N = 809.
Note: This table shows that there was a statistically significant change in the respondents' sense of institutional trust over time, with a few exceptions.

similar question after the general election, they reported undertaking an average of 4.1 actions. But, as can be seen in table 8.3, there was more change over time at the level of particular activities. An increase in activity was recorded in nine of the seventeen actions listed in the table. Not surprisingly, the largest increase was recorded for those claiming to have voted in a local government election, a rise from 58 to 74 per cent.[4] Most net change was small, however, and only the change in the percentage reporting voting in local government elections was significant.

Not only had our respondents become more politically active in some ways during these twelve months, but their potential for political action increased, as can be seen in part (a) of table 8.4. Asked whether they would consider undertaking any of the seventeen actions to influence political outcomes, in all but two of the potential actions the responses

[4] The local elections in 2001 were delayed as a result of the foot and mouth crisis, and therefore coincided with the general election, undoubtedly helping turnout (Butler and Kavanagh, 2001: 83).

Table 8.3 *Changes in Levels of Political Action*

	2000%	2001%	change	t	sig
Voted in local government election	57.8	73.8	16.0	7.84	0.00
Contacted a public official	28.7	31.4	2.7	1.37	0.17
Contacted a politician	15.6	17.4	1.8	1.24	0.22
Donated money to an organisation	62.8	64.0	1.2	0.59	0.55
Worn or displayed a campaign badge	23.4	24.2	0.8	0.53	0.59
Contacted a solicitor	19.2	20.0	0.8	0.53	0.59
Formed a group of like-minded people	4.7	5.1	0.4	0.37	0.71
Taken part in a strike	2.5	2.6	0.1	0.18	0.86
Signed a petition	47.2	47.3	0.1	0.06	0.95
Boycotted certain products	36.1	33.9	−2.2	−1.25	0.21
Bought products for ethical reasons	33.4	33.4	0.0	0.07	0.95
Participated in illegal protest	1.5	1.5	0.0	0.00	1.00
Attended rally or political meeting	6.9	6.4	−0.5	−0.49	0.63
Contacted an organisation	12.6	11.6	−1.0	−0.70	0.49
Contacted the media	10.6	9.6	−1.0	−0.85	0.39
Taken part in public demonstration	4.7	3.6	−1.1	−1.11	0.27
Raised funds for an organisation	32.0	30.3	−1.7	−0.84	0.40

'*During the last 12 months, have you done any of the following to influence rules, laws or policies?*'
Waves 1 and 2, 2000–01 Citizen Audit panel study, N = 809.
Note: This table shows that there was no significant change in political actions over time, except for voting in local elections.

were higher than one year earlier.[5] The most notable growth in potential for political action was recorded in contacting the media (+8 per cent) and contacting solicitors or judicial bodies (+7 per cent), contacting public officials and voting in a local government election (+6 per cent each), and contacting politicians (+6 per cent). Therefore a number of these individual net changes in potential actions were statistically significant. Taken as a whole, there was a significant increase in the overall level of potential activity. The mean number of potential actions rose significantly from 8.4 to 9.1 between wave 1 and wave 2 of the Citizen Audit.[6] It is interesting to note that potential political activity changes more than actual activity. The gap may be in part a feature of the nature of the 2001 election. The campaign helped raise the potential for political action, but, as the result of the election was never in doubt, it was harder to convert this potential into actual activity.

[5] The exceptions were donating money to organisations and forming a group of like-minded people.
[6] The means were compared using a t-test: t = 4.38, p = 0/000.

Table 8.4 *Changes in Levels of Potential Political Action*

(a) Would you:	2000%	2001%	change	t	sig
Contact the media	46.4	54.1	7.7	3.85	0.00
Contact a solicitor	62.2	68.7	6.5	3.36	0.01
Contact a public official	65.7	71.9	6.2	3.09	0.00
Vote in a local government election	79.6	85.2	5.6	3.46	0.00
Contact a politician	59.5	65.0	5.5	2.53	0.01
Contact an organisation	55.4	59.7	4.3	1.87	0.06
Buy products for ethical reasons	53.5	56.9	3.4	1.57	0.12
Wear a campaign badge	52.8	55.7	2.9	1.28	0.20
Attend a political rally	27.7	30.3	2.6	1.18	0.24
Boycott certain products	63.2	65.4	2.2	1.17	0.24
Take part in strike	25.3	27.4	2.1	1.25	0.21
Sign a petition	81.0	82.1	1.1	0.66	0.51
Raise funds for an organisation	57.2	58.0	0.8	0.61	0.54
Participate in an illegal protest	12.0	12.4	0.4	0.19	0.85
Take part in a public demonstration	34.5	34.8	0.3	0.07	0.95
Donate money to an organisation	78.0	76.4	−1.6	−0.77	0.44
Form a group of like minded people	26.5	23.5	−3.0	−1.96	0.05

Would you do any of the following to influence rules, laws or policies?

(b) Would you be willing to:	2000%	2001%	change	t	sig
Help local renovation	61.3	69.8	8.5	4.56	0.00
Donate blood	70.5	76.6	6.1	3.96	0.00
Assist with meals-on-wheels	50.1	55.7	5.6	2.07	0.04
Be a school governor	34.6	39.9	5.3	3.15	0.00
Serve on jury	76.0	79.6	3.6	2.75	0.01
Join Neighbourhood Watch	75.0	78.5	3.5	2.12	0.04
Be a local councillor	12.4	14.8	2.4	1.68	0.09

Would you be willing: to help renovate a local park or amenity; to donate blood; to assist a meals on wheels service; to serve as a school governor; to serve on a jury; to participate in a Neighbourhood Watch scheme; to stand as a local councillor?
Waves 1 and 2, 2000–01 Citizen Audit panel study, N = 809.
Note: This table shows that there was no significant change in most but not all of the potential political action measures over time.

Just as potential political actions grew between the two time points, so also did potential participation in a wider range of citizen activities. People at the later time point stated that they were more likely to participate in a Neighbourhood Watch scheme, assist with meals-on-wheels or with a local amenity renovation project. We noted in chapter 2 that the number of people willing to consider becoming a school governor or local councillor was low in 2000; the number remained low twelve months later but again, as we see in part (b) of table 8.4, the net participation potential has risen significantly.

Finally, do we detect changes in people's associational engagement, whether by belonging to organised groups, or participating in more informal friendship or support networks? As far as people's combined total of activities with organised groups are concerned, in other words, their membership, participation, volunteering and donating, there was a decline in activity in only four of the twenty-six types of organisation that we listed. These were peace groups, sports or outdoor activity groups, gymnasia and, finally, cultural organisations. In 2000 people belonged on average to one organisation and in 2001 they belonged to nearly two.

We see in figure 8.5 that our respondents' involvement in informal networks increased modestly during the twelve months. The percentage belonging to an informal friendship or acquaintance network, such as the pub quiz team, the reading group or the child support group, rose from 23 to 25 per cent, and providing regular neighbourhood support, such as shopping for neighbours or visiting old people, rose from 17 to 18 per cent. These increases are small. That said, both types of activity are community-oriented, not politically motivated. As a consequence, we would not therefore expect them to be affected much by a general election.

Finally, the total time people spent on associational activities and networks, formal and informal, in the previous month before they were interviewed stayed fairly constant, as can be seen in figure 8.6. There was a small rise in the percentage of people saying they had not spent any time during the last month associating with others, from 38 per cent to 39 per cent, but the change was not significant.

These results show, therefore, that civic attitudes and behaviour are far from being static. Even over the period of a year, net levels of attitudes and activity changed, sometimes substantially. But what underlies these changes? In chapters 5 and 6, we examined some theories of civic activism from the perspective of a single point in time. Here, we extend that investigation to examine change over time. We will focus mainly on change in two different areas: changes in people's perceptions of civic life – their trust in others, in state institutions, their sense of rights and obligations, and so on; and, secondly, changes in the actions they undertake. The aim is to explain who is likely to change their ideas or actions, and in which direction they are likely to move. As indicated above, a general election occurred between waves 1 and 2 of the Citizen Audit: what impact did it have on citizenship?

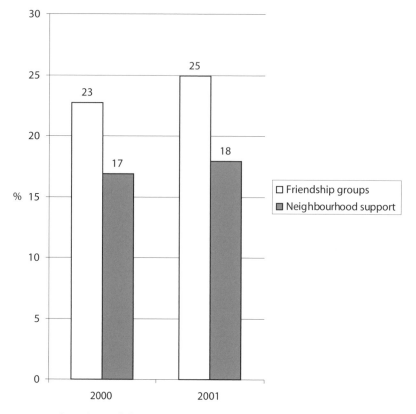

'. . . do you belong to an informal network of friends or acquaintances with whom you have contact on a regular basis . . . ? Do you actively provide any support beyond your immediate family for ill people, elderly neighbours, or acquaintances . . . ?'

Source: Waves 1 and 2, 2000–2001 Citizen Audit panel study, N = 809.

Figure 8.5 Changes in Informal, Personal Networks

Explaining the changes in civic attitudes and behaviour

The starting point of this analysis is an examination of the dependent variables in some detail. We will concentrate on change in two separate sets of factors. The first group comprises changes in individuals' attitudes and intentions concerning civic life. The second group concentrates on changes in their civic behaviour. These are outlined in table 8.5.

The attitudes and intentions measures cover a range of different aspects of civic life. The first three measures are related to different aspects of

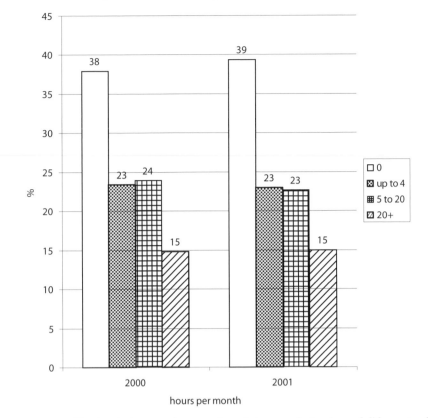

'*During the last month, approximately how much time in total did you spend on activities in clubs, associations, groups, networks, or in supporting other people?*'

Source: Waves 1 and 2, 2000–2001 Citizen Audit panel study, N = 809.

Figure 8.6 Changes in Time Devoted to Associational Engagement

trust: trust, which, as we saw in earlier chapters, is a key component of the social capital model. Although these measures are rather similar to measures used in earlier chapters, we employ slightly different methods of calculating the scales here to ensure complete comparability of scales between waves 1 and 2.[7] The three trust measures, trust in others, trust in

---

[7] The definitions used in earlier chapters depend, in several cases, on component scores from principal components analyses. These scores are based on the underlying relationships between the variables. But they are also affected by the exact component loadings of each variable on the underlying component. Principal components analyses of the

Table 8.5 *Net Change in Citizenship Scales*

	Means				Cronbach's alpha	
Attitudes	*2000*	*2001*	*t*	*p*	*2000*	*2001*
Trust in others[1]	19.31	19.40	0.48	0.63	0.81	0.85
Trust in elected politicians[2]	10.85	13.43	11.31	0.00	0.87	0.90
Trust in state institutions[3]	21.53	22.73	4.71	0.00	0.82	0.84
Political efficacy[4]	11.75	12.04	2.95	0.00	0.46	0.49
Satisfaction with democracy[5]	2.95	3.13	4.79	0.00	—	—
Interest in politics[6]	5.91	6.74	6.55	0.00	0.90	0.90
Exposure to politics on media[7]	3.66	4.88	11.60	0.00	0.72	0.63
Obligations: voluntary action scale[8]	1.86	2.04	4.61	0.00	0.58	0.63
Obligations: civic office scale[9]	0.47	0.55	2.99	0.00	0.45	0.50
Rights: state rights scale[10]	13.96	14.84	9.21	0.00	0.52	0.56
Civic activities						
Number of groups joined	0.72	1.35	11.36	0.00	0.57	0.56
Political conversations[11]	8.16	8.42	2.49	0.01	0.77	0.76
Number of political actions	3.97	4.14	1.65	0.09	0.76	0.74
Individualistic political actions	2.93	3.07	1.97	0.04	0.70	0.68
Contacting political actions	0.87	0.90	0.81	0.41	0.61	0.58
Collectivist political actions	0.18	0.17	0.57	0.56	0.48	0.47
Time for associational engagement	2.97	2.89	0.97	0.33	—	—

[1] sum q5a–q5c (wave 1): q2a–q2c (wave 2): high = high trust.
[2] sum q5d1, q5d2, q5d12 (wave 1): q2d1, q2d2, q2d12 (wave 2): high = high trust.
[3] sum q5d10 q5d11 q5d13 q5d14 (wave 1); q2d10 q2d11 q2d13 q2d14 (wave 2): high = high trust.
[4] sum q17a–q17d (wave 1)' q11a–q11d (wave 2): High = high efficacy.
[5] q8b (wave 1); q5b (wave 2): high = very dissatisfied.
[6] sum q16a1 to q16a5 (wave1): q10a1 to q10a5: high = interested.
[7] sum q44c1, q44c3 (wave 1): q1c1 q1c3: high = high exposure.
[8] sum q32c q32f q32g (wave 1): q18c q18f q18g (wave 2): high = high willingness.
[9] sum q32d q32e (wave 1); q18d q18e (wave 2): high = high willingness.
[10] sum q22d q22g q22g q35b (wave 1); q16c q16e q16g q20b (wave 2): high = high sense of rights.
[11] sum q61b1–q16b4 (wave 1): q10b1–q10b4 (wave 2): high = high conversation.
Waves 1 and 2, 2000–01 Citizen Audit panel study, N = 809.
Note: This table shows that there were statistically significant changes in most, though not all, of the citizenship scales over time.

relevant variables show the same underlying relationships between them at waves 1 and 2 of the Citizen Audit. However, the exact component loadings change. Not only that, but the component scores themselves are standardised measures, taken relative to the average for the component. For both these reasons, component scores are far from ideal when we want to measure change. We therefore create summative scales using the same variable definitions in both waves of the Citizen Audit.

elected politicians, and trust in state institutions, are based on responses to the series of 11-point scales discussed earlier and sum individual respondents' answers to the relevant questions in the Citizen Audit.[8] In all three cases, the higher an individual's score, the more trusting he or she is. As shown in table 8.5, in each case, Cronbach's alpha for the summary scales at both wave 1 and wave 2 confirms that the scales are robust.[9] Examining the averages for each of these scales at wave 1 and wave 2 confirms the patterns revealed earlier: on the whole, members of the Citizen Audit panel became more trusting of both elected and unelected political institutions between the two waves of the survey. As we would expect, however, there was no significant change over time in the trust in others scale. While an election might change people's minds about the political system, not surprisingly, it had no effect on people's personal evaluations of their fellow citizens.

The scale for political efficacy is based on the responses to four propositions: 'people like me have no say in what the government does'; 'people like me can have a real influence on politics if they are prepared to get involved'; 'sometimes politics and government seem so complicated that a person like me cannot really understand what is going on'; and 'it really matters which party is in power, because it will affect our lives'.[10] Echoing table 8.1, the results suggest a small but significant increase in individuals' sense of political efficacy between 2000 and 2001: people became more likely, on the whole, to feel their views mattered. A related issue, satisfaction with the way in which British democracy works, was measured using the 5-point scale displayed in figure 8.1, with 5 indicating greatest satisfaction: as the figure implied, there was a small but significant rise in levels of satisfaction with democracy between 2000 and 2001.

---

[8] The scales are coded so that the most 'trusting' reply possible is 10, and the least 'trusting' is scored 0. The trust in others scale is produced by summing responses to three of these scales: whether the respondent thinks other people can be trusted, will be helpful, or will be fair. 'Trust in elected politicians' is also the sum of three scales: trust in the government, trust in the House of Commons, and trust in politicians. And 'trust in state institutions' is the sum of: trust in the courts, the civil service, the police, and local government.

[9] Cronbach's alpha is a measure of the average correlation between each pair of items in a scale. It varies between 0 (where the items used to build the scale are not correlated at all with one another, and hence are not really suitable for inclusion in a common scale) and 1 (in which case the items making up the scale are perfectly correlated with each other). The closer Cronbach's alpha is to 1.0, the more robust and reliable the scale is.

[10] Responses were on a 5-point scale, from strongly agree to strongly disagree. They were coded so that 1 indicated low efficacy responses, and 5 high efficacy. So the higher an individual's score on the political efficacy scale, the greater his or her sense of political efficacy.

As we saw earlier, interest in politics generally, and the extent to which people followed political news both increased between 2000 and 2001. We have created scales for each of these at each wave of the panel.[11] The scales clearly demonstrate significant increases over time in interest in politics and in exposure to political news in the media.

The next two measures of respondents' views examined here look at attitudes to obligations and rights, introduced in tables 5.3 and 5.4. Some of the questions used to construct those scales were not asked in both waves of the survey, and we have therefore restricted our attention to those which were. Questions asked only in the first wave of the survey covered the following issues: whether it is ever justified to evade taxes; whether one should always obey the law; whether it is wrong to claim benefits to which one is not entitled; and whether one would consider working for a voluntary organisation. We are unable, therefore, to look at whether any changes occurred in attitudes regarding obeying the law. We are, however, able to examine the voluntary action dimension of obligations, which was analysed in chapter 6.[12] Comparing wave 1 and wave 2 scores reveals a small but significant increase in average scores over the course of the year: our respondents became slightly more willing to undertake voluntary activity. They become more public-spirited over time, not less.

[11] The 'interest in politics' scale is the sum of scores on five questions asking how interested individuals were in local, regional, national, European and international politics. Responses to each were coded from 0 (no interest) to 3 (very interested), giving a scale which has a theoretical range running from 0 to 15: higher scores suggest greater interest in politics. The scale measuring exposure to political news in the media, meanwhile, was constructed by summing responses to two questions asking respondents how often, in an average week, they read a newspaper, or used television or radio for political news. Responses to each were coded from 0 (never sought out political news) to 4 (sought out political news every day). The scale's theoretical range runs, therefore, from 0 to 8: the higher the score, the more frequent is the individual's exposure to political news. Both scales are robust in both waves of the panel, with good Cronbach's alphas.

[12] To ensure comparability between waves 1 and 2 of the survey, we have constructed scales for each by summing the number of occasions on which each individual said he or she would be willing to undertake a relevant action. For the voluntary action scale, we summed the number of times respondents said they would be willing to participate in: renovating a local park or amenity; helping with meals on wheels; or helping with a local Neighbourhood Watch scheme. We have no comparable measure for the work for a voluntary organisation measure in wave 2 of the Citizen Audit, but as can be seen in table 5.2, this was, in any case, the weakest element on the scale at the first wave. The civic service scale was constructed by summing the number of times individuals said they were willing to: serve on a jury; give blood; or vote in the next election. The first two questions were coded 1 for someone who was willing, and 0 for someone who was not; the vote question was coded on a scale of 1 to 4, where 1 indicated no chance of voting, and 4 indicated a definite vote. The voluntary action scale therefore has a theoretical range varying from 0 (not willing to engage in any activity) to 3 (willing to engage in them all), while the civic service scale varies from 1 to 6.

In addition, we have also looked at respondents' willingness to serve in a public office. We expect the intervention of the general election to have an effect here. Do people become more likely to want to run for office when an election happens? Does the election mobilise potential candidates as well as voters? In both waves of the panel survey, individuals were asked whether they would be willing to serve either as local government councillors or as school governors. Preliminary investigation reveals that responses to these questions are quite closely correlated: people who are willing to stand for the council are also likely to be willing to act as a school governor. We have therefore combined these two items into a 'civic office' scale, measuring the willingness to stand for public office.[13] Once again, there is a significant rise in the average score on this measure between 2000 and 2001, suggesting that respondents become more willing to stand for public office after the election than they were before. That said, the averages are low, around 0.5 on a scale which runs up to 2: even in 2001, most people are not willing to stand for public office.

Finally, for attitudes and intentions, we look at changes over time in individuals' sense of rights. Once again, several of the questions used in chapter 6 to construct the rights scale for the wave 1 survey were not repeated in wave 2 of the Citizen Audit. We do, however, have sufficient comparable questions to construct a version of the scale for rights to state action.[14] A high score on the scale therefore indicates that an individual believes strongly that citizens have a right to expect state action. Once again, there was a small but significant rise in the average score between 2000 and 2001: the implication is that people's expectations of what the state should deliver were growing.

The other area we focus on here is change in actual civic behaviour over time. Three different areas are examined: membership of clubs, societies and voluntary organisations; political conversations between citizens; and political activism – undertaking some act aimed at influencing laws, rules or policies. Associational engagement, as measured by the number of types of organisations joined in the previous year, also

---

[13] The scale adds the number of times individuals say they are willing to undertake these activities, and so ranges from 0 (undertake neither) to 2 (undertake both).

[14] In both waves respondents were asked whether: it was the government's responsibility to provide jobs for all; the government should reduce the income difference between rich and poor; government should provide housing for all who need it; and government should spend money to get rid of poverty. All questions were 5-point scales, and responses to each question were coded so that strong agreement scored 5 and strong disagreement scored 1. The summary scale was constructed by summing each respondent's score on each of the questions.

increased significantly between 2000 and 2001. As seen earlier, this form of activity almost doubled over the year.

Conversations about politics are important means through which individuals can express their opinions, and find out the views of others. It is also clear that, in electoral politics especially, political conversations between voters can mobilise support for particular parties and can also either encourage or discourage participation, depending on the composition of individuals' conversation networks (Huckfeldt and Sprague, 1995; Pattie and Johnston, 1999; Mutz, 2002). As demonstrated in figure 8.4, political conversations were, on the whole, more common in 2001 than in 2000, which is not surprising in an election year. Our scale measures the frequency of political discussion with four groups of people: family members, friends, neighbours and workmates.[15] In both 2000 and 2001, the average respondent scored just over 8, suggesting some political conversation was taking place, with moderate frequency, though, as figure 8.4 demonstrates, conversations were much more frequent with friends and family than with neighbours and co-workers (Pattie and Johnston, 1999). And there was a slight but significant increase in the political conversation scale between 2000 and 2001, consistent with a citizen body which was talking politics more often.

Clearly, we wish to know about changing levels of political action. We use the same four dimensions of political participation as employed in chapters 5 and 6. The first counts the total number of political activities undertaken by each panel respondent in both 2000 and 2001. Our remaining measures of political activism differentiate between the various forms of participation identified in chapter 5. The second measure concentrates on what we have termed individualistic political actions (petition signing, ethical consumption, etc.), and counts the number of such activities undertaken by each respondent. The third measure counts the number of contact actions undertaken (contacting politicians and officials). The fourth measure concentrates on the number of collective political actions (taking part in a demonstration, attending a meeting, etc.) undertaken. Intriguingly, table 8.5 shows there is little sign that most of these activities changed between 2000 and 2001. Only individualistic actions were significantly more frequent at the latter date than at the former. Voting in local elections is one of the most commonly conducted

---

[15] Respondents were asked how often they spoke to people in each group: never (coded 1), rarely (2), sometimes (3), or often (4). The political conversation scales were constructed by adding respondents' answers to all four questions: Cronbach's alphas are high, suggesting the scale is reliable. The theoretical range of the scale runs from 4, for respondents who never talk politics to anyone in any of the groups, to 16, for respondents who often have political conversations with people in all of the groups.

individualistic actions. We would expect a general election to boost interest in voting generally. But this is perhaps even more important for local electoral participation when, as in 2001, the local and general elections coincided in many parts of the country.

Finally, what of the time given to associational life? In both 2000 and 2001, panel members were asked how much time they had spent in the previous month on activities which involved some sort of associational engagement with others – in clubs, associations, groups, networks or in supporting others.[16] There was little change between 2000 and 2001 in the average amount of time spent in associational engagement, as can be seen in table 8.5. In each year, the average panel respondent scored just below 3, equivalent to spending just under five hours a month on this form of associational life.

The results

Our main interest is in accounting for change over time in civic attitudes and behaviour at the individual level. Even where there has been no net change, there may still have been considerable overall gross change. Some individuals may have become more active, or developed a more civic outlook, while others may have become less active or civic in their views. But if movement in one direction is cancelled by movement in the other, then the overall picture of volatility will not be well captured by examining average levels of activity in 2000 and 2001. One way of summarising that individual-level volatility is to look at how many respondents changed their attitudes and behaviour over time, and in which direction. Table 8.6 reports the percentage of respondents who became less civic-minded between 2000 and 2001, the percentage whose views and actions remained at the same level, and the percentage becoming more civic-minded. On average, just over a quarter of respondents became less civic-minded over time, though this varies substantially from measure to measure. Only 9 per cent said they had undertaken fewer collectivist political actions in 2001 than in 2000 (though relatively few had been active at the earlier date in any case), while 13 per cent reported being less willing to stand for a civic office, and just over one in five said they had paid less attention to political reporting on television or the radio. But almost 40 per cent of respondents reported feeling less politically efficacious in 2001 than in 2000, and around 40 per cent said they undertook fewer political actions – especially individualistic actions. But on the whole,

---

[16] Responses were coded on a 6-point scale: those who spent no time on such activities were coded as 1, while those who spent twenty hours or more were coded 6.

Table 8.6 *Total Change in Citizenship Scales*

	(N = 809)		
Attitudes	*Decline %*	*Same %*	*Increase %*
Trust in others	44.8	10.1	45.0
Trust in elected politicians	31.6	7.0	61.5
Trust in state institutions	41.5	5.1	53.4
Political efficacy	38.1	15.6	46.4
Satisfaction with democracy	22.4	43.5	34.1
Interest in politics	28.7	21.9	49.4
Exposure to politics on media	21.4	27.3	51.3
Obligations: voluntary action scale	21.9	44.3	33.9
Obligations: civic office scale	13.3	65.3	21.4
Rights: state rights scale	29.8	14.2	56.0
Civic activities			
Political conversations	35.0	23.1	41.9
Number of groups joined	14.6	41.2	44.3
Number of political actions	39.4	16.8	43.8
Individualistic political actions	37.6	20.3	42.2
Contacting political actions	25.8	46.5	27.7
Collectivist political actions	9.4	82.1	8.5
Time for associational engagement	32.4	35.1	32.5

Waves 1 and 2, 2000–01 Citizen Audit panel study, N = 809.
Note: This table shows how the citizenship scales changed over time, and measures the percentages of respondents indicating decreasing, unchanged or increasing activities and beliefs.

more people (40 per cent on average) reported becoming more civic-minded than reported becoming less so. The smallest increases were in the number of collectivist political actions (with only 8 per cent reporting becoming more active) and in trust in others (with 10 per cent feeling more trusting over time). But some of the increases were substantial, and, on three measures, over half of all respondents were more civic-minded in 2001 than they had been in 2000. Not surprisingly after an election year, 51 per cent said they had paid an increased amount of attention to political reporting on the media. Around 53 per cent reported an increase in their trust of state institutions. And an impressive 62 per cent became more trusting of politicians over time, which is not the cynical response one might expect.

So there is substantial individual-level volatility, with people changing their views and actions in both directions. We therefore need to model change at the level of the individual citizen. As in chapter 6, we rely on regression models for much of our analysis here. However, since we are now interested in change over time, we take a different approach to the modelling and estimate a panel regression model. As mentioned in chapter 7, the basic problem we face is one of causation: just because two factors are correlated, it does not mean that one causes the other. Nor does it mean that causation runs in a particular direction. So, for instance, does social capital cause civic participation, or does civic participation cause social capital? With cross-sectional data gathered at one point in time, it is very hard indeed to disentangle such conundrums. However, time-series and panel data, by providing information for two or more time points, do allow us to begin to unpick cause from effect. The approach used to achieve this here draws on recent work in econometrics, stressing so-called Granger causality (Granger, 1988). The idea rests on the analogy of time's arrow. Events in the past might cause events in the present, but events in the present cannot cause events in the past. So current income levels might reflect, say, educational qualifications gained in the past. But current income cannot cause past education – it has already happened.[17] More formally, 'x is a Granger cause of y, if present y can be predicted with better accuracy by using past values of x rather than by not doing so, other information being identical' (Charemza and Deadman, 1992: 165).

The analytical strategy adopted here, therefore, is to try to model variations in key variables measured at wave 2 of the panel using explanatory variables measured at wave 1 of the survey. Included among the explanatory variables is the wave 1 version of the dependent variable (Finkel, 1985; Greene, 2003).[18] So, for instance, we can model the effects of social capital at wave 1 on political activism at wave 2 by fitting the following model:

$$
\begin{aligned}
\textit{Political activism}_{i2} = {} & a_{11} + b_{11}\textit{Political activism}_{i1} + b_{12}\textit{Interpersonal Trust}_{i1} \\
& + b_{13}\textit{Trust in Institutions}_{i1} + b_{14}\textit{Membership of Groups}_{i1} \\
& + b_{15}\textit{Membership of an Informal Network}_{i1} \\
& + b_{16}\textit{Exposure to TV}_{i1} \\
& + b_{17}\textit{Ties to the local community}_{i1} + u_{i1} \qquad (8.1)
\end{aligned}
$$

---

[17] Clearly there are exceptions, usually involving some form of anticipated actions: in a well-known example, the sales of turkeys rise as Christmas approaches – but selling turkeys does not cause Christmas!

[18] This model creates bias in the estimates as the lagged endogenous variable is likely to be correlated with the predictors. The standard 'cure' for this is to use an instrumental variable or variables to stand in for the lagged endogenous measure. Unfortunately, this can be potentially worse than the disease if the instruments are not very good predictors, since the estimates will lack precision (see Greene, 2003: 80). Thus test statistics can be misleading – in effect, the instrumental variables approach trades bias against precision. Generally, there are few satisfactory instrumental variables in political science, although this is not true in economics. We therefore employ the lagged endogenous specification.

where:

> *Political activism*$_{i2}$ is the dependent variable, a measure of individual i's political activism from wave 2 of the panel;
>
> *Political activism*$_{i1}$ is the same measure of political activism, at wave 1 of the panel;
>
> *Interpersonal Trust*$_{i1}$ measures the extent to which individuals trust other people, at wave 1;
>
> *Trust in institutions*$_{i1}$ measures the extent to which individuals trust the institutions of the state at wave 1;
>
> *Membership of Groups*$_{i1}$ measures individual membership of interest groups at wave 1;
>
> *Membership of an Informal Network*$_{i1}$ measures individual membership of informal groups at wave 1;
>
> *Exposure to TV*$_{i1}$ measures the number of hours respondents watch TV in the average day at wave 1;
>
> *Ties to the Local Community*$_{i1}$ measures the length of residence and family ties in the community at wave 1; and
>
> u_{i1} is an error term in which $E(u_{i1}) = 0$ and σ_u^2 is constant.

Other independent variables, also measured at wave 1, can be added to the model. However, the key points to note are that we control for each individual's previous score on the dependent variable, and that all independent variables are measured using wave 1 data. Under these circumstances, the b_{1n} regression coefficients tell us whether each independent variable can effect change in the dependent variable, according to the principle of Granger causality.

There is a further step, however, in establishing Granger causality. The procedure just described establishes whether predictor variables at time 1 can influence dependent variables at time 2, controlling for the past history of the dependent variable at time 1. But we also need to test for reciprocal effects. In other words, are the dependent variables measured at time 1 able to predict the independent, predictor variables at the later time 2? Only if they cannot is it possible to claim Granger causality. So, for instance, to test for a possible reciprocal effect between political activism and interpersonal trust in the model specified above, we would evaluate the following model:

$$
\begin{aligned}
\textit{Interpersonal trust}_{i2} = {} & a_{11} + b_{21}\textit{Political activism}_{i1} + b_{21}\textit{Interpersonal Trust}_{i1} \\
& + b_{22}\textit{Trust in Institutions}_{i1} + b_{23}\textit{Membership of Groups}_{i1} \\
& + b_{24}\textit{Membership of an Informal Network}_{i1} \\
& + b_{25}\textit{Exposure to TV}_{i1} \\
& + b_{26}\textit{Ties to the local community}_{i1} + u_{i2} \qquad (8.2)
\end{aligned}
$$

For Granger causality to be established between interpersonal trust at wave 1 and political activism at wave 2, then two conditions must be met. First, the effect of interpersonal trust at wave 1 on political activism at wave 2 tested in equation 8.1 should be significant. Second, the effect of political activism at wave 1 on interpersonal trust at wave 2 tested in equation 8.2 should be non-significant. This provides a strong test of reciprocal causation which is only possible in a panel survey design. In the analyses which follow, the great majority of relationships discussed pass both tests of Granger causality. In the few cases where this is not true, we will draw attention to this fact in the discussion.

In the following analyses, we employ wave 1 measures of the independent variables used in chapter 6 to evaluate the various theories of civic engagement. Tables 6.11 and 6.12 provide guidance on which variables are likely to be important in the various models. From the cognitive engagement model (Dalton, 2002), we take age at which individuals left education, political knowledge scores, media exposure, interest in politics, and a measure of policy dissatisfaction. From the civic voluntarism model (Verba, Schlozman and Brady, 1995) come measures of political efficacy, mobilisation, free time, occupational status and partisanship. The equity–fairness model (Runciman, 1966) contributes measures of perceived outcomes and expectations, economic deprivation, and variables assessing whether respondents are members of a deprived group. The social capital model (Putnam, 2000) contributes measures of interpersonal trust, trust in institutions, membership of associational groups and informal networks, exposure to TV, and ties to the local community. And from the general incentives model (Whiteley and Seyd, 2002), we examine the effects of perceived costs and benefits (both collective and selective) of action, as well as of social norms towards participation.

For the most part, the independent variables are defined in the same way as their cross-sectional equivalents in chapter 6. There are two main sets of exceptions. One is party identification. In addition to the measure of strength of party identification employed earlier as part of the civic voluntarism model, we have also investigated which party an individual identifies with. We make this addition here to reflect the potentially important partisan impact of the 2001 election. The result of that contest was widely and correctly anticipated well in advance of the election itself: a second Labour landslide. If the election were to prove a factor in accounting for changes in civic activity over time, therefore, we might anticipate that supporters of different parties would be affected in different ways. Two different scenarios are possible. Conservative supporters, for instance, might have found the prospect of a second major defeat profoundly demotivating, while Labour supporters might have been more susceptible to mobilisation. One could also anticipate the opposite reaction, with Conservatives keen to minimise the damage to their party, and hence becoming more active, while Labour supporters, assured of victory, might have become complacent and so less likely to become active.

The second group of explanatory variables are calculated in a slightly different way here compared to our earlier definitions. These are wave 1 measures of inter-personal trust, trust in institutions and in politicians, political efficacy, and levels of individualistic, contact and collectivist civic action. As noted above, the versions adopted here are designed to allow strict comparability in these measures between waves 1 and 2 of the panel, by adopting exactly the same algorithms to calculate the measures in both waves.

A general to specific modelling strategy is adopted here to test each theoretical model. Although all independent variables have the potential to be entered into the model, only those which prove significant are retained. As such, this produces relatively parsimonious models. There is, however, a risk that, by allowing variable selection to be driven by statistical rather than theoretical considerations, spurious results might follow. We have therefore also conducted analyses which enter all possible independent variables into a global model simultaneously. The results of both exercises are very similar, reassuring us that we have neither missed something important nor misrepresented the results by adopting the general to specific procedure.

We start in table 8.7 by examining change over time in attitudes towards the political system. In particular, we are interested in changes in: interest in politics; exposure to political news on the media; levels of satisfaction with democracy (which is also our measure of collective benefits in the general incentives model); and political efficacy.

It will be recalled that the panel regression models all control for the dependent variable measured a year previously. As we would expect, in each case, this was the single most important variable accounting for 2001 scores on each issue. In all four equations, the respondent's score on the measure a year earlier is significantly and positively related to their score on the same measure in 2001 (the relevant coefficients are printed in bold in the table). In other words, people who were interested in politics in 2000 still tended to be interested in politics in 2001. Those who followed politics closely in the media in 2000 were on the whole still doing so in 2001. The more satisfied someone was with British democracy in 2000, the more likely he or she was still to be satisfied in 2001. And the greater a person's sense of political efficacy in 2000, the more likely it was that he or she would still feel efficacious in 2001.

Table 8.7 *The Dynamics of Participation: Changing Attitudes towards Politics*

	Perceptions and intentions scales 2001			
	Interest in politics	Media exposure	Satisfaction with democracy	Political efficacy
Independent variables (2000)				
Constant	1.88	3.86	2.04	7.87
Cognitive engagement				
Age left education				0.17***
Media exposure	0.12***	**0.31***		
Interest in politics	**0.40***	0.07***		0.10***
General incentives				
Collective benefits:				
Satisfaction with democracy			**0.35***	0.17**
Selective benefits:				
Process incentives	0.21***			
Group incentives		−0.12**		
Civic voluntarism				
Political efficacy				**0.25***
Party ID (comparison = no party ID)				
Conservative ID			−0.21***	
Labour ID				0.59***
Other ID			−0.67***	
Occupational status	0.25***			
Equity–fairness				
Outcomes and expectations				−0.37***
Retired		0.51***		
Social capital				
Trust elected politicians	0.06***			
Trust state institutions			0.02***	
Informal networks				0.56***
TV watching	−0.14**	−0.11***		−0.10**
Years in area		0.21**	−0.07**	
R^2	0.38	0.21	0.20	0.30

Waves 1 and 2, 2000–01 Citizen Audit panel study, N = 809.
Note: The table contains the unstandardised regression coefficients obtained from regressing the row variables on the column variables. Asterisks indicate the statistical significance of the coefficients with $p < 0.10^*$; $p < 0.05^{**}$; $p < 0.01^{***}$.

This is exactly what we would expect from panel data. Most people tend not to change their views radically over the course of a year. However, it is also worth noting that people's views in 2000 did not completely explain their views in 2001. The R^2 values, while respectable for survey data, are not overwhelming, suggesting that much of the variation in each of our measures in 2001 remains to be accounted for.[19] And, of more immediate interest to us, opinions in 2001 were related to a range of other factors from a year earlier, even when we control for people's views on the same measures in 2000. Because we have held constant the effect of the 2000 score on the dependent variable, these other significant coefficients tell us about who was likely to change their views, and in what direction.

Looking first at interest in politics, those who followed political news closely in 2000 were more likely to become more interested in politics over the ensuing year compared with those who did not make as much use of the media. However, perhaps not surprisingly, this failed the second test for Granger causality: other things being equal, interest in politics at time 1 was also positively related to media exposure to politics at time 2 – clear evidence of reciprocal causation. Apart from that, the more middle-class the individual (as measured by occupational status), the more likely it was that his or her interest in politics would grow. And people who scored relatively high on the scale for trust in elected politicians in 2000 were also more likely to become more interested in politics than were those who did not trust politicians. From the general incentives model, process incentives (related mainly to how rewarding an activity people think politics is) were positively related to interest in politics: the more process incentives a person could identify in 2000, the greater the increase in his or her interest in politics over the following year. But not everything increased interest in politics. Frequent television viewers in 2000 became less interested in politics over time, compared to those who watched little TV. This clearly works in the opposite direction to the effects of exposure to politics on the media, suggesting that Norris' (1996) critique of Putnam's (1995) indictment of television is correct. However, the important factor here is what is being watched. Television viewing in general takes in a very wide range of programmes. Frequent TV viewers are seeing not only the news and current affairs, but game shows, soap operas, dramas, comedies, films, and so on. While over-exposure to television

---

[19] Some of the lagged effects look modest here, as shown by the generally small regression coefficients uncovered in the models. However, this is because these measure immediate effects. The longer-term effects may be much larger, so that a year may be too short a period to fully assess the overall effect. In the equations, the slope coefficient b_{1i} gives the immediate effect. The long-term effect can be modelled as $1/(1 - b_{1i})$. Where b_{1i} is less than 1, the long-term effect must be larger than the immediate effect.

in general does seem demotivating, it depends on what sort of programmes are being watched. Those who use the media to follow politics
can actually be mobilised by it. As we will see, this turns out to be a fairly
consistent story.

The model for change in exposure to political reporting in the media
looks relatively similar. The more interested a person was in politics in
2000, for instance, the more likely he or she was to pay increased attention to political news over the following year – though again this failed the
second test for Granger causality, indicating reciprocal effects at work.
TV watching was once again a disincentive, however. The frequent TV
watchers in 2000 paid less attention to political news a year later than they
had done in 2000, while those who watched little TV at the first point
in time paid an increasing amount of attention to it subsequently. Perceptions of group incentives are also related to changing media exposure
to politics. Interestingly, this relationship was negative: the more likely
people were in 2000 to feel that politics was a good way of obtaining
benefits for groups they cared about, the greater the relative decline in
the attention they paid to political news between 2000 and 2001. This is
striking. It might be argued that it is a consequence of disillusion, if, for
instance, those who felt strong group incentives in 2000 felt let down by
the results of the 2001 election. However, the correlation between perceptions of group incentives in 2000 and in 2001 is positive and significant,
suggesting there is little sign of selective disillusion here.

Two other factors are associated with increasing exposure to political reporting in the media. First, those who were retired in 2000 were
more likely to increase their attention to political news than were those
not retired, perhaps related to the greater time flexibility enjoyed by the
retired, or perhaps to concerns over government pension plans which
became an issue during the 1997–2001 Parliament. And the longer people
had lived in their neighbourhoods in 2000, the greater their increase in
attention to television news.

Satisfaction with democracy, meanwhile, fell over time among those
who in 2000 had identified with the Conservatives or with some other
party, compared, in both cases, to those who identified with no party at all.
That supporters of the party which lost the 2001 election should become
less satisfied is hardly surprising. Conservative supporters were among
the least satisfied with British democracy at that time, which repeats a
finding occurring in 1997 (Pattie and Johnston, 2001b). And the longer
individuals had lived in their neighbourhood in 2000, the less their satisfaction with democracy increased. But the more people had trusted state
institutions in 2000, the more their satisfaction with democracy grew over
the subsequent year.

The sense of political efficacy, meanwhile, was, not surprisingly, related to partisanship. Labour supporters had seen their party win power for the first time in almost twenty years at the 1997 election. They had also watched the new Labour government apparently buck the electoral cycle: unlike previous governments, it was not unpopular in the mid-term, and it was re-elected in 2001 with another, barely reduced, landslide. Not surprisingly, therefore, Labour partisans were much more likely to feel an increase in their sense of political efficacy between 2000 and 2001 than were supporters of other parties. The feeling of efficacy also increased more among the relatively well-educated than among those who had left education early. It grew faster among those who had been interested in politics a year before than among those who had not. And being a member of an informal network in 2000 contributed to an improved sense of political efficacy: feelings grew more among those who were members of such networks in 2000 than among those who were not. However, in keeping with Putnam's claims, television watching made people feel relatively powerless. The more frequently individuals watched television in 2000, the less their sense of political efficacy grew over the following year. The more satisfied they had been with British democracy in 2000, the more their sense of political efficacy increased subsequently. Finally, the higher individuals scored on the relative deprivation outcomes and expectations measure in 2000, the less their sense of political efficacy grew (and for some it fell) between 2000 and 2001. The outcomes and expectations measure, based on responses to statements such as 'there is a big difference between what I expect from life and what I get', is coded so that high scores indicate a large disparity between expectations and results. In other words, those with high scores on the measure are the most disgruntled with their lot in life. It is hardly surprising, therefore, that they feel less politically effective as time goes on.

What of changes in levels of trust? Once again, not surprisingly, we see in table 8.8 that the more trusting people were in 2000 on each of our three trust scales, the more trusting they were a year later. All the relevant coefficients, picked out in bold, are positive and highly significant – indeed, they are the most significant variables in their respective equations. Two other factors stand out quite consistently in all three equations. First, the more satisfied with British democracy people were in 2000, the more likely they were to become more trusting of other people, of elected politicians and of state institutions over the subsequent year: satisfaction bred trust. It should be noted, however, that the relationship between trust in state institutions and satisfaction with democracy failed the second test for Granger causality, implying reciprocal causation. Second, the

Table 8.8 *The Dynamics of Participation: Changing Trust*

	Perceptions and intentions scales 2001		
	Trust others	Trust elected politicians	Trust state institutions
Independent variables (2000)			
Constant	7.92	6.38	12.14
Cognitive engagement			
Age left education		−0.31**	
Political knowledge	0.20**		
General incentives			
Collective benefits:			
Satisfaction with democracy	0.40**	0.65***	0.51**
Selective benefits:			
Process incentives	0.25**		
Outcome incentives	−0.28***		−0.27**
Civic voluntarism			
Strength of party ID			−0.49**
Party ID (comparison = no party ID)			
Labour ID		1.30***	
Occupational status	0.20**		
Equity–fairness			
Outcomes and expectations	−0.26	−0.80***	−0.93***
Retired	1.01***		
Social capital			
Trust others	**0.38***		0.13***
Trust elected politicians		**0.23***	
Trust state institutions		0.14***	**0.40***
TV watching	0.19**		
R^2	0.26	0.28	0.33

Waves 1 and 2, 2000–01 Citizen Audit panel study, N = 809.
Note: The table contains the standardised regression coefficients obtained from regressing the row variables on the column variables. Asterisks indicate the statistical significance of the coefficients with $p < 0.10^*$; $p < 0.05^{**}$; $p < 0.01^{***}$.

greater the perceived gap between outcomes and expectations in 2000, the less trusting did individuals become over time. On all three scales, trust fell most among those who in 2000 had felt they were receiving less than they expected, a measure from the relative deprivation model. It increased most among those who had felt their expectations and outcomes were more in balance. Relative deprivation, therefore, was inimical to growing trust.

But these were not the only factors affecting change in the trust scales. Trust in other people grew most among those who scored well on the political knowledge scale in 2000, those who felt there were strong process incentives to action, the more middle-class, the retired and (intriguingly) those who watched most television, though this is a rather weak effect. It fell among those who had felt there were strong outcome incentives to action in 2000. Trust in elected politicians fell among the best-educated, meanwhile. But, not surprisingly, given that their party had just won a second landslide victory, it grew among Labour partisans. It also grew more among those who had previously trusted other state institutions than among those who had not. And trust in state institutions also grew most among those individuals who trusted other citizens most. But it fell more among those with strong outcome incentives in 2000 than among those whose outcome incentives were weaker, presumably reflecting their general dissatisfaction with the state system: remember the outcome incentives scale is built from questions which tap into a sense that 'things would be better if I was involved in running them'. And it fell most, too, among those who were the strongest partisans.

What of change in people's sense of civic obligations, as measured by their willingness to undertake different forms of civic activity in our two attitudes to obligations scales and by the attitudes to rights scale? Table 8.9 reveals that, as ever, the best predictor of an individual's views on these scales in 2001 is his or her score on the equivalent scale the previous year; the relevant coefficients are in bold. Interest in politics is a consistent predictor of change in both obligations models. The more interested individuals said they were in politics at wave 1, the more likely it is that their voluntary action and civic office scores will increase between waves 1 and 2. Initial interest encourages a growing willingness to participate in voluntary actions and public office. Other factors play a part in particular models. Education emerges as an important factor accounting for change in willingness to seek civic office: the longer people had spent in education, the greater their willingness to stand for office increased over the year. Outcome incentives were also important – not surprisingly – in accounting for change in willingness to stand for civic office. Those who in 2000 had felt that people like themselves would do a good job as a councillor or an MP became more likely over time to claim a willingness to act in those capacities. But retired people's willingness to undertake voluntary actions declined over time relative to those who were not retired. This may reflect the relatively physical nature of several of the tasks in the scale: giving blood, renovating a park and helping with meals on wheels.[20]

---

[20] In fact, those older than the state retirement age are not allowed to donate blood.

Table 8.9 *The Dynamics of Participation: Changes in Attitudes to Obligations and Rights*

	Obligations scales 2001		Rights scale 2001
	Voluntary action	Civic office	Rights to state action
Independent variables (2000)			
Constant	1.22	−0.12	9.47
Voluntary action	0.42***		
Civic office		0.34***	
State action			0.39***
Cognitive engagement			
Age left education		0.06***	
Interest in politics	0.02**	0.02***	
General incentives			
Selective benefits:			
Outcome incentives		0.04***	
Civic voluntarism			
Strength of party ID			0.24***
Party ID (comparison = no party ID)			
Conservative ID			−0.76***
Other ID	0.44**		
Household income			−0.19***
Equity–fairness			
Female			0.40**
Retired	−0.26***		
R^2	0.23	0.20	0.23

Waves 1 and 2, 2000–01 Citizen Audit panel study, N = 809.
Note: The table contains the unstandardised regression coefficients obtained from regressing the row variables on the column variables. Asterisks indicate the statistical significance of the coefficients with $p < 0.10$*; $p < 0.05$**; $p < 0.01$***.

People who said they supported a political party other than one of the big three became more willing to engage in voluntary activities over time.

What of change over time in individuals' sense of their rights, in particular of rights to state action? As ever, past belief is a strong, positive, predictor of current belief: people tend to think now as they have in the past. Three factors from the civic voluntarism model all contribute to an explanation of change in sense of rights. The stronger an individual's sense of partisanship, for instance, the more that person's belief in state rights grows over time. But the direction, as well as the strength, of partisanship matters. Not surprisingly, given the party's now long-established desire to cut back on state provision, individuals identifying themselves as Conservative become less likely over time to support state rights. Similarly, affluence is negatively related to change in support for state-provided rights: the richer an individual was in 2000, the less his or her support for state rights grew over the following year, perhaps due to anxieties about tax burdens. Women's belief in state-provided rights grows more over the period than does men's, however.

The discussion so far has focused on changes in people's civic attitudes. What of their actions? Can we identify which factors mobilise people, and which demotivate them? We focus first in table 8.10 on people's associational lives. What influenced changes in organisational membership, time given to associational activities, and frequency of political conversations? Once again, unsurprisingly, levels of activity in 2001 were best predicted by levels of the same activity in 2000 (coefficients in bold). The more types of organisation people had joined in 2000, the more they joined a year later. The more time they spent associating in 2000, the more time they devoted to it in 2001. And those disposed to frequent political discussions in 2000 were also the most active political conversationalists in 2001. Education was positively associated both with group membership and with time spent in associational engagement: the better educated an individual was in 2000, the bigger the increase in the number of types of organisation he or she joined over the following year, and the more time he or she devoted to those activities. Occupational status, too, played a consistent role: more middle-class individuals became more active, spent more time associating, and became more frequent political discussants over time than did working-class individuals. And as we saw earlier, media effects were both evident and nuanced. In line with Norris' (1996) argument, the attention people paid to political news had a motivating effect: the greater a person's exposure to politics in the media in 2000, the greater the increase in his or her associational membership and in their political conversation over time. But, as suggested by Putnam, television viewing in general was demotivating. The more TV a person watched in 2000, the less his or her associational activity increased over time, and the less likely he or she was to spend more time on those activities, presumably because there was insufficient time to fit those activities and discussions around the demands of the TV schedules. Informal networking encouraged participation. Those in such a network in 2000 increased the time they spent associating more over the following year than those who did not belong to such a network. And the retired spent increasing amounts of time associating with others – but they became less frequent political

Table 8.10 *The Dynamics of Participation: Changing Civic Activities*

	Civic activities scales 2001		
	Number of groups joined	Time associational engagement	Political conversations
Independent variables (2000)			
Constant	0.08	1.55	2.74
Time associational engagement			**0.24*****
Political conversations			**0.41*****
Cognitive engagement			
Age left education	0.12***	0.14***	
Political knowledge	0.06**		
Media exposure	0.06***		0.13***
Interest in politics			0.06**
General incentives			
Selective benefits:			
Group incentives		0.08**	
Civic voluntarism			
Political efficacy			0.09**
Party ID (comparison = no party ID)			
Other ID		−0.94**	
Occupational status	0.10***	0.07**	0.11**
Free time		−0.05**	
Household income			0.11
Equity–fairness			
Retired		0.46***	−0.89***
Social capital			
Number groups joined	**0.39*****		
Informal networks		0.42***	
TV watching	−0.09***	−0.08***	
Years lived in neighbourhood	0.10**		
R^2	0.28	0.16	0.36

Waves 1 and 2, 2000–01 Citizen Audit panel study, N = 809.
Note: The table contains the unstandardised regression coefficients obtained from regressing the row variables on the column variables. Asterisks indicate the statistical significance of the coefficients with $p < 0.10^*$; $p < 0.05^{**}$; $p < 0.01^{***}$.

discussants, perhaps because of the loss of work colleagues with whom to talk.

Those most politically knowledgeable in 2000 were more likely to increase their membership of different types of groups over the following year than the less knowlegeable. And the more group incentives people saw in 2000, the greater was the time they gave to associational activities between then and 2001 – though this particular relationship failed the second Granger test for reciprocal links. But people who identified with parties other than Labour, Conservative or Liberal Democrat, and people with abundant free time in 2000, were less likely than their counterparts to increase the time spent associating in 2001 than in 2000. The more interested people were in politics in 2000, the greater the chance they would talk more about it to others over the coming year. And not surprisingly, perhaps, the greater the sense of political efficacy felt by individuals in 2000, the greater the increase in the frequency of their political conversations over the following year. People who felt that political activity mattered presumably saw political discussion as a key part of that activity, and responded to the 2001 election by talking more to their fellow citizens about politics.

There were also changes in the level of activities aimed at influencing rules, laws or policies. In table 8.11 we examine not only change in the total number of activities undertaken, but also change in the number of individualistic, contacting and collective actions. As before, levels of activity a year before were the best predictors: the more activities, both in total and of each kind, a person had undertaken in 2000, the more they undertook in 2001. Active people tended to stay active (coefficients in bold).

Education was associated with increasing levels both of total and of individualistic activism. The longer a person had spent in full-time education, the more likely it was that he or she would undertake more activities in total, and more individualistic activities in particular, in 2001 than in 2000. And television watching discouraged both. The more TV people had watched in 2000, the less their total level of civic activity grew between 2000 and 2001, and the less their levels of individualistic activity increased. The more middle-class someone's occupation, the greater the increase over time in total, contacting, and collective civic activities. The more trusting individuals were of state institutions at wave 1, however, the less likely they were to increase the total number of political activities they were involved in by wave 2. In this instance alone, then, trust discouraged action, perhaps by encouraging a view that the state was working effectively and so did not need the extra goad of public action. That said, this relationship failed the second test for Granger causality: trust in state institutions at wave 2 was significantly and negatively related to total levels of political activity at wave 1. Women were more likely than men to increase the level of their individualistic civic activities between 2000 and 2001. The more interested people were in politics in 2000, the greater was the likelihood that they would become more involved in

Table 8.11 *The Dynamics of Participation: Changing Political Activities*

	Number of political activities scales 2001			
	Political activities	Individualistic activities	Contacting activities	Collective activities
Independent variables (2000)				
Constant	2.92	1.94	0.05	0.12
N political activities	**0.42*****			
N individual political actions		**0.34*****		
N contacting political actions			**0.41*****	
N collectivist political actions				**0.19*****
Cognitive engagement				
Age left education	0.13**	0.15***		
Interest in politics		0.04**		
General incentives				
Collective benefits:				
Satisfaction with democracy				−0.04**
Costs				−0.02**
Selective benefits:				
Process incentives				0.03**
Outcome incentives			0.05**	
System (altruistic) benefits				0.02**
Civic voluntarism				
Party ID (comparison = no party ID)				
Conservative ID				−0.12***
Other ID				0.31***
Occupational status	0.10**		0.05***	0.02***
Equity–fairness				
Female		0.41***		
Social capital				
Trust state institutions	−0.02**			
TV watching	−0.13***	−0.12***		
R^2	0.29	0.25	0.22	0.11

Waves 1 and 2, 2000–01 Citizen Audit panel study, $N = 809$.

Note: The table contains the unstandardised regression coefficients obtained from regressing the row variables on the column variables. Asterisks indicate the statistical significance of the coefficients with $p < 0.10^*$; $p < 0.05^{**}$; $p < 0.01^{***}$.

individualistic political activities over time. Outcome incentives, meanwhile, were associated with change in levels of contacting: the more an individual thought politics would benefit from the involvement of a person like him- or herself in 2000, the greater the increase over the next twelve months in his or her levels of contacting. People who thought they could make a difference tried to do so.

Finally, what of increases in levels of collective action? General incentives rational choice factors played an important role here. Changes in levels of collective action were associated with dissatisfaction with democracy (our measure of collective benefits). Those who felt, in 2000, that British democracy was not working as well as they would like were more likely than those satisfied with it to increase the number of collective steps taken to remedy things. But, not surprisingly, those who perceived significant costs to involvement in 2000 were less likely to increase their collective activities than were those who saw few such costs. But the more process and altruistic benefits people could see in 2000, the more likely they were to increase their collective activism in 2001. Partisanship mattered here too. Conservative identifiers became less collectively active over time, compared to those with no party identification, while those who identified with 'other' parties were more likely than non-identifiers to increase their collective activities.

Conclusions

The period between the 2000 and 2001 waves of our panel was a dramatic one. British political life was stirred up not only by a general election in June 2001, but also by the fuel protests of autumn 2000, by protests over a proposed ban on fox hunting, and by the political fall-out of the foot and mouth crisis of the first half of 2001. International tensions grew dramatically after the events of 11 September 2001. Although we cannot completely disentangle the effects of each of these events from the others, our panel evidence does suggest that an unusually political year did have an effect on the civic attitudes and behaviour of the British public. In general, people became more concerned about politics, were more interested in it, paid greater attention to it, and did more about it. On a variety of measures, Britain was a more civic society after the 2001 election than it had been before it.

Accounting for that change is more difficult, however. Here we have focused on the attributes of individual members of the public. Who was likely to become more engaged with civic life, and who less? The various models of citizenship discussed throughout the second half of the book have all influenced change over time, as we can see if we highlight a few examples. Factors related to the cognitive engagement model help account for increased associational activity, for instance. General incentives factors encouraged collective action. Aspects of the civic voluntarism model were related to change in time spent on activities. On the whole, the more interested people were in politics to start with, the more they felt they got out of their lives, the greater the resources they had to draw on, and the better integrated they were into informal networks of friends and acquaintances, the more active they became over time, and the more positive they felt in their civic attitudes. In other words, the civic culture grew most among those who were already most likely to be civic-minded. To them that have shall be given.

The villain of the piece, however, comes from the social capital model: as Putnam (2000) suggested, it is television. In model after model, the more TV a respondent reported watching on average in 2000, the less likely he or she was to improve his or her civic commitment. Television is, of course, generally consumed in the privacy of the home. Frequent TV watchers just did not get out and get involved to the same extent as those not glued to the screen. But – again a feature of many models – not all media exposure was bad. Those who paid close attention to political news in 2000 generally became more active, and thought better of civic life, over the following year. Television may be a villain, therefore, but it is not always so. As with so many things, it isn't what you do, it's the way that you do it . . .

The analysis presented here of year-on-year change in civic activity in Britain suggests an intriguing picture, therefore. Contrary to those who would claim that the civic culture is in inexorable decline, our results show that there are positive as well as negative trends. Not only that, but it is clear that events can trigger activity. The 2001 general election does seem to have engendered a rise in civic-mindedness, even if this did not translate into voting. Parties, and other organisations and individuals, can still mobilise the public. That said, the diversity of different factors which influence change in the civic culture suggests that there is no magic bullet, no simple panacea to encourage civic virtue among the public, let alone to discourage civic vice. On the contrary, different factors influence different outcomes. Before deciding how to do it, one needs to know what one wants to do.

We have now looked at citizenship in contemporary Britain from a variety of perspectives: who gets involved and why; what difference it makes; and how it has changed over the short term. In the next, and final, chapter, we draw some wider conclusions.

9   Challenges to Citizenship in Contemporary Britain

In this concluding chapter we do three things. Firstly, we summarise some of the key findings from the earlier chapters as a way of addressing the question posed in chapter 1: 'What does it mean to be a British citizen in the early twenty-first century?' Secondly, we go on to examine some of the changes that have taken place in the key indicators of citizenship over time, linking these to some of the earlier findings. Thirdly, we consider the implications of our findings for citizenship in Britain in the future. These results pose challenges to British society and the political system, and so we spend some time considering these challenges.

What does citizenship mean?

The findings in this book make it possible to begin to answer the question posed in chapter 1. The starting point of an answer to this question is to divide citizenship into two related aspects involving attitudes and beliefs on the one hand and behaviour on the other. We explored the former in chapter 2 and the latter in chapters 3 and 4 before going on to discuss the determinants of such attitudes and behaviour in chapters 5 and 6.

We explored many facets of attitudes to citizenship in chapter 2, examining identities, inter-personal trust, institutional trust, tolerance, and perceptions of government among other things. The common thread running through the discussion was the attempt to understand the relationship between the individual and the state. This relationship concerns questions like: Do individuals identify with the state and feel that they belong to it? Do they trust its institutions and their fellow citizens? Do they believe that the government is responsive to their concerns or do they think it largely ignores them? These are all important for understanding what it means to be a citizen in contemporary Britain.

The analysis in chapter 2 suggested that on the whole Britons identified with their country rather more than they did with their locality or region. But surprisingly, less than a quarter of our sample identified themselves as British, indicating that in a sense national identity is fragmenting.

Citizens increasingly identify themselves with the country they are living in – England, Wales or Scotland – rather than with the British Isles as a whole.

If identity is one of the foundations of citizenship then so is trust – a sound civic culture involves individuals being willing to trust each other as well as the institutions of the state. The evidence suggests that people do tend to trust each other, and many trust the unelected institutions of the political system, such as the police and the courts. However, there is much less trust of elected institutions such as Parliament or the political parties. Curiously, while the elective principle legitimates democratic government, directly elected institutions are not trusted very much compared with their appointed rival institutions. One way of explaining this apparent paradox is that a healthy democracy requires people to be basically loyal to the system and to some extent be proud of it. At the same time they should have a healthy scepticism towards their elected representatives if government is to be held accountable. Britons certainly appear to share that scepticism.

Another important feature of democracy is tolerance, and with a few exceptions, citizens are tolerant towards other people and organisations. However, there are clear limits to this tolerance; they may be happy to allow dissenters to speak in public, but they are not happy to extend this to neo-nazis or to have a new age traveller camp housed next door. Tolerance operates in a context, and its limits are reached when it imposes real costs on the people involved.

A third feature of a healthy democracy is citizen attitudes to government. The key issue here is whether or not individuals feel that the government is responsive to their concerns. The evidence suggests that most people believe that government is not very responsive to them as individuals, and moreover it will not generally make decisions in accordance with their personal wishes. On the other hand, there is a widespread belief that government is relatively responsive to majority opinion. Again, if the institutions of democracy are to work well, government should be viewed in this light. While people may think that the government pays little attention to them as individuals, democracy will be safeguarded if they think it pays attention to a majority of citizens.

In this respect some of the most important findings in the Citizen Audit relate to attitudes to voting. Generally people disagree with the proposition that voting makes no difference, even though they do not see all types of voting as being effective. Majorities believe that voting in local elections, general elections and elections for the Scottish Assembly all have an influence on the decision-makers at these different levels of government. However, the same cannot be said about elections to the European

Parliament and to the Welsh Assembly, where voting is seen as having little influence on decision-makers. Ironically, more people believe that voting influences decision-makers in local authorities than believe it influences the House of Commons. This is surprising given the erosion of local authority powers over the past twenty-five years. The Welsh Assembly in particular does worse than the European Parliament in public perceptions of responsiveness to voters. This may, of course, change in the future as this relatively new institution becomes embedded in public consciousness, but apart from the Scottish Assembly the regional and European institutions have a long way to go before they are seen as responsive to public concerns.

As we made clear in chapter 1, citizenship is a very broad concept, and to make it tractable for empirical analysis it is important to concentrate on the key issues. We have suggested that a key issue from the point of view of civil society is the need to balance the demand for rights with a willingness to accept the obligations which accompany those rights. This is a key requirement for a successful political culture.

When it comes to accepting obligations it is clear that people's sense of civic duty is relatively high. This encompasses obedience to the state, a willingness to undertake voluntary activity, such as participating in a Neighbourhood Watch or a local renovation project, and a willingness to engage in civic service, such as going on a jury or giving blood. But for most people their sense of duty does not extend to more high-intensity forms of participation such as becoming a school governor or standing for the local council; on such matters, their commitment is much more limited. If democracy is to work properly it is important that some people are willing to run for public office, but this only need be a minority. What is much more important is that the vast majority of people feel obliged to operate by the rules of the game, to pay their taxes, and to obey the law. Generally, this is true in Britain.

If most people accept their obligations it is also true that most people are aware of their rights. There is widespread support for private rights such as paternity leave, women's right to choose an abortion and the right to die. However, there is scepticism about extending gay rights to make them equivalent to those enjoyed by married couples. In relation to state-provided benefits, such as housing, income maintenance for the poor and higher education, there is strong support for state action to maintain such rights. However, there is less public support for the notion that the government should find work for every person requiring it. Perhaps this reflects the fact that governments have increasingly acknowledged that they have only a limited influence on employment in the modern globalised economy.

When considering rights it is important to recognise that many people want the right to be left alone by government, so that the demand for rights is not always about asking government to intervene. This is apparent in the survey, since many people think that individuals should not expect the state to provide for their retirement, and many think that health care should not be universally provided for the affluent. Overall, this selective approach to rights, combined with the evidence of a strong sense of civic duty, makes the task of governing easier. The demand for benefits on the one hand tends to be balanced by the supply of support and resources on the other.

If public attitudes to rights and obligations are broadly supportive of democratic government, what of public willingness to participate? The first point to make is that it is important to define participation broadly since a narrow focus, say, on electoral participation, will miss much of the participation which is actually going on. It is apparent that macro participation – that is participation aimed at influencing actors or organisations which are direct representatives of the state – can be structured into three broad categories. These are individualistic forms of participation, such as voting and donating money to an organisation, contact participation, such as writing to the media or speaking to a Member of Parliament, and collective participation, such as attending a political meeting or taking part in a demonstration. Not surprisingly, in terms of the costs and benefits of participation, more people are involved in individualistic forms than in collective forms. The evidence in chapter 3 suggests that many of the individualistic forms have increased and many of the collective forms of participation have declined in importance since the early 1980s. Despite this, the evidence also suggests that participation potential – the willingness of people to get involved – is high and in the case of participating in demonstrations, it has increased over time.[1] Moreover, viewed in terms of the number of political actions undertaken over the previous twelve months, more than eight out of ten citizens have participated in some form.

Another important dimension of participation is membership and activism in organised and informal groups. In fact membership of organised groups is a minority activity, since 55 per cent of Britons are not members of any group. In addition, many of the people who are members of groups pay their dues and do very little else. While many of these groups have very little direct link with the political process, since they involve organisations like sports clubs and gymnasia, they are nonetheless training grounds for participation for many people. If individuals are

[1] See table 3.3.

actually involved in one of these groups, then many of them regularly attend meetings, speak, organise, and try to mobilise their fellow members to undertake tasks for the organisation. It is clear that such groups are places where people can learn the skills associated with more high-intensity forms of participation.

Beyond the organised groups is a whole world of informal groups which underpin civil society, and in some cases provide important services. About one person in five belongs to an informal group such as a pub quiz team or a book reading group, and about a third of people provide some sort of support for neighbours or friends beyond their immediate family. This type of activity is important because it helps build networks of civic engagement and also provides services which are of real value. There would be drastic political consequences for government if such informal provision of support for people in the community were no longer provided.

Another aspect of participation which has been largely invisible to researchers in the past is what we have termed micro political participation. This refers to actions designed to influence indirect agents of the state in the day-to-day world. For parents this means trying to influence their children's education in school, for patients it means trying to influence their medical treatment, or for the employed it means trying to influence their working conditions. Given that the state is becoming less and less a direct service provider and more of an overseer and regulator, this is an aspect of politics which is growing in importance. It is readily apparent that a lot of this type of participation is taking place. In the previous year almost one in two of our respondents in employment had tried to improve their working conditions, one in four parents had tried to change the way their children's education was provided, and one in ten patients had tried to change the way their health treatment was delivered. Not surprisingly, people tend to take action only when they are dissatisfied with these services or work conditions, and their actions are less likely to be channelled through the orthodox route of contacting a politician and more likely to involve contacting the professionals direct. It is also apparent that micro political activities are more likely to be conducted through personal contact and individualised forms of action, with the sole exception of employee participation via trade unions. Success rates for this type of action seem to be quite high, and on the whole people felt that they had been treated fairly in trying to influence politics at this level.

Overall, the Citizen Audit survey reveals that citizens have not contracted out of politics, but rather are engaged in a multiplicity of political activities beyond the traditional ones. The most common forms of political activity tend to be individualistic, like giving money, signing a petition, or purchasing particular types of goods. These can be done without the need to cooperate with other people in an organisation. While many observers are rightly concerned about the decline of electoral participation, it is important to remember that political engagement does not lie upon one single continuum. Rather, there are distinct individualistic, contact and collectively organised forms of political engagement. When these are viewed as a whole and micro political participation is also taken into account, there is a lot of participation going on in Britain.

This pattern of individualistic engagement makes it meaningful to talk about 'consumer citizenship'. This idea was first introduced into British politics by the Conservative government in the form of the Citizen's Charter, and has been promoted by successive governments since that time. In 1999 the Labour government published a White Paper crafted around the idea that consumers should be active citizens (HMSO, 1999), and the idea has become part of day-to-day discourse. For many politicians active citizenship means making the public services responsive to consumer preferences, but actually it is considerably wider than that. Individualistic action can involve citizens trying to influence the political process in relation to a wide array of governmental responsibilities. Whether the issue involves the environment, animal welfare, transport, or even foreign policy, when citizens use their purchasing power to try and influence policies they are actively participating in politics.

If the evidence suggests that civic engagement is healthy, there is also evidence of a darker side to citizenship. Some citizens do want rights without acknowledging their obligations, but it is important to note that these attitudes are not widespread. For the most part, it is the individuals who lack power and resources who are most likely to want the state to intervene on their behalf while at the same time being reluctant to get involved in the political process themselves. Aside from this group, powerful norms exist in British society which support the idea that individuals should not free-ride on the efforts of others. These norms are ultimately responsible for making civil society and the state effective.

We noted in chapter 6 that the demand for state intervention to provide redistributive rights is very much influenced by individual resources. It is the uneducated, the low-status and the low-income citizens who are most likely to make these demands. But their relative lack of interest in participation constitutes a real barrier to the implementation of policies which will promote state intervention to reduce inequality and redistribute income. As Peter Hall points out, Britain is 'divided between a well-connected group of citizens with prosperous lives and high levels of civic engagement and other groups whose networks, associational life and involvement in politics is very limited' (Hall, 2002: 53). The reality of democratic electoral politics is that non-participants are likely to be marginalised or ignored, since the electoral incentives are for parties to focus on participants. It is perhaps not surprising that inequality in Britain has grown over the last twenty-five years.[2] This is more or less inevitable in a democratic system where the demand for redistribution comes mainly from non-participants. The relatively contented majority will not be that concerned about such questions and as a consequence they will be neglected in the policy process (see Galbraith, 1992)

Another aspect of this dark side of contemporary political participation is the rise of 'cheque-book' participation. This goes beyond buying goods for ethical or political reasons and involves, in effect, subcontracting out one's participation to someone else. Much of the recent growth in interest groups such as Greenpeace, Friends of the Earth, Shelter and other cause groups can be explained by this development (Maloney, 1999). Such organisations have large numbers of supporters who donate money to the cause, but who do little else. Indeed the organisational structure of such groups militates against mass democratic participation in policy formation and implementation. For many of these organisations 'members are a non-lucrative distraction' (Skocpol, 2002: 134). Skocpol argues that many of these groups are created by political entrepreneurs who raise funds by direct mail and then use the money to hire pollsters and media consultants in order to frame policies and lobbying strategies. These policies are drafted with one eye on their mass marketing appeal as much as on the cause being advocated. This is not a deliberative, or for that matter an educative, form of participation from the point of view of the wider society. It narrows the dialogue to one between full-time professionals in the interest groups and in the policy-making networks in government. It tends to exclude the mass of citizens, except in the most general terms. It is not a recipe for building a grassroots activist type of politics.

In chapters 5 and 6 we turned our attention to the task of explaining citizen attitudes and behaviour using choice-based and structural-based theories and models. As we pointed out, this distinction pervades social theory and when it is translated into testable models the relevance of these alternative explanations of citizenship can be examined. In explaining citizen attitudes and behaviour, it is apparent that no single model dominates the picture, but it is also clear that some models are more important than others. In relation to attitudes to rights, two models in particular were important, the equity–fairness and the civic voluntarism models. As far as the former is concerned, a lack of resources encourages individuals

---

[2] See the Office of National Statistics website http://www.statistics.gov/.

to demand rights. However, this is inconsistent with the latter model, since the civic voluntarism model predicts that individuals with resources are likely to be the biggest advocates of rights. As mentioned earlier, the uneducated, the low status and those at the bottom of the income ladder are more likely to demand redistributive rights than the educated and high-status individuals. In addition, perceptions of costs, process incentives and altruistic motives from the general incentives model are also important variables in explaining the demand for rights. In the case of rights, structure-based and choice-based theories are equally important.

The obligation to volunteer model is rather different from the rights model. In this case the general incentives and social capital models appear to be most important of the incentive variables, altruistic motives appear to have marginally the strongest influence on obligations, but outcome incentives and social norms also play a positive role. As far as the social capital model is concerned, membership of groups has the biggest impact on obligations, with informal group membership and community ties being relevant also for promoting a sense of obligations. Other models make minor contributions to explaining obligations as well. From the cognitive engagement model, those who are politically knowledgeable, those who are interested in politics, and individuals who are exposed to politics in the media all have a stronger sense of obligations to volunteer than the population in general. It is also apparent that policy dissatisfaction motivates individuals to volunteer.

The biggest contrast between the rights and obligations models is that a lack of resources creates a demand for rights, whereas obligations to participate are much more about being interested in politics and being rooted in the community. Putting this the other way round, those with a strong sense of obligations are inclined to take political action, whereas supporters of rights are more likely to want the state to act on their behalf.

Turning next to the participation models, while all five models contribute to explaining variations in participation, the general incentives model appears to be more important than its rivals in explaining individualistic participation. However, the political interest and knowledge variables from the cognitive engagement model, and the community and group attachments variables from the social capital model, all contribute to explaining individualistic forms of participation. On the other hand, with the exception of the mobilisation measure, the civic voluntarism model makes very little contribution to explaining individualistic action. A similar point can be made about the equity–fairness model.

In relation to collective action, the general incentives model is rather less important than is true of individualistic participation and the cognitive engagement and equity–fairness models play a more important role.

From the cognitive engagement model, interest in politics and higher education promote collective action. From the equity–fairness model a gap between individuals' expectations and their life experiences motivates them to participate in collective action. Equally, mobilisation is an important factor in explaining this type of participation, although in other respects the civic voluntarism model plays no role in explaining collective action. Finally, the effects arising from the social capital model appear to be inconsistent with the theory.

In the case of small-scale democratic political action, the social capital model appears to be quite important; inter-personal and institutional trust influences participation as does membership of groups. TV exposure appears to inhibit participation as it does in the individualistic participation model. The general incentives, cognitive engagement and equity–fairness models play modest roles in explaining small-scale participation, while once again the civic voluntarism model appears to be largely irrelevant, except in relation to mobilisation.

Stepping back from the detailed estimates of the models and looking at the picture as a whole, it is clear that choice-based models are more important than structural-based models for explaining political participation. In many respects the opposite is true for attitudes to rights. In the case of rights, a clear majority of the important effects come from structural-based models, with equity–fairness and civic voluntarism being particularly important. In the case of participation, the general incentive and cognitive engagement models are particularly important.

Chapters 7 and 8 address the key question as to whether citizenship has any effects on policy outcomes. In chapter 7 we distinguished between outputs and outcomes, with the former referring to things like spending on services like education, health and transport, and the latter referring to perceptions of the quality of these services or to objective measures of such quality. The results in chapter 7 indicate that citizenship has clear payoffs from the point of view of the wider political system. However, these payoffs really come in terms of influencing outcomes rather than outputs. In one sense this is not surprising, since much local government spending is tightly controlled by central government or by legal restrictions, so the scope for local variations in spending on outputs is limited. However, when it comes to perceptions of the quality of local services or actual quality of life measures, areas of the country characterised by 'good citizenship' get a better quality of service than areas characterised by 'poor citizenship'. This is particularly apparent in relation to educational performance, health, and satisfaction with life and with democracy.

Chapter 8 focused on the dynamics of citizenship, aiming to address the broad question as to whether a general election can act as a stimulus to good citizenship. Traditionally, research into electoral behaviour has focused on the task of explaining participation. In chapter 8 we reversed this focus by looking at the extent to which citizenship in Britain is renewed and refreshed by electoral participation. The period between the 2000 and 2001 waves of our panel saw some dramatic changes. In addition to the general election of June 2001, there were the fuel protests of autumn 2000, widespread protests about countryside issues focusing particularly on fox hunting, and the political fall-out of the foot and mouth crisis of the first half of 2001. International tensions grew dramatically after the attack on the World Trade Center in New York on 11 September 2001. Although we cannot completely disentangle the effects of each of these events from each other, the panel evidence suggests that these events did have cumulative influence on civic attitudes and behaviour in Britain. In general, people became more interested in politics, paid greater attention to it, and participated more. On a variety of measures, Britain was a more civic society at the end of 2001 than it was at the start, making civic attitudes and behaviour dynamic rather than static phenomena.

In the light of this brief review of our findings, we return to the question of exploring the long-term dynamics of citizenship, looking next at some evidence on the evolution of attitudes and participation over time.

Change in citizenship over time

An examination of trends in the attitudinal and behavioural indicators of citizenship over time provides key insights into how civil society is changing. In chapter 6 we suggested that choice models of participation and perceptions of obligations most commonly provide a better explanation than do structural models. This has an important implication, namely that citizenship is more of a dynamic phenomenon with a potential for change than would be predicted by the relatively slow processes of social structural change. However, one problem for assessing change of this type is that there is a dearth of data on many of our indicators from earlier time periods. We saw in chapter 8 that there can be considerable changes in attitudes and behaviour over the period of a year, but it is harder to assess longer-term changes. On the other hand, the data available on attitudes to rights and obligations as well as in relation to participation over a long period of time are limited.

We have suggested that perceptions of rights and obligations are at the heart of citizenship in modern Britain. What trends exist over time in these measures? It is quite difficult to measure this since there are only limited data available on these attitudinal dimensions of citizenship.

Table 9.1 *Changes in Attitudes to Obligations 1959–2000*

1959	Active participation %	Passive participation %	Other types of participation %	Do nothing %	Don't know %
	39	31	5	6	17

'We know that the ordinary person has many problems that take his time. In view of this, what part do you think the ordinary person ought to play in the local affairs of his town or district?' (Almond and Verba, 1963: 127)

2000	Strongly agree %	Agree %	Neither %	Disagree %	Strongly disagree %
	8	37	34	18	3

'Every citizen should get involved in politics if democracy is to work properly' (Citizen Audit 2000, weighted face-to-face wave 1 survey).

In their 1959 survey of civic attitudes Almond and Verba included an interesting indicator of perceptions of obligations which can be compared with an indicator used in the Citizen Audit.

Table 9.1 contains the responses to the question about obligations asked in the 1959 and 2000 surveys. It can be seen that in 1959 some 70 per cent of respondents thought that citizens had a duty either to be active or at least passively involved in their local communities. In contrast, in the 2000 survey only 44 per cent of respondents thought that citizens had a duty to get involved if democracy was to work properly. These indicators are not directly comparable to each other of course, but they are nonetheless suggestive that a decline has taken place in the norms which support citizen participation. Since passive participation is a rather ambiguous term, a comparison of the percentage of those advocating non-participation in both surveys is worth making. In 1959 some 6 per cent believed in doing nothing, but by 2000 18 per cent disagreed with the idea that people should be involved. It would seem that there has been a three-fold increase in the number unwilling to become engaged over this forty-year period.

There are no comparable indicators of rights in the 1959 and 2000 surveys, but in this case we can compare responses to the British Election Study survey of 1983 with the Citizen Audit in relation to attitudes to various types of rights. It can be seen in table 9.2 that the evidence of change over this period is somewhat mixed. In relation to combating poverty and promoting equality, the belief that government should do

Table 9.2 *Changes in Attitudes to Rights 1983–2000*

	Year	Should %	Doesn't matter %	Should not %
Government should encourage the growth of private medicine	1983	36	8	47
	2000	49	23	29
Government should spend more money to get rid of poverty	1983	80	3	11
	2000	89	6	5

	Year	Agree %	Neither %	Disagree %
Income should be redistributed*	1983	47	15	37
	2000	64	22	14
Government should create jobs*	1983	73	8	19
	2000	49	21	30

(*Note that there are differences in wording of these indicators in the two years)

	Year	Should %	Doesn't matter %	Should not %
Government should increase the standard of living of pensioners	1983	80	3	13

	Year	Agree %	Neither %	Disagree %
People shouldn't rely on the state for retirement	2000	37	25	38

British Election Study survey, 1983 and Citizen's Audit 2000 weighted face-to-face wave 1 survey.

more has grown over time. On the other hand, in relation to employment, there has been a drastic reduction in the number of people who believe that government should try to create jobs. Equally, the idea that the government should encourage private health care receives more contemporary support than was true in 1983. Similarly, the evidence hints at a growing awareness that individuals are going to have to provide for their own retirement and that they cannot rely solely on the state to do this.

Table 9.3 *Trends in Attitudes to Taxation and Spending 1979–2001*

	Cut taxes and spending %	Doesn't matter/ don't know %	Keep up services and taxes %
1979	26	13	61
1983	19	39	43
1987	13	27	59
1992	12	21	65
1997	8	17	72
2001	10	24	65

British Election Study surveys.

Thus on some issues the demand is for greater government intervention to support rights, whereas on others the demand is for less intervention.

At the centre of almost all political debates in Britain there is a conflict over levels of public expenditure and taxation. The balance between taxation and spending is a key issue which divides the political parties and it is the basis of electoral politics. Arguably this is the area in which the conflict between rights and obligations is most acute. It is interesting to see how attitudes to the trade-off between taxation and spending have evolved over time and this is shown in table 9.3. The data in table 9.3, which are drawn from various British Election Study surveys, tell an interesting story.[3] Firstly, in viewing these figures it is important to note that large majorities of voters favoured higher taxes and spending to the alternative of lower taxes and spending cuts. This is true throughout the whole of the period. Thus there is not much evidence that the British electorate are in favour of downsizing government in order to avoid paying taxes. Just as there is strong support for rights and obligations, there is strong support for government spending to maintain important social programmes. A second point is that these measures have an important dynamic to them over time. At the start of the Thatcher era there was more support for tax and spending cuts than was true in any subsequent period. But this support eroded continuously until the arrival of New Labour in 1997

---

[3] The scales used to measure the taxation versus spending trade-off in the election studies have varied over time. They are all variants of an 11-point 0 to 10 scale, where a score of 0 means that a respondent strongly supports cuts in taxation and spending, and a score of 10 means the opposite. These scales have all been recoded so that a low score (usually 0 to 3) is labelled 'cut taxes and spending', an intermediate score (4 to 6) is labelled 'doesn't matter' and a high score (7 to 10) is labelled 'keep taxes and spending'.

(Crewe, 1988; Heath, Jowell and Curtice, 2001). This suggests that the public became more and more conscious of the need to spend money on services even if this meant higher taxes, during the eighteen years of the Conservative government. It is interesting to note that the Thatcher government advocated tax cutting for most of its period of office and sought to roll back the state in line with its New Right agenda (Riddell, 1989).[4] The evidence in table 9.3 suggests that citizens in Britain reacted to this agenda by gradually becoming more in favour of taxing and spending rather than less in favour.

The longitudinal evidence is limited and there are problems of comparability between some of the indicators. It is nonetheless possible to draw some conclusions about trends from this evidence. It appears that, with the possible exception of protest demonstrations, collective forms of participation have declined in Britain over this period and that this decline has been reinforced by a weakening of the norms which sustain such participation. Put simply, individuals are less likely to believe that citizens should participate, and because of this fact they are less likely to actually get involved. This is what is implied by table 9.1. At the same time, perceptions of rights have not changed in a similar direction during this period. While there is some evidence to suggest that individuals support a reduction in government activities in certain policy areas, this view is certainly not universally held. In relation to issues of redistribution it appears that the demand for government intervention to promote equality has grown rather than diminished over time. Similarly, large majorities are in favour of public expenditure, even if this means higher taxation, and while attitudes to taxation have evolved over time, they have been evolving in favour of more spending rather than tax cuts. In the light of the evidence from the Citizen Audit we conclude that Britons are atomised citizens.

The atomised citizen

This book could have been entitled 'The Atomised Citizen' since this reflects many of the trends we are observing in contemporary Britain. The rise of individualistic forms of participation at the expense of collectivist forms characterises this process. There are clearly costs associated with this development. They are, firstly, a weakening of the institutions which support collective action, such as political parties. We have documented

---

[4] Although it should be said that cuts in government spending were much more a matter of rhetoric for that government than actual policy.

elsewhere the decline of the grassroots political parties in Britain (Seyd and Whiteley, 1992, 2002a; Whiteley and Seyd; 2002; Whiteley, Seyd and Richardson, 1994). Since parties are the most important institutions in civil society, their decline means a weakening of collective action. The rise of cheque-book participation referred to earlier reinforces this trend. As pressure groups cease to represent large and encompassing groups of citizens, they either become vehicles for narrow special interests or alternatively professional advocacy groups which speak *about*, rather than *on behalf of*, various social groups.

The importance of parties and encompassing representative interest groups is that they help to aggregate interests in society. In a world of special interest groups or narrow advocacy groups, actors seek benefits for the particular constituencies they represent while at the same time trying to avoid paying the costs. The classic strategy of such groups is to seek policies which concentrate the benefits of collective action on their favoured constituencies while at the same time spreading the costs of such policies throughout society (Olson, 1982). In a fragmented, individualistic political system no one has an incentive to accept costs whereas everyone has an incentive to seek benefits. The risk is that policy-making will become gridlocked by ever-increasing demands for particularistic benefits alongside a growing reluctance of society to pay for those benefits. As Mancur Olson pointed out some twenty years ago, society needs encompassing groups like the mainstream political parties, or large trade unions in which demands for benefits have to be matched with a willingness to share the costs of collective action. If a party seeks to represent a majority of the citizens then it cannot walk away from its responsibility to pay for the benefits which it is advocating.

The growth of atomised citizenship runs the risk of a growth of policy fragmentation and policy failure. The best example of this process is in relation to NIMBYist politics. Whether it is car owners who want faster travel times but oppose local motorway construction, or holiday-makers who regularly fly to Europe while bitterly opposing local airport expansion schemes, or newlyweds who turn into staunch opponents of local building projects once they have bought their first house, all illustrate the problem. If the institutions of civil society become weak, then it becomes harder to counteract these tendencies, and individuals will not have to face the logic of their own choices in a fragmented individualistic political system.

One consequence of this trend is that the state is likely to retreat from the collective provision of goods and services and leave this increasingly to the marketplace. Since marketisation is driving the atomisation process, a rational response by governments is to hand over responsibility to the market for collective provision. The historian Philip Bobbitt has written about the rise of what he terms the market state. He writes:

What are the characteristics of the market-state? Such a state depends on the international capital markets and, to a lesser degree, on the modern multinational business network to create stability in the world economy, in preference to management by national or transnational political bodies . . . Like the nation-state, the market-state assesses its economic success or failure by its society's ability to secure more and better goods and services, but in contrast to the nation-state it does not see the State as more than a minimal provider or redistributor. Whereas the nation-state justified itself as an instrument to serve the welfare of the people (the nation), the market-state exists to maximize the opportunities enjoyed by all members of society. (Bobbitt, 2002: 229)

Since his theme is the relationship between war and statehood, he goes on to make the point that it is much harder to get the citizens of a market state to risk their lives on its behalf, since it no longer champions their cultural values. Such a state does not try to cultivate the sense that citizens are part of a common community of values and interests, but merely tries to hold the ring in a competing marketplace of values, ideas and consumer desires.

The key problem for this development is that markets cannot provide the resources they need to sustain themselves. The most basic requirement for markets is that contracts are enforced and property rights protected, which means the rule of law is enforced. As we pointed out in chapter 1, the rule of law is a pure public good, characterised by jointness of supply and the impossibility of exclusion. The attributes of law, such as the equality of all citizens, blindness to status and impartiality of treatment cannot be delivered by markets, but only by a political authority. Historically, market-provided law means rule by the Mafia, with the rich and powerful buying justice at the expense of the poor and vulnerable. In game-theoretic terms, defection by the powerful overrides cooperation.

The problem for the market state is that if it ceases to cultivate common values and community cohesion and withdraws from attempts to sustain a common culture, there is no reason why the process of withdrawal should stop there. If the state is thought to be incompetent in managing the economy and in providing welfare for its citizens and it increasingly withdraws from these activities, there is no reason why it should be seen as competent in providing basic security and the rule of law either. In this situation, citizens will seek private solutions to the problem of security in the form of gated communities and private police forces. The threat of an underclass created by growing inequality and social exclusion will be solved by coercion rather than by social inclusion, and eventually this will destroy democratic politics.

In Britain the trend towards the privatisation of state institutions began in the early 1980s but it continues today even though many state assets have now been transferred to the private sector, or to quasi-non-government organisations. What started out as a device for filling the Treasury's coffers, and weakening public sector trade unions has become a bipartisan policy. Even in highly controversial areas like the air traffic control system, where opponents of privatisation argue that safety will be put at risk if public service norms are replaced by profit-seeking, the policy nonetheless drives forward. Ultimately, this is caused by the process of state withdrawal from collective provision. Apart from raising funds and saving public expenditure, politicians hope that this process will serve to reduce their accountability. Since no one holds the state responsible for the provision of private goods like cars or televisions, the argument is that people will not hold the state responsible for a privatised railway system. This allows decision-makers to avoid the blame for failure in a context in which electoral consequences follow from such failure. This is an inevitable consequence of the market state in which the resources for supporting collective provision are in decline.

Yet another consequence of weakening institutions of civil society is the decline in the dialogue between the rulers and the ruled – a decline of deliberation. Increasingly, debates about policy-making take place between professionals and largely exclude citizens and the wider community. When political parties, for example, were mass organisations then one of the most important functions they fulfilled was to communicate the beliefs of ordinary voters to political decision-makers in a two-way process of dialogue. As parties have atrophied, so has this process of dialogue. Of course, much contemporary policy-making involves sampling public opinion and getting feedback from focus groups on the likely response to public initiatives. But this is the management of opinion rather than a deliberative dialogue between the decision-makers and the public. Elites are seeking legitimation for their initiatives rather than a dialogue about what should or should not be done in the future. In this context the public are seen as a constraint on political action – one more problem to be managed – rather than as partners or stakeholders in a process of policy formation and implementation. The growth of protest potential and the proliferation of demonstrations may be a reaction to this development as the mass public feel a lack of ownership of policy initiatives and as a consequence end up protesting about them. This is made worse by the tendency of elites to ignore such protests if they think they are a passing fashion.

Atomised citizenship has positive aspects as well, which is why the state is moving in this direction. As is well known, collective provision of goods and services by the state has often meant a world of little choice and a one-size-fits-all model of provision. Atomised citizens expect choice and diversity and this is certainly the hallmark of market provision. British citizens want to be able to choose between different schools for their children, choose the hospital they will attend to get an operation and choose their means of travelling to work. Markets bring diversity and choice albeit at the cost of the exclusion of those unable to afford these choices.

A second advantage of the growth of the market state involves efficiency. As Lane argues, markets have 'efficiency norms' (1991: 13) which gives participants an incentive to innovate and reduce costs in order to widen profit margins. Nationalised industries and the public sector more generally do not have these norms to the same extent, and so are often poor at innovating. Moreover, in some cases state-owned industries were captured by producer interests who were not particularly interested in giving the customer what they wanted. An extreme example of this is provided by the old Soviet centralised planning system, which eventually collapsed under the weight of its own inability to innovate and to promote efficiency (see Nove, 1991). Markets promote efficiency and innovation in a way which government finds it hard to emulate.

A third advantage of market provision is the direct link between the costs of a service and the benefits received by individuals. If the state provides goods and services, paying for them out of general taxation, this link is broken. Individuals then have an incentive to demand more than they are willing to pay, because they hope to transfer the costs to someone else. In this situation government over-supplies services and can waste resources if it is too responsive to demands from special interest groups.

Broadly, the state provides four types of activities: regulatory services, pure public goods such as national defence, quasi-public goods such as education and health care, and finally, the administration of transfer payments (Wolf, 1990). Some of these are absolutely essential if the market is to operate at all – particularly the regulation and enforcement of contracts. Similarly, the provision of pure public goods is essential if they are to be adequately supplied. But the other functions are contested, particularly the provision of quasi-public goods and transfer payments. If the state tries to do too much and extends its activities into areas where the market operates much more effectively, then it is likely to fail. In this situation inefficiency undermines legitimacy. However, the retreat by the state into providing only vestigial functions is not possible either, since it is the provision of quasi-public goods and transfer payments which makes the rule of law possible, because these are essential for sustaining citizenship.

In the light of this discussion, what can be done to strengthen citizenship in the future? How might we tackle some of the problems we have observed in this discussion of the foundations of citizenship? We examine this issue next in a final section.

Strengthening citizenship in the future

To return to the discussion of chapter 1, we defined citizenship in terms of norms and practices aimed at solving collective action problems, and set out the conditions under which individuals are likely to cooperate to provide solutions to such problems. What can be done to strengthen and sustain such cooperation? It will be recalled that the cooperative solution in the prisoner's dilemma game required four conditions to be met: an absence of myopia, repeated interaction between actors, uncertainty about when the game ends, and the ability to punish defectors. As we pointed out, these conditions are most likely to be met in relatively small, homogeneous and stable communities in which actors frequently meet each other on a more or less equal basis, and in which they have enough common values to agree on policies and to sanction defection. Clearly, these conditions are less likely to be met in large, heterogeneous societies, where individuals are highly mobile, there is great inequality and a weak common culture.

Changes in British society in the late twentieth and early twenty-first centuries are making the conditions for cooperative action relatively harder to achieve over time. This is because Britain is now a rapidly changing, multicultural society, with a lot of geographical mobility and diverse values. The long-term changes in attitudes and behaviour discussed above are moving us in the direction of declining collective participation and weakening social norms which support participation. Arguably, the market state promotes a culture of instant gratification and this brings with it a myopia of needs – individuals want benefits now and are not prepared to wait. Frequent interaction between actors becomes more difficult as society becomes more socially and ethnically segmented as well as geographically mobile. Common values are weakened as class solidarity and religion decline, culture diversifies and moral relativism grows stronger. Sanctioning defection becomes harder as a result of these developments and if more people are prepared to free-ride on the efforts of others. Finally, growing inequality undermines one of the important preconditions for citizenship – that actors are willing to cooperate because relative equality between them ensures that they face common problems.

It is important to stress that none of these developments prevents solutions to collective action problems being achieved, since an authoritarian government can impose solutions. But they do make democratic solutions harder to achieve, and we have argued that healthy citizenship is closely linked to democracy. In this situation governments are increasingly likely to act arbitrarily and without proper democratic consultation, to try to manipulate opinion and to attempt to impose solutions. This in turn undermines the long-term legitimacy of the state, and in any case such approaches to public policy are likely to fail if citizens feel no ownership of these policy solutions.

On the other hand, there are some positive things which government can do to move us in the direction of a more civic culture. One such innovation is the introduction of citizenship studies into the core curriculum in schools. Given that children have to be socialised into reading and numeracy and have to be taught how to live with other people in schools, it is extraordinary that the state has largely ignored the task of socialising them into citizenship. As we pointed out in chapter 1, citizenship has been about the realm of the *polis* since the time of the ancient Greeks, so it is very strange that the family has been given the sole task of transmitting the values and behaviour associated with good citizenship. It is important to remember that citizenship education is not a panacea, but it should improve political knowledge, stimulate political interest and encourage voluntary activity, if it is imaginatively implemented.

A second and very important way of promoting good citizenship is to devolve power from the centre to the locality and regions. For the reasons examined in chapter 1, cooperation between actors to solve collective action problems works better in small communities than in large ones. If comparisons are made between Britain and other advanced democracies like Germany and the United States, the British state continues to be a very over-centralised system. Over the last couple of decades formerly very centralised states such as Spain and Italy have radically devolved decision-making down to the regional and local levels, seeking the advantages of decentralisation. The British state resists this in the belief that common standards and managerial efficiency will be undermined by these developments. The evidence that citizens are more satisfied with their locally provided services than they are with the nationally provided services should give pause to this belief. The fact is that the centre is often incompetently trying to micro-manage activities which should rightly be devolved down to a much lower tier of government. As a consequence, outcomes are neither efficient nor supportive of good citizenship. Of course, in a complex globalised world, key policies like defence, macro-economic management and foreign affairs cannot be devolved down, but many other domestic policies can be. This is a big agenda which is likely to take a long time to implement, but it is one of the most important ways in which the civic culture can be renewed and strengthened.

A third way of promoting good citizenship is to rein in the continuous election campaign which has now become such a feature of contemporary political life. When such campaigns are never-ending, information is seen as a propaganda weapon rather than as a means of informing people, and this corrodes public discourse. Such campaigns are about manipulation and agenda-setting rather than about public dialogue, so it is not surprising that the public discourse at the heart of citizenship is damaged by the continuous campaign. There is evidence from the 2001 general election that this type of campaigning demobilises voters and switches them off politics (Clarke et al., 2004). The short-term advantages of spin give way to the long-term disadvantages of declining trust in government and political alienation, particularly among the young. Genuine discourse is only likely to be restored when these campaigning pressures are eased, and this will happen when the actors involved begin to realise that they are counterproductive. The media has a responsibility in the process as well, since it has the task of providing information and helping to socialise citizens into participating in a public discourse. The print media is all to often raucously biased, reflecting the priorities and preoccupations of its powerful owners rather than providing a balanced account of the alternative policy choices which society needs to make.

A fourth concern is the relationship between citizenship and equality. We have suggested that if society becomes too heterogeneous then the common norms and values which underpin citizenship are likely to be weakened. Perhaps the most important source of such heterogeneity is the growing income inequality in Britain which is an inevitable product of a marketised society. Civic values are best protected by an egalitarian ethic which emphasises social inclusion. The fact that everyone's vote counts the same in a democracy provides legitimacy to governance. If individuals are marginalised in a system which depends increasingly on financial power in the marketplace rather than voting power in the *polis*, then citizenship will be fatally weakened. In an extreme case government itself will be seen as irrelevant in such a system, as the well-resourced attempt to buy their way out of the insecurities produced by extreme inequality and social exclusion, and the excluded fight back against the injustices resulting from these developments. Thus, when government intervenes to redress the inequalities of the market society, it is strengthening citizenship and promoting social inclusion.

We finish on a cautiously optimistic note. Citizenship in Britain is not in deep crisis and in some respects is quite healthy. On the other hand, some developments such as the decline in a sense of civic duty and in collectivist forms of participation bode ill for the future. However, if the cultivation of civic values and practices is taken seriously by all concerned, there is no reason why citizenship in Britain cannot be renewed in the future.

Appendices

Appendix A The Citizen Audit: Technical Details

Sampling method

The Citizen Audit is a stratified, clustered, random sample of adults aged 18 or over. The sampling frame for the face-to-face part of the survey was the Postcode Address File (PAF). Private households only were selected from the PAF; people living in institutions were excluded. For the mail survey the sampling frame was the 1999 electoral register. The selection of respondents involved three separate stages:

Selection of local authorities

At the first stage, 101 local authorities were selected in England, Scotland and Wales. Using Census sources local authorities were stratified on the basis of:
• population density
• region of the country

Selection of addresses

For the face-to-face survey, three postal districts were selected randomly in each local authority by Business Geographic. Within each of these postal districts twenty households (sixteen to be contacted, plus four spare ones to substitute for missing households) were selected at random. In the mail survey 238 addresses were selected per local authority.

Selection of individuals

Interviewers called at each selected address and listed all those eligible for inclusion in the sample, that is all persons currently aged 18 or over and resident at the selected address. The interviewer then selected the person within the household who had the next birthday. In the mail survey names and addresses were selected randomly from the 1999 electoral registers.

Weighting

The raw data file was weighted by age, sex and employment status to make them consistent with Census data in order to compensate for non-response. All the analysis in this book uses weighted data.

Fieldwork

Interviewing took place in two stages. For the face-to-face part of the survey, the interviews were conducted between 4 September 2000 and 8 December 2000. The mail survey commenced in January 2001. Initial introduction letters were mailed out on 3/4 January 2001. The question-naires were then mailed out on 10/11 January 2001. Two sets of reminder letters were mailed out, the first on 17/18 January, and the second on 31 January/1 February. Finally, a third reminder and questionnaire was sent out to non-respondents on 2/3 April. The cut-off date for the return of questionnaires was 11 May (the end of the week the general election was called).

Response rates

The response rate for wave 1 of the face-to-face survey was 62 per cent, and the unweighted N = 3,258 and the weighted N = 3,262. For cost reasons a 50 per cent random sample of the first wave respondents were selected for reinterviewing for the second wave of the panel. The response rate for this second wave of the panel survey was 50 per cent.

The response rate for the mail survey was 38 per cent (24,038 sent out, 9,959 returned, 2,180 moved/deceased).

For details of socio-demographic characteristics see table 2.13.

Appendix B   The Questionnaires

1.   *Face-to-face questionnaire* (Wave 1)

fieldcontrol
"The Old Laundry"
36 Berrymede Road
Chiswick
London W4 5JD
Tel: 020 8994-9192

FINAL 24/8/00

CITIZENS AUDIT – STAGE 1

Edited By..

SAMPLE/RESPONDENT NO.

(11–15)

FC:105898/00

<u>PLEASE WRITE ALL DETAILS IN *BLOCK CAPITALS*</u>

NAME: Mr/Mrs/Ms/Miss _____

ADDRESS: _____

POSTCODE: (16 – 22)   TELEPHONE NO. _____
(AT LEAST 4 DIGITS NEEDED FOR ANALYSIS)   (INCLUDE DIALLING CODE)

INTERVIEWERS DECLARATION

I DECLARE THIS QUESTIONNAIRE WAS COMPLETED AND CHECKED BY ME, WITHIN THE CODE OF CONDUCT OF THE MARKET RESEARCH SOCIETY AND THE JOB INSTRUCTIONS. THE INFORMANT WAS UNKNOWN TO ME AT THE TIME OF THIS INTERVIEW.

INTERVIEWER SIGNATURE: _____   DATE: _____

INTERVIEWER NAME (*PLEASE PRINT*) _____   INT. No. [   ] (23 – 28)

TIME INTERVIEW BEGAN _____AM/PM   TIME INTERVIEW ENDED _____ AM/PM

OFFICE USE ONLY

RESPONDENT
S.O.C [ ][ ] / [ ][ ]   (29–34)

PARTNER
S.O.C [ ][ ] / [ ][ ]   (35–40)

INTERVIEWER NOTE - CONFIDENTIALITY

WHEN INTRODUCING YOURSELF AND THIS SURVEY, PLEASE ENSURE THE RESPONDENT KNOWS THAT THIS RESEARCH AND ANY INFORMATION THEY GIVE ARE, AND WILL REMAIN, STRICTLY CONFIDENTIAL

SHOWCARD
1) **How long have you lived at this address?**

	(41)
Under 1 year	1
From 1 year and under 5 years	2
From 5 years and under 10 years	3
From 10 or more years	4

2) **Do you have family who live nearby?**

	(42)
Yes	1
No	2

ATTACHMENT TO PLACE

SHOWCARD
3) I would now like to ask you some questions about your feelings of attachment to the place where you live. How strong are your feelings of attachment to your neighbourhood, town, region, country and Europe?

Some people feel a <u>very strong attachment</u>. They would give themselves a score of <u>ten</u>.

Other people feel no attachment. They would give themselves a score of <u>zero</u>.

Others feel <u>somewhere in between.</u> (If you have no preference either way give a score somewhere in between)

Please give a number which comes closest to your views about your attachment to each of the places referred to below.

	NO ATTACHMENT AT ALL									VERY STRONG ATTACHMENT		DON'T KNOW	
	0	1	2	3	4	5	6	7	8	9	10		
Your neighbourhood or village	0	1	2	3	4	5	6	7	8	9	X	V	(43)
Your municipality or town	0	1	2	3	4	5	6	7	8	9	X	V	(44)
Your region	0	1	2	3	4	5	6	7	8	9	X	V	(45)
Your country	0	1	2	3	4	5	6	7	8	9	X	V	(46)
The European Union (The Common Market)	0	1	2	3	4	5	6	7	8	9	X	V	(47)

SHOWCARD
4) **Do you think of yourself first and foremost as (please Code <u>ONE</u> only)**

	(48)
English	1
Scottish	2
Welsh	3
Irish	4
British	5
European	6
Other (Write In)	7
Don't know	8

TRUST

I would now like to ask you some questions about your views of other people.

SHOWCARD
5a) Thinking for a moment about whether people with whom you have contact can be trusted. Please use the 0-10 scale where 10 means definitely can be trusted and 0 means definitely cannot be trusted.

	MOST PEOPLE CANNOT BE TRUSTED									MOST PEOPLE CAN BE TRUSTED		DON'T KNOW	
	0	1	2	3	4	5	6	7	8	9	10		
CODE HERE→	0	1	2	3	4	5	6	7	8	9	X	V	(49)

SHOWCARD

5b) Would you say that most of the time people you come into contact with try to be helpful or that they are mostly looking out for themselves?

	LOOKING OUT FOR THEMSELVES									TRY TO BE HELPFUL	DON'T KNOW	
	0	1	2	3	4	5	6	7	8	9	10	
CODE HERE →	0	1	2	3	4	5	6	7	8	9	X	V	(50)

SHOWCARD

5c) Do you think that most people you come into contact with would try to take advantage of you if they got the chance or would they try to be fair?

	TRY TO TAKE ADVANTAGE									TRY TO BE FAIR	DON'T KNOW	
	0	1	2	3	4	5	6	7	8	9	10	
CODE HERE →	0	1	2	3	4	5	6	7	8	9	X	V	(51)

SHOWCARD

5d) And now your views on various institutions. Do you trust:

	DO NOT TRUST AT ALL									TRUST COMPLETELY	DON'T KNOW	
	0	1	2	3	4	5	6	7	8	9	10	
✓ ☐ The Government	0	1	2	3	4	5	6	7	8	9	X	V (52)
House of Commons	0	1	2	3	4	5	6	7	8	9	X	V (53)
Scottish Parliament (Ask Scotland Only)	0	1	2	3	4	5	6	7	8	9	X	V (54)
Welsh Assembly (Ask Wales Only)	0	1	2	3	4	5	6	7	8	9	X	V (55)
Conservative Party	0	1	2	3	4	5	6	7	8	9	X	V (56)
Labour Party	0	1	2	3	4	5	6	7	8	9	X	V (57)
Liberal Democrat Party	0	1	2	3	4	5	6	7	8	9	X	V (58)
Scottish Nationalist Prty **(Ask Scotland Only)**	0	1	2	3	4	5	6	7	8	9	X	V (59)
Plaid Cymru **(Ask Wales Only)**	0	1	2	3	4	5	6	7	8	9	X	V (60)
The Courts	0	1	2	3	4	5	6	7	8	9	X	V (61)
The Civil Service	0	1	2	3	4	5	6	7	8	9	X	V (62)
(IN OTHER WORDS, DEPARTMENTS SUCH AS INLAND REVENUE OR HEALTH AND SOCIAL SECURITY)												
Politicians	0	1	2	3	4	5	6	7	8	9	X	V (63)
The Police	0	1	2	3	4	5	6	7	8	9	X	V (64)
Local Government	0	1	2	3	4	5	6	7	8	9	X	V (65)
The European Union (The Common Market)	0	1	2	3	4	5	6	7	8	9	X	V (66)
✓ ☐ The Banks	0	1	2	3	4	5	6	7	8	9	X	V (67)

ORGANISATIONAL ACTIVITY

SHOWCARD

6a)   I will read you a list of different types of organisations. <u>In the last 12 months</u>, have you been a <u>member</u> of this type of organisation (in other words you have paid a membership fee if it is required), have you <u>participated in an activity</u> arranged by this type of organisation, have you <u>donated money</u> as an individual to this type of organisation, or have you <u>done voluntary or unpaid work</u> for this type of organisation? If none of these apply to you, please say so.

	MEMBER (PAID SUBSCRIPTION IF REQUIRED)	PARTICIPATED	DONATED MONEY	CARRIED OUT VOLUNTARY OR UNPAID WORK	NONE OF THESE APPLY	
Youth organisation (e.g. Scouts)	1	2	3	4	5	(68)
Environmental organisation (e.g. Greenpeace)	1	2	3	4	5	(69)
Conservation organisation (e.g. The National Trust)	1	2	3	4	5	(70)
Organisation for animal rights or protection (e.g. RSPCA)	1	2	3	4	5	(71)
Peace organisation (e.g. CND)	1	2	3	4	5	(72)
Humanitarian aid/Human Rights organisation (e.g. Amnesty Internat.)	1	2	3	4	5	(73)
Social Welfare organisation (e.g. Shelter)	1	2	3	4	5	(74)
Organisation for medical patients, specific illnesses or addictions (e.g. British Heart Foundation)	1	2	3	4	5	(75)
Organisation for disabled (e.g. Royal National Institute for the Blind)	1	2	3	4	5	(76)
Pensioners or retired persons organisation (e.g.Help The Aged)	1	2	3	4	5	(77)
Ex-Service Clubs (e.g. Royal British Legion)	1	2	3	4	5	(78)
Sports club or outdoor activities club	1	2	3	4	5	(79)
Gymnasium	1	2	3	4	5	(80)
Trade Union (e.g. UNISON)	1	2	3	4	5	(11)
Business or Employers Organisation (e.g. British Chamber of Commerce)	1	2	3	4	5	(12)
Professional Organisation (e.g. British Medical Association)	1	2	3	4	5	(13)
Consumer organisations (e.g. The Consumer Association)	1	2	3	4	5	(14)
Parent and Teachers organisation	1	2	3	4	5	(15)
Cultural/Musical/Dancing/ Theatre organisations	1	2	3	4	5	(16)
Hobby organisation (e.g. Stamp Collecting Group)	1	2	3	4	5	(17)
Motoring Association (e.g. AA)	1	2	3	4	5	(18)
Residents/Housing or Neighbourhood organisations (e.g. N'bourhood Watch)	1	2	3	4	5	(19)
Ethnic organisation (e.g. Black Resource Centre)	1	2	3	4	5	(20)
Religious or Church organisation	1	2	3	4	5	(21)
Women's organisation (e.g. Women's Institute)	1	2	3	4	5	(22)
Social Club (e.g.Working Men's Clubs)	1	2	3	4	5	(23)
Member of other organisations not listed above	1	2	3	4	5	(24)

If NOT A MEMBER of any organisation go to question 6e

SHOWCARD

6b) Thinking about the ONE organisation which is <u>most important</u> to you, how often do you?

	OFTEN	SOMETIMES	RARELY	NEVER	DON'T KNOW	
Attend its meetings	1	2	3	4	5	(25)
Participate in decision making at its meetings	1	2	3	4	5	(26)
Speak at its meetings	1	2	3	4	5	(27)
Plan or chair its meetings	1	2	3	4	5	(28)
Write a report about its meetings	1	2	3	4	5	(29)

SHOWCARD

6c) Again, thinking about the ONE organisation which is <u>most important</u> to you, how often do you do any of the following with other members of the organisation?

	OFTEN	SOMETIMES	RARELY	NEVER	DON'T KNOW	
Talk about the organisation's problems or goals	1	2	3	4	5	(30)
Call upon fellow members for practical help or assistance	1	2	3	4	5	(31)
Disagree with other members about the organisation's problems or goals	1	2	3	4	5	(32)
Meet each other socially	1	2	3	4	5	(33)

SHOWCARD

6d) Thinking about the ONE organisation which is <u>most important</u> to you. Would you call yourself very strongly, fairly strongly or not very strongly attached to this organisation?

	VERY STRONG	FAIRLY STRONG	NOT VERY STRONG	DON'T KNOW	
	1	2	3	4	(34)

6e) Apart from these organisations we have talked about do you belong to an informal network of friends or acquaintances with whom you have contact on a regular basis (for example, Pub Quiz Team, Book Reading Group, Parent/Toddler group, Child Care group)?

	YES	NO	DON'T KNOW	
	1	2	3	(35)

SHOWCARD

6f) Do you actively provide any support beyond your immediate family for ill people, elderly neighbours, acquaintances without doing it through an organisation (for example, shopping for neighbours, visiting old people)?

	YES, REGULARLY	YES, OCCASIONALLY	NO	DON'T KNOW	
	1	2	3	4	(36)

SHOWCARD

6g) During the <u>last month</u>, approximately how much time <u>in total</u> did you spend on activities, in clubs, associations, groups, networks or in supporting other people?

	(37)
None	1
Less than 1 hour in a month	2
1 to 4 hours in a month	3
5 to 10 hours in a month	4
11 to 20 hours in a month	5
More than 20 hours in a month	6
Don't know	7

I am now going to talk to you about your attempts to influence rules, laws or policies.

SHOWCARD

7ai)   <u>During the last 12 months</u> ha*ve you done* any of the following to influence rules, laws or policies?

7aii)   And *would you do* any of the following to influence rules, laws or policies?

		(7ai) HAVE DONE		(7aii) WOULD DO		
		YES	NO	YES	NO	
Contacted a politician (for example, a member of parliament or local councillor)	(38)	1	2	1	2	(39)
Contacted an organisation (for example, Shelter or Help the Aged)	(40)	1	2	1	2	(41)
Contacted a public official (for example, a person from the housing or social security offices)	(42)	1	2	1	2	(43)
Contacted the media	(44)	1	2	1	2	(45)
Contacted a solicitor or judicial body	(46)	1	2	1	2	(47)
Worn or displayed a campaign badge or sticker	(48)	1	2	1	2	(49)
Signed a petition	(50)	1	2	1	2	(51)
Taken part in a public demonstration	(52)	1	2	1	2	(53)
Taken part in a strike	(54)	1	2	1	2	(55)
Boycotted certain products	(56)	1	2	1	2	(57)
Bought certain products for political, ethical or environmental reasons	(58)	1	2	1	2	(59)
Donated money to an organisation	(60)	1	2	1	2	(61)
Raised funds for an organisation	(62)	1	2	1	2	(63)
Attended a political meeting or rally	(64)	1	2	1	2	(65)
Voted in a local government election	(66)	1	2	1	2	(67)
Participated in illegal protest activities	(68)	1	2	1	2	(69)
Formed a group of like minded people	(70)	1	2	1	2	(71)

7b)   In the past twelve months have you received any request <u>directed at you personally</u> to do any of these things?

YES	NO	DON'T KNOW	
1	2	3	(72)

If <u>No</u> go to Q8a

SHOWCARD

7c)   Thinking about the last occasion this happened, was the person who asked you:

	(73)
Family	1
A close friend	2
A work colleague	3
Someone you didn't know	4
None of these	5
Don't know	6

7d)   **Did you respond positively to the request?**

YES	NO
1	2

(74)

LIFE SATISFACTION

SHOWCARD
8a)   **Thinking about yourself, how satisfied are you with your life as a whole these days?**

VERY SATISFIED	SATISFIED	NEITHER SATISFIED NOR DISSATISFIED	DISSATISFIED	VERY DISSATISFIED	DON'T KNOW
1	2	3	4	5	6

(75)

SHOWCARD
8b)   **Thinking about Britain, how satisfied are you with the way democracy works?**

VERY SATISFIED	SATISFIED	NEITHER SATISFIED NOR DISSATISFIED	DISSATISFIED	VERY DISSATISFIED	DON'T KNOW
1	2	3	4	5	6

(76)

(Ask in Scotland and Wales only)

SHOWCARD
8c)   **Thinking about (Scotland) (Wales), how satisfied are you with the way democracy works?**

VERY SATISFIED	SATISFIED	NEITHER SATISFIED NOR DISSATISFIED	DISSATISFIED	VERY DISSATISFIED	DON'T KNOW
1	2	3	4	5	6

(77)

*Start card 3

SHOWCARD
9)   **Are you satisfied or dissatisfied with the delivery of the following services provided by your local authority?**

	VERY SATISFIED	SATISFIED	NEITHER SATISFIED NOR DISSATISFIED	DISSATISFIED	VERY DISSATISFIED	DON'T KNOW	
Schools	1	2	3	4	5	6	(11)
Care for the elderly	1	2	3	4	5	6	(12)
Road maintenance	1	2	3	4	5	6	(13)
Street cleaning	1	2	3	4	5	6	(14)
Social Services	1	2	3	4	5	6	(15)
Parks & sports facilities	1	2	3	4	5	6	(16)
Libraries	1	2	3	4	5	6	(17)

CHILD'S EDUCATION

10a)   **Do you have any children of school age?**

YES	NO
1	2

(18)

(If no children of school age go to question 11a)

SHOWCARD

10b) I will now ask you some questions about the quality of your children's schooling. <u>During the last 12 months</u> to what extent have you felt satisfied or dissatisfied with any of your children's education at school?

VERY SATISFIED	SATISFIED	NEITHER SATISFIED NOR DISSATISFIED	DISSATISFIED	VERY DISSATISFIED	DON'T KNOW	
1	2	3	4	5	6	(19)

10c) <u>During the last 12 months</u> have you done anything to try and change the way education is provided at any of your children's schools?

YES	NO	DON'T KNOW	
1	2	3	(20)

(If No go to Q 10g)

10d) Which of the following did you do to change the way education is provided at any of your children's schools?

	YES	NO	
I approached a teacher or other member of staff at the school	1	2	(21)
I approached a politician	1	2	(22)
I approached the Parents Teachers Association	1	2	(23)
I approached the School Governors	1	2	(24)
I approached a local council official	1	2	(25)
I approached a solicitor	1	2	(26)
I approached the media	1	2	(27)
I approached other parents with children in the same school	1	2	(28)
I approached family, relatives or friends	1	2	(29)
I approached the Office for Standards in Education (OFSTED)	1	2	(30)

10e) Were you successful?

YES	NO	DON'T KNOW	
1	2	3	(31)

SHOWCARD

10f) Do you think you were treated fairly in your attempt to change the way education is provided at any of your children's schools?

NOT TREATED AT ALL FAIRLY									TREATED VERY FAIRLY	DON'T KNOW	
0 1	2	3	4	5	6	7	8	9	10		
0	1	2	3	4	5	6	7	8	9	X	V	(32)

SHOWCARD

10g) More generally with regard to any of your children's schooling, do you think you are able to:

	NOT AT ALL	SOME	A GREAT DEAL	DON'T KNOW	
Influence the choice of school?	1	2	3	4	(33)
Influence the teaching in the school?	1	2	3	4	(34)
Influence the running of the school?	1	2	3	4	(35)

<u>MEDICAL TREATMENT</u>

I would now like to ask you some questions about the quality of any medical treatment you or any relative have received <u>over the last 12 months.</u>

<u>During the last 12 months</u> have you or a relative...

11a) Sought or obtained medical treatment (for example, your general practitioner, dentist or as a hospital patient)?

YES	NO	DON'T KNOW	
1	2	3	(36)

(If no to question a) move to question 12a)

SHOWCARD
11b) <u>During the last 12 months</u>, to what extent have you felt satisfied or dissatisfied with your medical treatment?

VERY SATISFIED	SATISFIED	NEITHER SATISFIED NOR DISSATISFIED	DISSATISFIED	VERY DISSATISFIED	DON'T KNOW	
1	2	3	4	5	6	(37)

11c) <u>During the last 12 months</u> have you done anything to try and change the way medical treatment was provided?

YES	NO	
1	2	(38)

(If no, move to question 11g)

11d) Which of the following did you do to try to influence the way medical treatment was provided? (Code all those that apply)

	YES	NO	
I approached the Doctor or Member of staff responsible for the medical treatment	1	2	(39)
I approached an official in the Health Service or Company which provided treatment	1	2	(40)
I approached a politician	1	2	(41)
I approached an association e.g. a patients association	1	2	(42)
I approached a solicitor	1	2	(43)
I approached the media	1	2	(44)
I approached other patients in the same hospital or practice	1	2	(45)
I approached other family, relatives or friends	1	2	(46)

11e) Were you successful?

YES	NO	DON'T KNOW	
1	2	3	(47)

SHOWCARD
11f) Do you think you were treated fairly in your attempt to influence the treatment?

NOT TREATED AT ALL FAIRLY									TREATED VERY FAIRLY	DON'T KNOW	
0	1	2	3	4	5	6	7	8	9	10	
CODE HERE→ 0	1	2	3	4	5	6	7	8	9	X	V (48)

SHOWCARD
11g) Did you or your relative use the National Health Service or Private Health Care?

NATIONAL HEALTH SERVICE	PRIVATE	BOTH	DON'T KNOW	
1	2	3	4	(49)

11h)   With regard to the medical treatment that you or your relative received during the last 12 months, did you:

	YES	NO	DON'T KNOW	
Obtain prompt treatment	1	2	3	(50)
Influence the medical treatment	1	2	3	(51)
Obtain adequate medical information about your treatment	1	2	3	(52)
Choose the doctor you wanted	1	2	3	(53)
Obtain a second opinion	1	2	3	(54)
Change to the private sector	1	2	3	(55)
Refuse treatment	1	2	3	(56)

THE WORKPLACE

12a)   Are you in paid employment?

YES	NO	
1	2	(57)

If YES answer question 12b, and then continue with question 12d. If NO answer question 12c, and then move to 13a.

SHOWCARD
12b)   If yes, are you?

(58)

In a full time job	1
In a part time job	2
On leave of absence for studies	3
Currently on parental leave of absence	4

SHOWCARD
12c)   If no, are you?

(59)

Temporarily unemployed (less than 6 months)	1
Unemployed for a long period (more than 6 months)	2
On disability pension	3
On early retirement arrangement	4
Retired pensioner	5
Currently a student in further or higher education	6
Currently a pupil in school	7
A houseperson	8
Not employed for other reasons	9

SHOWCARD
12d)   During the last 12 months to what extent have you felt satisfied or dissatisfied with your working conditions?

VERY SATISFIED	SATISFIED	NEITHER SATISFIED NOR DISSATISFIED	DISSATISFIED	VERY DISSATISFIED	DON'T KNOW	
1	2	3	4	5	6	(60)

12e)   During the last 12 months have you done anything to try and improve your working conditions?

YES	NO	
1	2	(61)

(If no, move to question 12i)

12f)   If yes, which of the following did you do to try and improve your working conditions? (Code all that apply)

	YES	NO	
I approached my boss or employer	1	2	(62)
I approached a politician	1	2	(63)
I approached a public official	1	2	(64)
I approached a Trade Union official	1	2	(65)
I approached a solicitor	1	2	(66)
I approached the media	1	2	(67)
I approached other employees in my workplace	1	2	(68)
I approached family, relatives or friends	1	2	(69)
I changed work place or department	1	2	(70)

12g)   Were you successful?

	YES	NO	DON'T KNOW	
	1	2	3	(71)

SHOWCARD

12h)   Do you think you were treated fairly in your attempt to try and improve your working conditions?

	NOT TREATED AT ALL FAIRLY									TREATED VERY FAIRLY	DON'T KNOW	
	0	1	2	3	4	5	6	7	8	9	10	
CODE HERE →	0	1	2	3	4	5	6	7	8	9	X	V	(72)

SHOWCARD

12i)   Here are a few things that people sometimes do as part of their job. As part of your work how often do you:

	OFTEN	SOMETIMES	RARELY	NEVER	DON'T KNOW	
Attend a meeting?	1	2	3	4	5	(73)
Participate in decision making at a meeting?	1	2	3	4	5	(74)
Speak at a meeting?	1	2	3	4	5	(75)
Plan or chair a meeting?	1	2	3	4	5	(76)
Write a report on a meeting?	1	2	3	4	5	(77)

*Start card 4

SHOWCARD

12j)   Some people have a lot of contact with their fellow workers or colleagues, and others have only limited contact. How about you? How often do you:

	OFTEN	SOMETIMES	RARELY	NEVER	DON'T KNOW	
Talk with your fellow workers about problems at work?	1	2	3	4	5	(11)
Call upon fellow workers to give practical help or assistance?	1	2	3	4	5	(12)
Express disagreement about work issues with fellow workers?	1	2	3	4	5	(13)
Meet fellow workers socially?	1	2	3	4	5	(14)

SHOWCARD
12k)   With regard to your work can you:

	NOTATALL	SOME	A GREAT DEAL	DON'TKNOW	
Influence the time when your work will begin or end for the day?	1	2	3	4	(15)
Influence how your own daily work will be organised?	1	2	3	4	(16)
Influence your working conditions? (e.g. rest periods, safety conditions)	1	2	3	4	(17)

POLITICS AND PARTICIPATION

SHOWCARD
13a)   Talking to people about the last general election in 1997 (the one when Labour was elected to Government), we have found that a lot of people didn't manage to vote. How about you – did you manage to vote in the general election?

	(18)
Yes	1
No	2
Was not eligible to vote	3
Don't know	4
Refuse to answer	5

SHOWCARD
13b)   If you did vote which party did you vote for?

	(19)
Conservative	1
Labour	2
Liberal Democrat	3
Scottish National Party	4
Plaid Cymru	5
Green Party	6
Other	7
None	8
Don't know	9
Refuse to answer	0

SHOWCARD
13c)   How likely is it that you will in the future:

	NOT AT ALL LIKELY	NOT VERY LIKELY	FAIRLY LIKELY	VERY LIKELY	DON'T KNOW	
Vote in the next general election?	1	2	3	4	5	(20)
Vote in the next election for the European Parliament?	1	2	3	4	5	(21)
Vote in the next election for the Scottish Parliament/Welsh Assembly? (Ask Scotland & Wales Only)	1	2	3	4	5	(22)
Vote in the next local government elections?	1	2	3	4	5	(23)

SHOWCARD
14a)   Generally speaking do you think of yourself as Conservative, Labour, Liberal Democrat, Scottish or Welsh Nationalist or what?

	(24)
Conservative	1
Labour	2
Liberal Democrat	3
SNP	4
Plaid Cymru	5
Other	6
Don't know	7
None	8

(If None or Don't Know go to Q15)

SHOWCARD
14b)   Would you call yourself very strong (quote party), fairly strong or not very strong?

VERY STRONG	FAIRLY STRONG	NOT VERY STRONG	DON'T KNOW	
1	2	3	4	(25)

SHOWCARD
15)   Thinking about <u>voters in general</u> to what extent does voting allow people to influence decisions made by:

	NOT AT ALL	SOME	A GREAT DEAL	DON'T KNOW	
Local Authorities (in other words, the elected council)	1	2	3	4	(26)
Scottish Parliament/Welsh Assembly **(Ask Scotland & Wales Only)**	1	2	3	4	(27)
House of Commons	1	2	3	4	(28)
European Parliament	1	2	3	4	(29)

SHOWCARD
16a)   How interested are you <u>personally</u> in each of the following levels?

	VERY INTERESTED	FAIRLY INTERESTED	NOT VERY INTERESTED	NOT AT ALL INTERESTED	DON'T KNOW	
Local Politics	1	2	3	4	5	(30)
Regional Politics	1	2	3	4	5	(31)
National Politics	1	2	3	4	5	(32)
European Politics	1	2	3	4	5	(33)
International Politics	1	2	3	4	5	(34)

SHOWCARD
16b)   How often would you say you <u>discuss political matters</u> when you get together with the following groups of people?

	OFTEN	SOMETIMES	RARELY	NEVER	DON'T KNOW	
Your Friends	1	2	3	4	5	(35)
Your Family	1	2	3	4	5	(36)
Your Neighbours	1	2	3	4	5	(37)
Your Fellow Workers	1	2	3	4	5	(38)

SHOWCARD
16c)   At the time when you were growing up how often was politics discussed at home?

OFTEN	SOMETIMES	RARELY	NEVER	DON'T KNOW	
1	2	3	4	5	(39)

SHOWCARD
16d)   At the time when you were growing up, how active was your <u>mother</u> in politics ?

VERY ACTIVE	FAIRLY ACTIVE	NOT ACTIVE AT ALL	DON'T KNOW	
1	2	3	4	(40)

SHOWCARD
16e)   At the time when you were growing up how active was your <u>father</u> in politics?

VERY ACTIVE	FAIRLY ACTIVE	NOT ACTIVE AT ALL	DON'T KNOW	
1	2	3	4	(41)

SHOWCARD

17) I will now give you a series of statements. Please read and indicate whether you strongly agree/ agree/ neither agree nor disagree/ disagree/ strongly disagree with them by *Ticking* the appropriate boxes.

		STRONGLY AGREE	AGREE	NEITHER AGREE NOR DISAGREE	DISAGREE	STRONGLY DISAGREE	
17a)	People like me have no say in what the government does	☐1	☐2	☐3	☐4	☐5	(42)
17b)	People like me can have a real influence on politics if they are prepared to get involved	☐1	☐2	☐3	☐4	☐5	(43)
17c)	Sometimes politics & government seem so complicated that a person like me cannot really understand what is going on	☐1	☐2	☐3	☐4	☐5	(44)
17d)	It really matters which party is in power, because it will affect our lives	☐1	☐2	☐3	☐4	☐5	(45)
17e)	The government generally treats people like me fairly	☐1	☐2	☐3	☐4	☐5	(46)
17f)	When people like me all work together we can really make a difference to our local community	☐1	☐2	☐3	☐4	☐5	(47)
17g)	My vote makes no difference to the outcome of an election	☐1	☐2	☐3	☐4	☐5	(48)
17h)	If people like me work together we can really change Britain	☐1	☐2	☐3	☐4	☐5	(49)

SHOWCARD

18a) How much do you think the British Government <u>listens personally to people like yourself</u>? If you think that it doesn't listen at all you would give it a score of 0 whereas if you think it listens a great deal you would give it a score of 10. Or you might give it a score in between.

	NOT AT ALL									A GREAT DEAL	DON'T KNOW	
	0	1	2	3	4	5	6	7	8	9	10	
CODE HERE→	0	1	2	3	4	5	6	7	8	9	X	V	(50)

SHOWCARD

18b) How much do you think the British Government <u>takes decisions in accordance with your personal wishes</u>?

	NOT AT ALL									A GREAT DEAL	DON'T KNOW	
	0	1	2	3	4	5	6	7	8	9	10	
CODE HERE→	0	1	2	3	4	5	6	7	8	9	X	V	(51)

SHOWCARD

18c) How much do you think the British Government <u>listens to majority opinion</u>?

	NOT AT ALL									A GREAT DEAL	DON'T KNOW	
	0	1	2	3	4	5	6	7	8	9	10	
CODE HERE→	0	1	2	3	4	5	6	7	8	9	X	V	(52)

SHOWCARD

18d) How much do you think the British Government <u>takes decisions in accordance with majority wishes</u>?

	NOT AT ALL									A GREAT DEAL	DON'T KNOW	
	0	1	2	3	4	5	6	7	8	9	10	
CODE HERE→	0	1	2	3	4	5	6	7	8	9	X	V	(53)

SHOWCARD

19) I will now give you a series of statements. Please read and indicate whether you strongly agree/ agree/ neither agree nor disagree/ disagree/ or strongly disagree with them by *Ticking* the appropriate boxes.

		STRONGLY AGREE	AGREE	NEITHER AGREE NOR DISAGREE	DISAGREE	STRONGLY DISAGREE	
19a)	The only way to be really informed about politics is to get involved	☐1	☐2	☐3	☐4	☐5	(54)
19b)	Participating in politics is not much fun	☐1	☐2	☐3	☐4	☐5	(55)
19c)	I enjoy working with other people on common problems in our community	☐1	☐2	☐3	☐4	☐5	(56)
19d)	Participating in politics is a good way to meet interesting people	☐1	☐2	☐3	☐4	☐5	(57)
19e)	Being active in politics is a good way to get benefits for oneself and one's family	☐1	☐2	☐3	☐4	☐5	(58)
19f)	The government is doing a good job in managing public services like health care and education	☐1	☐2	☐3	☐4	☐5	(59)
19g)	A person like me could do a good job as a local councillor	☐1	☐2	☐3	☐4	☐5	(60)
19h)	The government is doing a bad job in managing the economy	☐1	☐2	☐3	☐4	☐5	(61)
19i)	There is a big difference between what people like me expect from life and what people like me actually get	☐1	☐2	☐3	☐4	☐5	(62)
19j)	Politics would be a lot more effective if more people like me were elected to Parliament	☐1	☐2	☐3	☐4	☐5	(63)
19k)	Being active in politics is a good way to get benefits for groups that I care about	☐1	☐2	☐3	☐4	☐5	(64)
19l)	Getting involved in politics can be tiring after a hard day's work	☐1	☐2	☐3	☐4	☐5	(65)
19m)	Being involved in politics would take time away from one's family	☐1	☐2	☐3	☐4	☐5	(66)
19n)	People like me are so busy these days that they don't have the time to vote	☐1	☐2	☐3	☐4	☐5	(67)
19o)	Every citizen should get involved in politics if democracy is to work properly	☐1	☐2	☐3	☐4	☐5	(68)
19p)	If a person is dissatisfied with the policies of the government, he/she has a duty to do something about it	☐1	☐2	☐3	☐4	☐5	(69)
19q)	It is every citizen's duty to vote in elections	☐1	☐2	☐3	☐4	☐5	(70)
(19r)	It doesn't really matter which party is in power, in the end things go on much the same	☐1	☐2	☐3	☐4	☐5	(71)
19s)	Generally speaking those we elect as MPs lose touch with people pretty quickly	☐1	☐2	☐3	☐4	☐5	(72)
19t)	Politicians only look after themselves	☐1	☐2	☐3	☐4	☐5	(73)

ECONOMIC POLICY PERFORMANCE

SHOWCARD

20a) How do you think the <u>general economic situation</u> in this country has changed over the last 12 months? Has it...

SHOWCARD

20b) How does the <u>financial situation of your household</u> now compare with what it was 12 months ago? Has it...

SHOWCARD

20c) How do you think the <u>general economic situation</u> in this country <u>will develop</u> over the next 12 months? Will it...

SHOWCARD

20d) How do you think the <u>financial situation of your household will change</u> over the next 12 months? Will it...

	(20 A) (74)	(20 B) (75)	(20 C) (76)	(20 D) (77)	*Start card 5
Got a lot better	1	1	1	1	
Got a little better	2	2	2	2	
Stayed the same	3	3	3	3	
Got a little worse	4	4	4	4	
Got a lot worse	5	5	5	5	
Don't know	6	6	6	6	

FOR QUESTION 21...
Ask a) to people living in England.
Ask b) to people living in Scotland.
Ask c) to people living in Wales.

SHOWCARD

21a) Which <u>one</u> of the following do you think most affects the standard of living of people in *Britain*?

	(11)	
Local government	1	*-Punchers Note No Codes 2 or 3*
The British government	4	
The European Union	5	
The International economy	6	
Don't know	7	

SHOWCARD

21b) Which <u>one</u> of the following do you think most affects the general standard of living of people in *Scotland* ?

	(12)	
Local government	1	*-Punchers Note No Code 3*
Government of Scotland	2	
The British Government	4	
The European Union	5	
The International economy	6	
Don't know	7	

SHOWCARD

21c) Which <u>one</u> of the following do you think most affects the general standard of living of people in *Wales*?

	(13)	
Local government	1	*-Punchers Note No Code 2*
Government of Wales	3	
The British Government	4	
The European Union	5	
The International economy	6	
Don't know	7	

RIGHTS AND OBLIGATIONS

SHOWCARD

22) I will now give you a series of statements. Please read and indicate whether you strongly agree/ agree/ neither agree nor disagree/ or strongly disagree with them by *Ticking* the appropriate boxes.

		STRONGLY AGREE	AGREE	NEITHER AGREE NOR DISAGREE	DISAGREE	STRONGLY DISAGREE	
22a)	Fathers should have the right to three months paid paternity leave following the birth of a child	☐1	☐2	☐3	☐4	☐5	(14)
22b)	The Government should remove present legal restrictions on the right to strike	☐1	☐2	☐3	☐4	☐5	(15)
22c)	In order to preserve the right to higher education student tuition fees should be abolished	☐1	☐2	☐3	☐4	☐5	(16)
22d)	It is the government's responsibility to find a job for everyone who wants one	☐1	☐2	☐3	☐4	☐5	(17)
22e)	Individuals should not rely on the state to provide for their own retirement	☐1	☐2	☐3	☐4	☐5	(18)
22f)	Gay relationships should have an equal status to marriage	☐1	☐2	☐3	☐4	☐5	(19)
22g)	Government should reduce income differences between the rich & poor	☐1	☐2	☐3	☐4	☐5	(20)
22h)	Individuals who can afford it should meet the cost of their own health care when they are sick	☐1	☐2	☐3	☐4	☐5	(21)
22i)	Government should provide housing for those who cannot afford it	☐1	☐2	☐3	☐4	☐5	(22)
22j)	Women should have the right to abortion on demand	☐1	☐2	☐3	☐4	☐5	(23)
22k)	Everyone should have the right to choose to die	☐1	☐2	☐3	☐4	☐5	(24)
22l)	Censorship of films & magazines is necessary to uphold moral standards	☐1	☐2	☐3	☐4	☐5	(25)
22m)	Smoking should be banned in all public places	☐1	☐2	☐3	☐4	☐5	(26)
22n)	To be classified as a full citizen an individual should have to have been born in Britain	☐1	☐2	☐3	☐4	☐5	(27)

SHOWCARD
23)   To what extent should the following groups be allowed to speak out in public?

	DEFINITELY NOT	POSSIBLY NOT	POSSIBLY YES	DEFINITELY YES	DON'T KNOW	
Neo-nazi and racist groups	1	2	3	4	5	(28)
Religious fundamentalists	1	2	3	4	5	(29)
Animal Liberation groups	1	2	3	4	5	(30)
Environmental groups	1	2	3	4	5	(31)

24)   Recently there has been debate about the limits to trial by jury. Some would like to introduce trial by Judges alone as a means of saving money and time. Do you think that those accused of the following crimes should always have the right to a jury trial?

	YES	NO	DON'T KNOW	
shoplifting	1	2	3	(32)
car theft	1	2	3	(33)
burglary	1	2	3	(34)
violent assault	1	2	3	(35)
fraud	1	2	3	(36)
murder	1	2	3	(37)

SHOWCARD
25)   If one of the following were proposed in your locality or neighbourhood, would you support or oppose it?

	STRONGLY SUPPORT	SUPPORT	NEITHER SUPPORT NOR OPPOSE	OPPOSE	STRONGLY OPPOSE	DON'T KNOW	
A new school	1	2	3	4	5	6	(38)
A retirement home	1	2	3	4	5	6	(39)
A resettlement centre for young offenders	1	2	3	4	5	6	(40)
A new age travellers camp site	1	2	3	4	5	6	(41)
A sex offenders rehabilitation centre	1	2	3	4	5	6	(42)

SHOWCARD
26)   How important do you feel it is?

	NOT AT ALL IMPORTANT	NOT VERY IMPORTANT	FAIRLY IMPORTANT	VERY IMPORTANT	DON'T KNOW	
Never to evade paying taxes	1	2	3	4	5	(43)
Always to obey the law	1	2	3	4	5	(44)
To make regular charity donations	1	2	3	4	5	(45)
To work for local voluntary organisations	1	2	3	4	5	(46)

27)   Are you a driver? (car, motorbike, lorry)

	YES	NO	
	1	2	(47)

If No go to Q 29

SHOWCARD
28)   Some drivers ignore the speed limit, while others always observe it. How about you? Which of the following options applies to you?

(48)
I always stay within the speed limit   1

I sometimes exceed the limit, but never by much   2

I sometimes exceed the limit by a great deal.   3

Don't know

29)   Some service providers accept cash as a means of avoiding VAT.

29a)   Have you ever paid cash in order to avoid VAT? *Code Below*

29b)   Have you offered a cash-payment service and avoided VAT? *Code Below*

29c)   Suppose the Inland Revenue makes a mistake in your favour. Would you tell them about it? *Code Below*

	(29A) (49)	(29B) (50)	(29C) (51)
Yes	1	1	1
No	2	2	2
Don't know	3	3	3

30a)   What would you do if you saw a person being robbed in the street? Would you...

	YES	NO	DON'T KNOW	
Intervene to prevent the crime	1	2	3	(52)
Call the police and give your name	1	2	3	(53)
Call the police, but not give your name	1	2	3	(54)
Make yourself available as a potential trial witness	1	2	3	(55)
Ignore it	1	2	3	(56)

30b)   What if you saw someone dropping litter in the street? Would you...

	YES	NO	DON'T KNOW	
Ask that person to pick it up	1	2	3	(57)
Pick it up yourself	1	2	3	(58)
Ignore it	1	2	3	(59)

SHOWCARD
31a)   Consider the following: please tell me if you think they can be justified or not?

		NEVER JUSTIFIED	RARELY JUSTIFIED	SOMETIMES JUSTIFIED	ALWAYS JUSTIFIED	DON'T KNOW	
✓ i)	claiming government benefits which you are not entitled to	1	2	3	4	5	(60)
ii)	buying something you know is stolen	1	2	3	4	5	(61)
iii)	taking cannabis	1	2	3	4	5	(62)
iii)	keeping money that you found in the street	1	2	3	4	5	(63)
v)	lying in your own interests	1	2	3	4	5	(64)
vi)	having an affair when you are married	1	2	3	4	5	(65)
vii)	having sex under the legal age of consent	1	2	3	4	5	(66)
viii)	failing to report accidental damage you've done to a parked vehicle	1	2	3	4	5	(67)
ix)	throwing away litter in a public place	1	2	3	4	5	(68)
✓ x)	driving under the influence of alcohol	1	2	3	4	5	(69)

SHOWCARD

31b)   Thinking about things that might happen to you. Would you expect…

		NEVER	RARELY	SOMETIMES	ALWAYS	DON'T KNOW	
i)	To get your wallet returned if you lost it in the street?	1	2	3	4	5	(70)
ii)	To have someone come to your assistance if you were robbed in the street?	1	2	3	4	5	(71)
iii)	To have someone report that they hit your car in a car park?	1	2	3	4	5	(72)

32)   Would you be willing

	YES	NO	DON'T KNOW	
To serve on a jury?	1	2	3	(73)
To donate blood?	1	2	3	(74)
To help renovate a local park or amenity?	1	2	3	(75)
To serve as a school governor?	1	2	3	(76)
To stand as a local councillor?	1	2	3	(77)
To assist a meals on wheels service?	1	2	3	(78)
To participate in a Neighbourhood Watch scheme?	1	2	3	(79)

*Start card 6

SHOWCARD

33)   Please say whether you strongly agree/ agree/ neither agree nor disagree/ disagree or strongly disagree that the following individuals should receive welfare benefits?

	STRONGLY AGREE	AGREE	NEITHER AGREE NOR DISAGREE	DISAGREE	STRONGLY DISAGREE	
An asylum seeker	1	2	3	4	5	(11)
An unemployed person who refuses training	1	2	3	4	5	(12)
A teenage unmarried mother	1	2	3	4	5	(13)
A well off pensioner	1	2	3	4	5	(14)
A gypsy who refuses a local authority house	1	2	3	4	5	(15)

SHOWCARD

34)   Here is another set of statements. Please say whether you strongly agree/ agree/ neither agree nor disagree/ disagree/ or strongly disagree with them.

		STRONGLY AGREE	AGREE	NEITHER AGREE NOR DISAGREE	DISAGREE	STRONGLY DISAGREE	
34a)	Protecting the environment is so important that environmental improvements must be made regardless of costs	1	2	3	4	5	(16)
34b)	The National Health Service is so important that improvements in health care must be made regardless	1	2	3	4	5	(17)
34c)	Education is so important that improvements in education must be made regardless of cost	1	2	3	4	5	(18)

SHOWCARD

35) Please indicate whether you think the government should or should not do the following things, or doesn't it matter either way?

		DEFINITELY SHOULD	PROBABLY SHOULD	DOESN'T MATTER	PROBABLY SHOULD NOT	DEFINITELY SHOULD NOT	
35a)	Get rid of private education	1	2	3	4	5	(19)
35b)	Spend more money to get rid of poverty	1	2	3	4	5	(20)
35c)	Encourage the growth of private medicine	1	2	3	4	5	(21)
35d)	Put more money into the National Health Service	1	2	3	4	5	(22)
35e)	Reduce government spending generally	1	2	3	4	5	(23)
35f)	Introduce stricter laws to regulate trade unions	1	2	3	4	5	(24)
35g)	Give workers more say in the places where they work	1	2	3	4	5	(25)
35h)	Spend less on defence	1	2	3	4	5	(26)

SHOWCARD

36) Thinking about what it means to be a citizen of Britain today, would you say that you were very proud, somewhat proud, not very proud or not at all proud to be a British citizen?

VERY PROUD	SOMEWHAT PROUD	NOT VERY PROUD	NOT AT ALL PROUD	DON'T KNOW	
1	2	3	4	5	(27)

ISSUES

Taxation and Spending

SHOWCARD

37) We now want to ask you questions on a range of issues.

Some people feel that the government should put up taxes and spend much more on health, education and social services. Other people think that the government should cut taxes a lot and spend much less on health, education and social services.

If you feel that the government should put up taxes and spend more on health, education and social services you would give a high score. If you feel that the government should cut taxes a lot and spend much less on health, education and social services you would give a low score. If you feel something in between you would give a score somewhere in the middle.

Please tell me which score comes closest to your own views about taxes and government spending.

Own views

	CUT TAXES SPEND LESS									RAISE TAXES SPEND MORE		DON'T KNOW	
37a)	0	1	2	3	4	5	6	7	8	9	10		
CODE HERE ⟶	0	1	2	3	4	5	6	7	8	9	X	V	(28)

And where do you think the political parties stand on this issue:

The Labour Party

	CUT TAXES SPEND LESS									RAISE TAXES SPEND MORE		DON'T KNOW	
37b)	0	1	2	3	4	5	6	7	8	9	10		
CODE HERE ⟶	0	1	2	3	4	5	6	7	8	9	X	V	(29)

The Conservative Party

	CUT TAXES SPEND LESS									RAISE TAXES SPEND MORE		DON'T KNOW	
37c)	0	1	2	3	4	5	6	7	8	9	10		
CODE HERE →	0	1	2	3	4	5	6	7	8	9	X	V	(30)

The Liberal Democrats

	CUT TAXES SPEND LESS									RAISE TAXES SPEND MORE		DON'T KNOW	
37d)	0	1	2	3	4	5	6	7	8	9	10		
CODE HERE →	0	1	2	3	4	5	6	7	8	9	X	V	(31)

Scottish National Party (Ask Scotland Only)

	CUT TAXES SPEND LESS									RAISE TAXES SPEND MORE		DON'T KNOW	
37e)	0	1	2	3	4	5	6	7	8	9	10		
CODE HERE →	0	1	2	3	4	5	6	7	8	9	X	V	(32)

Plaid Cymru (Ask Wales Only)

	CUT TAXES SPEND LESS									RAISE TAXES SPEND MORE		DON'T KNOW	
37f)	0	1	2	3	4	5	6	7	8	9	10		
CODE HERE →	0	1	2	3	4	5	6	7	8	9	X	V	(33)

RIGHTS OF THE ACCUSED AND CRIME

SHOWCARD
38)   Some people think that protecting the rights of people accused of committing crimes is more important than reducing crime. Other people think that reducing crime is more important than protecting the rights of people accused of committing crimes.

If you feel that protecting the rights of people accused of committing crimes is more important than reducing crime you would give a high score. If you feel that reducing crime is more important than protecting the rights of people accused of committing crimes you would give a low score. If you feel something in between you would score somewhere in the middle.

Please Code which score comes closest to <u>your own views about the rights of people accused of committing crimes</u>

OWN VIEWS

	REDUCE CRIME									PROTECTING RIGHTS		DON'T KNOW	
38a)	0	1	2	3	4	5	6	7	8	9	10		
CODE HERE →	0	1	2	3	4	5	6	7	8	9	X	V	(34)

And where do you think the political parties stand on this issue:

The Labour Party

	REDUCE CRIME									PROTECTING RIGHTS		DON'T KNOW	
38b)	0	1	2	3	4	5	6	7	8	9	10		
CODE HERE →	0	1	2	3	4	5	6	7	8	9	X	V	(35)

The Conservative Party

	REDUCE CRIME									PROTECTING RIGHTS		DON'T KNOW	
38c)	0	1	2	3	4	5	6	7	8	9	10		
CODE HERE →	0	1	2	3	4	5	6	7	8	9	X	V	(36)

The Liberal Democrats

	REDUCE CRIME									PROTECTING RIGHTS	DON'T KNOW	
38d)	0	1	2	3	4	5	6	7	8	9	10	
CODE HERE →	0	1	2	3	4	5	6	7	8	9	X	V	(37)

The Scottish National Party (Ask Scotland Only)

	REDUCE CRIME									PROTECTING RIGHTS	DON'T KNOW	
38e)	0	1	2	3	4	5	6	7	8	9	10	
CODE HERE →	0	1	2	3	4	5	6	7	8	9	X	V	(38)

Plaid Cymru (Ask Wales Only)

	REDUCE CRIME									PROTECTING RIGHTS	DON'T KNOW	
38f)	0	1	2	3	4	5	6	7	8	9	10	
CODE HERE →	0	1	2	3	4	5	6	7	8	9	X	V	(39)

PROTECTING THE COUNTRYSIDE AND DEVELOPMENT

SHOWCARD
39)   Some people think that protecting the countryside is more important than providing new housing and roads. Other people think that providing new housing and roads is more important than protecting the countryside.

If you feel that protecting the countryside is more important than providing new housing and roads you would give a high score. If you feel that providing new housing and roads is more important than protecting the countryside you would give a low score. If you feel somewhere in between you would score somewhere in the middle.

Please Code which score comes closest to your own views about the countryside

Own views

	MORE ROADS & HOUSES									PROTECTING THE ENVIRONMENT	DON'T KNOW	
39a)	0	1	2	3	4	5	6	7	8	9	10	
CODE HERE →	0	1	2	3	4	5	6	7	8	9	X	V	(40)

And where do you think the political parties stand on this issue:

The Labour Party

	MORE ROADS & HOUSES									PROTECTING THE ENVIRONMENT	DON'T KNOW	
39b)	0	1	2	3	4	5	6	7	8	9	10	
CODE HERE →	0	1	2	3	4	5	6	7	8	9	X	V	(41)

The Conservative Party

	MORE ROADS & HOUSES									PROTECTING THE ENVIRONMENT	DON'T KNOW	
39c)	0	1	2	3	4	5	6	7	8	9	10	
CODE HERE →	0	1	2	3	4	5	6	7	8	9	X	V	(42)

The Liberal Democrats

	MORE ROADS & HOUSES									PROTECTING THE ENVIRONMENT		DON'T KNOW	
39d)	0	1	2	3	4	5	6	7	8	9	10		
CODE HERE →	0	1	2	3	4	5	6	7	8	9	X	V	(43)

The Scottish National Party (Ask Scotland Only)

	MORE ROADS & HOUSES									PROTECTING THE ENVIRONMENT		DON'T KNOW	
39e)	0	1	2	3	4	5	6	7	8	9	10		
CODE HERE →	0	1	2	3	4	5	6	7	8	9	X	V	(44)

Plaid Cymru (Ask Wales Only)

	MORE ROADS & HOUSES									PROTECTING THE ENVIRONMENT		DON'T KNOW	
39f)	0	1	2	3	4	5	6	7	8	9	10		
CODE HERE →	0	1	2	3	4	5	6	7	8	9	X	V	(45)

EUROPEAN MONETARY SYSTEM

SHOWCARD

40)   Some people think that Britain should never replace the pound with the European Currency Unit (the Euro). Other people think that Britain should replace the pound with the Euro.

If you feel that Britain should never replace the pound with the European Currency Unit (the Euro) you would give a high score. If you feel that Britain should replace the pound with the Euro you would give a low score. If you feel somewhere in between you would score somewhere in the middle.

Please Code which score comes closest to <u>your own views about the pound and the Euro.</u>

Own views

	REPLACE POUND WITH EURO									KEEP THE POUND		DON'T KNOW	
40a)	0	1	2	3	4	5	6	7	8	9	10		
CODE HERE →	0	1	2	3	4	5	6	7	8	9	X	V	(46)

And where do you think the political parties stand on this issue:

The Labour Party

	REPLACE POUND WITH EURO									KEEP THE POUND		DON'T KNOW	
40b)	0	1	2	3	4	5	6	7	8	9	10		
CODE HERE →	0	1	2	3	4	5	6	7	8	9	X	V	(47)

The Conservative Party

	REPLACE POUND WITH EURO									KEEP THE POUND		DON'T KNOW	
40c)	0	1	2	3	4	5	6	7	8	9	10		
CODE HERE →	0	1	2	3	4	5	6	7	8	9	X	V	(48)

The Liberal Democrats

	REPLACE POUND WITH EURO									KEEP THE POUND		DON'T KNOW	
40d)	0	1	2	3	4	5	6	7	8	9	10		
CODE HERE →	0	1	2	3	4	5	6	7	8	9	X	V	(49)

The Scottish National Party (Ask Scotland Only)

	REPLACE POUND WITH EURO									KEEP THE POUND	DON'T KNOW	
40e)	**0**	**1**	**2**	**3**	**4**	**5**	**6**	**7**	**8**	**9**	**10**		
CODE HERE →	0	1	2	3	4	5	6	7	8	9	X	V	(50)

Plaid Cymru (Ask Wales Only)

	REPLACE POUND WITH EURO									KEEP THE POUND	DON'T KNOW	
40f)	**0**	**1**	**2**	**3**	**4**	**5**	**6**	**7**	**8**	**9**	**10**		
CODE HERE →	0	1	2	3	4	5	6	7	8	9	X	V	(51)

SHOWCARD

41)   Nowadays people talk a lot about the Left and the Right in politics. How about you? On the following scale where would you place yourself?

	LEFT									RIGHT	DON'T KNOW	
41a)	**0**	**1**	**2**	**3**	**4**	**5**	**6**	**7**	**8**	**9**	**10**		
CODE HERE →	0	1	2	3	4	5	6	7	8	9	X	V	(52)

And where would you place...

The Labour Party

	LEFT									RIGHT	DON'T KNOW	
41b)	**0**	**1**	**2**	**3**	**4**	**5**	**6**	**7**	**8**	**9**	**10**		
CODE HERE →	0	1	2	3	4	5	6	7	8	9	X	V	(53)

The Conservative Party

	LEFT									RIGHT	DON'T KNOW	
41c)	**0**	**1**	**2**	**3**	**4**	**5**	**6**	**7**	**8**	**9**	**10**		
CODE HERE →	0	1	2	3	4	5	6	7	8	9	X	V	(54)

The Liberal Democrats

	LEFT									RIGHT	DON'T KNOW	
41d)	**0**	**1**	**2**	**3**	**4**	**5**	**6**	**7**	**8**	**9**	**10**		
CODE HERE →	0	1	2	3	4	5	6	7	8	9	X	V	(55)

Scottish National Party (Ask Scotland only)

	LEFT									RIGHT	DON'T KNOW	
41e)	**0**	**1**	**2**	**3**	**4**	**5**	**6**	**7**	**8**	**9**	**10**		
CODE HERE →	0	1	2	3	4	5	6	7	8	9	X	V	(56)

Plaid Cymru (Ask Wales only)

	LEFT									RIGHT	DON'T KNOW	
41f)	**0**	**1**	**2**	**3**	**4**	**5**	**6**	**7**	**8**	**9**	**10**		
CODE HERE →	0	1	2	3	4	5	6	7	8	9	X	V	(57)

SHOWCARD

42) Now I want you to think about those people whose opinions are especially important to you, for example your spouse, partner or friends. Think about what THEY would say in response to the following statements. Would you say that they agree or disagree with the following statements:

		STRONGLY AGREE	AGREE	NEITHER AGREE NOR DISAGREE	DISAGREE	STRONGLY DISAGREE	
42a)	People who get involved in politics are often a bit odd	1	2	3	4	5	(58)
42b)	Members of Parliament are respected figures in the community	1	2	3	4	5	(59)
42c)	The only way to change anything in our society is to get involved	1	2	3	4	5	(60)

POLITICAL QUIZ

Here is a quick quiz. For each of the following statements I say tell me if it is true or false. If you do not know just say and we will skip to the next one.

		TRUE	FALSE	DON'T KNOW	
43a)	The minimum voting age is 21	1	2	3	(61)
43b)	Britain has separate elections for the European parliament & the British parliament	1	2	3	(62)
43c)	The number of members of parliament is about 100	1	2	3	(63)
43d)	Britain's electoral system for Westminster is based on proportional representation	1	2	3	(64)
43e)	No one may stand for parliament unless they pay a deposit	1	2	3	(65)
43f)	The House of Lords has equal powers to the House of Commons	1	2	3	(66)
43g)	The European Union (The E.U.) is composed of 15 states	1	2	3	(67)

MEDIA

Now I would like to ask you some questions on the media.

44a) Do you regularly read a morning newspaper every day?

YES	NO	
1	2	(68)

SHOWCARD

44b)   If yes, which <u>daily morning</u> newspaper do you read <u>most</u> often? (Code the <u>one</u> you read most often)

	(69)
Daily Express	1
Daily Mail	2
Mirror	3
Daily Star	4
The Sun	5
Daily Telegraph	6
Financial Times	7
The Guardian	8
The Independent	9
The Times	0
Daily Record	X
The Scotsman	V
	(70)
The Herald (Glasgow)	1
The (Aberdeen) Press and Journal	2
The Western Mail	3
Other (WRITE IN)	4

SHOWCARD

44c)   In an average week how often do you...

	EVERY DAY	4 TO 6 DAYS A WEEK	1 TO 3 DAYS A WEEK	LESS THAN ONCE A WEEK	NEVER	
Read a newspaper for political news	1	2	3	4	5	(71)
Read a newspaper for other news or sports	1	2	3	4	5	(72)
Listen to radio or watch television for political news	1	2	3	4	5	(73)
Listen to radio or watch television for other news or sports	1	2	3	4	5	(74)
Use the Internet to obtain information about politics	1	2	3	4	5	(75)

*Start card 7

SHOWCARD

44d)   How many hours of television do you normally watch...

	NONE	UP TO 1 HOUR	1 UP TO 2 HRS	2 UP TO 3 HRS	3 UP TO 4 HRS	4 UP TO 5 HRS	5 UP TO 6 HRS	6 UP TO 7 HRS	7 UP TO 8 HRS	8 UP TO 9 HRS	9 UP TO 10 HRS	10 UP TO 11 HRS	11 OR MORE HRS	
In an average weekday?	1	2	3	4	5	6	7	8	9	0	X	V (11)	1	(12)
In an average day during the weekend?	1	2	3	4	5	6	7	8	9	0	X	V (13)	1	(14)

Note Total Weekday Hours

SHOWCARD

45)   And now I would like to ask you about other ways that you spend your time on an average weekday. Think about How many hours do you spend on:

	NONE	UP TO 1 HOUR	1 UP TO 2 HRS	2 UP TO 3 HRS	3 UP TO 4 HRS	4 UP TO 5 HRS	5 UP TO 6 HRS	6 UP TO 7 HRS	7 UP TO 8 HRS	8 UP TO 9 HRS	9 UP TO 10 HRS	10 UP TO 11 HRS	11 OR MORE HRS	
Work in the home and for the family	1	2	3	4	5	6	7	8	9	0	X	V (15)	1	(16)
Paid employment in an average day, including commuting & work that you take home	1	2	3	4	5	6	7	8	9	0	X	V (17)	1	(18)
Studying on an educational course	1	2	3	4	5	6	7	8	9	0	X	V (19)	1	(20)
Other leisure activities such as playing Sports etc.	1	2	3	4	5	6	7	8	9	0	X	V (21)	1	(22)
Sleeping	1	2	3	4	5	6	7	8	9	0	X	V (23)	1	(24)
Other	1	2	3	4	5	6	7	8	9	0	X	V (25)	1	(26)

Note Total Hours

Note to Interviewer..
PLEASE ENSURE THAT THE TOTAL HOURS FOR QUESTION 44D) (WEEKDAY ONLY) AND 45 ADD UP TO APPROXIMATELY 24 HOURS.

SOCIAL BACKGROUND

EDUCATION – PLEASE think for a moment about the educational experiences of you and your parents.

SHOWCARD

46a)   At what age did you finish full time education?

	15 (AND UNDER)	16	17	18	19 (AND OVER)		
CODE HERE →	1	2	3	4	5		(27)

SHOWCARD

46b)   At what age did your father leave full time education?

	15 (AND UNDER)	16	17	18	19 (AND OVER)	DON'T KNOW	
CODE HERE →	1	2	3	4	5	6	(28)

SHOWCARD

46c)   At what age did your mother leave full time education?

	15 (AND UNDER)	16	17	18	19 (AND OVER)	DON'T KNOW	
CODE HERE →	1	2	3	4	5	6	(29)

47a) Do you have any educational or work related qualifications?

	YES	NO	DON'T KNOW	
	1	2	3	(30)

If no, go to question 48

SHOWCARD
47b) If yes, what is the highest qualification you have?

	(31)
Youth training certificate/Skillseekers	1
Recognised trade apprenticeship completed	2
Clerical and commercial qualifications (e.g. typing/shorthand/book-keeping/commerce)	3
City & Guilds Certificate – Craft/Intermediate/Ordinary/Part I/ Or Scotvec National Certificate Modules/ or NVQ1/SVQ1	4
City & Guilds Certificate – Advanced/Final/Part II/ Or Scotvec Higher National Units/ or NVQ2/SVQ2	5
City & Guilds Certificate – Full Technological/Part III/ Or Scotvec Higher National Units/ or NVQ3/SVQ3	6
Ordinary National Certificate (ONC) or Diploma (OND), BEC/TEC/BTEC/ Scotvec Higher Certificate or Higher Diploma/ or NVQ4/SVQ4	7
CSE grades 2–5	8
CSE grade 1, GCE O level, GCSE, School Certificate	9
Scottish Ordinary/Lower Certificate	0
GCE A level or Higher Certificate	X

	(32)
Scottish Higher Certificate	1
Nursing qualifications (e.g. SEN, SRN, SCM RGN)	2
Teaching qualifications (not degree)	3
University diploma	4
University or CNAA First Degree (e.g. BA, BEd, BSc)	5
University or CNAA Higher Degree (e.g. MSc, PhD)	6
Other technical, professional or higher qualifications	7

(PLEASE GIVE DETAILS) ....

I am now going to ask you some questions about your current work/job, or if not now working your last MAIN work/job.

48)   Are you or were you self-employed?

	YES	NO
	1	2

(33)

49)   Do you or did you supervise other workers?

	YES	NO
	1	2

(34)

If no go to Q 51a

50)   If yes, how many employees are you or were you responsible for?

	UNDER 25	25 OR MORE
	1	2

(35)

51a)   What is or was YOUR job title?.. (36 – 37)

51b)   Can you describe YOUR working tasks? (note for interviewer, Probe what materials/machinery used if relevant and what training/qualifications are required for the job)

....

....

.... (38 – 43)

51c)   What is/was the main business activity at the place you work/worked? By that we mean precisely what is/was made, sold or provided there? (note for interviewer, Probe for Manufacturing; Retail; Wholesale; Services etc. and for Products/Services. Please ensure you record what they manufacture or retail)

....

....

....

51d)   Including yourself, approximately how many people are/were employed at the site you work/worked?

1 Respondent only	1
2 – 4	2
5 – 24	3
25 – 29	4
100 – 99	5
200+	6

If single with no husband, wife or partner go to question 53

52a)   What is or was your husband's, wife's or partner's job title?

.... (44 – 45)

SHOWCARD
52b)   Can you describe your husband's, wife's or partner's working tasks? (note for interviewer, Probe what materials/machinery used if relevant and what training/qualifications are required for that job)

....

....

....   (46–51)

SHOWCARD
52c)   Does or did your husband, wife or partner supervise other workers and if so how many?

	(52)
No, do not supervise	1
Yes, supervise under 25	2
Yes, supervise 25 or more	3
Don't know	4

52d)   What is/was the main Business activity at the place of work of your husband, wife or partner where they work/worked? By that we mean precisely what is/was made, sold or provided there? (note for interviewer, Probe for manufacturing; Retail; Wholesale; Services etc. and for Products/Services. Please ensure you record what they manufacture or retail)

....

....

....

52e)   Approximately, how many people are/were employed at the site where your husband, wife or partner works/worked?

Husband/Wife/Partner only	1
2 – 4	2
5 – 24	3
25 – 29	4
100 – 199	5
200+	6

Socio-Economic Status

SHOWCARD
53)   From this card please tell me which best describes the sort of work YOU do. (If not working now, please tell me what YOU did in your last job.) Then, from this card do the same to show which best describes the sort of work your husband, wife or partner (where appropriate) does or did. (Note to interviewer, please skip this question if the person has never worked full-time (e.g. a student) and has no husband, wife or partner)

		Yourself (53)	Your Husband, Wife or Partner (54)
A)	Professional or technical work (e.g. doctor, accountant, schoolteacher, social worker, computer programmer)	1	1
B)	Manager or administrator (e.g. company director, manager, executive officer, local authority officer)	2	2
C)	Clerical (e.g. clerk, secretary, telephone operator)	3	3
D)	Sales (e.g. commercial traveller, shop assistant)	4	4
E)	Foreman	5	5
F)	Skilled manual work (e.g. plumber, electrician, fitter, train driver, cook, hairdresser)	6	6
G)	Semi-skilled or unskilled manual work (e.g. machine operator, assembler, postman, waitress, cleaner, labourer)	7	7
H)	Other (please describe)	8	8

SHOWCARD

54) From this card please tell me which type of organisation **YOU** do or **YOU** did work for. Then, do the same to show which type of organisation your husband, wife or partner (where appropriate) does or did work for.

		YOURSELF (55)	YOUR HUSBAND, WIFE OR PARTNER (56)
A)	Self-employed	1	1
B)	Private sector firm or company (e.g. limited companies, small unlimited companies and plcs)	2	2
C)	Nationalised industry or public corporation (e.g. Post Office, BBC)	3	3
D)	Other public sector employer (e.g. Central Government, Civil Service, Local Authorities, Universities, LEA, NHS, Police, Armed Forces)	4	4
E)	Charity/voluntary sector (e.g. charitable companies, churches, trade unions)	5	5

SHOWCARD

55) From this card please indicate which of the following categories represents the total annual income of your family in this household from ALL sources before tax.

		(57)
A)	Under £10,000	1
B)	£10,000 up to £19,999	2
C)	£20,000 up to £29,999	3
D)	£30,000 up to £39,999	4
E)	£40,000 up to £49,999	5
F)	£50,000 up to £59,999	6
G)	£60,000 up to £69,999	7
H)	£70,000 plus	8

56a)   Apart from yourself does anyone else live in your home?

YES	NO
1	2

(58)

If No go to Q57a

56b)   Do you have any children living here in your home?

YES	NO
1	2

(59)

If Yes go to Q56c
If No go to Q57a

SHOWCARD
56c)   How old are the children living in your home? Please start with the youngest and continue upwards.

	UP TO 2 YRS OLD	2 AND UP TO 4	4 TO 6	6 TO 8	8 TO 10	10 TO 12	12 TO 14	14 TO 16	16 TO 18	18 AND OVER	
First Child	1	2	3	4	5	6	7	8	9	0	(60)
Second Child	1	2	3	4	5	6	7	8	9	0	(61)
Third Child	1	2	3	4	5	6	7	8	9	0	(62)
Fourth Child	1	2	3	4	5	6	7	8	9	0	(63)
Fifth Child	1	2	3	4	5	6	7	8	9	0	(64)
Sixth Child	1	2	3	4	5	6	7	8	9	0	(65)

*Start card 8

If over six, write in their ages	(11-12)	(13-14)	(15-16)	(17-18)	(19-20)	(21-22)	(23-24)	(25-26)	(27-28)	(29-30)

57a)   Do you regard yourself as belonging to any particular religion?

YES	NO
1	2

(31)

If Yes ask question 57b
If No go to question 58

SHOWCARD
57b)   If yes, which denomination?

	(32)
Church of England/Anglican/Episcopal	1
Roman Catholic	2
Presbyterian/Church of Scotland	3
Methodist	4
Baptist	5
United Reform Church or Congregational	6
Free Presbyterian	7
Brethren	8
Jewish	9
Hindu	0
Islam/Muslim	X
Sikh	V
	(33)
Buddhist	1
Other (*WRITE IN*)	2

SHOWCARD
57c)   How religious do you consider yourself to be?

	(34)
Very religious	1
Somewhat religious	2
Not very religious	3
Not at all religious	4

SHOWCARD
58)   Ethnic origins (interviewer to complete).

	(35)
White/European	1
Asian (e.g Indian or Pakistani)	2
East Asian (e.g. Chinese, Japanese or Malaysian)	3
Black (e.g West Indian or African)	4

59)   What language do you usually speak at home?

	ENGLISH	OTHER (WRITE IN)	
	1	2	(36)

60)   Gender (interviewer to complete)

	MALE	FEMALE	
	1	2	(37)

61)   In what year were you born?   19............   (38 – 41)

62)   Thank you for participating in this survey. We guarantee that the details in this survey will not be passed on to any outside organisations. Would you be willing to answer similar sorts of questions in the future?

	YES	NO	
	1	2	(42)

If Yes – Please Ask Respondent To Sign As Confirmation...

RESPONDENT SIGNATURE: ....   DATE:.....................

THANK RESPONDENT & CLOSE INTERVIEW

PLEASE ENSURE ALL RELEVANT QUESTIONS ARE CODED & WRITTEN ANSWERS ARE LEGIBLE

THANK YOU

2.   *Mail-back questionnaire*

The following questions contained in the wave 1, face-to-face questionnaire above were *not* included in this questionnaire: 13 (c), 16 (c–e), 23, 24, 26, 28, 29 (a–c), 30 (a–b), 31a (i–x), 31b (i–iii), 33, 35 (a–h),

38 (a–f), 39 (a–f), 40 (a–f), 41 (a–f), 42 (a–c), 43 (a–g), 44 (a–c, and dii), 46 (b–c), 49, 50, 51 (a–d), 52 (a–e), 56c.

One question not included in the face-to-face, wave 1, questionnaire but added to this questionnaire was: 'If you answered "don't know" or "none" to the previous question ("Generally speaking do you think of yourself as Conservative, Labour, Liberal Democrat, Scottish National-ist, Plaid Cymru or what?"), do you think of yourself as a little closer to one of the parties than the others? If yes please tell me which party?'

3.   *Face-to-face questionnaire* (Wave 2)

The following questions contained in the wave 1, face-to-face question-naire were *not* included in this questionnaire: 1, 2, 3, 4, 10 (a–g), 11 (a–h), 12 (a–k), 16 (c–e), 24, 25, 26, 27, 28, 29 (a–c), 30 (a–b), 31a (i–x), 31b (i–iii), 34 (a–c), 38 (a–f), 39 (a–f), 46 (b–c), 47 (a–b), 48, 49, 50, 51 (a–d), 52 (a–c), 54, 55, 56 (a–c), 57 (a–c), 58, 59.

A further organisation (Political Party) was added to the list in Q 6a.

The wording on Q13a was modified to ask respondents about their voting behaviour in the 2001 general election rather than the 1997 general election.

Three additional questions were asked:

> Q 7b 'People have different reasons for not voting. Which of the statements on the card comes closest to your reason for not voting in the general election of 2001?' The statements were: 'I really intended to vote but circumstances on the day prevented me'; 'I'm just not interested in politics'; 'There is no point in voting because there is no real democracy in Britain'; 'There was no point in voting because it was obvious that Labour would win the election'; 'The party I used to support no longer stands for what I believe in'; 'None of the above'.
>
> Q 8b 'Do you generally think of yourself as a little closer to one of the parties than the other?'
>
> Q8e 'If you answered yes to being a member of a political party in question 3a which political party are you a member of?'

Bibliography

Abramson, Paul R. and Ronald Inglehart. 1995. *Value Change in Global Perspective*. Ann Arbor: University of Michigan Press.

Almond, Gabriel A. and Sidney Verba. 1963. *The Civic Culture: Political Attitudes and Democracy in Five Nations*. Princeton, NJ: Princeton University Press.

Andrews, Geoff (ed.). 1995. *Citizenship*. London: Lawrence and Wishart.

Axelrod, Robert. 1984. *The Evolution of Cooperation*. New York: Basic Books.

—1997. *The Complexity of Cooperation*. Princeton, NJ: Princeton University Press.

Banducci, Susan A. and Jeffrey A. Karp. 2003. 'How Elections Change the Way Citizens View the Political System: Campaigns, Media Effects and Electoral Outcomes in Comparative Perspective', *British Journal of Political Science*, 33, 3: 443–68.

Barnes, Samuel and Max Kaase. 1979. *Political Action*. London: Sage.

Beetham, David. 1994. *Defining and Measuring Democracy*. London: Sage.

Beetham, David, Iain Byrne, Pauline Ngan and Stuart Weir. 2002. *Democracy under Blair*. London: Politicos.

Beiner, Ronald (ed.). 1995. *Theorizing Citizenship*. Albany: State University of New York Press.

Bellah, Robert, Richard Madsen, William Sullivan, Ann Swindler and Steven Tipton. 1985. *Habits of the Heart*. Berkeley: University of California Press.

Bennett, Stephen E., Richard S. Flickinger and Staci L. Rhine. 2000. 'Political Talk Over Here, Over There, Over Time', *British Journal of Political Science*, 30.

Blunkett, David. 2001. *Politics and Progress*. London: Politicos.

—2003. *Civic Renewal: A New Agenda*. CSV Edith Kahn Memorial Lecture. Home Office.

Bobbitt, Philip. 2002. *The Shield of Achilles: War, Peace and the Course of History*. London: Penguin Books.

Boothroyd, Betty. 2000. *House of Commons Official Report*. 26 July, Cols. 1113–14. London: TSO.

Boyne, G. A. 1984. 'Output Disaggregation and the Quest for the Impact of Local Politics', *Political Studies*, 32: 451–58.

Bradshaw, Jonathan. 1992. 'Social Security', in David Marsh and R. A. W. Rhodes (eds.), *Implementing Thatcherite Policies*. Buckingham: Open University Press.

Brady, Henry, E., Sidney Verba and Kay L. Schlozman. 1995. 'Beyond SES: A Resource Model of Political Participation', *American Political Science Review*, 89: 271–94.

Brehm, John and Wendy Rahn. 1997. 'Individual-Level Evidence for the Causes and Consequences of Social Capital', *American Journal of Political Science* 41, 3: 999–1023.

Brody, Richard A. 1978. 'The Puzzle of Political Participation in America', in Antony King (ed.), *The New American Political System*. Washington, DC: American Enterprise Institute.

Bromley, Catherine and John Curtice. 2002. 'Where Have All the Voters Gone?' in Alison Park, John Curtice, Katarina Thomson, Lindsey Jarvis and Catherine Bromley (eds.), *British Social Attitudes: The 19th Report*. London: Sage.

Bromley, Catherine, John Curtice and Ben Seyd. 2001. 'Political Engagement, Trust and Constitutional Reform', in Alison Park, John Curtice, Katarina Thomson, Lindsey Jarvis and Catherine Bromley (eds.), *British Social Attitudes: The 18th Report*. London: Sage.

Brubaker, Roger. 1992. *Citizenship and Nationhood in France and Germany*. Cambridge, MA.: Harvard University Press.

Butler, David and Dennis Kavanagh. 2001. *The British General Election of 2001*. Basingstoke: Palgrave/Macmillan.

Campbell, Angus, Philip E. Converse, Warren E. Miller and Donald E. Stokes. 1960. *The American Voter*. New York: Wiley.

Charemza, Wojciech and Derek Deadman. 1992. *New Directions in Econometric Practice*. London: Edward Elgar.

Chisholm, M. 2000. *Structural Reform of British Local Government: Rhetoric and Reality*. Manchester: Manchester University Press.

Claibourn, M. P. and P. S. Martin. 2000. 'Trusting and Joining? An Empirical Test of the Reciprocal Nature of Social Capital', *Political Behavior*, 22: 267–91.

Clarke, Harold D. and Allan Kornberg. 1992. 'Do National Elections Affect Perceptions of MPs' Responsiveness? A Note on the Canadian Case', *Legislative Studies Quarterly*, 17: 183–204.

Clarke, Harold D., David Sanders, Marianne C. Stewart and Paul Whiteley. 2004. *Political Choice in Britain*. Oxford: Oxford University Press.

Clarke, Paul Barry. 1994. *Citizenship*. London: Pluto Press.

—1996. *Deep Citizenship*. London: Pluto Press.

Coleman, James S. 1988. 'Social Capital in the Creation of Human Capital', *American Journal of Sociology*, 94, supplement S95–S119.

Conover, Pamela Johnston and Donald D. Searing. 2002. 'The Elusive Ideal of Equal Citizenship: Political Theory and Political Psychology in the United States and Great Britain'. Paper presented to the Annual Meeting of the American Political Science Association, Boston.

Crewe, Ivor. 1981. 'Electoral Participation', in D. Butler, H. R. Penniman and A. Ranney (eds.), *Democracy at the Polls: A Comparative Study of Competitive Elections*. Washington: American Enterprise Institute for Public Policy Research.

—1988. 'Has the Electorate become Thatcherite?' in Robert Skidelsky (ed.), *Thatcherism*. London: Chatto and Windus: 25–50.

Crewe, Ivor, Pamela Johnston Conover and Donald D. Searing. 1994. 'The "Good" Citizen in Theory and Practice: American and British Perspectives on Political Tolerance'. Paper presented to the Annual Meeting of the American Political Science Association.

Crick, Bernard. 2002. 'Education for Citizenship: The Citizenship Order', *Parliamentary Affairs*, 55, 3: 488–504.

Curtice, John and Roger Jowell. 1995. 'The Sceptical Electorate', in Roger Jowell, John Curtice, Alison Park, Lindsay Brook and Daphne Ahrendt (eds.), *British Social Attitudes: The 12th Report*. Aldershot: Dartmouth.

—1997. 'Trust in the Political System', in Roger Jowell, John Curtice, Alison Park, Lindsay Brook, Katarina Thomson and Caroline Bryson (eds.), *British Social Attitudes: The 14th Report*. Aldershot: Ashgate.

Dalton, Russell, J. 1999. 'Political Support in Advanced Industrial Democracies', in Pippa Norris (ed.), *Critical Citizens*. Oxford: Oxford University Press.

—2002. *Citizen Politics*. New York: Seven Bridges Press.

Dalton, Russell J. and Martin P. Wattenberg. 2000. *Parties without Partisans*. Oxford: Oxford University Press.

Dalton, Russell, Scott C. Flanagan and Paul Allen Beck. 1984. *Electoral Change in Advanced Industrial Democracies*. Princeton, NJ: Princeton University Press.

Denters, B. 2002. 'Size and Political Trust: Evidence from Denmark, the Netherlands, Norway and the United Kingdom', *Environment and Planning C: Government and Policy*, 20: 793–812.

Department for Education and Employment. 1999. *Citizenship: The National Curriculum for England*. London: Qualifications and Curriculum Authority.

Dorling, D. 1997. *Death in Britain: How Local Mortality Rates Have Changed, 1950s–1990s*. York: Joseph Rowntree Foundation.

Dorling, D. and M. Shaw (eds.) 2001. 'Life Chances and Lifestyles', in C. Gardiner and H. Matthews (eds.), *The Changing Geography of the United Kingdom* (3rd edition). London: Routledge.

Etzioni, Amitai. 1995. *The Spirit of Community: Rights, Responsibilities and the Communitarian Agenda*. London: Fontana Press.

Finkel, Steven E. 1985. 'Reciprocal Effects of Participation and Political Efficacy', *American Journal of Political Science*, 29: 891–913.

Frandsen, A. G. 2002. 'Size and Electoral Participation in Local Elections', *Environment and Planning C: Government and Policy*, 20: 853–69.

Frank, Robert H. 1988. *Passion within Reason: The Strategic Role of the Emotions*. New York: W. W. Norton.

Franklin, Mark. 1996. 'Electoral Participation', in Larry Le Duc, Richard Niemi and Pippa Norris (eds.), *Comparing Democracies: Elections and Voting in Global Perspective*. London: Sage.

Fraser, Nancy and Linda Gordon. 1998. 'Contract versus Charity: Why is There No Social Citizenship in the United States?' in Gershon Shafir (ed.), *The Citizenship Debates*. Minneapolis: University of Minesota Press.

Fukuyama, Francis. 1995. *Trust: The Social Virtues and the Creation of Prosperity*. London: Hamish Hamilton.

Galbraith, John Kenneth. 1992. *The Culture of Contentment*. Boston: Houghton Mifflin.

Glazer, Nathan. 1988. *The Limits of Social Policy*. Cambridge, MA: Harvard University Press.

Goldstein, Harvey. 2001. 'Using Pupil Performance Data for Judging Schools and Teachers: Scope and Limitations', *British Educational Research Journal*, 27: 433–42.

Granger, Clive, J. 1988. 'Some Recent Developments in a Concept of Causality', *Journal of Econometrics*, 2: 111–20.

Gray, John, D. Jesson and B. Jones. 1984. 'Predicting Differences in Examination Results between Local Education Authorities – Does Local School Organisation Matter?', *Oxford Review of Education*, 10: 45–68.

Gray, John, D. Jesson and N. Sime. 1990. 'Estimating Differences in the Examination Performance of Schools in Six LEAs: A Multilevel Approach to School Effectiveness', *Oxford Review of Education*, 16: 137–58.

Greene, William H. 2003. *Econometric Analysis*. Upper Saddle River, NJ: Prentice-Hall.

Gurr, Ted Robert. 1970. *Why Men Rebel*. Princeton, NJ: Princeton University Press.

Hall, Peter. 1999. 'Social Capital in Britain', *British Journal of Political Science*, 29, 3: 417–62.

—2002. 'The Role of Government and the Distribution of Social Capital', in Robert D. Putnam (ed.), *Democracies in Flux*. Oxford: Oxford University Press.

Hammer, Tomas. 1986. 'Citizenship: Membership of a Nation and of a State', *International Migration*, 24: 735–47.

Heater, Derek. 1990. *Citizenship: The Civic Ideal in World History, Politics and Education*. London: Longman.

Heath, Anthony, Roger Jowell and John Curtice. 2001. *The Rise of New Labour: Party Policies and Voter Choice*. Oxford: Oxford University Press.

Heclo, Hugh. 1974. *Modern Social Policy in Britain and Sweden*. New Haven: Yale University Press.

Held, David. 1989. 'Citizenship and Autonomy', in David Held and John Thompson (eds.), *Social Theory of Modern Societies*. Cambridge: Cambridge University Press: 162–84.

Hendry, David. 1995. *Dynamic Econometrics*. Oxford: Oxford University Press.

HMSO. 1999. *Encouraging Citizenship: Report of the Commission on Citizenship*. London.

Hoggart, K. 1991. *People, Power and Place: Perspectives in Anglo-American Politics*. London: Routledge.

Home Office. 2002. *Safe Borders, Safe Haven: Integration with Diversity in Modern Britain*. London: TSO.

House of Commons. 2001. *Select Committee on Public Administration First Report*. London: TSO.

Huckfeldt, Robert and John Sprague. 1995. *Citizens, Politics and Social Communication: Information and Influence in an Election Campaign*. New York: Cambridge University Press.

Huntingdon, Samuel P. 1991. *The Third Wave: Democratization in the Late Twentieth Century*. Norman and London: University of Oklahoma Press.

Inglehart, Ronald J. 1997. *Modernization and Postmodernization*. Princeton, NJ: Princeton University Press.

—1999a. 'Trust, Well-being and Democracy', in Mark E. Warren (ed.), *Democracy and Trust*. Cambridge: Cambridge University Press.

—1999b. 'Postmodernization Erodes Respect for Authority, but Increases Support for Democracy', in Pippa Norris (ed.), *Critical Citizens*. Oxford: Oxford University Press.

Janoski, Thomas and Brian Gran. 2002. 'Political Citizenship: Foundations of Rights', in Engin F. Isin and Bryan S. Turner (eds.), *Handbook of Citizenship Studies*. London: Sage.

Johnston, Michael. 1988. 'The Price of Honesty', in Roger Jowell, Sharon Witherspoon and Lindsay Brook (eds.), *British Social Attitudes: The 5th Report*. Aldershot: Gower.

Johnston, Michael and Roger Jowell. 2001. 'How Robust is British Civil Society?' in Alison Park, John Curtice, Katarina Thomson, Lindsey Jarvis and Catherine Bromley (eds.), *British Social Attitudes: The 18th Report*. London: Sage.

Johnston, Ron. 1991. *A Question of Place: Exploring the Practice of Human Geography*. Oxford: Blackwell.

Johnston, Ron, Charles Pattie, D. J. Rossiter, D. Dorling, H. Tunstall and I. McAllister. 1998. 'Anatomy of a Labour Landslide: The Constituency System and the 1997 General Election', *Parliamentary Affairs*, 51: 131–48.

Jones, Kathleen Marion. 1998. 'Citizenship in a Woman-Friendly Policy', in Gershon Shafir (ed.), *The Citizenship Debates*. Minneapolis: University of Minnesota Press.

Jowell, R. and R. Topf. 1988. 'Trust in the Establishment', in Roger Jowell, Sharon Witherspoon and Lindsay Brooks (eds.), *British Social Attitudes: The 5th Report*. Aldershot: Gower.

Katz, Richard S. and Peter Mair. 1992. *Party Organizations: A Data Handbook on Party Organizations in Western Democracies*. London: Sage.

Kavanagh, Dennis. 1980. 'Political Culture in Britain: The Decline of the Civic Culture', in Gabriel A. Almond and Sidney Verba (eds.), *The Civic Culture Revisited*. London: Sage.

Klingemann, Hans-Dieter. 1999. 'Mapping Political Support in the 1990s: A Global Analysis', in Pippa Norris (ed.), *Critical Citizens*. Oxford: Oxford University Press.

Knack, S. 2002. 'Social Capital and the Quality of Government: Evidence from the States', *American Journal of Political Science*, 46: 772–85.

Knack, S. and P. Keefer. 1997. 'Does Social Capital Have an Economic Payoff? A Cross-country Investigation', *The Quarterly Journal of Economics*, 112: 1251–88.

Knight, Barry and Peter Stokes. 1996. *The Deficit in Civil Society in the United Kingdom*. Foundation for Civic Society. Working Paper Number 1.

Knight, Jack and Itai Sened. 1995. *Explaining Social Institutions*. Ann Arbor: University of Michigan Press.

Kymlicka, Will. 1995. *Multicultural Citizenship*. Oxford: Clarendon Press.

—1998. 'Multicultural Citizenship', in Gershon Shafir (ed.), *The Citizenship Debates*. Minneapolis: University of Minnesota Press.

Lane, Robert. 1991. *The Market Experience*. Cambridge: Cambridge University Press.

Leamer, Edward E. 1983. 'Let's Take the Con out of Econometrics', *American Economic Review*, 73, 1: 31–43.

Levy, F., A. J. Melttsner and A. Wildavsky. 1974. *Urban Outcomes*. Berkeley: University of California Press.

Maloney, William A. 1999. 'Contracting Out the Participation Function: Social Capital and Chequebook Participation', in Jan Van Deth, Marco Marraffi, Ken Newton and Paul F. Whiteley (eds.), *Social Capital and European Democracy*. London: Routledge.

Mann, Michael. 1987. 'Ruling Class Strategies and Citizenship', *Sociology*, 21: 339–54.

Marsh, Alan. 1977. *Protest and Political Consciousness*. Beverly Hills, CA: Sage.

Marsh, David. 2002. 'Understanding Young People's Understanding of Politics'. Paper presented to the Democracy and Participation Programme workshop, University of Essex.

Marshall, T. H. and Tom Bottomore. 1992. *Citizenship and Social Class*. London: Pluto Press.

Mayer, Nonna. 2001. 'Social Capital, Trust and Civicness'. Paper presented to the Social Capital conference, University of Exeter.

McAllister, Ian. 1992. *Political Behaviour: Citizens, Parties and Elites in Australia*. Melbourne: Longman Cheshire.

—1999. 'The Economic Performance of Governments', in Pippa Norris (ed.), *Critical Citizens*. Oxford: Oxford University Press.

Miller, A. and O. Listhaug. 1999. 'Political Performance and Institutional Trust', in Pippa Norris (ed.), *Critical Citizens*. Oxford: Oxford University Press.

Miller, Warren and J. Merrill Shanks. 1996. *The New American Voter*. Cambridge, MA: Harvard University Press.

Milner, Henry. 2002. *Civic Literacy: How Informed Citizens Make Democracy Work*. Hanover: University of New England Press.

Mortimore, Roger. 1995. 'Politics and Public Perceptions', in F. F. Ridley and A. Doig (eds.), *Sleaze: Politicians, Private Interests and Public Reaction*. Oxford: Oxford University Press.

Muller, Edward. 1979. *Aggressive Political Participation*. Princeton, NJ: Princeton University Press.

Mutz, Diana. 2002. 'The Consequences of Cross-cutting Networks for Political Participation', *American Journal of Political Science*, 46: 838–55.

Newton, Kenneth. 1999. 'Social and Political Trust in Established Democracies', in Pippa Norris (ed.), *Critical Citizens*. Oxford: Oxford University Press.

Newton, Kenneth and Pippa Norris. 2000. 'Confidence in Public Institutions: Faith, Culture or Performance?' in Susan J. Pharr and Robert D. Putnam (eds.), *Disaffected Democracies: What's Troubling the Trilateral Democracies?* Princeton, NJ: Princeton University Press.

Norris, Pippa. 1996. 'Does Television Erode Social Capital? A Reply to Putnam', *PS: Political Science and Politics*, 29.

—(ed.). 1999. *Critical Citizens*. Oxford: Oxford University Press.

—2002. *Democratic Phoenix: Reinventing Political Activism*. Cambridge: Cambridge University Press.

Norris, Pippa, John Curtice, David Sanders, Margaret Scammell and Holli A. Semetko. 1999. *On Message*. London: Sage.

Nove, Alex. 1991. *The Economics of Feasible Socialism Revisited*. London: HarperCollins.

Nye, Joseph, Philip Zelikow and David King. 1997. *Why People Don't Trust Government*. Cambridge, MA: Harvard University Press.

O'Connor, James. 1973. *The Fiscal Crisis of the State*. New York: St. Martin's Press.

Oliver, J. Eric. 1999. 'The Effects of Metropolitan Economic Segregation on Local Civic Participation', *American Journal of Political Science*, 43: 186–212.

—2000. 'City Size and Civic Involvement in Metropolitan America', *American Political Science Review*, 94: 361–73.

—2001. *Democracy in Suburbia*. Princeton, NJ: Princeton University Press.

Olson, Mancur. 1965. *The Logic of Collective Action*. Cambridge, MA: Harvard University Press.

—1982. *The Rise and Decline of Nations*. New Haven: Yale University Press.

O'Neill, Onora. 2002. *A Question of Trust*. Cambridge: Cambridge University Press.

Opp, Karl Dieter. 1990. 'Postmaterialism, Collective Action and Political Protest', *American Journal of Political Science*, 34: 212–35.

Parry, Geraint, George Moyser and Neil Day. 1992. *Political Participation and Democracy in Britain*. Cambridge: Cambridge University Press.

Pattie, Charles and Ronald Johnston. 1999. 'Context, Conversation and Conviction: Social Networks and Voting at the 1992 British General Election', *Political Studies*, 47: 877–89.

—2001a. 'A Low Turnout Landslide: Abstention in the British General Election of 1997', *Political Studies*, 49: 286–305.

—2001b. 'Losing the Voters' Trust: Evaluations of the Political System and Voting at the 1997 British General Election', *British Journal of Politics and International Relations*, 3: 191–222.

Pharr, Susan and Robert D. Putnam (eds.) 1999. *Disaffected Democracies*. Princeton, NJ: Princeton University Press.

Pinch, S. P. 1985. *Cities and Services: The Geography of Collective Consumption*. London: Routledge & Kegan Paul.

Pocock, J. G. A. 1998. 'The Ideal of Citizenship since Classical Times', in Gershon Shafir (ed.), *The Citizenship Debates*. Minneapolis: University of Minnesota Press.

Prime, Duncan, Meta Zimmeck and Andrew Zurawan. 2002. *Active Communities: Initial Findings from the 2001 Home Office Citizenship Survey*. London: Home Office.

Putnam, Robert D. 1993. *Making Democracy Work: Civic Traditions in Modern Italy*. Princeton: Princeton University Press.

—1995. 'Tuning In, Tuning Out: The Strange Disappearance of Social Capital in America', *PS: Political Science and Politics*, 28: 664–83.

—2000. *Bowling Alone*. New York: Simon and Schuster.

—2002. *Democracies in Flux*. Oxford: Oxford University Press.

Putnam, Robert D., Susan J. Pharr and Russell J. Dalton. 2000. 'Introduction', in Susan J. Pharr and Robert D. Putnam (eds.), *Disaffected Democracies: What's Troubling the Trilateral Democracies?* Princeton, NJ: Princeton University Press.

Rahn, Wendy, John Brehm and Neil Carlson. 1999. 'National Elections as Institutions for Generating Social Capital', in Theda Skocpol and Morris P. Fiorina (eds.), *Civic Engagement in American Democracy*. Washington, DC: Brookings Institution.

Rawls, John. 1971. *A Theory of Justice*. Oxford: Oxford University Press.

Riddell, Peter. 1989. *The Thatcher Decade*. Oxford: Basil Blackwell.

Riker, William H. and Peter C. Ordeshook. 1968. *An Introduction to Positive Political Theory*. Englewood Cliffs, NJ: Prentice-Hall.

Rose, L. E. 2002. 'Municipal Size and Local Nonelectoral Participation: Findings from Denmark, the Netherlands and Norway', *Environment and Planning C: Government and Policy*, 20: 829–51.

Runciman, W. G. 1966. *Relative Deprivation and Social Justice*. London: Routledge & Kegan Paul.

Samuelson, Paul. 1954. 'The Pure Theory of Public Expenditure', *Review of Economics and Statistics*, 36: 387–89.

Seyd, Patrick and Paul F. Whiteley. 1992. *Labour's Grassroots: The Politics of Party Membership*. Oxford: Clarendon Press.

—2002a. *New Labour's Grassroots*. Basingstoke: Palgrave.

—2002b. 'Party Election Campaigning in Britain: The Labour Party'. Paper presented to the Annual Meeting of the Canadian Political Science Association, University of Toronto.

Shafir, Gordon (ed.). 1998. *The Citizenship Debates*. Minneapolis: University of Minnesota Press.

Sharpe, L. J. and Kenneth, Newton. 1984. *Does Politics Matter?* Oxford: Oxford University Press.

Skocpol, Theda. 2002. 'United States: From Membership to Advocacy', in Robert D. Putnam (ed.), *Democracies in Flux*. Oxford: Oxford University Press.

Soysal, Yasemin. 1998. 'Towards a Postnational Model of Membership', in Gershon Shafir (ed.), *The Citizenship Debates*. Minneapolis: University of Minnesota Press.

Spinner, Jeff. 1994. *The Boundaries of Citizenship: Race, Ethnicity and Nationality in the Liberal State*. Baltimore: Johns Hopkins University Press.

Steinmo, Sven. 1993. *Taxation and Democracy*. New Haven: Yale University Press.

Swaddle, K. and Anthony Heath. 1989. 'Official and Reported Turnout in the British General Election of 1987', *British Journal of Political Science*, 19: 537–50.

Tarrow, Sidney. 1996. 'Making Social Science Work across Space and Time: A Critical Reflection on Robert Putnam's *Making Democracy Work*', *American Political Science Review*, 90: 389–97.

—1998. *Power in Movement*. Cambridge: Cambridge University Press.

Taylor, Michael. 1987. *The Possibility of Cooperation*. Cambridge: Cambridge University Press.

Tocqueville, Alexis de. 1990. *Democracy in America*, Vol. 1. New York: Vintage Books.

Tonnies, F. 1957. *Community and Society*. East Lansing: Michigan State University Press.

Toynbee, Polly and David Walker. 2001. *Did Things Get Better?* Harmondsworth: Penguin.

Tullock, Gordon. 1971. 'The Paradox of Revolution', *Public Choice*, 11: 89–99.

Van Deth, Jan, Marco Maraffi, Kenneth Newton and Paul Whiteley (eds.). 1999. *Social Capital and European Democracy*. London: Routledge.

Van Gunsteren, Herman. 1978. 'Notes towards a Theory of Citizenship', in F. Dallmayr (ed.), *From Contract to Community*. New York: Marcel Decker.

—1998. *A Theory of Citizenship*. Boulder, CO: Westview Press.

Vanhanen, Tatu. 1997. *Prospects of Democracy*. London: Routledge.

Verba, Sidney and Norman H. Nie. 1972. *Participation in America*. Chicago: University of Chicago Press.

Verba, Sidney, Norman Nie and Jae-On Kim. 1978. *Participation and Political Equality: A Seven Nation Comparison*. Cambridge: Cambridge University Press.

Verba, Sidney, Kay Lehman Schlozman and Henry E. Brady. 1995. *Voice and Equality: Civic Voluntarism in American Politics*. Cambridge, MA: Harvard University Press.

Webb, Paul. 2000. *The Modern British Party System*. London: Sage.

Weir, Stuart and David Beetham. 1999. *Political Power and Democratic Control in Britain: The Democratic Audit of the UK*. London: Routledge.

Whiteley, Paul. 1999. 'The Origins of Social Capital', in Jan Van Deth, Marco Marraffi, Kenneth Newton and Paul Whiteley (eds.), *Social Capital and European Democracy*. London: Routledge.

—2000. 'Economic Growth and Social Capital', *Political Studies*, 48, 3: 443–66.

Whiteley, Paul, Harold Clarke, David Sanders and Marianne Stewart. 2001. 'Turnout', in Pippa Norris (ed.), *Britain Votes 2001*. Oxford: Oxford University Press.

Whiteley, Paul F. and Patrick Seyd. 2002. *High-Intensity Participation: The Dynamics of Party Activism in Britain*. Ann Arbor: University of Michigan Press.

Whiteley, Paul, Patrick Seyd and Jeremy Richardson. 1994. *True Blues: The Politics of Conservative Party Membership*. Oxford: Clarendon Press.

Wolf, Charles. 1990. *Markets or Governments: Choosing between Imperfect Alternatives*. Cambridge, MA: MIT Press.

Worms, Jean-Pierre. 2002. 'Old and New Civic and Social Ties in France', in Robert D. Putnam (ed.), *Democracies in Flux*. Oxford: Oxford University Press.

Wuthnow, Robert. 2002. 'United States: Bridging the Privileged and the Marginalized', in Robert D. Putnam (ed.), *Democracies in Flux*. Oxford: Oxford University Press.

Yang, M., Harvey Goldstein, W. Browne and G. Woodhouse. 2002. 'Multivariate Multilevel Analyses of Examination Results', *Journal of the Royal Statistical Society Series A – Statistics in Society*, 165: 137–53.

Zaller, John R. 1992. *The Nature and Origins of Mass Opinion*. Cambridge: Cambridge University Press.

Index